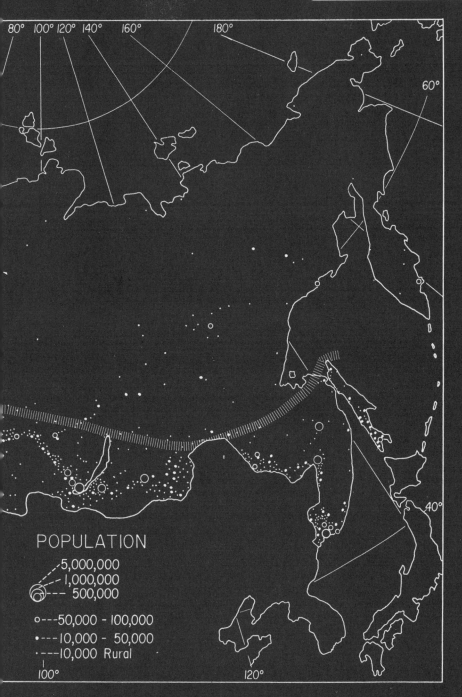

80° 100° 120° 140° 160° 180° 60° 40°

100° 120°

POPULATION

5,000,000
1,000,000
500,000

○--- 50,000 - 100,000
•--- 10,000 - 50,000
--- 10,000 Rural

THE SOVIET UNION
people and regions

THE SOVIET UNION
people and regions

DAVID HOOSON

University of California, Berkeley

Wadsworth Publishing Company, Inc.
Belmont, California

Wadsworth Publishing Company, Inc.
Belmont, California

Published in England by the University of London Press Ltd.

Printed in the United States of America

L.C. Cat. Card No.: 66-25892

Preface

THE regional geography in this book has been written mainly in the course of seeking to understand the reasons for the location of people in the Soviet Union. This necessitates above all a historical approach to the peopling process, and also assessment and constant re-evaluation of the character of the natural environments as they appear to the people who inhabit them. Since the chief purpose is an understanding of present conditions, the growth of cities, which expresses geographically most of what is dynamic and internationally significant, has been accorded particular attention. Further, though the geographer is no less vulnerable as a forecaster than other students of the human scene, it is his duty to collect his thoughts on probable future directions and trends, and the economic and regional chapters close with a brief review of 'Prospects'.

The scheme of regional divisions used here is meant to embody in itself a geographical statement about the changing relative importance, significant links and differences in character between the various parts of this very large country. The criteria for their delimitation are outlined in the Introduction to Part II; it should however be reiterated here that such regional units are inevitably neither self-contained nor permanent, but only tools of analysis. Apart from the world itself, the most fundamental of geographical units today is the sovereign state, so that the regional chapters, intended as the book's main contribution, have been preceded by systematic background studies on a national scale and are hardly intelligible except in the context of these.

Since the regions, in general, coincide neither with the Soviet official economic-administrative units nor the units traditionally used by foreign geographers, the compilation of as accurate statistical foundations as possible for the regions, for several critical points of time, has involved painstaking research. Although it was decided, in the interests of readability, to introduce a minimum of figures into the text itself, most of the statements and generalizations are nevertheless based on the results of this statistical compilation. An attempt has been made to combine geographical judgement with statistical data, as for instance in the population maps, where the dots have been distributed within the smallest censal units according to the best available statistical and non-statistical evidence.

The book has taken shape in the course of teaching the subject to students over a number of years, and has been modified considerably as

5

a result of their reactions and comments. Its chief purpose is to satisfy their needs but a conscious attempt has been made to eliminate technical jargon in the hope that it will also appeal to the general unspecialized reader with an interest in the contemporary world.

In addition to the general debts to my students, including a number of graduate students writing theses on Soviet topics, some specific acknowledgements must be made. Among my students, Mr R. N. North, now Lecturer in Geography in the University of Glasgow, should be singled out. He is largely responsible for the basic statistical research both for the regions and for the transport flow maps. Mr J. Wiedel of the University of Maryland has drawn the final maps. Thanks are also due to the United States Inter-University Committee on Travel Grants for enabling me to travel widely in the Soviet Union; to the Geographical Branch of the Canadian Government for supporting work on Soviet geography at the University of British Columbia; and to several Soviet geographers, particularly at Moscow University, for their help and interest.

Acknowledgement should also be made of the fact that some of the material in the book, notably that concerning the zone from the Middle Volga to Lake Baykal, appeared in my paperback *A New Soviet Heartland?*, published by D. Van Nostrand Company in 1964.

Mr Theodore Shabad, *New York Times* correspondent in Moscow and editor of *Soviet Geography: Review and Translation,* one of the busiest as well as the best informed of foreign students of Soviet geography, generously took the time to read most of the manuscript and offered very useful comments and criticism, though of course he is in no way responsible for any errors, omissions, or for the opinions expressed in the book. Finally, my wife has given much help in matters of editing and style, throughout the years during which this book has been on the horizon of our domestic life.

David J. M. Hooson

Contents

Maps and Diagrams

Plates

Introduction

THE accession of the Soviet Union to 'super-power' status has introduced a fundamentally new, long-term element into the contemporary political world. The victories of the Second World War, leading to Soviet control of Eastern Europe, brought the first clear signs of the new situation and, by 1950, with the successful reconstruction of the war-ravaged Soviet economy and the Communist victory in China, there seemed to be little doubt about it. It is the rapid growth of industry since then, bolstered by development of newly found resources and scientific research, which has been particularly striking and which has reached the public consciousness of the rest of the world through the symbolism of the earth satellites.

In spite of its European roots the Soviet Union is new as America is new and has, for the most part, found itself geographically even more recently than has its great continental rival. Sheer size is its most staggering characteristic, though this can be misleading unless quality is considered as well as quantity. More than twice as large as any other country, it stretches half round the world—a vast realm on which the sun scarcely sets. Britain would fit into the Soviet Union a hundred times and the continental U.S.A. (excluding Alaska) nearly three times. In many respects North America affords the closest and most meaningful yardstick. The total Soviet area (8½ million square miles) is a little more than that of the whole American continent from Panama to the Arctic and its population (230 millions) is roughly equal to that of North America north of Mexico City. Only China and India have more people—the Soviet population is four times as numerous as that of the U.K. and 20% higher than that of the U.S.A. The tremendous demographic setback of the Second World War is reflected in the fact that the Soviet population exceeded that of the U.S.A. by 45% in 1939: Soviet deaths attributable to the War are estimated at about 15 million, compared with about 300,000 for the U.S.A., and the proportion in the reproductive age-groups was clearly high. Birth rates in the U.S.S.R. since 1950 have been as high as in the U.S.A. and considerably higher than the average for Western Europe.

Apart from considerations of size of land and population, position in the world has a pervading influence upon the fortunes of any country, both by determining, to a large extent through climate, the value of the land at the disposal of the people, and by fixing certain geographical relationships with other countries which affect profoundly, through accessibility, exchange of goods, people and ideas in peace and military strategy in war (Fig. 2).

13

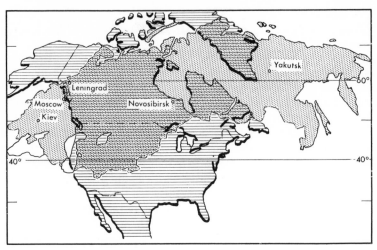

FIG. 1—The northerliness of the Soviet Union, compared with North America

Less obvious but as significant as the fact of size in the Soviet Union is its predominantly high-latitude position (Fig. 1). This factor, together with its land-locked continental nature, goes a long way towards explaining (a) that with a greater area than that possessed by any other country, good farm land is relatively scarce and (b) that with the longest coastline of any country, a maritime, naval or trading tradition has hardly developed. Basic comparisons of the U.S.S.R. and the U.S.A., so topical today, can do no better than begin with latitude, from which it soon appears that Canada is in many ways a more analogous case. Moscow itself (with 6 million inhabitants) is further north than Edmonton, Alberta, the most northerly city of any real importance (over 100,000 people) in Canada, while in Britain its opposite number is Edinburgh. Leningrad (3 million inhabitants), for two centuries the capital of Imperial Russia, is on the latitude of southern Alaska or the Shetland Islands. Only the southern Ukraine, the Caucasus regions and Soviet Middle Asia are in latitudes comparable with those of the northern part of the United States (e.g. Tashkent = Chicago; Baku = Salt Lake City). Whereas the entire U.S. coastline is normally ice-free, hardly any of the Soviet coastline is so fortunate. Even Odessa and Vladivostok on the southern edges of the country (comparable latitudes to Seattle and Boston respectively) are troubled by ice in winter although they are normally kept open artificially. However a notable anomaly is the completely ice-free port of Murmansk, by far the largest city in the world within the Arctic Circle, and there are small corners of the Soviet Union which are almost as mild as California or Florida. Thus, although natural patterns are writ large, with a uniformity and continentality of landscape and climate inconceivable in England, the straitjacket does not fit with equal tightness over all the regions of the Soviet Union.

The Soviet Union's geographical relationships with its neighbours can be understood properly only with the help of a globe. The Soviet Union is a massive Eurasian state but it is noteworthy that while three-quarters of its land lies in Asia, three-quarters of its population still lives in the European part (i.e. west of the Urals) in spite of the easterly displacements in this century. Thus Europe, of all major neighbouring land areas, is the nearest to the Soviet 'effective national territory', has always had the closest contact with it, and is physically unseparated from it by mountains or seas. Like America, Russia is fundamentally European, and the two most all-pervading themes in the Soviet Union today, Marxist theory and the techniques of the industrial revolution, are unmistakably European in origin. Since the war, the so-called 'Iron Curtain' has assumed the role of the most effective and significant frontier in Europe, cutting across previous groupings. The Eastern part has been, to some extent, integrated with and oriented to the Soviet Union (though there are signs that the bonds are now weakening), while the Western part has in general looked across the Atlantic for its economic and military connections. Europe west of the 'Iron Curtain', in spite of its comparatively tiny area, has almost precisely the same population (about 300 millions) as Eastern Europe and the Soviet Union combined. Trade and other currents of activity between the two areas have increased recently, but the dichotomy remains.

The geographical relationship between the Soviet Union and its great rival, the United States, can be seen most dramatically though not entirely realistically by looking down on the north polar sea (Fig. 2). From a 'conventional' map one might not guess that Moscow is equidistant from Washington, D.C., and from Seattle, or that Seattle is equidistant from Moscow and Vladivostok. But the geographical separation of the two giants is still formidable. New York is three times as far from Moscow as London is, and nature has interposed vast insulators of ocean, ice or wasteland between the inhabited cores of the two nations. Each country increasingly symbolizes the bi-polar character, ideologically, economically and strategically, of the post-war world.

Beyond the long southern frontier of the U.S.S.R., in Asia, over half the world's population is concentrated. Nearly half of these are in China,

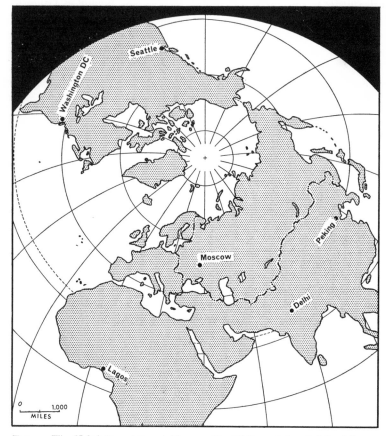

FIG. 2—The U.S.S.R. and its neighbours. (An Oblique Azimuthal Equidistant
projection centred on Moscow.)

which cannot now be regarded, except in the most formal sense, as being
part of the same Communist world as the Soviet Union, or anything but a
threat to the latter. The remainder, often called 'underdeveloped' and
'uncommitted' and for the most part newly emerged from colonial status,
view the growth and development of Soviet Asia with varying degrees of
admiration and apprehension. The Soviet Union presents itself as an
Asian country, a Moslem country, an 'anti-colonial country' and one which
has apparently transformed itself within a generation from a dominantly
agrarian and illiterate condition similar to that prevailing over much of
Southern Asia today. In Africa too, which has the same total population

as the Soviet Union, the same attitude prevails, and Lagos, Nigeria, is no further from Moscow than is Peking. Finally Latin America, which, with the South West Pacific, is the remotest inhabited land from the Soviet Union, also has a comparable population total, and is emerging from varying degrees of economic dependence and agrarian poverty. A similar ambivalent attitude to the U.S.S.R. is found there, and the case of Cuba has shown the potency of Soviet influence even at that distance

In the mid-nineteenth century, in terms of power, wealth and influence, Britain was unchallenged in the world. In the incomparably broadened and yet shrunken world of the mid-twentieth century the U.S.A. has become heir to this position. Whether the twenty-first will be the Russian century is, to say the least, not entirely ruled out. The permanence and relative power of states rest in the long run on the basic wealth of their lands and the way in which their people use it. Thus any valid assessment of the Soviet Union of today and tomorrow demands, among other approaches, that of the regional geographer, whose concern is to analyse and interpret the character of the country's component parts, from the standpoint of significance to their inhabitants.

PART I: GENERAL

CHAPTER ONE

The Natural Habitat

LANDFORMS

THE popular image of Russia as a land of vast, more or less level plains has more than a grain of truth in it. And yet one can find, within the borders of the Soviet Union, a wide variety of scenery. There are rugged peaks higher than any in the western hemisphere and salt flats well below sea-level; glaciers and volcanoes; vast marshes on permanently frozen ground and hot sandy deserts; gently rolling, domesticated landscapes and coasts reminiscent of the French Riviera.

This section is concerned with the basic skeleton of the country, with the major relief units or land forms upon which the flesh—soils, plant, animal and human life—has developed. It is hoped to avoid treatment of details which properly belong in the regional chapters and to consider only those aspects of origins and sequence in the development of the land forms which add to our understanding of their present character and human significance.

Major Relief (Fig. 3)

The 'Tees–Exe' line in Britain or a line along the Rocky Mountain foot-hills in North America separate in broad but meaningful terms highlands from lowlands. In the Soviet Union the division may be said to follow the River Lena from mouth to source and thenceforth run parallel to and about three hundred miles from the southern frontier as far as the Black Sea.

To the west and north of this line, covering more than two-thirds of the country, the relief is characteristically low, the landforms subdued and un-spectacular and nowhere does the elevation exceed about 6,000 feet. It is noteworthy that in all these respects North America east of the Rockies is similar. However, an important distinction is that in the Soviet region really low land (less than 600 feet) is predominant, while in the American region the average level is considerably higher. The significance of this Soviet stretch of lowland, much the largest on the earth, lies mainly in its mitigating effect upon the country's northerliness, especially in agri-culture.

Whereas the upland areas west and north of the dividing line have the character of plateaux of low and fairly uniform height, those to the east and south are typically ranges with steep slopes and jagged crests of uneven height—from 6,000–10,000 feet in the north-east and from 10,000–15,000 feet in the mountains of Middle Asia and the Caucasus. Isolated peaks exceed 18,000 feet in the Caucasus and 24,000 feet in Pamir. While the Urals may be compared with the Appalachians in height, age and appearance, the ranges which girdle the Soviet Union on the south are of the Alpine or Rocky mountain type (Fig. 4).

The nature of the rocks

The great Russian plain is underlain almost everywhere by a very ancient platform of hard crystalline rocks, but only in a few places does it outcrop at the surface. In European Russia the most extensive of such outcrops is in the north-west, in Karelia and the Kola peninsula. It is very similar to the 'shields' of Scandinavia and Eastern Canada and the hardness of the rock combined with the action of ice has led to the occurrence of innumerable lakes and has provided a poor basis for soil formation. Further south this rock outcrops in much smaller patches, notably in the southern Ukraine where, for example, it forms the sill over which the Dnieper river tumbles to produce electricity. Granite and mica schists are prominent among the economically valuable types of rock and as in the Canadian shield the regions where this platform emerges or is hardly buried have proved rich in metals such as iron, manganese and nickel. This latter characteristic doubly applies to the rather younger Ural mountains, where the rocks yield as great a variety of metals as any comparable area on earth.

The more recent beds of horizontal or gently folded sedimentary rocks which predominate on the surface of the Great Russian Lowland include various types of limestone, chalk, clay, shale and sandstone. They house the great reserves of petroleum and coal, as well as raw materials for the chemical, cement and steel industries. In some parts of European Russia these rocks stand out as low plateaux or escarpments, giving birth to the river systems and being dissected by them.

The recently folded Alpine mountains of the south and north-east, while a homogeneous group in their morphology, are exceedingly heterogeneous in their rock types. Though they are less rich in accessible mineral resources than the ancient eroded plateaux, such items as sulphur, mercury, gold and diamonds are obtained and also some small but rich deposits of oil, especially on the flanks of the Caucasus. These mountains are good collectors of snow and ice and this, together with their precipitous slopes, makes them the greatest repository of hydro-electric power in the Soviet Union. Finally, it should be noted that the geological youth of the mountains results in their being subject to earthquakes and volcanic activity. Volcanic eruptions are confined at present to Kamchatka and the Kuril Islands and geothermal steam is becoming an economic asset there. Hot sulphurous springs have long been used in the spas of the North Caucasus and elsewhere. The earthquakes are often disastrous—Ashkhabad, capital of the Turkmen republic, was wrecked by one in 1948.

The legacy of the Ice Age

Most of the landscape of the Soviet Union bears the clear imprint of the recent Ice Age, in one way or another. The later advances and retreats coincided with the early attempts of man to make a living on this land. The northern part of European Russia bore the brunt of the glacial invasion. When fully extended the ice-sheet sent two broad lobes down the Dnieper and Don valleys (Fig. 3). This was 300 miles further south than the limit reached by the ice in England but 700 miles short of the North American equivalent. In Siberia the continental ice-sheet was much less extensive, and east of the Taymyr peninsula actually disappeared. Local glaciers, as in the Alps, developed and crept down mountains like the Caucasus, Tien Shan, and Altay, and the shrunken remnants can be seen today. In the unglaciated regions water-bodies were immensely swollen. The ice-front blocked the flow of the Ob and Yenisey systems, creating a vast lake which spilled over into the Caspian and Aral Sea areas. (Incidentally the Russians have a plan for partly recreating this condition, by substituting concrete for ice across the lower Ob.) The Caspian, Aral and Black Seas were joined together and an arm of this sea apparently stretched up the Volga to the present site of Kazan.

In terms of today's physical landscape in the plain of European Russia the most fundamental distinction is between the glaciated (and incidentally mostly forested) country north of a rough line from Lvov to Perm and the southern unglaciated and unforested lands. To the north the ice has left in its wake a chaotically unkempt drainage system, with extensive marshlands and lakes and great morainic dumps of unsorted earth and boulders. Some of the more prominent terminal moraines have been used as routeways, for instance the road well-trodden by French and German soldiers, through Minsk and Smolensk to Moscow. Near the southern edges of the ice-sheets deposition by melt-water streams and by the strong winds which characteristically blow out from ice-sheets have had the effect of sorting and spreading out the finer material. Thus the Ukraine, with its thick spread of fine

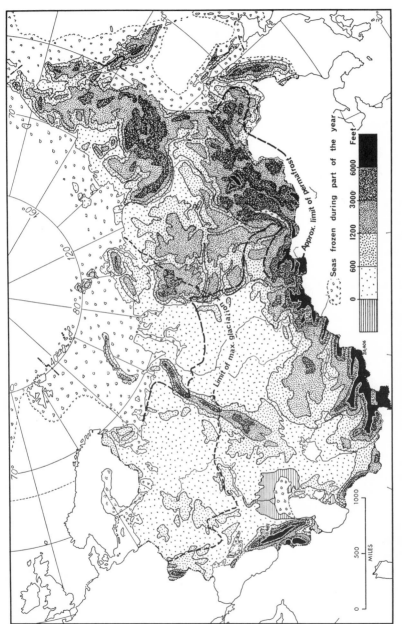

FIG. 3—The height of the land and the impact of freezing conditions

löss (loess), has benefited at the expense of its northern neighbours in the same way as has southern England or the U.S. Corn Belt. The softness of this *löss* has facilitated the formation of the widespread gullies and ravines (*ovragi*) of the Ukrainian landscape, which hinder communications and farming.

Nearly half the total area of the Soviet Union today has permanently frozen ground (*merzlota*) which may extend from a few feet to a thousand feet in depth. Most of this 'permafrost' is in Eastern Siberia, which was not covered by a continental ice-sheet. In fact it seems that this area acquired its frozen ground because of the very light snowfall which, in the Ice Age as today, prevents the formation of a protecting 'blanket' and permits excessive radiation and the prolonged severe temperatures to put the land into a deep freeze (Fig. 3).

The great extent of permanently frozen ground obviously has tremendous significance for the development of the Soviet land. Not only agriculture but the construction of buildings, roads and railways comes up against difficult problems peculiar to this region. However, an important silver lining to this cloud is the fact that the presence of trees over much of this region is permitted only by the permafrost which confines the limited moisture to the top soil. Further, one may mention the potential food storage possibilities of a system which has proved its worth by preserving mammoths intact and fresh for several thousands of years.

The rivers and lakes

Russia began on its rivers and to this day they remain a vital part of the national fabric. And yet many of them are physically crippled from the point of view of man. Some of the longest, broadest and least useful rivers in the world are in the Soviet Union.

The most coherent group of rivers and the most prominent throughout history is that of European Russia. It forms a radial pattern with its hub in the Central Russian uplands just west of Moscow. This pattern has been a crucial factor in the ultimate supremacy of Moscow, and low 'portages' and later connecting canals have knit the rivers into an integrated transport system. All the rivers north of the Caucasus are paralysed by ice for a period varying from about two months in the Dniester of the south-west to seven months in the Pechora of the north-east. All have highly irregular natural régimes, with high flood levels following the spring thaw which are swollen further by the spring rains, and a drastic lowering of levels in the latter part of the summer. However, this condition is being ironed out by the systems of dams and reservoirs which have been constructed since 1939.

The Volga–Kama is almost a string of lakes and so is the Dnieper. A gentle gradient is common to most of the big rivers but there is a notable difference between the longitudinal profiles of those in the glaciated country and the smoother profiles of the southern rivers. The rapids of the Dnieper bend are unique in the south but would be quite normal in the north-west. Even the Volga has many rapids in its upper reaches. The generally softer rock in the south also helps to increase the difference between the high right and low left banks as compared with many of the northern rivers. This phenomenon, which has had an important influence on the siting of towns, is considered to be due to the normal tendency for all moving bodies to be deflected to the right of their course in the northern hemisphere (Ferrel's Law).

The Siberian rivers are similar to those of European Russia in their general régime and rank among the longest rivers in the world. Of the three giants the Yenisey is much the most valuable. It is more practically navigable than the Lena because the latter has an exceptionally irregular flow due to its rapid run-off over permanently frozen ground. The Lena also suffers from a longer frozen period and reaches a part of the Arctic which is always full of wind-packed ice, through a tortuous delta which is sometimes blocked even in midsummer. Summer sea ice conditions are much freer to the west of the Taymyr peninsula. Although the Ob–Irtysh system, the longest in the Soviet Union (3,000 miles) shares with the Yenisey this comparative advantage, this is nullified by the fact that it dawdles endlessly through the almost flat swamps of its basin, taking 1,200 miles to descend 300 feet, and becoming braided, shallow and stagnant. Finally the Yenisey, which has easily the greatest volume of all the Soviet river systems, shares with the Nile and St Lawrence the great asset of a natural holding reservoir in Lake Baykal which, lying in a rift valley, is the deepest lake on earth, and twice the size of Wales or Lake Ontario. This circumstance has contributed towards making the Yenisey system the greatest potential hydro-electric power-house in the Soviet Union.

With one exception the Siberian rivers experience especially chaotic spring flooding conditions because of the fact that the thaw comes to their upper before their lower reaches. The exception is the Amur, which flows from west to east, and is troubled by ice for only five months, compared with ten to twelve in the lower Lena. The Amur is also unique in its régime; because of the monsoon climate the flood levels come in July and August rather than in the spring.

In the southern part of the country there is an inland drainage area nearly as large as the U.S.A. It includes the Volga system, which although now connected with the oceans for transport purposes still drains exclusively into the landlocked Caspian. The surface of this salt lake, the world's largest inland body of water, is half as large again as the combined Great Lakes of North America, and is nearly 100 feet below mean sea level. Moreover, its level has been falling steadily over the last thirty years, as it has done intermittently in recent geological times, and this, coupled with the encroachment of the Volga delta and the creation of the new reservoirs upstream, is causing the shallow northern part of the Caspian, one of the richest of the Soviet fishing grounds, to shrink. Much of the Caspian is only one-third as saline as normal sea-water: this is due partly to the shallow natural evaporating lagoon of Kara-Bogaz-Gol, which is almost as salty as the Dead Sea or the Great Salt Lake, and which is liable to be left high and dry if the Caspian level falls much further.

The Aral Sea, which is even less saline than the Caspian, receives the only two important rivers in the Middle Asian desert, the Syr Darya and the Amu Darya, which are fed by mountain ice and snow. The former discharges only about one-third as much water as the latter, but is more manageable for the all-important function of irrigation. The Aral Sea has also begun to shrink seriously in recent years, largely as a result of accelerated use of the inflowing rivers for purposes of irrigation. Like the Caspian it partly freezes in winter. Lake Balkhash is a long and very shallow lake which is fresh in its western half, where the river Ili feeds it, and slightly brackish in its eastern part. Most of the other streams of Middle Asia are either seasonal in flow or eventually peter out in the sands as a result of evaporation and irrigation.

The coastline and the Soviet seas

No country on earth is anything like as hamstrung by its coastline or shut in by its own seas as the Soviet Union. In proportion to area Britain has seventy times as long a coastline as the Soviet Union whereas the United States and Soviet figures are much the same. The valuable portions of the Soviet coastline are few and far between. The only direct year-round access to the high seas, apart from some of the tiny Kuril Islands, is obtained through the short Murman coast of the far north-west, where the Gulf stream just manages to keep the winter sea ice at bay. Archangel, the great port three hundred miles further south, in the White Sea, is paralysed by ice from November to May. The Arctic coast west of the Taymyr peninsula is passable for a short summer season, but beyond this point only the occasional well-protected and well-equipped ship of the Northern Sea Route Administration can pass in midsummer, with luck. Virtually all the long mainland Pacific coast is frozen up—the southern edge of the frozen sea coincides, in an uncanny way, with the southern border of the Soviet Union. Even on the western and south-western margins of the U.S.S.R., within reach of the moderating breath of the Atlantic, the premier Soviet port, Leningrad, is frozen for several months, while Riga and Odessa are also troubled by ice for a short period. In the Baltic Kaliningrad (Königsberg), which was acquired from Germany in 1945, is the only major ice-free port, and in the Black Sea only the ports of the Crimean and Caucasian coasts are similarly favoured.

There are very few good natural harbours with deep water and solid elevated land accessible to well-peopled and good trading country; no New Yorks or San Franciscos. Most of the coastline is low and marshy with few indentations and often choked with sand or gravels. In important parts of the Baltic and Black Seas, sandspits built by currents have almost sealed up potentially usable anchorages. Of the few good natural harbours there should be mentioned Sevastopol on the southern tip of the Crimea, Murmansk in its rocky fjord, and Vladivostok on the Bay of the Golden Horn.

Finally, two general points may be made about the Soviet seas—first that the Soviet Union is one of the world's chief sea-fishing nations, abutting on and sharing in the rich grounds of the north-west Pacific as well as the north-east Atlantic, and secondly that from three of the most valuable of the Soviet seas access to the open ocean can easily be impeded by a foreign power.

PHYSICAL REGIONS

By way of summary it seems desirable to try to distinguish broad regions which are relatively homogeneous in their landforms, including drainage characteristics. It should be clear, however, that such generalized regions always conceal within them distinct sub-regions which can be more appropriately recognized in the regional chapters.

A. *Mountainous country*

1. *The Ranges of Eastern Siberia.* The character of this region is dominantly one of young folded mountain ranges with crests varying between 6,000 and 10,000 feet, some of which, like the Chersky, have only been fully discovered and mapped in the Soviet era. There has been much faulting and Lake Baykal (5,000 feet deep) lies in a rift valley. There is volcanic activity in the Kamchatka area (one volcano is 16,000 feet high) and earthquakes are common. Crystalline rocks are prominent and this is

the chief Soviet source of gold and diamonds. Apart from Kamchatka and the south-east fringe all of this land is permanently frozen. Most of it is drained, through marshy coastal plains, to the ice-choked eastern Arctic by the Lena and Kolyma systems and in the south via the Amur into the Okhotsk Sea.

2. *The Sayan and Altay mountains* differ from those of the last group in that they have the appearance of high and wide plateaux varying from 9,000 to 14,000 feet, with dome-like summits. They are deeply dissected by the headwaters of the Yenisey, Ob and Irtysh. There are numerous glaciers in the Altay, and this is the chief Soviet source of lead and zinc, while the chief coalfield is on its northern flank.

3. *The Middle Asian folded ranges* (Tien Shan, Alay and Pamir) are the highest of all—everywhere over 10,000 feet, and reaching 24,600 feet. The snow-line begins at 11,000–15,000 feet and extensive snow and ice-fields feed the desert rivers. The Kopet Dag range (10,000 feet) is everywhere below the snow-line.

4. *The Caucasus* main range is highly precipitous, particularly in the west, and reaches 18,000 feet. Present and past glaciation is much in evidence as well as earthquakes and sulphurous springs. Many torrential rivers descend on both sides. The southern 'lesser Caucasus' is lower, plateau-like, and has no glaciers. There are rich deposits of petroleum and manganese. The Crimean mountains and the Soviet Carpathians are Alpine fold mountains of a lower elevation (4,000–6,000 feet), more subdued relief and with no permanent snow or ice.

B. *Low eroded plateaux of old hard rock*

5. *The shield of Karelia and the Kola peninsula* is a little below 1,000 feet high, with one plateau-like massif, the Khibiny mountains, standing above the general level, at 3,000 feet. Heavy glaciation on hard rock has left thousands of lakes, with rapids on the rivers. It is rich in minerals, especially apatite (phosphate rock), the valuable columbium group, iron and nickel.

6. *The Urals* is a middle-aged mountain range of rounded relief features. Except at a few points the crest is only about 2,000 feet high in the inhabited southern half and a little higher further north. Rocks include limestones as well as crystallines, with many mineral veins. It is the chief Soviet source of bauxite, platinum, nickel, chrome, asbestos and has rich iron deposits, with oil and coal on its flanks.

7. *The Central Siberian Plateau* has been deeply dissected by big rivers of the Yenisey and Lena systems, so the landforms appear as a series of

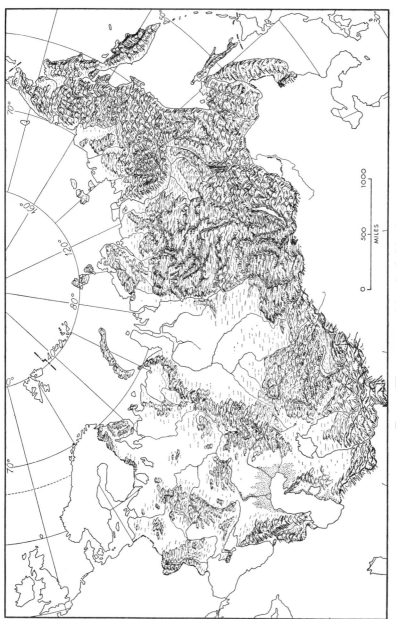

Fig. 4—The anatomy of the physical landscape

table mountains at a general level of about 2,000 feet, with occasional peaks exceeding 4,000 feet. The rocks include crystallines, coal and extensive lava fields. Nickel, cobalt, platinum and copper are mined on the north-western edge of the plateau. The ice-sheet was confined to the north-west corner, but virtually the whole region is in the permafrost zone.

8. *The Kazakh Upland* is a plateau of old hard rocks similar in levels to the Central Siberian Plateau, but much less dissected. It forms the watershed between the Ob system and the inland drainage area. It is the chief Soviet source of copper and has a coalfield on its northern flank.

C. *Lowlands of predominantly soft and recent rocks*

9. *The plain of European Russia roughly north of the Lvov–Perm line* has been glaciated and its land and water features are related to this experience. There are extensive marshes, lakes and confused drainage, with morainic dumps. The basic rocks are generally soft and most of the land is well below 600 feet high. Peat and brown coal are widespread.

10. *The southern part of the European Russian lowland* consists of the valleys of south-flowing rivers and intervening low plateaux or escarpments. Limestone and chalk are common and there is a thick covering of fine silty *löss* which has often been carved into ravines. There are a few outcrops of old hard rock, and rich deposits of iron and manganese, coal and oil.

11. *The West Siberian Plain* is the largest stretch of really low land in the world, drained by the Ob system. Marshes cover most of the area, except on the southern margins. The rocks are soft and recent, with coal and iron on the southern margins. Only the northern quarter is permafrozen.

12. *The Caspian Aral lowland* is a region of inland drainage and predominantly desert landscapes, including sand dunes, bare rock, clay hollows and salt flats. Much of the land is below sea-level and all water-bodies are somewhat saline. Oil and mineral salts are obtained.

This survey has been confined to the sheer framework of land and water in the Soviet Union. From it a dismal picture has emerged of large parts of the country which at present seem too mountainous, too rocky, too water-logged, too frozen, too salty, too sandy to be attractive to man as colonizer. But the huge size of the country allows for a prodigal writing-off of at least half the area for normal settlement, while retaining it as a rich repository of minerals, and there still remains a usable portion at least as large as that of any other country.

CLIMATE

The prime characteristic of the Soviet climate, continentality, results in the first place from the sheer mass of land involved and its position in the northern hemisphere. The country is wide open to the Arctic and, unlike North America, is cut off from the tropical air to the south by a continuous mountain rim. The general westerly airstream makes the Atlantic, not the Pacific, the tempering influence, and continentality (as measured by annual range of temperature) is intensified from south-west to north-east. But, although the Atlantic air has easy access to the Soviet Union, intervening Europe takes the lion's share of its moderating and moistening beneficence. Looked at from the British Isles or the American west coast, all of the Soviet Union, apart from a few miles of the Black Sea coast, has an emphatically continental climate.

A facet of the climate often overlooked but no less significant is its dryness. All parts of the British Isles receive at least 20 inches precipitation in the year and well over half the United States is so favoured, but less than a quarter of the Soviet land area comes up to this level. Even allowing for differences of evaporation, the U.S.S.R. is more similar to Australia in this respect than to any other important power. Moreover, there are hardly any areas which are really wet. In absolute terms, those areas which have more than 40 inches in the Soviet Union are less extensive than those in Britain and only a tiny fraction of the United States equivalent. However in terms of practical significance much of this sparsity of precipitation is ameliorated or nullified by permanently frozen ground, low evaporation, and because other factors make much of the dry land of little use anyway.

A theme of the Russian climate which cannot fail to be noticed is its uniformity. In January it would be perfectly feasible to skate on rivers and canals from the Arctic to the Caspian or travel by sledge from Leningrad to Vladivostok, and almost all Russians can be happy in shirtsleeves in July. But though this general uniformity is an inevitable result of the peculiar nature of the Russian plains, its completeness can be exaggerated. At sea level, in July, without leaving Soviet territory, one can experience the temperatures of both Greenland and Arizona, and in January of the North Pole and the south of France.

Winter conditions

Winter is without doubt the dominant season—a heavy cross that the Russians have always had to bear. Over half the Soviet area experiences continuous freezing temperatures and snow-cover for over half the year.

During the winter there develops over Siberia and Middle Asia a high pressure system of an intensity unique in the world at any season. In the windless centre of this system intense radiation leads to the stagnation of very cold air which drains down into the valleys. Two such sites are Verkhoyansk and Oymyakon where the coldest temperatures on earth, outside the Antarctic, are consistently recorded. The January average at these places is −60° F. and extreme minima of −90° F. or even −100° F. have been recorded. The fact that Oymyakon is only 300 miles from the Pacific reveals the complete subjection of the Soviet east coast to landward air in winter. This outflowing air also extends over European Russia and on occasion crosses the North Sea to paralyse eastern England, but throughout this region its dominance is challenged by the inflowing air from the Atlantic. The latter's tempering influence is clearly reflected in the pattern of the January isotherms, which run predominantly from north-west to south-east in European Russia, rather than west to east as in Siberia and Middle Asia. Whereas almost all of European Russia has average temperatures below freezing point, those of almost all of Siberia are below 0° F., which is colder than any part of the United States. The isotherm for −15° F. more or less coincides with the limit of the permanently frozen ground and within this region the mercury drops steeply towards the 'Cold Pole' of the north-east.

Winter can be differentiated by length as well as severity. Excluding those special areas which escape regular freezing altogether, the frozen period varies from one or two months in the southern Ukraine to ten months or more in the Taymyr peninsula. It should also be noted that the northernmost point of the mainland is half way between the Arctic Circle and the North Pole and that a land area ten times the size of Britain experiences up to three months total darkness in winter. The gulf of winter warmth which encloses the British Isles gives Murmansk the same winter temperature as Astrakhan, 2,000 miles to the south.

There are a few small areas where the mean midwinter temperature is above freezing point. These are the southern coast of the Crimea, the eastern coastlands of the Black Sea, the lowlands around the southern edge of the Caspian Sea and some parts of the middle Amu Darya region near the Afghan border. Altogether these areas are considerably smaller than those areas of the British Isles with comparable winter temperatures. The only

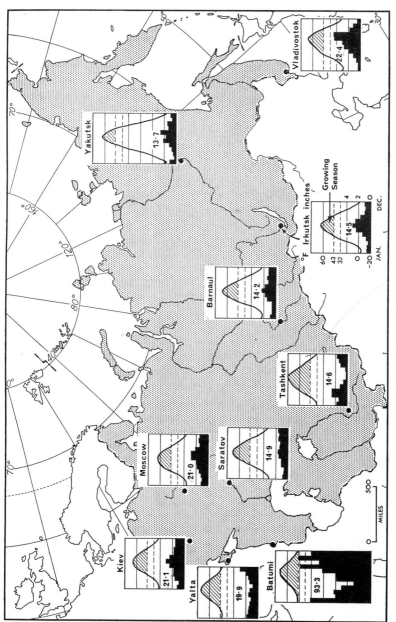

FIG. 5—Some climatic types

part of the Soviet Union which has a January mean temperature in the 40s is the south-eastern corner of the Black Sea, but even this area is slightly cooler than southern California or Florida and, like the latter, is not entirely free from the risk of frost.

Except for the southern margins just mentioned, the winter half-year is the dry season in the Soviet Union. Most of eastern Siberia and the Pacific coast has less than 2 inches of precipitation (or more specifically 2 feet of snow) during the winter, and virtually all the Soviet land east of the Volga has less than 5. A corollary to this is that eastern Siberia is, on the average, only one-third as cloudy as European Russia in winter. The penetration of the Atlantic depressions is reflected in the fact that from 5 to 10 inches are recorded over most of the plain of European Russia. Considerably heavier precipitation, associated largely with depressions which have come from the Mediterranean, occurs at the eastern end of the Black Sea, where the precipitous seaward-facing Caucasus and the funnel-shaped Georgian lowlands form the greatest rain and snow trap in the country. Some depressions even wander across the Caspian and bring much needed rain and snow to the mountains and foothills of Middle Asia. This region and the southern Crimea, which has a modified Mediterranean climate, are the only two parts of the Soviet Union which receive the bulk of their precipitation in winter.

Summer conditions

Spring is a fleeting season in most parts of the Soviet Union. The temperatures in Kiev or Moscow jump about 15° F. between March and April, compared with 5° in London or Glasgow. The thaw is rapid and soon transforms rivers into overflowing torrents and roads into quagmires. It arrives in March in the south-west Ukraine and moves gradually north-eastwards across the country, reaching the Lena mouth in late June. Thus the accumulated winter precipitation, since there are few winter thaws, is being distributed through the soil as the growing season begins. The heating of the land soon leads to the replacement of the high pressure system of Siberia by a low pressure system which invites inflowing winds from the oceans. In addition the quick rise in temperature leads to local convectional activity, and heavy thunderstorms and even hailstorms occur frequently. Thus at least 10 inches are recorded during the summer over most of the plains of European Russia and western Siberia. However, some important farming areas, especially the southern Ukraine, the lower Don and Volga valleys and the 'new lands' of western Siberia, fall short of this figure, and their totals are notoriously variable from year to year. The whole of Soviet Middle Asia is practically rainless in summer, and the Lena basin and neighbouring parts of eastern Siberia have a very light rainfall which is preserved near the surface by the permanently frozen subsoil.

Although the low pressure system is not as intense as the one which forms over northern India in summer, it is enough to ensure that the Soviet Far East receives the benefit of the last gasp of the south-west monsoon. August and September are the wettest months at Vladivostok and several parts of this region receive more than 20 inches during the summer. The Black Sea-facing Georgian Transcaucasus, in summer as in winter, is the wettest part of the Soviet Union.

In July most of the U.S.S.R. is warmer than London though not as warm as most of the U.S.A. Temperatures soar almost everywhere to unusual heights for the latitudes, and one vital criterion for differentiating region from region climatically is the length of the summer. A critical mean daily temperature is $43°$ F. when the growing season is set in train (Fig. 5). By this index the coastal plain of the western Transcaucasus has a continuous season while that of the Lena delta has none. In the Ukraine Kiev has as long a growing season as Chicago or London. Moscow, however, is more comparable to Winnipeg, and most of the southern agricultural land of western Siberia is similar to that of Minnesota in this respect. Tashkent, in Central Asia, has as long a growing season as Nashville, Tennessee, or Milan (9 months). Even Verkhoyansk has a three-month growing season which is enough for the ripening of special crops, and may be compared with Dawson City in the Canadian Yukon, which has a similar constricted inland valley position. The long summer days of the Arctic Circle do stretch the effective length of the growing season, but on the other hand the chilling effect of the proximity of the frozen ocean and the fact that the northern coastland is the most clouded part of the U.S.S.R. in summer are factors which reduce and in many places eliminate growth.

Length of growing season is not the only test of a summer. Reykjavik in Iceland has as long a growing season as Moscow, but almost all useful plants require warmer temperatures than Iceland's summer can provide. Taking $56°$ F. as a somewhat arbitrary measure, it appears that Moscow has about $3\frac{1}{2}$ months above this temperature, which compares closely with Glasgow on the same latitude, although Moscow rises to a higher maximum in midsummer. Kiev corresponds with London and the only regions which have at least six months 'summer' by this definition (equivalent to New York's) are the southern Crimea and the lower parts of the Transcaucasus and Middle Asia. Finally, a higher standard can be set—that of a hot summer in which the mean monthly temperature stays above $70°$ F. for

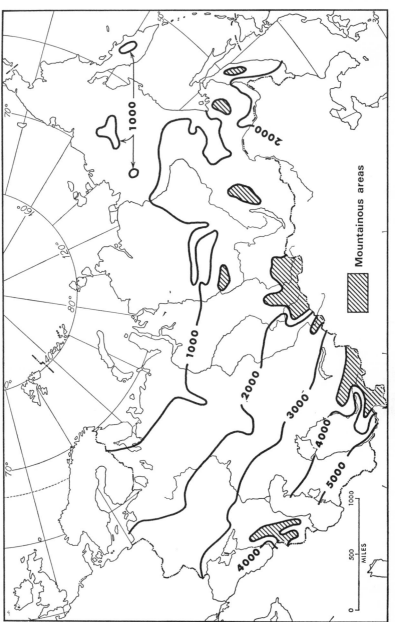

FIG. 6—Distribution of accumulated temperatures—day-degrees, centigrade, above 10° C (50° F)—(after C. T. Selianinov)

three or four months, a quite typical pattern in the United States (e.g. St Louis). In the Soviet Union only the Middle Asian desert area and a few lowlands near the Caspian Sea measure up to this standard. For comparison it may be noted that no part of the British Isles reaches 70° in any month.

Conclusions

While one can be quite precise about the delimitation of landform regions, climatic regions are difficult to define in this land of broad uniformity and hardly perceptible transition zones. On the other hand, many of the significant regional variations are faithfully reflected in the soil and vegetation zones which will be described in the next section. It will be more useful here, by way of summary, to attempt to assess the significance of the blessings and curses of the Soviet climate in their net effect upon the people who have to live with it.

The two elements of the climatic budget are heat and moisture, but each is largely wasted except in combination with the other.

The outstanding reservoir of heat in the Soviet Union is the Middle Asian desert. Here the cloudless, scorching summer days and short winter build up the highest totals of accumulated temperatures (above 50° F.) in the country, comparable with most of the southern part of the United States (Fig. 6). Given irrigation water, as in the latter regions, these temperatures are ideal for cotton and other sub-tropical crops, but only a fraction of the generated heat is captured by man, which lends a sense of wistful urgency to schemes for siphoning off to the south some of the surplus water of the northern marshes.

The lowlands on both sides of the Caucasus range and in the Crimea accumulate heat on much the same scale as southern California or the borderlands between the U.S. Corn and Cotton Belts, and grow the same crops. The southern part of the Ukraine resembles the northern fringes of the Corn Belt in this respect, while the northern Ukraine around Kiev and Kharkov, for long the most intensively farmed region of Russia, has a heat income more like that of North Dakota and northern Minnesota, and this would apply to most of the new wheat lands of western Siberia which have been broken in since 1954. The older farmed land of western Siberia, as well as the cleared forest land of the Moscow region and the Baltic Republics and the Far Eastern strip north of Vladivostok, are in the same heat category as the Canadian Prairies or south-east England. North of these regions is an area, covering a good half of the U.S.S.R., which is relatively short of heat and crippled by the winter, but even here, except for the

Arctic coastlands, there is enough heat to support agriculture in certain places where other factors permit. For instance the Yakutsk area of the Middle Lena is as cumulatively warm as the Edmonton region of the Canadian prairies, while Archangel and even Verkhoyansk compare favourably with north-east Scotland in this respect.

In the case of the distribution of effective moisture income (i.e. precipitation minus evaporation) the most important fact is that most of the lands where there is a positive net balance are at least marginally deficient in heat (Fig. 7). Regions of superabundant moisture comparable to the mountains of western Britain or western North America are Karelia, the lower Ob and Yenisey valleys and the Pacific coastlands, all of which are very sparsely peopled and where water stands about in swamps or lakes. One small and important outlier of this moisture category, the only one in a warm region, is the western Transcaucasus, where drainage of the swamps is the chief pre-requisite to the extension of sub-tropical agriculture. Somewhat drier regions, where the moisture is everywhere adequate, comparable to lowland England or the U.S.A. east of the Mississippi, include all of European Russia north of Kiev and Kuybyshev, the Far Eastern monsoonal strip and much of Siberia. A dry zone in north-east Siberia stands out, but the permafrost considerably ameliorates the practical results of this condition.

Broadly speaking, one can say that south of a line from Odessa to Lake Baykal, and always excepting the western Caucasus, shortage of moisture is more or less of a problem and an obstacle to the progress of farming. In this respect the Ukraine, the Middle Volga and the farming strip along the Trans-Siberian railway can be compared with the western wheat-growing margins of the North American Great Plains which similarly grade into semi-desert ranching country and eventually into waterless desert.

Thus the major climatic misfortune in the Soviet Union, probably even transcending the paralysing winters in economic cost, is the lack of geographical correspondence between the reservoir of heat and that of moisture. There is nothing quite comparable to the great mass of the eastern United States where adequate heat is married to adequate moisture. The problem of bringing water to the parched southern lands is perhaps *the* agricultural problem and one which is being steadily attacked with irrigation, dry farming methods and special plant breeding. In absolute terms, the Soviet Union has about the same amount of climatically usable (and used) farmland as the United States but more of the Russian farmland is climatically marginal in one way or another.

While agriculture is the most completely dependent on climate of all

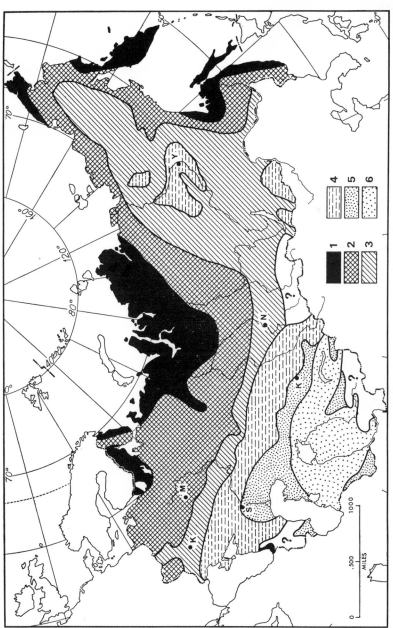

Fig. 7—Distribution of effective moisture, $\dfrac{\text{Precipitation}}{\text{Evaporation}}$

100 = equilibrium. Legend: 1 = over 150, 2 = 100–149, 3 = 60–99, 4 = 30–59, 5 = 13–29, 6 = below 12 (after Ivanov)

economic activities, others, particularly transport, are also profoundly affected. Finally there are many hypotheses, most of them private, about the effect of an extreme continental climate on the character and capability of people. Ellsworth Huntington, the eloquent protagonist of the stormy yet equable climate of North-West Europe as a civilizing influence, recommended the shipment of the Russian peasants to Mesopotamia for the winter for the good of their souls. One can deplore the long enforced idleness of the peasant's winter, which was often passed in an overheated drowse, broken only by the periodic necessity to take a stroll in order to freeze out the vermin. It is certainly a far cry from the British experience, where the very heating systems embody a perennial hope that the existence of winter may be ignored altogether.

However, since Huntington wrote, the Russian 'type' has been rapidly changing from the illiterate peasant to the literate urban year-round indoor worker. If the British climate is something to grumble about, the Russian climate is something to be reckoned, even wrestled, with. Far from producing a stultifying effect, its challenge may turn out to produce a response in terms of national development as great as that sometimes attributed to the successive cyclonic storms of North-West Europe.

NATURAL REGIONS

The Russian landscape is stamped in the image of its climate. The divisions which really meant something to man as he strove to colonize this land were not the hills and the vales but the forests and the grasslands. On no other landscape has the climate been able to use such a broad brush. Thus it is not surprising that Russian scientists were the first to reveal the perfectly balanced interacting system which binds climate, soil and vegetation together and is expressed in the natural regions. These regions form the basic framework of Russian physical geography, which continues to provide a more integrated picture of the living physical environment than is usually achieved in other countries.

Moisture and heat are the climatic elements which create a particular soil, first by breaking up the parent rock and later moving its various ingredients up and down and secondly by providing the correct conditions for the growth of a certain type of vegetation which in turn helps to build up and add distinctive character to the soil. But this all takes time and because the climate itself has been gradually assuming its present pattern during post-glacial times some of the soil and vegetation associations have not yet reached a mature stage and the boundaries of the natural regions are often blurred.

In a country with a severe and uniform climate and vast plains the parent rock has much less influence upon the character of its offspring soil than it does in Britain with its varied climate and relief. However, particularly in the drier lands of the south, some underlying formations like limestone or *löss* do make themselves felt.

The Russians recognize nine major natural regions (also called 'landscape zones') in their country, each of which will be described below. But first attention should be directed once again to the primary division of the country by a line joining the north-west Ukraine with the neighbourhood of Lake Baykal and the Amur valley. To the north of this line there is adequate moisture but inadequate heat, the soils are leached and acidic ('pedalfers') and trees are ubiquitous. To the south, always excepting the eastern Black Sea coastlands, there is enough heat but not enough moisture, the soils are well-supplied, often too well-supplied, with soluble salts (the 'pedocal' group), and grass and drought-resisting shrubs characterize the treeless landscapes. The trend of the natural regions is latitudinal, following that of the climate, but in the mountain areas of the south and east the zoning of landscapes and climate becomes vertical (Fig. 8).

The Tundra

This is the most cramped and hopeless of all the natural regions. It covers at least a tenth of the Soviet area and forms a continuous strip from the Norwegian border to Kamchatka. It is underlain almost everywhere by a permanently frozen subsoil. The winters are long and severe and the midsummer temperatures, in spite of the continuous daylight within the Arctic Circle, stay below 50° F. as a rule. It is this summer coolness rather than the long winter which keeps trees, except for midget birches, out of the tundra (Plate XXXI). Although precipitation is generally scanty, the low evaporation and permafrozen layer make this region one of surplus moisture during the short summer. The generally waterlogged surface favours the formation of peat, but no soil worthy of the name. Aeration, the work of bacteria and other creatures in the soil, plant decomposition and humus formation are all at a minimum. However, those local sites in the tundra which are both better drained and have a sheltered southerly aspect do allow for the formation of an acidic type of soil and for plant growth. Almost all the plants of the tundra are perennials; mosses, lichens, dwarf shrubs and berry-bearing bushes are common, and in some places a brightly coloured carpet of polar flowers appears in summer. The reindeer is *the* animal of the tundra, making the most of the sparse vegetation and supplying all the basic needs of the native people. Mosquitoes and other insects emerge from the marshes and flocks of birds migrate north in summer to eat them. Animals such as the lemming and the fur-bearing foxes are quite common and several species migrate seasonally between forests and the tundra.

In a few suitable places specially hardy grains and potatoes may ripen with the help of the 'midnight sun', and greenhouse fruits and vegetables are produced near the few settlements, in almost wholly man-made soil and climate.

The Tayga

About half the country is covered by trees—a greater area than Canada or the U.S.A. Of this all but a small fraction is coniferous forest or tayga (Plate XXIX). It begins on the southern fringe of the tundra as the mid-summer temperatures begin regularly to rise above 50° F., and eventually gives way to deciduous forest and grass when the effective moisture starts to decline and the summers become longer.

The most valuable part of the tayga is still the European part, which has been a rich source of wealth for Russians from their very beginnings. Scots pine, Norway spruce and Siberian fir are common here, and there is no permanently frozen ground. In most of Siberia the larch, which is well adapted to the permanently frozen ground, is much more prevalent. Birch is common on the northern and southern fringes and it usually contrives to make a first appearance in second-growth forest, for instance, following a fire. Bogs, often with moss and peat formations, are very widespread in the tayga of Western Siberia and many parts of European Russia, but not in Eastern Siberia.

The bogs are often created or aggravated by the widespread occurrence of hardpan a little way below the surface. This is one symptom of the fact that throughout the tayga there is a net loss of minerals and plant foods from the top soil by the process known as leaching. In spite of the generally low precipitation, there is a positive balance of moisture due to the low evaporation, the permafrozen layer and the long winters which result in a great spring thaw which acts like heavy rain as soon as the soil is opened up to water action. Owing to the coolness bacterial action is weak, the cones and needles of the trees make a poor humus contribution and decomposition is long drawn out.

The typical soil formed in the coniferous forests is the *podzol*, which is common over most of Canada and the hilly west of Britain. Its name

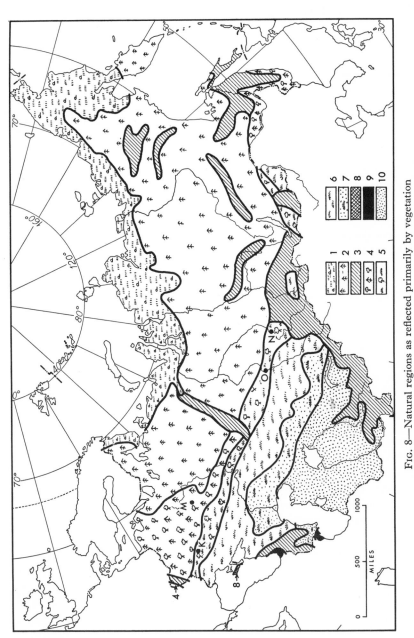

FIG. 8—Natural regions as reflected primarily by vegetation

1 = tundra, 2 = tayga, 3 = mountain (vertical zoning), 4 = mixed forest, 5 = wooded steppe, 6 = steppe, 7 = semi-desert, 8 = Mediterranean, 9 = wet sub-tropical, 10 = desert

(meaning 'ash colour') refers to its typical feature which is a grey-white layer one or two feet down, composed largely of sand and leached of its humus, clay and salts. These have been deposited below, beyond the reach of the plough. The thin surface mat or largely undigested conifer waste is not particularly rich in humus.

It was the fur-bearing animals like the ermine, sable and beaver that first lured man into the tayga, but the more valuable of these have retreated further and further eastwards. Elk, deer, hare, squirrel, lynx and bear are common, as well as birds such as grouse, woodpecker and pelican.

Most of the tayga is unpopulated and unused, and in places forest fires can rage for weeks without being detected. Much of the timber is poor and inaccessible. Except in a few dry pockets like the Middle Lena basin and along the southern margins, agriculture is absent. However, as in the tundra, the demand for fresh food near lumber or mining camps makes it worth while to plaster the soil with lime and raise expensive crops.

The Mixed Forests

All the remaining regions differ from the tundra and the tayga in two important respects. First, they fail to straddle the country from coast to coast. Second, they have very little 'natural' vegetation left.

The mixed forest region illustrates these points well. Its main part forms a triangular wedge in European Russia with its base against the western frontier and its apex just west of the Urals. Then there is a great gap in Siberia until this type is encountered again, in a slightly different form, in the Middle Amur and Ussuri valleys of the Far East.

The mixed forest of European Russia (Plate II), like its analogues in peninsular Europe, has been gradually cleared and pressed into agricultural service over the past thousand years or so. It was in such clearings that the first seeds of Russian nationality germinated. Why was this region populated so early while the tayga is still empty and likely to remain so? Soviet soil maps show both regions combined as undifferentiated podzols but this conceals important distinctions. The soils of the mixed forests are generally leached because, although evaporation is higher than in the tayga, this is partly counterbalanced by higher precipitation. However, the leaching is not as ruinous, and there is much less pan development, while the higher summer temperatures and shorter winters encourage more bacterial activity. Then the presence of such broad-leaved deciduous trees as oak, ash and maple as well as conifers means that more humus is added to the soil in the 'fall', and brown earths similar to those of England or north-east North America are found together with some grey, less fertile podzols and even some modified or 'degraded' black earths. In the Far East the same variety of soil and vegetation is found within a much smaller area, with the added difference from Europe that the deciduous trees and shrubs are of Manchurian and Japanese species, and that the tiger and wild boar replace the lynx and rabbit of the west. Both regions are essentially transition zones and for the European zone, centred on Moscow, this has been a source of strength in the struggle to bring under its control a wider area.

The Steppe

Between the forest of the north and the desert of the south lies a virtually treeless expanse of the grassland (the *steppe*) with its rich *chernozem* or black earth. On either side the steppe is flanked by transition zones, the wooded steppe, which will be included with it here, and the semi-desert, which will be treated with the desert. Since very little of the original vegetation remains, it is .the black earth which expresses the character of the region. This is one of the most productive soils in the world and the Soviet Union has more of it than any other country. It began to be cultivated centuries later than the mixed forest lands, but today it carries well over half of the Soviet arable land.

How has this soil, truly the bread-basket of the Soviet Union, been created? Essentially it results from a lower net balance of moisture than is found in the forest but higher than that in the desert. The warmer and longer summers allow for greater bacterial activity, and this, together with a rather lighter precipitation, reverses the dominance of the leaching process. While leaching does occur, particularly in the spring, the summer heat recaptures the leached materials for the topsoil by capillary action, and there is normally a net accumulation in the surface layers over the year. The blackness of the soil is an indication of its proverbially rich store of humus, built up by centuries of annual decay of the thick growth of tall grasses and further preserved and enriched by the acquisition of lime, löss and clay constituents from the parent rocks. The soils have an excellent texture, which favours proper aeration, permeability and easy cultivation, though in the drier southern margins they bake rather hard, and there are patches of unduly saline (*solonets*) soils.

While in the steppe proper trees are confined to the riversides, where the water table is high, in the wooded steppe, a distinctive hybrid region to the north, they are common, usually in clumps separated by patches of grassland. They consist predominantly of oak in European Russia, much of which has been cleared, and birch in Western Siberia. The soil is transitional but is usually classed mainly as *chernozem*. The densest strip of rural population and of intensive and productive farming in the Soviet Union follows the wooded steppe and the neighbouring part of the steppe in the northern Ukraine. Apart from having a very fertile soil its rainfall is somewhat heavier and more reliable than it is over much of the steppe proper. An irony which is probably not lost on the cultivators of the Russian steppes or the North American prairies is that the climate which has made them a superlative soil cannot always be relied on to ripen their crops.

The Desert

As the climate becomes drier towards the depression around the Caspian and Aral Seas, the black earth slowly degenerates into the less fertile chestnut-coloured soil of the semi-desert. Drought-resisting bushes begin to replace grasses and the vegetation becomes more sparse. This means that there is less of the raw material for humus and a thinner topsoil which is often over-supplied with soluble salts by the summer heat. However, the 'Virgin Lands' plough-up programme of recent years has penetrated some of the northern fringes of this zone, with by no means unmixed success so far.

South of the Aral Sea and Lake Balkhash, in the desert proper, the soil cover is highly variable and sometimes non-existent, the surface consisting of pieces of bare rock or shifting sand-dunes. As noted earlier, the nature of the parent rock becomes more significant in differentiating soil-types, the drier the climate becomes. Clay hollows, which collect and retain whatever water there is and may alternate from temporary lakes to a sun-baked parquet-floor surface, contrast with hard porous limestone which aggravates the aridity. Salts inevitably collect at the surface after a shower of rain and in some places form a solid crust several feet thick known as *solonchak*. Some of the richest soils in the Soviet Union are encountered in the desert area, in particular the strip of löss *sierozems* at the piedmont of the high mountains, and the irrigable alluvium of the big rivers, from which the people of Middle Asia have derived their sustenance for thousands of years. Even in the thirstiest parts of this land, except where the sand is very mobile, there is a surprising profusion of salt-loving shrubs and trees, such as the *saksaul*, many of which can provide some food for sheep and camels. Moreover, the chance shower of the desert, like the fleeting summer of the tundra, can conjure up a magic carpet of ephemeral flowers and grasses.

The Sub-tropical landscapes

This category comprises three small and rather distinct regions in European Russia. On the southern coastal slopes of the Crimea the moist warm winters and hot dry summers have led to the formation of a thin, quite fertile, reddish soil something like that of the Mediterranean, but forest brown earths are rather more common. Mediterranean trees such as olive, juniper and fig are present, as well as oak, beech and pine (Plate VII). The vegetation is well adapted to the summer drought.

The Kolkhida lowland of the western Transcaucasus, is the wettest part of the Soviet Union as well as the warmest in winter. Rain is heavy at all seasons and the soils of the low-lying parts are often waterlogged, though better drained reddish soils are found on slightly higher ground. The forests and undergrowth are very luxuriant and monsoonal plants such as rice, tea, tung and bamboo thrive, as well as citrus fruits (Plate XX).

On the Caspian border of Iran is a narrow strip of similar character—the Lenkoran lowland. The rainfall is not quite as heavy or as well distributed as in Kolkhida and has definite monsoon characteristics, while the winters are slightly cooler, but tea has also been introduced successfully and the forest is dense. The Indian character of the region is suggested by the presence of zebu cattle, wild boars and tigers.

The Mountainous Regions

Although the general principle is that the same natural zones are passed through on ascending a mountain as when moving latitudinally across the plains, this is a generalization which only takes temperature into account. Much depends, of course, on the rainfall; for instance the western Caucasus changes from sub-tropical forests to beech and then to coniferous, after which there are alpine grasslands and finally bare rock and ice-fields, while in the drier plateau-like eastern Caucasus a steppe type of vegetation with very little forest is predominant. On most of the ranges of Eastern Siberia the conifers are succeeded by alpine grasses and tundra, but in the Far East forest prevails even near the summits. On steep slopes, especially on the drier mountain areas such as those of Middle Asia, the frost-bitten scree tends to be as slippery for the soil and vegetation-making processes to grip as the sand-dunes of the desert.

Conclusions

Only the European mixed forest among the Soviet natural regions has a fairly close counterpart in the British Isles. On the other hand, the Soviet regions are reflected in North America from the Yukon to Florida and Quebec to Arizona. The differences are to be discovered by measuring how large each region looms in the continental scheme. In the U.S.S.R. the natural grain is east-west, while in America it is north-south, the former extending half round the world in quite high latitudes and the latter longitudinally joining the polar and tropical seas. Thus, in proportion to size, the Soviet Union has much more tundra and podzolic coniferous forest, and slightly more black earth grassland and arid lands, than North America, while their tracts of mountain landscapes are similar. To balance the slightly podzolized mixed forests around Moscow there are those in the north-east United States and eastern Canada, and the southern Crimea is a very miniature California. Conspicuous by its absence in the U.S.S.R except perhaps in tiny corners of the Transcaucasus, is an analogue to the well-watered, well-heated, generally fertile forest land of the south-east quadrant of the United States. In both continental areas the nature, extent and position of the natural regions, summing up as they do the character of the physical environments, have had a profound effect upon the history of human colonization. In the process they have themselves been significantly modified, and present to each succeeding generation a face that is fresh and yet enduring.

CHAPTER TWO

Historical Background

THE GROWTH OF THE RUSSIAN STATE

THE nation-state of Russia, to which the Soviet Union has become heir, is both old and new—a Europe and a North America rolled into one. Russian national consciousness emerged from a melting-pot of immigrant peoples and took geographical root at about the same time as this was happening in England. On the other hand the 'frontier' in the social rather than the strictly political sense has been as pervading and continuous a feature of national development as it has in North America.

Precursors

Long before the Russians had been heard of, people were roaming over the lands now included in the Soviet Union and were occasionally to be found in relatively civilized settlements. Samarkand in Middle Asia has been an important centre of its region off and on for five thousand years and there were several offshoots of Hellenic civilization along the northern Black Sea coast. But these were exceptional cases, climatically favoured, and on the beaten tracks of the ancient world. The inhabitants of the more northerly lands were few and scattered, much less civilized and characteristically on the move.

As the ice-sheet retreated northwards the natural regions gradually adapted to the changing climates and man followed suit. To the north this resulted in a somewhat milder and more expansive environment for the hunters of the forests. In Middle Asia, the wet period following the retreat of the ice seems to have given way to drier conditions which would have reduced inexorably the animal-carrying capacity of the grasslands. Whatever the reasons, wave after wave of livestock-herding nomads moved out from Mongolia and neighbouring areas along the steppeland route of south Russia towards the rich sedentary edges of Europe (e.g. the Huns in the fifth century A.D.) and also battered on the gates of the Chinese Empire. These peoples, often but not always pillagers, were powerfully organized and were for many centuries a thorn in the side of the embryo Russian state.

The birth of the nation

By the eighth century A.D. Slavic-speaking peoples were moving eastwards from about the Carpathians into the mixed forest region of Russia, following river courses like the Dnieper, Volkhov and upper Volga and clearing patches of forest in the better drained districts. At first they were primarily hunters and collectors and accumulated furs, skins and honey for trading, but later turned to a system of 'shifting cultivation' on burnt-over forest land similar to that now common in Africa. Most of the families lived scattered in hamlets, but one or two towns sprang up at well-defended river trading sites which became centres of power, wealth and influence and seedbeds of the idea of Russian nationhood. The name 'Russia' actually derives from 'the men of Rus', Scandinavian immigrants who came to settle among the Slavic tribes at the same time as their kinsmen were settling in Britain and Normandy, and many of whom became leaders.

Kiev, on a bluff overlooking the Dnieper on the southern edge of the forests, was the first citadel of political, economic and military power and is rightly regarded as the cradle of Russia. But soon there emerged a rival—Novgorod, on the Volkhov river at the northern edge of the mixed forest region. The alignment of these two towns was along the major trading route between the rich northern forests and the civilized centres of Constantinople and the Arab world. Kiev's strategic trading position depended on the varying strength and hostility of the nomadic tribes who roamed across the broad grasslands lying between it and the Black Sea. The city rose from the ashes several times but after the Mongol conquest of the early thirteenth century went into a long decline and remained quite outside the Russian fold for over four centuries. However, during its heyday it had effectively lighted the lamp of Russian nationhood and endowed it with many Byzantine characteristics, the foremost being the national Orthodox Church.

Novgorod survived for over two centuries after the eclipse of Kiev and was the only part of Russia which did not labour under the so-called 'Tatar yoke' of this period. It had become a great commercial centre whose dominion extended over the northern forests as far as the Urals. It was for a time a member of the Hanseatic League but often had to beat off attacks from Teutonic invaders and had a very tenuous outlet on the Baltic. It was the northern collecting-point for furs and other forest products and its most lucrative trade outlet lay through Kiev (which it conquered more than once) to the Black Sea and beyond.

The rise of Moscow

The demise of Kiev and increasing pressure from the nomadic tribes to the south caused the nucleus of the emerging Russian nation to shift northwards, particularly to the region between the upper Volga and its tributary the Oka. To the refugees from the Kiev region this must have seemed an unsmiling land, with its marshes and chaotic streams, heavier, stonier soil and thicker forests. But these people were for the most part more interested in finding a fairly sheltered haven for colonization than in trading, and this land was by no means beyond the pale for the farmer, as was the great forest to the north. Moreover, although this region was off the beaten tracks of the period, it turned out to be potentially the most strategically placed, at the hub of great rivers radiating out to the four seas.

In the heart of this region the little settlement of Moscow was founded, three or four centuries after Kiev or Novgorod, and within a short time it became the nucleus and rallying-point for the new Russian state and the springboard for its massive expansion up to the present time (Fig. 9). The princes of Moscow were clever politicians who made the most of the possibilities of their position. On them the 'Tatar yoke' rested lightly, since they insinuated themselves into the Great Khan's favour, became recognized by him as the sovereign princes of all Russia and were made collectors of Russian tribute. In this way they built up their power, and further prestige was added when the Orthodox Church, driven from Kiev, made Moscow its headquarters. Thus, although the little Muscovite state seemed to be encircled by alien peoples (not only the Tatars but the powerful Lithuanians on the south-west who were eating into their territory) it had by the end of the fifteenth century built its house upon a rock. From this base it began to build a vast continental empire, just as those states of maritime Europe, which were also finding their feet, were preparing to set out across the oceans.

The beginnings of Russian expansion

Although Tamerlane had, in the early fifteenth century, partly reconstituted the unitary continental empire of Genghis Khan two centuries earlier, the Tatar power soon afterwards began to wane and the empire broke up into several sections. The year 1480 marked the last payment of tribute to them by Moscow and two years earlier great Novgorod with its spacious forested dominions had fallen to Moscow's armies. Thus these years mark a clear turning of the tide in the affairs of the Russian state, which seemed suddenly conscious of its newly-found adult strength, independence and national and religious mission. (The new Muscovite

Tsars looked upon themselves all the more as the custodians of the Eastern Orthodox faith after the fall of Constantinople to the Turks in 1453.)

During the sixteenth century the most notable expansion was perforce to the east. The way to the west was blocked by Lithuania (allied with Poland) which still held the Dnieper valley including Kiev, and by Sweden, which effectively denied to Russia any outlet on the Baltic. To the south access was denied to the Black Sea by the Crimean Tatars, who were under the command of the Ottoman Empire, newly in control of the Straits. A high premium was therefore put upon the opening up of the northern coasts which had fallen to Moscow with Novgorod, and Chancellor's trading ships from England, which penetrated to Archangel in 1553, provided timely encouragement as well as further recognition of the new state by the outside world.

The decisive event in the eastward thrust was the capture in 1552 of Kazan on the Volga, a Tatar stronghold. This opened the way for the rapid advance down the river to Astrakhan and also to the central Urals whose low passes led easily to Siberia.

The dash across Siberia

Within a century after the fall of Kazan, Russians had penetrated to the Pacific, over 3,000 miles to the east, establishing a chain of trading forts at strategic points en route. This feat more than trebled the size of the Muscovite Empire, making it by far the largest in the world (Fig. 9), though it entailed little in the way of permanent colonization. The magnet was fur, as it had been for centuries, and the motley crew of Cossacks, soldiers and hunters kept to the forests, being as yet unconcerned about the fertile steppes to the south, where in any case the Tatars held sway. The rapidity of the advance can be put down to the familiarity of the landscape and the river communication linked by portages, and to the fact that, for the most part, there were only a few ill-equipped native peoples to offer resistance. However, in one region, the Amur valley of the Far East, the Russians did meet their military match in the Manchu Empire, and after bitter fighting for over twenty years had to acknowledge Chinese sovereignty east and south of the Stanovoy Mountains, which was respected for nearly two centuries.

The growing internal power of the new centralized state was responsible in several ways for the drive across Siberia. In the first place the crystallization of the feudal system meant that there emerged rich families prepared to finance mercantile expeditions and more and more escapees from the lower end of the system who were often well-suited to the career of

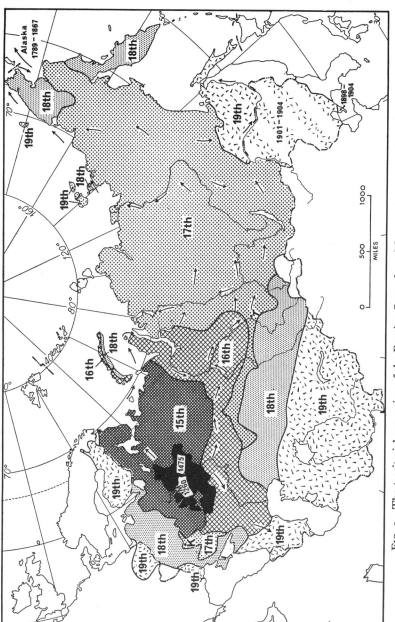

Fig. 9 —The territorial expansion of the Russian State, from Moscow, between 1260 and 1904

freebooter and merchant adventurer. Secondly, the government was increasingly hungry for wealth (which still spelt fur to a large extent) and attempted both to encourage such expeditions and to tax them as heavily as it could.

Russia turns westwards

Thus during the first two centuries after the young Muscovite Russian state had become confident of its strength and independence, expansion was directed primarily towards the east and almost exclusively across forested land. In effect this was due to a combination of the continuing lure of the lucrative products of the forest and of the existence of the organized military power of the Lithuanian–Polish, Ottoman and Chinese empires which effectively blocked the advance along otherwise tempting fronts. The net geographical effect was a marked displacement of the Russian state into Asia and away from Europe. Russia seemed to turn her back on Europe and such fermenting movements as the Renaissance, Reformation and the stirrings of scientific discovery were passing her by.

However, towards the end of the seventeenth century, the reign of Peter the Great marks a clear turning point in the history of Russia. He wrenched her head round towards Europe, while as a massive symbol of this new orientation he built his 'window on the west', St Petersburg, on a swampy, northerly site at the head of the Gulf of Finland, to replace Moscow itself as the capital of his increasingly centralized state. He was bent on industrializing Russia, and travelled widely in Western Europe, collecting knowledge personally to this end. The mining of metals within Russia, especially in the Urals, added a new aspect to the economic picture of the country, and European experts were brought to St Petersburg, inaugurating a feature of the Russian scene which has been characteristic down to our own day.

In the realm of territorial expansion the Baltic was the scene of Peter's most prolonged efforts and conspicuous successes. When he came to the throne Russia had no territory on this sea but before he died he had broken Sweden's hegemony, made the Gulf of Finland virtually a Russian lake, established his capital there, and brought the Estonians and Latvians into the Russian Empire. These peoples, with their German ruling-class (non-Russian, non-Orthodox and 'Western') were acquisitions greatly valued by Peter. He was less successful in his attempts to dislodge Poland and Lithuania from their line along the Dnieper, although his father had in fact brought Kiev itself back into the Russian fold.

Towards the end of the eighteenth century, however, Poland and

Lithuania became fatally weakened by internal dissensions, and the Russia of Catherine the Great was able, in partnership with Austria and Prussia, to make extensive territorial gains at their expense. A few years later, during the period of the Napoleonic Wars, the Russian Empire was extended to take in the whole of Finland (from Sweden), Bessarabia (from Turkey) and finally the heart of a Poland which had been completely dismembered among the Powers. Thus the European frontier of the Russian Empire in 1815, as a century later, extended considerably further to the west than does that of the present Soviet Union.

The advance to the south

The most significant and insistent direction taken by Russian territorial expansion in the nineteenth century was southwards, as that of the previous century had been westwards and the one before eastwards. This expansion involved two concomitants on a much greater scale than hitherto: permanent migration and agricultural colonization by Russians, and the incorporation of long-settled communities of Asian peoples into the Empire. By 1900 the Russian tide of empire-building had come up against the more-or-less 'natural' frontier formed by the southern rim of high mountains and had also reached the sphere of influence of the British Empire and in the Far East of the new imperial power of Japan.

1. *The Black Sea and the Caucasus.* Towards the end of the eighteenth century the Empress Catherine realized a dream which had stirred the Russian nation since its beginnings at Kiev—control of the northern coastlands of the Black Sea. Thus ended, for European Russia at least, the struggle between the farmer and the nomad which had throughout the centuries lain at the heart of its history. The Tatars of the steppes and especially of the strategic Crimea had long been the instrument of the Ottoman Turks from the southern shore of the Black Sea, whose interests obviously clashed diametrically with those of an expanding Russia clearly interested in gaining control of the narrow passage to the Mediterranean. The rich black-earth steppes of the southern Ukraine and the neighbouring Don and Kuban regions, still sometimes referred to as 'New Russia', were at last brought under the plough and supplied the massive wheat exports of the nineteenth century. Large estates were established, often owned by families of Cossack origin who had become pillars of support for the Tsar, and the rural population was less dense, serfdom less developed, and agriculture more progressive than in the wooded steppe to the north. A policy of bringing in settlers from Central Europe, particularly Germany, was a novel feature of the colonization of these regions, as well as that of the

lower Volga, which although nominally under Russian control since the sixteenth century, had been as precarious for agricultural settlement as its early American equivalents in 'Indian' territory.

The next objective was the Caucasus region, a bewildering mosaic of landscapes, languages, religions and races—a meeting-place and warring-place of peoples for ages. This region was very different from the previous scenes of Russian advances, for here were non-Russians, under the varying control of neighbouring great powers and with no empty spaces to invite the Russian colonist. During the first quarter of the nineteenth century western Georgia was wrested from the Turks and eastern Georgia, Azerbaijan and Armenia from the Persians. The present Soviet boundary in this region had been reached, but in the mountain regions the Russians found that they had a situation similar to that of the British on the Indian North-West Frontier, and it was only in the latter part of the century that the mountain peoples were finally subdued. Britain and France had become concerned over the Russian advance in this area in relation to the route to India, and contrived thenceforth to support the Turks (for instance in the Crimean War) and also mountain guerilla activity.

2. *Western Siberia and Middle Asia.* The first tentative settler-farmers in the good black-earth regions of western Siberia arrived during the eighteenth century, a collection of Cossacks, runaways from serfdom or religious persecution and a few government officials. They were so few in number that for some time they just took possession of land as they needed it. But as in the lower Volga, fortified lines had to be built against the nomadic Kazakhs, and communications with Russia proper were very difficult.

The end of serfdom in 1861 and the increased Russian control of the nomads changed the trickle of settler-immigrants into a steady stream and land in the better areas had to be allocated to the newly organized village communes. But the flood-gates were really opened only in the early 'nineties when exceptional famines in Russia coincided with the construction of the Trans-Siberian railway and the beginnings of government encouragement and financial aid to intending settlers. It is notable that this rush to the east and the railway building which encouraged it came several decades after the North American westward migration towards similar landscapes under not too dissimilar conditions. The very name 'Siberia' has in the West a strong association with deportees, and in fact perhaps a million people were deported there in the nineteenth century. But most of these went to eastern Siberia (to which there was very little free agricultural migration), rarely to the rich farmlands of western Siberia. The convict element in the broad history of settlement in Siberia has probably been no more important than it was in Australia. In any case who can say that both countries have not gained from the considerable leaven of innovating and idealistic spirits among their company of involuntary visitors?

The conquest of Middle Asia was a very different affair. This took place during the second half of the nineteenth century, and bore more resemblance to the colonial history of the Western powers in Africa than to that of North America. Instead of the ocean a broad desert separated colonizer and colonized and had precluded any but the most tenuous cultural interchange beforehand. Similarly 'indirect rule' was practised, so that in many respects the pre-existing Moslem Khanates and Emirates retained their independence, and the territory was quickly organized to provide one basic crop, cotton, for Russian industry. As the habitable land in this region had been closely occupied for centuries, there was obviously limited scope for Russian rural colonization on the Siberian model, but some did occur, notably that of the Cossacks in the foothills near Alma Ata. As in the Caucasus the Russian bear and the British lion had come within snarling range, and in 1895 representatives of both fixed the frontier between Russia and the buffer state of Afghanistan.

3. *The Far East.* The only significant part of the huge territory of the Soviet Union east of the Yenisey suitable for agricultural colonization is the Amur region and this was cordoned off by Chinese power until the mid-nineteenth century.

There was some activity during the two centuries following the first formal annexation of eastern Siberia for Russia, notably in fur-trading and later precious metals. Moreover, the region was prominent as a penal settlement. But perhaps most significant was the primary establishment of Russia as a power on the Pacific. Russian explorers and merchant adventurers were active in the northern Pacific in the later eighteenth century when permanent Russian settlements were established in Alaska and outposts along the west coast just north of San Francisco. But Russia became more and more reluctant to pursue its colonizing and trading activities in North America and it retired gracefully with the cheap sale of Alaska to the United States just before gold was discovered there.

At the time when this sale was being negotiated, apparently much richer fruit was being plucked in the Far East which had been forbidden since the treaty with the Manchus in 1689. The time chosen (1858–60) was certainly propitious. Chinese power had declined considerably in relation to Russia, and Britain had recently forced China to open her doors to European influence and had set a precedent by annexing Hong Kong. On the other hand, Japan, whose star was quite soon to be in the ascendant, had only just been similarly forced open by the United States and had not yet had time to reshape her policy. Thus the Russian Empire acquired the monsoonal farmlands of the Amur and Ussuri valleys, together with Sakhalin Island, and clinched its position as a naval power on the Pacific by acquiring Vladivostok with its good harbour on the Sea of Japan.

But this annexation could only be safeguarded by the construction of better communications with European Russia and the Russian colonization which they would be expected to bring. The Trans-Siberian railway did not reach the Amur until the very end of the century and by this time events were moving quickly. Japan had just defeated China over Korean sovereignty and had annexed Port Arthur, but very soon afterwards the European Powers, including Russia, forced Japan to hand Port Arthur back to China. Then Russia acquired rights to build the last section of the Trans–Siberian railway straight across Manchuria to Vladivostok and also a southern extension to Port Arthur, which China was forced to lease to her. Finally, following the anti-European 'Boxer' rising of 1900 Russia occupied the whole of Manchuria, which had recently been an empty land but which was then filling up with Chinese peasants. As Mongolia had also passed effectively from the Chinese to the Russian sphere of influence, this added up to a tremendous extension of Russian power in the Far East. However, in 1905 the young Japanese state, in a 'Pearl Harbor' attack on Port Arthur, put a sharp halt to this advance. As a result Russia was rolled back to the Amur, and even had to surrender the southern part of Sakhalin.

Thus the year 1904 saw the high water mark of the Russian Empire, when its area was larger than that of the Soviet Union of today. Russia had grown continuously without setbacks, except temporarily in wars, ever since the fifteenth century, when the nuclear Muscovite state first became independent. It was, incidentally, in 1904 that the British geographer Mackinder read his famous paper on the 'Geographical pivot of history'[1] in which he drew attention, against the background of world history, to a 'Heartland' region in Eurasia (most of which lay within the Russian Empire) which had a commanding position in the Old World and therefore the world itself. During the nineteenth century for the first time the empire-building sea powers, especially Britain, had become acutely aware of this growing land-power colossus which came uncomfortably close at several points. However, its feet of clay were partly revealed by its rebuff in 1905 at the hand of an upstart Asian power, which experience shook the Russian state apparatus to its foundations and paved the way for collapse a decade later.

[1] See bibliography for Chapter 18.

The massive empire was in 1900 still loosely knit together and unco-ordinated, like some outsize prehistoric monster with a small head. In spite of unprecedented development in industry, rail building and large-scale agriculture around the turn of the century, its level was well below that of the other major world powers. Moreover, the wealth of its natural resources was scarcely suspected. New wine was beginning belatedly to flow like water, but it was all going into old bottles. The great achievement of the previous four centuries had been the straddling of two continents by an emergent people, comparable with the British achievement over the same period. During the four centuries before Muscovy the settler was constantly at the mercy of the nomad and was hard put to it to keep contact with the seas. By 1900 the tables had been turned, and the railway had almost completed the primary framework for a unified state. Most of the elements of a first-class world power were there—great size and man-power, natural wealth, communications, commanding position. Only the keystone seemed to be effectively lacking—organization—and the Soviet Union, building on the massive foundations bequeathed by the Russian Empire, seems to have supplied it.

THE CHANGING POLITICAL FRONTIERS
IN THE TWENTIETH CENTURY

The unprecedented setback to Russian expansion of the war with Japan in 1905 failed to galvanize the nation behind the government. On the contrary, it led to a series of revolutionary outbreaks which widened the cracks in the foundations of Tsarism. The attempts at political and economic reform during the following decade largely fell into the category of 'too little and too late', and Russia drifted into the general European war in a dangerously unprepared condition.

Seven years of war

Between 1914 and 1921 the country was in a continuous state of war, either external or civil or both. In the middle of this period the Tsarist empire collapsed and the Bolsheviks grasped the reins of power. At times the continued existence of an independent and viable Russia was in the balance, and in 1921 the young Soviet state, though still surviving, was economically on its knees and severely truncated geographically.

The ruinous treaty of Brest–Litovsk with Germany in 1917 provided for the surrender not only of Poland and the Baltic states, but of the Ukraine itself and part of Belorussia. Finland had also just been made independent, while Bessarabia was later transferred to Romania. Thus Russia was divested of much of its richest lands just when it was reeling from three years of disastrous foreign wars and was becoming embroiled in civil war.

The insurgents against the Bolshevik government included, besides hostile Russians of many different persuasions, those non-Russian minorities of the old Empire who were reasserting their independence of Moscow. British, French, American and Japanese troops intervened at various points in support of the anti-Bolshevik movements, but were uncertain of their aims and, by pinning a foreign label on the 'Whites', may have helped to undermine their strength. In the Caucasus area, 'White' republics were set up but did not survive long, while the Turks temporarily occupied the oil town of Baku in 1918 and later managed to annex the small districts of Kars and Ardahan, which parts of the old Russian Empire they still hold.

The recreated Polish state declared its intention of regaining its 1772 boundaries with Russia. In 1920 it actually occupied Kiev and although it eventually withdrew from this city, it was able to force Russia to accept a boundary which lay well east of the ethnic line just delimited by Lord Curzon. The ultimate result of the seven-year war period was a loss of territory to the Russian state amounting to more than twice the size of Britain. On the Baltic only the narrow approaches to Leningrad were retained and, except on the southern fringes, the Russian frontiers had reverted to those of the latter part of the eighteenth century. The southern frontier in Asia and the Caucasus was held firm except for the small cession to Turkey mentioned above, and for the granting of independence to Tuva, in the upper Yenisey region, which had been incorporated into the Russian Empire in 1911.

The turn of the tide

Between 1921 and 1939 the Soviet Union neither lost nor gained any territory and attention was concentrated upon the economic development and socialization of the country, which will be considered in later chapters. However, during the period 1939–45 it regained most, though not all, of the territory of the old Russian Empire of 1904, besides two areas which had never before been under Russian sovereignty (Fig. 10). Moreover, the accession, in 1945 and the years following, of Communist governments in neighbouring states of Europe and Asia gave the Soviet Union a greater effective territorial range than the Russian Empire had ever possessed.

The tide began to flow again in 1939 when the Soviet Union invaded Poland simultaneously with Germany and advanced to a line slightly to the west of the present Russo–Polish boundary but by no means as far west as that of 1914. In fact the great majority of the people in this annexed area spoke the Russian group of languages and much of it had been over-run by the Poles in 1920. For the series of Soviet occupations which followed in 1940, historical and strategic, rather than ethnic, claims were invoked. Estonia, Latvia and Lithuania, which had become independent as part of a deliberately created tier of buffer states in 1918, were reincor-porated under pressure into the Soviet Union and Bessarabia (Moldavia) was ceded by Romania. Finland, however, whose 'Mannerheim' defence line was within 30 miles of Leningrad, rejected the Russian ultimatum, and only after a bitter war was forced to evacuate from the Viipuri (Vyborg) and Lake Ladoga region and two small strips in the north, one of which con-tained Petsamo (Pechenga), Finland's only outlet to the Arctic Ocean.

These acquisitions were obviously regarded by Stalin as a cushion against the impending German invasion of Russia which actually began in June 1941. Within a short time the Germans had made great inroads into the Russian lands, reaching the gates of Moscow, the lower Volga and the Caucasus. However, in spite of the fact that this occupied land con-tained nearly half the population and productive capacity of the country, the Russian armies were able eventually to stem and then roll back the invasion. The wave which originated at Stalingrad carried the Red Army and Soviet influence on its crest back to the border and on to the Elbe.

At the Potsdam conference the Soviet Union confirmed the retention of the lands she had reclaimed in 1939–40 (except for a narrow strip of Poland) and the acquisition of two areas which had never been under Russian rule. The most valuable of these was the northern part of the former German province of East Prussia, including the ancient ice-free port of Königsberg which was renamed Kaliningrad. The other was the tail-end of inter-war Czechoslovakia, then called Ruthenia, now called Transcarpathia, where the language spoken is largely Ukrainian.

As a consequence of its brief war against Japan the Soviet Union re-gained the southern part of Sakhalin Island and the whole chain of the Kuril Islands. In addition a lease was obtained of Port Arthur and a privileged position on the Manchurian railways, similar to that held in the early years of this century, but these concessions were returned in 1955 to a China which was then counted as the Soviet Union's chief ally. (A similar extra-territorial base, Porkkala, near Helsinki, which was leased from Finland after the war, was also evacuated in 1955.)

An odd reacquisition was made, in 1944, when Tuva, which had been made an independent state in 1921, came back, apparently voluntarily, into the Soviet Union. Apart from this, no changes occurred on the long southern boundary from the Pacific to the Black Sea. The Soviet Union has recently renounced its claims to the Turkish districts of Kars and Ardahan, which formed part of the Russian Empire from 1878 to 1917.

The character of the present Soviet frontiers

The Soviet Union abuts, either directly or across narrow straits of water, upon fourteen countries, half of them non-Communist, from the U.S.A. to Norway. Another (Pakistan) is only a few miles away across the narrow Afghanistan 'panhandle'.

The distinction between 'natural' and 'artificial' frontiers is less meaningful than it was. Airpower has reduced the barrier quality of mountain ranges, and rivers may as often as not be bonds rather than barriers. In general perhaps frontiers passing through sparsely populated areas are less inflammable than those passing through densely populated zones, though there are notable exceptions to this over the world. But there are so many different factors such as historical tradition, ethnic affinity, economic resources and the relative strength of the contiguous states, that it is hazardous to generalize. One must consider the stability of specific stretches of frontier separately.

It would be wrong to regard the Soviet Union's frontiers with other Communist states as unimportant. It is now quite clear that a common ideology is often unable to submerge the anti-Russian traditions and strong feelings of nationalism and independence in Poland or China, for instance. It seems certain that maintenance, at least, of their present frontiers is a prime article of faith for such re-emerging nation-states.

The European frontier

The western is the most open and ill-defined by physical geography of any of the Soviet frontiers. Lying astride the eastern marshlands of Europe, it has ebbed and flowed over the centuries, with the relative power of Russia and its neighbours.

Apart from the area of the Pripyat (Pripet) marshes, a traditional no-man's land, most of this frontier zone has been long settled by many mobile nationalities and the ethnic question has been thrust into prominence, especially since the 'self-determination' pronouncements of 1918. However, leaving aside the special question of Estonia, Latvia and Lithuania, these problems are now much less acute than they were in the interwar years or in the nineteenth century. This is partly due to the recent policy of cutting the knot by wholesale transfers of people to the 'right' side of

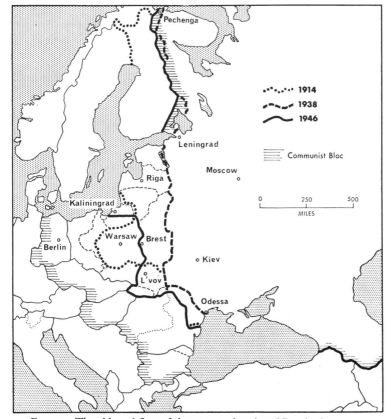

FIG. 10—The ebb and flow of the western frontier of Russia since 1914

the line, either voluntarily or otherwise. Examples of this are the former Finnish region around Lake Ladoga and Vyborg and the former German region of Königsberg, which have been evacuated by their previous inhabitants and resettled by Russian immigrants since the war. As Poland's new eastern frontier follows the Curzon line, much less mass migration was involved than in its new western border zone, where a large area of former German territory was annexed in 1945.

The Moldavians are probably the only notable group of people along the western frontier of the Soviet Union who have stronger ethnic affinities with a larger group of people on the other side of the frontier than with their Soviet neighbours. However, although they speak Romanian, they use the Cyrillic script which distinguishes them from their kinsfolk.

Three strategic underpinnings of the present western Soviet frontier may be noted. First the spacious Baltic frontage has been strengthened, from Vyborg to Kaliningrad (Königsberg), the southern part of which is always ice-free. Second, the newly acquired foothold on the Carpathian Mountains has given the Soviet Union direct frontiers with Hungary and Czechoslovakia for the first time and control of several well-worn routes into those countries. Third, the Soviet advance to the Danube delta (the Russian Empire was forced to withdraw twenty miles from the river after the Crimean War) makes it a Danubian power in its own right. A result of the latter is that the Soviet Union since the war has been able to prevent the resumption of the pre-war 'open', international character of navigation on this river. However, there seems to be evidence that the smaller Danubian states are now reasserting their independence to some extent.

The Asian frontier

The long southern frontier from the Black Sea to the Pacific has, by comparison with the western frontier, been comparatively stable throughout the Soviet period. However, in the present state of Sino–Soviet relations it has considerable potentiality for instability.

On a continental scale it appears that the southern boundary follows a remarkable 'natural' rim of highlands. Some stretches, notably in Middle Asia, form insulating barriers of almost uninhabited territory. However, on closer inspection, especially in South-West Asia, this generalization appears much less significant. For instance the rivers Araks and Amu Darya form for a long way the boundary with Iran and Afghanistan respectively, being no more of a physical frontier than is the Rio Grande between the U.S.A. and Mexico. But, as in the latter case, a notable difference between the 'cultural landscapes' on opposite sides of these borders has developed in the last few decades.

The most striking difference has been created by the rapid industrialization of the Soviet republics, which is making a profound impression upon their southern neighbours. The Tadzhiks and Azerbaijanis of the Soviet Union, for instance, are very closely akin in language, race, religion and traditions to their neighbours across the border. During the latter part of the war, when the Soviet Union was occupying northern Iran, moves were made to form a 'Greater' Azerbaijan by the amalgamation of the Iranian and Soviet Azerbaijanis. The project was withdrawn but the ethnic pretext remains, as it does in the case of the Tadzhiks and their kinsmen in Afghanistan.

64

Neither physical geography nor ethnology were much concerned in the drawing of the Russian boundary in South-West Asia. It resulted essentially from the clash of Russian land-power and British sea-power in the area. Recently the decline of British influence in the Middle East has led to something of a power vacuum (which the U.S.A. is uncertainly trying to fill) and the position of 'buffer' states like Afghanistan and Iran has become more ambiguous. But it may be assumed that Russia is as vitally concerned as ever in the situation in the Turkish straits, the Suez Canal and the Persian Gulf, and can claim to be a Middle Eastern state with one of the largest Moslem populations in the world.

For over 2,000 miles from Pamir to the Amur the Soviet frontier lies against one of the most extensive semi-deserts of the world, separating inhabited Russia from inhabited China. Although most of this region is under Chinese sovereignty, Russian influence has been gaining ground during the past century or so. The Mongolian People's Republic, though nominally independent, has much closer ties with the U.S.S.R. than with China, to which it formerly belonged. This seems inevitable now, in that the Mongolian capital and the most densely peopled zone lies against the rapidly developing Baykal region of the U.S.S.R, where their Mongol kinsmen, the Buryats, live, whereas the Gobi desert occupies the part of Mongolia next to China.

Similarly, whatever the reason for its erstwhile independent status, Tuva is unquestionably bound up geographically with the Soviet Union. The position of Sinkiang, which has been a tenuous province of China since the late nineteenth century, is anomalous since, like Mongolia, it has more often been oriented to the 'effective national territory' of the U.S.S.R. than of China. Russian influence has been considerable and the inhabitants are Turkic speaking Moslems, close kin of the Kazakhs and Kirgiz over the Soviet border. Border incidents have recently occurred, and sponsored immigration of Chinese into the area has been greatly increased.

It is only along the Amur–Ussuri border in the Far East that Russian-settled land adjoins Chinese-settled land. Since the short-lived Russian adventure in Manchuria at the turn of the century, that province has become the scene of steady immigration from the south and has now emerged as China's chief industrial region. Although there may be small groups of Manchurian or Chinese racial types on the 'wrong' side of the border, particularly in the Ussuri valley, there is no evidence that they form a majority in any part of the Soviet Far East.

In the Kuril Islands and South Sakhalin, regained from the Japanese, it seems that, as in the case of the East Prussians, there has been wholesale repatriation of Japanese people and immigration by Russians. The Japanese still lay vigorous claim to the southern Kurils. The Sea of Okhotsk has become virtually a Russian lake. So also, in effect, has almost half the Arctic Ocean, where the Soviet Union has rigorously applied the unofficial 'sector principle', involving not only claims to all islands north of any part of the Soviet mainland but also implicit jurisdiction over the sea as far north as the Pole. Thus the Soviet Arctic is enclosed by the meridians running due north from the Bering Straits (where the Soviet Union and the U.S.A. are only three miles apart) and due north from the Norwegian border except for a slight step eastwards to exclude one or two islets of the Norwegian administered Svalbard (Spitsbergen) archipelago.

Obviously the integrity of the present Soviet frontiers is underwritten by the strength of the Union. Although the Soviet Union of today is a little smaller in area than the Russian Empire of the early twentieth century, it occupies an incomparably more powerful position in the world. Its frontiers have an air of stability, even maturity, and there seem to be no openly festering problems at any point. However, the establishment of ethnic 'tidiness' along the western border has involved some painful surgery and there are some small national minorities such as the Baltic republics who would probably prefer to be independent, even though their independent existence is difficult to envisage realistically in the context of the modern world. The long southern Soviet frontier, although superficially more 'natural' than the western, is quite likely to stand the test of time less well.

CHAPTER THREE

Farming

BETWEEN 1954 and 1958 a tract of virgin land larger than that of the entire sown area of Canada was brought under cultivation in the Soviet Union. However, even now little more than one-tenth of the Soviet national acreage is cultivated. A further fifth is classified as pasture and hay meadow, leaving over two-thirds effectively 'beyond the pale' from the farming point of view. Nevertheless, the sown area of the U.S.S.R. is, in absolute terms, larger than that of the United States and Canada combined, but size is, of course, by no means the whole story. The average quality of the cultivated land in the Soviet Union is considerably lower than that of the United States (more like Canada) and so is productivity (per acre or per man-hour). In climatically normal years, the Soviet Union is able to feed its people largely from its own land. Though this is at an adequate level of nourishment it does not yet afford the dietary range, especially in fresh fruit and vegetables and animal protein, which has recently become prevalent in North America and Western Europe. Moreover, there are none of the surpluses which have become normal in North America, and which have recently been called upon to help fill the serious consequences of climatic disasters aggravated by shortcomings of organization in Soviet farming.

Agriculture has been recognized throughout the Soviet era as the weakest sector in the economy—in fact it has been used deliberately as a means of financing the building of the industrial and scientific structure of a modern state at a rapid rate. This being so, agriculture was bound to suffer deeply, even apart from the ravages of war and the way in which collectivization was implemented.

There has been considerable improvement in Soviet agriculture from its abysmal state at the death of Stalin, but its retarded condition continues to be implicitly recognized in the disproportionate investment and belated concessions to the collective farmers still being made in the post-Khrushchev era.

ORGANIZATION

The collectivization of farming in the early 1930s was pushed through with a ruthlessness which evoked intense opposition and sabotage among the peasants. However, it should be noted that throughout Russian agricultural history some form of communal, rather than personal, way of working the land has been the experience of the vast majority of the rural population—either in the feudal system, which persisted until 1861, or the commune (*mir*) system which preceded and followed it.

Following the collectivization of the newly annexed territories after the Second World War, very few private farms remain. The collective farm (*kolkhoz*) is the dominant unit and produces the bulk of the country's output of food. Amalgamation of farms has been proceeding rapidly since 1950, the total number being reduced from 200,000 to 50,000 by 1960, the average size of unit now being about 6,000 acres. The principle is that the collective farmers (*kolkhozniki*) share the net proceeds of their kolkhoz in proportion to the skill and the hours of their labour contribution. In addition, each household is allowed a private garden plot with a few animals, the produce from which it can sell on its own account in the free market. The vital importance of these private plots in the nation's food supply is indicated by the fact that they account for nearly half the Soviet output of vegetables, including potatoes, and that at least one-third of the Soviet livestock head (fully half the milking cows) is privately owned. These proportions have been substantially reduced since the War with the recovery of the public sector, while the private plot is hardly in line with Marxist theory, but the intensity of production on these plots, which amount to barely one-twentieth of the national sown area, indicates that there is considerable slack to be taken up in the productivity of the collective lands. An important step in the reorganization of the collective farms was the abolition in 1958 of the all-powerful 'machine-tractor stations' and the sale of their equipment to the farms themselves.

The other major unit is the state farm (*sovkhoz*) which are less numerous, but are multiplying more quickly and are much larger in size than the collective farm. These are run like a factory, with no collective principle, but with payment by results on a salary basis. They are scattered through the agricultural triangle serving an educational and scientific, as well as economic function, but the newest and largest are in the Virgin Lands, specializing in wheat and averaging over 150,000 acres each.

THE NATURAL LIMITS

More than two-thirds of the Soviet arable land is in black-earth (*chernozem*) country. The core or axis of the chief agricultural belt follows the 'wooded steppe' from Moldavia to the Altay (with a short break at the Urals), extending southwards into those parts of the steppe proper which receive adequate moisture, and northwards into the warmer and less leached parts of the mixed forests.

The wooded steppe zone is in fact the most favoured by climate for farming activity. It occupies the narrow zone of overlap between that of adequate and reliable moisture and that of adequate and reliable heat and length of growing season. Moreover, the climate which is so suitable for growing crops has also made for a good lime-accumulating, humus-rich soil, since precipitation is regularly slightly less than evaporation.

Outside this black earth region the arable areas are notably less dense and more discontinuous, including the long-settled podzolic mixed forest zone around Moscow, the Baltic and White Russia, and some patches in Trans-Caucasia, middle Asia and Eastern Siberia.

To the North of about 61° latitude in European Russia, about 57° in Western Siberia and 53° in Eastern Siberia lies a great non-agricultural wilderness, covering well over half the Soviet Union and much larger than Canada. Given a special incentive, crops can be grown in most of this region, but only through the kind of massive investment in the amelioration of nature which would be extremely uneconomic elsewhere.

The agricultural belt wedged between these Northlands and the deserts of Middle Asia, has been broadening notably in recent years, primarily on its southern edge in connection with the Virgin Lands Project, but the effective limits even of intermittent 'dry farming' have now been reached —probably even overreached.

Apart from limited schemes for irrigation or drainage, it seems clear that the agricultural belt has been essentially marked out for the forseeable future, up against the climatic limits, and that intensification of agriculture in the already established optimum areas will account for future increases in production.

THE EVOLUTION OF THE AGRICULTURAL BELT

The black-earth country, now so dominant in the Soviet agricultural scheme, was destined to remain dormant for many centuries, while the early Russian farmers struggled to make a living in the much poorer forest-clearings north of it. This was because the steppe and the relatively open wooded-steppe were the domain of the livestock-herding nomads and, so long as their power persisted, farming settlement in their territory was out of the question.

After the decisive defeat of the Tatars in the sixteenth century the way finally lay open, and pioneer bands of 'Cossacks' moved into the wilderness of the wooded steppe and engaged in farming, hunting and military activity. The present farming core had at last begun to be settled, but by the early eighteenth century two-thirds of the Russian population was still to be found in the podzolic forests around Moscow and the north-west. By the mid-nineteenth century, however, this proportion had been reduced to one-third, and the period 1725–1875, broadly speaking, saw the great southward shift of the Russian population into the black-earth zone of European Russia, down to the Black Sea and the North Caucasus.

During the third quarter of the nineteenth century, following the abolition of serfdom, it had become clear that the European wooded-steppe was overpopulated and since the new lands to the south had also been largely taken up, the direction of rural migration, which had been southerly for at least three centuries, turned towards the east.

The more favourable parts of the black-earth country of Siberia, in particular the Altay Steppe and the narrow strip of wooded steppe followed by the Trans-Siberian railway, have caught the limelight in respect of rural settlement ever since, culminating in the extremely ambitious (probably over-ambitious) government-sponsored Virgin Lands extension in the mid-twentieth century. With this it would seem probable that the last major chapter of the centuries-old record of the occupation of the Russian farmland has been written.

PRESENT CROP DISTRIBUTIONS

Just before the First World War nine-tenths of the sown area was in grain. In spite of the massive absolute increase in grains due to the Virgin Lands Project and the maize drive of recent years grain now amounts to less than two-thirds of the sown area, which is rather less than the Canadian proportion and slightly more than that of the United States. However, in the U.S. the bulk of the grain (in particular maize) is fed to livestock whereas in the Soviet Union the bulk of the crop is still for direct human consumption. The main weight of government policy since the death of Stalin has been directed to achieving an emphasis more like that of the United States, but with substantially poorer natural endowments.

Grain Crops

Wheat still accounts for over half the total grain acreage in the U.S.S.R. and the production equals that of North America and much of Western Europe combined. Since the eighteenth century the traditional wheatland has been the black-earth zone of European Russia, in particular the

Ukraine and North Caucasus, where the winters are mild enough for autumn sowing and a large-scale export trade had been built up by the end of the nineteenth century. But during the present century a relative shift has been made to the black-earth zone between the Volga and the Yenisey, this being effected in three main bursts of colonization—(a) the period when the Trans-Siberian railway was built, (b) the Second World War when the older European wheat-lands were overrun and (c) the Virgin Lands project which was designed primarily to free the older areas for maize production (Plate XI). As a result of this the wheat acreage east of the Volga is at least double that of the European zone, although the yields in the east are considerably lower and more variable owing to unreliable rainfall and the necessity of spring-sowing. These two wheat areas are now about equal in average annual production, and together dominate the nation's output. Attempts have been made to encourage wheat-growing in the mixed forest zone of European Russia, but the actual results have been quite unimpressive.

This mixed forest zone, with its damper and more acid soil, has been the traditional home of rye, which can stand up to these conditions better, and which has long provided the main breadstuff of the peasants. However, rye sowings have declined steadily during the Soviet period and a large part of them is now found in the northern fringes of the black-earth belt of European Russia. Rye is virtually absent east of the Urals. Oats and barley are also very important as feed grains, the latter largely in the European black-earth region and the former in the damper conditions of the mixed forest. Buckwheat is another traditional crop of the forest zone and millet is important in the drier areas of the Volga and Western Siberia. Irrigated rice is grown on a comparatively small scale in the Kuban delta, Middle Asia, and the Far East.

The most highly publicized and encouraged crop after the death of Stalin was maize (corn). The acreage was multiplied six-fold between 1954 and 1956, but only a third in the latter year was harvested for grain, the rest being necessarily cut for silage and 'green mass'. The only areas with enough heat and moisture to ripen the grain regularly are the Ukraine, the Kuban valley of the North Caucasus and Georgia, and even these areas do not quite equal the natural endowments of Iowa, which has been held up as the model and from which much of the seed has been procured. There have been massive sowings as the main base of the livestock drive and green maize has appeared along the forest margins from Leningrad to Lake Baykal, although the fall of Khrushchev has resulted in a sharp reaction against its excessive planting in unsuitable areas.

Other food crops

Potatoes have long been a staple food, grown throughout the mixed forest and wooded steppe zones of European Russia, though less in Siberia. Sugar-beet is largely concentrated in the Ukrainian wooded steppe which provides the best climatic and soil conditions (Plate IV), but there is some irrigated beet in southern Kazakhstan. In normal (i.e. pre-Cuba) times the U.S.S.R. provides all its sugar requirements this way and is easily the world's largest beet producer. Sunflowers are a traditional and decorative feature in the drier steppe country of the Ukraine and Middle Volga, and supply two-thirds of the country's edible oils.

Alongside the drive for more meat and dairy products for the Russian table, the production of fruits, vegetables and particularly wine is being greatly expanded. (Vineyard acreage was doubled between 1956 and 1959 and was scheduled to further quadruple in the Seven Year Plan.) The chief wine districts are in the southern Ukraine and Moldavia, the Crimea and Georgia and parts of Middle Asia, while fruits range from the apples and plums of the mixed forests to the melons of the south. Lemons, oranges and tea are confined to the Georgian Black Sea coast and the Lenkoran lowlands on the Caspian. The Soviet Union *can* grow the whole range of crops except purely tropical ones like cacao, coconuts or bananas, but sub-tropical crops are more precarious than in the U.S.A.

Livestock

Owing to the violent peasant reaction to collectivization and the subsequent ravages of the war the livestock population in 1953 was less numerous than it was in 1928, but since then there has been a notable increase of pigs, cattle and sheep, with a steady decline in goats and horses, the latter numbering barely a quarter of the 1928 figure. Fodder-crops now account for a quarter of the Soviet sown area, compared with 3% in 1913.

While the Soviet production of milk and butter already exceeds that of the U.S.A., the latter's meat output remains twice as large. There is much less functional specialization in livestock, e.g. in beef or dairy cattle, than in North America. However, the damper urbanized parts of European Russia stand out for dairying and so do the wetter parts of Western Siberia which have had a large butter surplus since before the Revolution. By contrast, sheep are heavily concentrated in the drier south, especially Caucasia, where the merino is now common, and Middle Asia, where the karakul is an important traditional breed. The pig population has more than doubled since 1953, a faster growth than that of any other major farm animal. Highest densities are in the maize-growing Ukraine and Kuban (the chief poultry areas too), with secondary concentrations in the Baltic republics and the dairying zones. For religious reasons the pig is rare in Middle Asia. Of negligible commercial significance, but of vital importance to the lives of the indigenous peoples, are the reindeer of the Northlands, the camels of the southern deserts and the yaks of the Middle Asian mountains.

Traditionally the most lucrative of Russian animals have been those bearing fur. In spite of a long record of uncontrolled exploitation of this resource, the U.S.S.R. is still the world's greatest exporter of furs, though these are increasingly being farmed instead of hunted. Presumably the silkworm can be classed with the sheep and the mink as textile-bearing livestock. The production of cocoons, an ancient industry, is still rising slowly, in spite of competition from synthetics, and two-thirds of this output comes from Middle Asia, most of the remainder coming from Transcaucasia. The mulberry trees, on which the 'worms' feed, line the edges of the cotton fields.

Fisheries

The catch of fish doubled during the 1950s and the Soviet Union is now one of the world's most prominent fishing nations. But, whereas the Caspian Sea accounted for two-thirds of the total catch in Tsarist times, almost the same proportion is now taken by the sea fisheries based on the Barents Sea and the Soviet Far East. Each of these regions now lands twice as much fish as does the Caspian, where the falling level has damaged the fishing grounds. The Baltic and the Sea of Azov are of minor significance but one of the most interesting of recent developments has been the appearance of Soviet fishing and whaling fleets as far afield as Newfoundland and Antarctica. Fresh-water fisheries account for less than one-twentieth of the total catch.

Non-food crops

These account for barely 2% of the national sown acreage. Cotton is by far the most important, and predominates among the textile materials worked up in Soviet industry. As in the late Tsarist era, it is entirely grown on irrigated land in Middle Asia and Transcaucasia—attempts to grow it without irrigation in the Ukraine and North Caucasus in the 1930s failed. Nearly nine-tenths comes from Middle Asia, chiefly the row of Uzbek oases from Fergana valley to Khiva, and the remainder chiefly from Azerbaijan.

While cotton acreage has expanded three-fold since 1913, the older staples, flax and hemp, have declined or stagnated in the Soviet times. The traditional home of flax is in the European mixed forests, especially in the damp soils west of Moscow, and here it remains. Hemp is found chiefly in the wooded steppe. Small amounts of imported Indian fibres like jute and *kenaf* are grown in Middle Asia, but several varieties of rubber-bearing plants, grown widely in the thirties, seem to have disappeared. The native Russian *makhorka* tobacco is still grown in the black-earth region, but the better-quality Turkish tobacco comes mainly from the Caucasus and Crimea.

FARMING REGIONS

Out of the detail of the geography of particular crops and livestock it is possible to construct major agricultural regions which stand out for particular crop combinations and for their relative productivity and importance to the whole economy. In doing this one must recognize that the boundaries are necessarily thick lines and that each region contains a number of subdivisions (Fig. 11).

A. THE MAIN AGRICULTURAL TRIANGLE

Region 1

The European black-earth. This is the agricultural heart of the Soviet Union, accounting for about half the country's farm output by value. Although natural conditions are not uniform throughout this area, with more heat and less moisture towards the south-eastern borderlands, and each district may have its speciality, there are strong common features. Most important of these are the soil fertility and the dominance of a relatively intensive type of mixed farming. This region produces the great bulk of the country's winter wheat, barley, maize for grain, sunflowers, sugar-beet, hemp, fruit and wine, and also of pigs and poultry, while a majority of the country's cattle and even such 'hardy' crops as potatoes, rye and buckwheat are probably accounted for too. It is the nearest counterpart to the Middle West in the U.S.A. (though significantly less rich in absolute natural endowments) and probably represents the soundest potentiality for increasing the Soviet output of food.

Region 2a

The European mixed forest zone. This is the agricultural hearth within which the early Russian farmers were confined until the seventeenth

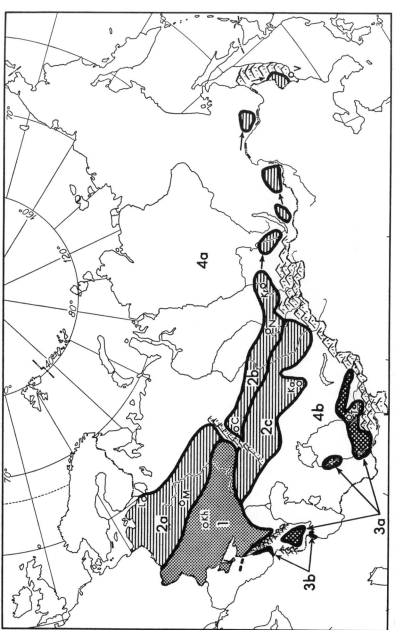

FIG. 11—Farming regions, as outlined in this chapter: 1 = European black-earth, 2a = European mixed forest zone, 2b = mixed farming zone of Siberia, 2c = the Virgin Lands, 3a = irrigated oases, 3b = humid sub-tropical districts, 4a = North-lands, 4b = southern arid zone

century, in between the tayga and the *chernozem*. It is now very second-grade land even by Russian standards and its agriculture is notably less intensive and productive than in Region 1. However the soil and climatic conditions, together with the large urban market are favourable enough to make agriculture an economic proposition, which is not the case in the northern forests. The traditional emphasis on rye, oats, potatoes and flax is giving way steadily to fodder crops, including green-cut maize, as the basis for dairying and related activities, and intensive market-gardening belts around the urban centres.

Region 2b

The mixed farming zone of Siberia. This region (rather similar to the Canadian Prairies), although consisting to a large extent of black earth, is more comparable in agricultural range and productivity to Region 2a, owing to the longer and more severe winters and cooler, shorter summers which rule out winter-sown crops and the full ripening of maize, for instance. However, dairying and grain-growing have made considerable strides and some districts, like the 'Altay Steppe', are decidedly better quality farmlands than the European mixed forests.

Beyond the Yenisey this zone becomes a series of discontinuous pockets along the length of the Trans-Siberian railway and, within the semi-permafrost zone, environmental conditions are more inimical to agriculture than in Western Siberia. Only in the Far East, in the rice and soy-bean areas, are conditions comparable to those of West Siberia, but the areas involved are very limited.

Region 2c

The Virgin Lands. This region, stretching from the Volga to the Altay, is at present largely a monocultural wheat producer and has for the most part been created very recently. The environmental problems combine some of those of the Canadian Prairies, such as short growing season and the necessity of spring-sowing with those of the 'dust-bowl' western margin of the American Great Plains. Thus productivity is relatively low, subject to fluctuations and is on a markedly lower level than the grain-lands of Region 1. Nevertheless it is of great importance to the nation and has facilitated the agricultural intensification of Region 1.

B. THE SPECIAL AREAS OF THE SOUTH

Region 3a

The irrigated oases. These consists of intensive but discontinuous patches of first-class land along the foothills of the Central Asian mountains and along certain river valleys running through the arid lands of Middle Asia and eastern Transcaucasia. Availability of irrigation water is almost everywhere the factor which decides whether the long summer heat can be capitalized. Cotton is the dominant crop everywhere except on the northern slopes of the Tien Shan, but fruit and fodder crops are also grown. Conditions are similar to those in Egypt or the Imperial Valley of California, not the so-called 'Cotton Belt' of the American South.

Region 3b

The humid sub-tropical districts. These enclaves—the Kolkhida lowland facing the Black Sea and the Lenkoran lowland on the Caspian—have a significance out of all proportion to their tiny area, because they are the only parts of the Soviet Union which escape regular frost and also have a heavy, well-distributed rainfall. They are the counterparts of Southern California and Florida in the U.S. economy, and with a climate more similar to Florida than California—but much less highly developed than either. Tea, lemons, oranges and tung-oil are the chief products, and drainage and other improvements could greatly extend the sown area. However, the frequency of occasional killing frosts discourages a great extension of citrus plantings.

C. THE NEGATIVE AGRICULTURAL AREAS

Region 4a

The Northlands. This vast area, which covers nearly two-thirds of the Soviet Union, is a wilderness from the agricultural point of view, making a negligible contribution to the national output of food. This does not mean of course, that farming is physically impossible or that the celebrated farm patches near lumber-camps, mining towns or on the Arctic coast are not highly important to the health and welfare of these settlements, as in similar situations in Canada. But physical obstacles like the shortness of the growing season and frost-free period, heavily leached soils, permafrost, bogs and boulders, make necessary an exorbitant capital investment which can only be justified by very special incentives. Thus, even Yakutia, which possesses unusually favourable physical conditions (for the Northlands) actually cultivates barely one out of every 2,000 of its acres. However, there are large areas of natural pastures, and reindeer herding, with hunting and forestry might be considered the only commercially viable activities of the northlands for which the environment makes provision.

Region 4b

The Southern arid zone. This is the area to the south of the 'Virgin Lands' wheat country, excluding the irrigated oases of Region 3a, but taking in both shores of the Caspian as well as the lower Volga, yet mainly in Middle Asia. Evaporation would everywhere absorb at least three times as much precipitation as actually occurs. The land only supports extremely sparse grazing for sheep and camels, traditionally based on nomadism. The mountainous zones of the southern frontier, though they are less arid and transhumance is practised, can be put in this same farming region.

THE PROSPECT

The roughly triangular Soviet farm base (Leningrad–Yenisey–Caucasus) seems to represent the effective limits beyond which it will generally be uneconomic or risky to extend. This position was reached soon after the First World War in North America and the modest retreat from marginal lands which has been evident there may well be repeated in the Soviet Union. However, drainage schemes such as in the Pripyat marshes and the Kolkhida lowlands, and further extension of irrigation in Middle Asia, the lower Volga and Don and the Trans-Caucasus can be expected to add significant tracts of farmland capable of intensive use (it may be noted that the national irrigated acreage has nearly trebled since Tsarist times).

But the main increase in output which could be forthcoming, given a proper application of research and a more sensible organization of labour, would be almost certain to come from the already relatively intensive black-earth core, especially in European Russia. The change of emphasis from bread-grains and starches to livestock products will continue, but the substitution of maize and other fodder crops for the ancient *travopolie* or grass-fallow system may now be expected to proceed more slowly.

There is no reason why, given intelligent management and liberal investment, the Soviet Union should not be able to provide its growing population with a more varied diet for the foreseeable future from its own land. However, on purely economic grounds it would probably pay to import some foodstuffs from other countries where natural conditions are more suitable and the price therefore lower. It seems distinctly possible that the Soviet Union, like other countries which have built up an export trade in manufactured goods and industrial raw materials, will forego the doubtful blessings of complete national self-sufficiency in food—if not to the same degree as Britain—at least to a significant extent. This would be in line with the increasing pragmatism, internationalism and self-confidence which the country has been exhibiting in recent years.

CHAPTER FOUR

Industry

THE Herculean strivings of the Soviet government and the labour and privations of the Soviet people since 1928, have largely been bent towards the massive and rapid industrialization of the country. Collectivization of agriculture (as a means of ensuring an initial capital accumulation as well as urban food supply), the scientific-educational programme, Lenin's 'electrification', the building of railways and canals, imports of foreign capital equipment, technical personnel and strategic raw material—all these and more were primarily harnessed to the overriding end of industrial growth.

Whatever the human cost, the cumulative fruits of this policy in terms of national strength and world status have been impressive. In little more than the decade of the 1930s Russia was changed from a largely agrarian, illiterate and military disorganized nation into an industrial power which was able to withstand the full onslaught of the German war machine. Moreover, in the decade following the post-war reconstruction, the Soviet Union had established itself as clearly second only to the United States in industrial, scientific and military terms, and the only real counterpoise to American power on the world scene. Its average annual rate of industrial growth between 1928 and 1937 was about 11% and since 1937 has averaged about 6%. In spite of the colossal setbacks of collectivization and a disastrous war, these rates were apparently not equalled by any other major country in either period. However, the rate has inevitably slackened lately —between 1955 and 1961, it was barely half as great as Japan's, although it was four times the American rate. More recently still, the rate of growth has declined more sharply.

THE ORIGINS AND SPREAD OF INDUSTRY

About a third of the Soviet working force is now classified as industrial, compared with less than one-tenth in the closing years of the Tsarist period and also in 1928. In spite of this dramatic change, however, it is hardly correct to portray Russia at the turn of the century as an industrially 'underdeveloped' country of the type prevailing in Africa and Asia today.

The last two or three decades of the Tsarist period were in fact

79

characterized by impressive rates of industrial growth and it may be said, with W. W. Rostow,[1] that Russia had 'taken off', even if rather erratically and creakingly, on its industrial revolution before 1917. This was to some extent due to certain dominant governmental personalities, in particular Witte, and to direction by foreign capital and technical personnel, while this combination of influences had also been responsible for an earlier burst of activity in the early eighteenth century (under Peter the Great). Nevertheless, there is no denying that Russia was decidedly backward in industrial and scientific matters in the early twentieth century by West European or North American standards and, taken all round, a gap, even though drastically narrowed, still exists.

From the early days of Muscovy to the Bolshevik Revolution the chief region in both scale and variety of industrial development was the Moscow region, still called the 'Central Industrial District'. Here at the hub of the river system of European Russia, near the centre of political power and convenient for assembly of raw materials and distribution to markets, industries, mainly of the cottage or *kustarny* type, based on grain, fur, wood or flax, developed early. This region remained eminently central to the populated part of the State—indeed *contained* almost all the major parts of it—until the eighteenth century.

Then the personal drive of Peter the Great put under way the first major extensions of industry outside the region. His new capital of St Petersburg, during the eighteenth and nineteenth centuries, intercepted many of the expanding industries which would otherwise have accrued to Moscow, particularly those based on imported raw materials. His obsession with the modernizing and arming of Russia led to the utilization of the rich iron ores of the Urals which later in the eighteenth century made Russia the world's leading iron producer.

Most of the nineteenth century saw expansion in the Ural iron industries and the diversification and growth of consumer industries in the Moscow and St Petersburg regions, in particular cotton textiles which became the chief industrial employer in the Empire. It was only towards the end of the century that a relative shift of industry to the south occurred, when Donets coke and Krivoy Rog iron were combined with modern technology to supplant the charcoal-based Urals as the chief Russian metallurgical base, and Baku oil became the main fuel supplier for Russian industry as well as the major world exporter.

Apart from local processing of agricultural commodities and some mining of gold and non-ferrous metals, there was very little industrial development

[1] *Stages of Economic Growth.* Cambridge, 1961.

in Asiatic Russia by 1913. The Moscow and St Petersburg regions were still the chief industrial employers and the textile industry (especially cotton), accounted for over 40% of the industrial employment of the whole country. This concentration of scarce skilled industrial manpower in the Moscow and Leningrad areas has continued to have its localizing effect on industrial location well into the Soviet period.

The Soviet easterly industrial movement dates from 1930 when the decision to build the 'Ural–Kuzbas Combine' was taken, involving the modernized resurrection of the Urals iron industry and the first serious utilization of the greatest Soviet accessible coal reserves in the Kuzbas. But the full impact of the easterly shift became really strong only after about 1939, and in the 1960s, except for certain specialized branches, its force seems to have been largely spent.

ENERGY

The Soviet Union may well possess greater total reserves of energy—coal, oil, gas and water—than any other country. As in the case of the heat and water balance for agriculture, however, there is a striking lack of coincidence between the location of most of this industrial energy and the present centres of consumption. At least two-thirds of the population and industry are in European Russia including the Urals, whereas at least four-fifths of the energy resources are in Siberia.

On the other hand the real significance of this maldistribution is by no means as great as might appear at first glance. Firstly, a large part of these technical reserves, mainly of coal and water-power, is illusory, because severe handicaps like sheer inaccessibility, ruggedness, and permafrost conditions, preclude utilization in the foreseeable future. Secondly, the present trend is to put an increasing relative emphasis on oil and gas, most of the reserves of which are in the European area. Thirdly, Soviet scientists are making notable advances in the long-distance transmission of electricity, which would greatly affect the feasibility and scale of exploitation of the rich and cheap *accessible* reserves of the East. Fourthly, as industry and urban population have been moving east in any case, the market imbalance has tended to become somewhat ameliorated. Nevertheless, in spite of all these qualifications, the poor correspondence between location of industry and of energy reserves is a problem to the Soviet Union and has placed a severe strain on its transport system.

The changing fuel balance

The total consumption of energy has increased some fifteen-fold since

1913 or 1927 and there have been significant changes in the relative importance of its various forms.

Before the 1890s wood had always been the chief source of fuel in Russia, but then came the phenomenal development of Donets coal and Baku oil and these two sources have been paramount until quite recently. Except for a short time at the very beginning of the century, when half the world's oil was coming from Baku, coal has been the chief energy producer throughout this century, but in the early sixties it is rapidly losing ground to oil and gas, as it is in Western Europe and as it has been in North America for several decades. But it should be noted how very recent is the relative demise of coal in the U.S.S.R. During the pre-war plans it contributed at least half the national energy needs and throughout most of the 1950s it was nearer two-thirds. However, a far-reaching and overdue decision was taken in 1958 to concentrate thenceforth upon oil and gas, which together were scheduled to increase their proportion of the national energy contribution from little more than a quarter to two-thirds by the early 1970s—coal declining inversely; and hydro-power maintaining a fairly constant and minor relative position. By 1961 coal was already supplying less than half the Soviet energy, probably for the first time since before the Revolution.

A secondary fuel and power policy change of recent years has involved a relative playing down of grandiose hydro-electric projects in favour of more thermal-electric plants based on cheap, low-quality coal and oil and gas. The Soviet fuel and power situation must thus be seen as in a state of transition. Moreover, the regional balance of the various types of fuel have been altered profoundly during the Soviet era and a summary of these changes may therefore be useful.

Coal

The Donets Basin (Donbas), in the Ukraine has been, from the beginnings of modern coal-mining, the chief producing field in Russia. However, whereas it accounted for nine-tenths of the national output in 1913 and nearly two-thirds even in 1940 its contribution has now dropped to one-third, although its output is still expanding and is still twice as large as that of its nearest rival. Moreover, it still produced 60% of the Soviet coking coal as well as anthracite. The fact that the Donbas has maintained its lead, even if a heavily reduced one, in spite of the war devastation and the high cost of its coal (now that the best seams are worked out), is a tribute to its position with reference to market and to iron ore, and also to historical inertia and concealed subsidization.

The new counterpoise to the Donets basin, contributing about another third of Soviet coal, is the group of Central Siberian fields from Karaganda to Lake Baykal, with its core in the Kuznetsk basin (Kuzbas). Although coal was known and mined to a small extent here before the Revolution, its national significance dates from the establishment of the Ural–Kuzbas Combine in 1930 and was greatly enhanced by the wartime evacuation.

This zone contains well over half of the Soviet reserves of both good-quality coking coal and of extremely cheap brown coal. From the cost viewpoint the thickness of the seams and the widespread feasibility of opencast mining gives this zone easily the cheapest coal in the country. (Kuzbas coking coal is said to be one-third the cost of its Donbas equivalent and the brown coal near Krasnoyarsk less than a tenth of that of the Moscow basin.) Karaganda coking coal is gradually replacing Kuzbas coal in the Urals metallurgical industries, being much closer. The factor of distance is the major one limiting the scale of development of this Siberian coal—largely owing to overloading of the available transport facilities, as the coal can be delivered even in parts of European Russia at a price fully competitive with its Donbas equivalent. A recent trend has been to build large power-stations to use the low-cost coal at source to encourage the immigration of power-intensive industries, and to experiment with long-distance electrical transmission. The Ekibastuz coalfield, north of Karaganda, is planned to fuel several massive power-stations on the spot—with the energy being transmitted to southern European Russia.

Outside these two major zones coal has either a purely local or else an ephemeral significance. In only one case is the coal moved any distance, viz from Vorkuta (Pechora) in the European tundra, which was connected to the south by rail during the Second World War and worked largely by forced labour. At present it sends coking coal to the steel works at Cherepovets near Leningrad, but in view of the high costs it would not be surprising if it were soon restricted to local purposes, like the few workings in the enormous coal reserves of permanently frozen north-east Siberia.

Similarly the high-cost brown coals and peats of the Moscow basin, and the sub-bituminous coals of the Urals are only used locally in power-stations because of the acute demand and shortage of alternative sources of fuels and the piping in of natural gas is tending to displace them. As part of a policy of encouraging a minimum degree of regional self-sufficiency coal is mined in the Far East, Middle Asia, Northern Siberia and Transcaucasia, but to a very limited degree.

Petroleum

Reference has been made to the radical policy change favouring oil in the U.S.S.R. This has in part undoubtedly stemmed from the dramatic changes in the geographical pattern and indeed general fortunes of the Soviet oil industry since the war. When the Germans invaded the U.S.S.R. in 1941 over four-fifths of the country's oil was still coming from the Caucasus (in particular Baku). Such a strategically vulnerable state of affairs quickly stimulated intensive prospecting in the Volga–Ural area, which was known to contain oil. The picture which emerged was, however, far more glowing than expected, revealing an oil-bearing region of the size and promise of the U.S. Mid-Continent fields. The result is that the Volga–Ural region now accounts for four-fifths of the Soviet output, which is moreover four times what it was in 1940. Apart from the scale of the new oil base, it is much more centrally situated on the national map of population and industry than is the Caucasus, and pipelines radiate from it to the Moscow region, the Urals and deep into Siberia. Outside the Volga–Ural and Caucasus regions less than a tenth of the Soviet oil comes from Middle Asia, Sakhalin, the western Ukraine and a few other points. Much of Siberia is geologically likely to produce oil eventually and significant production has recently begun in the Ob lowlands, north of Omsk, as well in the upper Lena valley.

Gas

If anything, the expansion of natural gas consumption has been more meteoric than that of oil—output having increased fifteen-fold in the last decade. Natural gas and also petroleum gas, which was largely wasted before, has assumed a most important place in Soviet fuel planning and can be expected to increase its relative position rapidly—in fact as soon as the main limiting factor, shortage of piping, is eliminated. The main developments have taken place in the Ukraine, the Volga–Ural and on the north and south flanks of the Caucasus—each of these three regions contribute over a quarter of the national output. In Siberia gas has been discovered under the lower Ob swamps, but the most notable recent developments have been at Bukhara in Middle Asia, where a pipeline has been constructed to the Urals, drastically reducing the need for coal in that fuel-deficit area and thus relieving the Siberian railways. The injection of gas into many of the areas such as the Moscow or Leningrad regions which have previously depended on poor-quality local coal or long-haul coal imports, is effecting fundamental savings for industry.

Water-power

The importance of hydro-electric power in the Soviet Union has probably been magnified by the peculiarly symbolic impact of huge dams, although it is a mistake of course, to evaluate these dams solely on their electrical output, without taking into account flood control, navigation, irrigation and other benefits. Only about a fifth of the Soviet electrical capacity is hydro (about the same proportion as in the U.S.A.) and only about one-twentieth of the national energy demand is supplied from this source.

As in the case of coal, most of the accessible hydro-power resources are in Central Siberia, while to date most of the developed capacity is in European Russia. Owing to Lenin's intense belief in electrification as a panacea, several small hydro-stations were built soon after the Revolution, mainly in the rapids-zone north-east of Leningrad, but the first large dam, which became an early symbol, was built on the Dnieper in 1933 (and has been rebuilt and expanded since its destruction by the Germans). The next major project, the 'Great Volga' system, materialized mainly in the late 1950s and included two dams (Volgograd and Kuybyshev) which have a capacity, fully operating, of $2\frac{1}{2}$ million kw each—or four times the size of the Dnieper dam. Since then the emphasis has shifted to Siberia, where in the early 1960s, following the commissioning of several small projects on the Ob and Irtysh, two dams with an ultimate capacity twice as large as the largest on the Volga have spanned the Angara (at Bratsk) and the Yenisey (at Krasnoyarsk). When these both reach their full projected capacity, their combined hydro-power will be as great as that of the whole of European Russia at present. But, although this Siberian hydro-power is very much cheaper than its European counterpart, it is competing against even cheaper open-cast coal and the problems of installing appropriate consuming industries on the spot and/or the transmission of very high voltages for long distances have not yet been fully solved.

The mountains of the Caucasus and Middle Asia have considerable potential, some of which has been developed, but in general it can be said that the Soviet Union has still harnessed a smaller proportion of its potential accessible water-power than any other major industrialized country.

The new energy axis

In 1900 and again in 1930 more than four-fifths of the energy production of the country was derived from a narrow axis stretching between the Donbas coalfield and the Baku oilfield, and when the invasion came in 1941 it still accounted for a vulnerable two-thirds (Fig. 12).

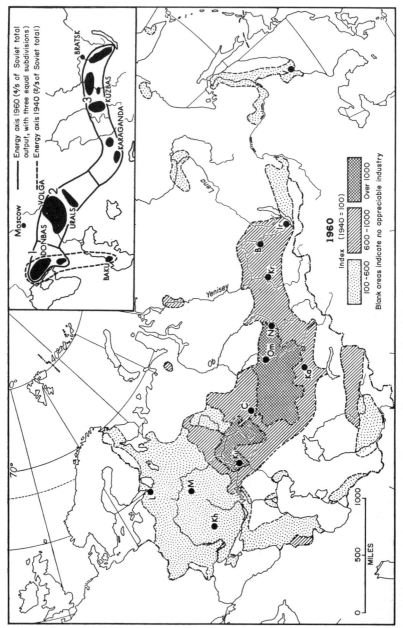

FIG. 12—Growth of industrial and energy output, 1940–60

However, since the war a radically different geographical orientation of energy production has emerged. While the western end of the new energy axis remains, as before, the Donbas coalfield, its trend has been swivelled away from the Caucasus and towards Central Siberia. Whereas the Donbas Baku axis accounted for at least two-thirds of the Soviet energy in 1940, the new Donbas–Angara axis contributed about four-fifths of the national output in 1960. Compared with the 1940 axis the 1960 one is three times as long, has three times the output and has a more variegated and balanced energy structure. It is made up of three energy regions which are of about equal importance—the Donbas coalfield, the Volga–Ural and Kuban oil and gas fields and the Central Siberian coal and water-power reserves.

The first two alone account for about half the energy and, with the Moscow region, their main consumer, they now form part of the European electrical grid. The eastern zone however is still out on a limb, though much less than formerly, and is being welded together in a grid of its own. The eventual aim is to link the Central Siberian and the European grids, and thus be able to make full use of the much cheaper eastern energy, take advantage of the differences in Time Zones, capture the benefit of seasonal floods and avoid transporting bulky solid fuels. If this is actually done, and technology is not the only stumbling-block, some four-fifths of the accessible energy and over three-quarters of the Soviet people will be woven together, to form a formidably effective national territory.

THE RANGE OF RAW MATERIALS

We have seen in the case of energy resources that the problem is not so much one of physical shortages of these resources on the territory of the U.S.S.R. (Eastern Europe is largely irrelevant to Soviet energy needs) but of conquering sheer distance and pipeline and rail bottlenecks between certain supply areas and the demand areas. So it is in the case of industrial raw materials. Although there were acute shortages of industrial essentials, not only in the thirties but even in the early fifties, it now appears that the Soviet Union has adequate reserves of virtually all the raw materials needed for modern industry on its own doorstep, which cannot be said for any other country. However, many of them are of less than first-class quality or are located awkwardly with reference to one or other of the factors with which they have to be combined. This can often be coped with—for instance nephelite, which is a poorer aluminium ore than the bauxite of the Urals, will probably be used around Krasnoyarsk because of the immensely cheap and plentiful fuel and power for smelting in the vicinity.

Again, free sulphur is one of the few chemical raw materials which is relatively scarce in the U.S.S.R., but most of their sulphuric acid is obtained from pyrites and smelter-gases, while some sulphur is imported. Substitution is widely practised, and it seems safe to say that, as with Cuban sugar or Egyptian cotton, such Soviet imports of metals and other industrial raw materials as now occur could be discontinued without any particularly serious effects. This was certainly not the case a few years ago, but the Soviet Union's compulsive dreams of complete self-sufficiency in industrial materials seem actually to have become a reality and the country now exports a variety of metals and minerals, increasingly to non-Communist co untries.

Metal ores

Iron is still very much the basic metal and it occurs widely in the Soviet Union. The rich Krivoy Rog mines of the Ukraine (the equivalent of the Mesabi range of Minnesota) still contribute at least half of the Soviet iron ore, but the proportion was three-quarters in 1928. The bulk of the remainder is mined in the Urals, notably still the rich magnetite of Magnitogorsk, although this is showing signs of exhaustion. In fact a very important trend of recent years, consequent on the impending depletion of such rich accessible reserves as Krivoy Rog and Magnitogorsk, is the growing emphasis on the open-cast mining of enormous low-grade ore bodies, most of which need concentrating before entering the furnace. In 1962, for the first time open-cast mined, concentrated ore outweighed the deep-mined unconcentrated rich ore. Thus, as in Minnesota, Krivoy Rog is moving rapidly over to its quartzites, while the concentrate from the enormous ore bodies around Kustanay in Kazakhstan is increasingly stepping into the breach at nearby Magnitogorsk. Similarly the Kachkanar deposits, even though only 16% metallic content, are estimated to contain half the Urals reserves and are just beginning to be concentrated and to provide the main base for the steel industry of the northern Urals. Finally, in the long run perhaps the most significant development for the Soviet ferrous industry has been the initiation of large-scale exploitation of the 'Kursk Magnetic Anomaly' (K.M.A.) in south central European Russia since 1959. Though known for nearly a century, these immense reserves of ferrous quartzite, overlain by water-logged strata, were technologically out of reach until very recently. Now accessible, their excellent location is ensuring a prominent place for them in the industrial planning of the next few decades.

Thus there are two general areas which stand out in iron ore mining, past, present and prospective—south-central European Russia and the eastern Urals. Other deposits likely to become more important are those of the Angara region and other parts of fuel-rich Central Siberia, while there are expensive or poor quality deposits which are nevertheless worked to a limited extent in the Crimea, the Kola peninsula and Transcaucasia.

The Soviet Union now appears to be self-sufficient in virtually the entire range of ferro-alloys, and it dominates the world production of the most important and indispensable of these, manganese, mined in the Ukraine and Georgia. Nickel and chrome are chiefly obtained from the Urals, though the former is also mined at Norilsk and Kola, in the Far North. As in other countries, aluminium is increasingly substituted for steel. Since the war the main source has been the Urals (bauxite) but secondary sources are the Kola peninsula, Transcaucasia and the new nephelite deposits of Central Siberia.

Although the Urals dominates the output of many non-ferrous metals and probably has as wide a variety of them as any comparable area on earth, other Soviet regions have come into prominence as 'polymetal' areas. Chief among these are the Kazakh uplands (particularly copper) the Altay mountains (lead and zinc—mined in Tsarist times), the Lena basin (gold and diamonds), Norilsk, Kola peninsula and Transcaucasia. In spite of this wide range though, it seems probable that the core of Soviet non-ferrous metal production extends from the southern Urals through the Kazakh uplands to the Altay, whereas the ferrous metal core runs in the opposite direction from the southern Urals to the eastern Ukraine.

Chemical raw materials

In the Seven Year Plan the chief change of emphasis in the material bases of the greatly expanding chemical industries was towards natural gas and the by-products of petroleum refining—but this is largely directed towards synthetic fibres, including rubber, plastics and other 'new' consumer-oriented commodities. Some of the more traditional industries, such as fertilizers, however, still depend largely on the rich phosphate (apatite) deposits of the Kola peninsula and the long-worked potash and other salts of the Kama valley. Nitrogen fertilizers have been located near coke-ovens but the transition to natural gas is taking place rapidly. There are immense reserves of 'Glauber's salts' in the Kara-Bogaz Gulf of the Caspian and some salt lakes of Middle Asia, and also common salt from Lake Baskunchak, near the lower Volga, and in the Donbas.

Timber

The natural textile materials have been discussed in the chapter on farming, but it remains to mention a raw material which over the course of Russian history has probably been used more widely than any other, wood. The Soviet Union claims at least a fifth of the world's forested area, but the areas of active timber-working are restricted. As in the case of other raw materials, three-quarters of the timber production takes place in European Russia while three-quarters of the nominal reserves are in Siberia. The four chief economic areas are the Moscow region, the northern Urals, the Dvina basin in northern European Russia, and Central Siberia from the Ob to Lake Baykal.

LOCATION OF INDUSTRIES

Throughout the Soviet period there has been an unusually heavy emphasis, by Western standards, on the metallurgical industries and on capital goods, as compared with light industry, chemicals and consumer goods generally. In the mid-fifties the metal industries, including mining, steel and engineering claimed nearly 40% of the Soviet industrial investment and labour force, while fuel and power, intimately tied up with these

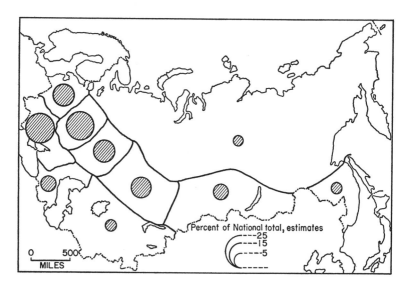

Percent of National total, estimates
----25
----15
----5
----

0   500
MILES

FIG. 13—Relative importance for manufacturing of the regional units used in the main part of this book (based partly on Lonsdale and Thompson)

industries, claimed a further 30% of the investment and 10% of the labour force. However, times are changing rapidly—there has been a notable increase in the emphasis on consumer goods since then and in 1962 there was a major policy decision to invest more funds in chemicals than in metals—a change comparable with, and to some extent associated with, the recent one in the national fuel balance. This is indicative of a new drive to modernize and diversify industry, to reduce the former over-emphasis on steel and, broadly speaking, to aim at something more like the American structure of industry as well as energy. Although the scale of Khrushchev's chemical 'crash programme' has been reduced somewhat by his successors, the fundamental change of emphasis is not in question.

In the discussion of energy and raw materials a repeated theme was the lack of geographical correspondence between those resource bases for industry and the present concentrations of population and industry. As a broad generalization we may say that half the industry is in the old-established zones of the Moscow and Leningrad regions and the Ukraine, while a third is in the zone between the Volga and Lake Baykal, the remainder being scattered about the southern, northern and eastern margins. On the other hand half of the accessible resources for industry are in the Volga–Baykal zone. The market, and inertia generally, are inevitably powerful, but there has been for two or three decades a deliberate policy of bringing the location of industry more in line with the location of resources and the disproportionate allocation of investment funds given to the Volga–Baykal zone in the Seven Year Plan testifies to its continuing force. The distribution of the major groups of industry will now be summarized.

Steel

As in 1913 and again in 1940 two regions—the Ukraine and the Urals—produced three-quarters of the Soviet steel. However the notable change is that, while at the earlier dates the Ukraine's output was two or three times that of the Urals, they are now roughly equivalent. The Ukrainian plants, from Krivoy Rog to the Donbas, with coke, iron, manganese and limestone all available, are closer together than those of the Urals. The latter may be divided into a northern group around Nizhnii Tagil, still dependent on Kuznetsk coking coal, and a southern group, depending on the nearer Karaganda coking coal and Kustanay iron ore and now receiving gas from Middle Asia. A 'third metallurgical base' is being actively extended from the pre-war nucleus on the Kuzbas to include integrated plants working on local ore and coke, at Karaganda and the Kuzbas. Technically, the conditions for efficient steel production are greater here than in most of the older places, but distance is always a drawback. Outside these three main bases about a tenth of the Soviet steel production, and undoubtedly the most expensive, comes from marginal plants in the Trans-Caucasus, Middle Asia, the North and the Far East, where they testify to the Soviet desire for a certain minimum degree of self-sufficiency in those bulky goods which would tax the limited transport facilities.

Though there is a dearth of statistics on non-ferrous metal smelting and related industries, it seems certain that most of this is in Asiatic Russia, in particular along the eastern flank of the Urals, in northern Kazakhstan, Central Siberia and Norilsk in the far north.

Engineering

Heavy machinery, such as locomotives and mining equipment, is naturally anchored by the sources of steel, so that the Donbas, Urals and Kuzbas, in that order, are most prominent. Then there are other specialized market localizations of long standing, such as textile machinery north-west of Moscow, coal-mining equipment in the Donbas, oil refining machinery at Baku and agricultural machinery dotted throughout the *chernozem* belt from the Ukraine to Krasnoyarsk. However, the inertia of a long-standing, concentrated market and a pool of skilled labour is still very powerful in keeping precision engineering, electrical industries and motor vehicles within the orbit of Moscow (including Gorky) and Leningrad. As in other high-density industrial regions of the world there is quite a high degree of specialization here, with inter-dependent factories making parts of a final product in which cost of raw materials is insignificant compared with that of skilled labour. However, with the general move to the east and the diffusion of scientific and technical education, other centres like Kuybyshev, Sverdlovsk or Novosibirsk have grown into minor Moscows or Gorkys in this respect and this kind of development is likely to be cumulative.

Chemicals

As noted above, this has been the most rapidly growing sector of industry in recent years, and indeed the Soviet Union has much leeway to make up, being far behind the United States, and even behind some of the other western countries in several items. Up to now, there have been three distinct types of locations for chemical industries—near coking and metallurgical operations, in the Moscow and Leningrad regions, and at rock sources such as the Kama potash deposits. However, the main·

trend is now towards use of gas and oil by-products, so that the Volga–Ural area, Baku, the North Caucasus and Ukrainian gasfields are prominent in new constructions—together with far-distant centres like Omsk and Irkutsk, which are linked up with the oil or gas sources by pipeline. Mineral fertilizers form the chief traditional branch of the industry, being concentrated largely in the non-*chernozem* belt of European Russia and secondarily in the cotton-lands of Middle Asia, where the demand is greatest and where the supply of Kama potash and Kola phosphates on the one hand and the Middle Asian phosphates and sulphur on the other, are reasonably accessible. However, the concentration of nitrogen fertilizers on the Donbas coalfield also remains notable.

Synthetic rubber has been made largely from industrial alcohol since the thirties, but until recently it was entirely derived from potatoes and grain and the plants were therefore concentrated in the agricultural zone south of Moscow (e.g. Voronezh). Now the emphasis has switched to the oil and gas fields, especially Volga–Ural, but also Baku and along the Siberian pipeline at Omsk. Rubber is also made from wood at Krasnoyarsk.

Other synthetic fibres are being greatly expanded under the current plan, especially in the Moscow region and the Volga–Ural—woollen and silk textiles now being almost entirely synthetic.

Textiles

In spite of the inroads of synthetic materials, cotton goods are still far more important than those of all the other fibres together, and this was the case even before the Revolution, when cotton was the largest single industry of any kind in terms of employment. It has since dropped sharply in the industrial hierarchy, inevitably, although production has doubled. It has remained, like all the textiles, heavily concentrated in Moscow and the upper Volga zone (e.g. Ivanovo), where nearly four-fifths of the cotton cloth is made in spite of much advertised new mills in Tashkent and parts of Siberia, nearer the source of the raw material. Linen is the only textile industry which is well located for raw-material as well as market. Fur and sheepskin are traditional and, considering the climate, highly desirable alternatives to woven textiles in Russia and are produced on the northern and southern margins of the populated belt respectively.

Timber

Again the great bulk of timber-using industries are located in northern and central European Russia, together with the northern Urals. Archangel is the chief timber export port and although most of the timber-processing centres are, naturally enough, in the forest zone, the importance of the rivers as the main timber-highways is indicated by the prominence of cities in the treeless south such as Volgograd and Rostov. In Central Siberia, in the upper reaches of the Ob, Yenisey, Angara and Lena, especially where these rivers are crossed by the railway and where electric power has been developed, timber-based industries are expanding rapidly.

Although much of the Soviet timber production is disposed of for fuel (still about a third) and as sawn lumber and plywood, paper constitutes a growing outlet. Three areas stand out—southern Karelia, the northern Urals and the Moscow region—amounting together to about two-thirds of the national output. However, there was a definite planned movement towards Siberia in the recent Seven Year Plan and southern Sakhalin, developed first under the Japanese, is important in the Far East.

Food and drink

There is a natural locational compromise here between the market and producing areas, which puts a premium on the northern Ukraine and the southern part of the Moscow region for such staples as flour-milling, sugar-refining and meat processing. However, in addition there is processing at the often outlandish sources of the raw materials, such as butter-making in Western Siberia, meat packing in Kazakhstan, wine-making in Moldavia and the Caucasus and, of course, fish-canning in the ports of the Far East and White Sea.

INDUSTRIAL REGIONS

Manufacturing in general is difficult to measure accurately and meaningfully, as particular industries show up more prominently if the number of employees is used as an index, while others show up better with amount of invested capital, value added in the manufacturing process, and so on. The difficulty is aggravated as far as the Soviet Union is concerned by the fact that the basic statistics for some of these indices are not available, either on the national or regional level. Further, even when they are, the regional units used are often so large and heterogeneous that the dimensions of the nationally significant industries are obscured by those of ubiquitous or purely local importance.

Nevertheless, the main features of the U.S.S.R.'s developing industrial geography are clear enough and from them the significant industrial regions may be distinguished. Disregarding as far as possible those regions in which the industrial activity is overwhelmingly directed towards securing ·

local self-sufficiency, one can discern three main groupings of industrial regions of significance on the national scene (Fig. 14).

Groups 1 and 2

There are five quite widely separated industrial concentrations, each of which was making a notable contribution to the national economy before the Second World War, and which can therefore be said, on the rapidly changing industrial landscape of the Soviet Union, to be reasonably well-established. To these several other major cities in the European zone may be added. Together by any yardstick, these still represent about half of the national manufacturing output (Fig. 13).

Group 1. Long-established centres of market-oriented, labour-intensive industries

1A. The Moscow region. As an industrial region this, which probably still ranks first of them all, is to a large extent a product of historical inertia. The fact that Moscow, at the hub of the medieval route system became the capital early and combined an admirable nodality in pre-eighteenth-century Russia with the immense fillip of political patronage, made it a precious reserve of experience, invested capital, skill and literacy. These gave it a head-start similar to that of London and Paris in their imperial days, which has quickly been reasserted after St Petersburg's long usurpation. Thus, although the region itself and its surrounding neighbourhood has hardly any resources of fuel or industrial raw materials, it has been, and remains, strong enough to command the 'import' of these requirements, and has become the hub of the significant routeways—first water, then railway, and now pipelines. Apart from Greater Moscow itself, the clusters of industrial cities included in this region are almost entirely to the east of the metropolis, notably Gorky (the 'Soviet Detroit') and the 'Soviet Lancashire' cities along the upper Volga. This is in line with the main set of Soviet industrial growth—however, there is a secondary set southwards, towards the Ukraine.

The present industrial specialization is therefore on skilled-labour-intensive, highly capitalized industries of the precision, scientific and consumer type, the longest established (on a substantial scale) being textiles, which remain remarkably tenacious. Moscow's position as the scientific and educational Mecca, as well as an expanding and influential market, is bound to prove a powerful industrial draw, as in other metropolises. However, the diffusion of technical education and know-how to the provinces seems likely, as costing becomes more rigorous, to work

95

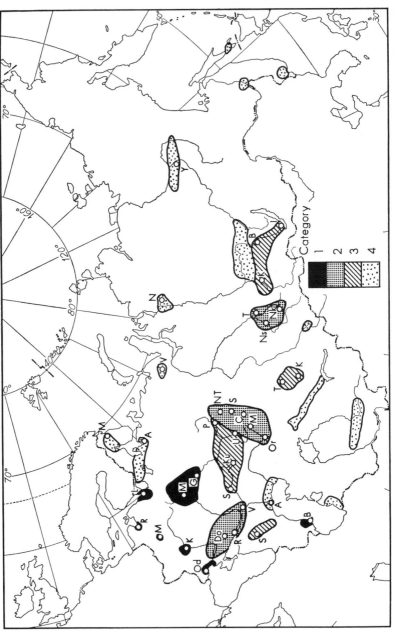

Fig. 14—Industrial regions, as outlined in this chapter: Categories: 1 = long-established centres of market-oriented, labour-intensive industries, 2 = centres of heavy industry, 3 = emerging industrial regions, 4 = outlying resource-oriented industries

eventually in Moscow's competitive disfavour, especially at the inter-mediate technical levels.

1B. Leningrad. Unlike the Moscow region, this is just one city, and a planted one at that, but its industrial structure is very similar to Moscow's, and its future problems in the Soviet industrial scheme are further ag-gravated by its position away from the main stream of national development. Even after two centuries as the national capital during an unprecedented period of empire-building and centralization, St Petersburg was still much less important than Moscow industrially, and the gap has rapidly widened in the Soviet period.

1C. Other industrial cities. There are a few cities which, standing on their own, partaking to a limited extent in the historical advantages which have been attributed to Moscow, make a significant, though of course minor, industrial contribution on the national plane. These are Kiev, Minsk and Riga, each of which is the capital of a republic, with a relatively long record of technical skills and literacy and 'Western' connections. To these may be added the Black Sea port of Odessa, the third city of the Russian Empire in 1900, and Baku, the Caspian oil city, which still has a role, albeit a relatively shrunken one, in the national economy.

Group 2. The centres of heavy industry

These are, of course, poles apart from the regions of Group 1 in their youth, historical development and present industrial character. How-ever, together they may be said to be at least as important as those of the first group combined. They have been literally basic to the very rapid advances of the industrial revolution in both the late Tsarist period and most of the Soviet period.

2A. The Eastern Ukraine. This region takes pride of place both chrono-logically in relation to the modern development of heavy industry, and also, even though not by much of a margin, as regards current output. Its core is the Donbas coalfield and it extends to Krivoy Rog on the west, Kharkov on the north, the Sea of Azov on the south and can be stretched, with some justification, to Volgograd on the east. The juxtaposition of good coal and iron resources, as well as a large market (especially if Communist Eastern Europe is considered) is unique in the Soviet Union. However, costs are high compared with many heavy industry centres further east, and its dominance over competitors has been greatly reduced in the Soviet times.

2B. The Eastern Urals. This is well situated in the context of the Soviet easterly industrial drift (not to mention strategic questions) but it is short of coking coal and much of its best iron ore is becoming exhausted.

However, new nearby metal ore sources of many types and the inflow of gas and oil from outside seem almost certain to preserve its importance as a highly organized and specialized metallurgical region.

2C. The Kuzbas. The newest of the coal/steel regions was set up deliberately in connection with the Urals, with which its links have subsequently been steadily reduced. Rich resources, especially of coking coal and the resulting unusually low costs, have to be weighed against the sheer distance separating the region from the main markets. However, as newer industrial regions of great promise spring up all round it, the local market is growing rapidly and there is no real sign that industrial expansion in the area will be appreciably slowed down in the foreseeable future. In industrial scale, the Kuzbas (including Novosibirsk) is to the Eastern Ukraine much as Leningrad is to Moscow. The crucial difference is, however, that whereas Leningrad has steadily lost ground to its 'rival' in the Soviet period, the Kuzbas has just as steadily gained ground.

Group 3. *Emerging industrial regions*

In contrast to the regions in the first two groups, there are some whose industrial significance was very dim before the war but which have subsequently burst into the limelight and are now emerging, not just as power or raw material storehouses but as major industrial regions.

3A. Volga–Ural. This is undoubtedly the most important of the regions in this category. It lies essentially between the middle reaches of the Volga and the Ural crest, centred somewhere between Kuybyshev and Ufa in the heart of the great oil-bearing zone which, more than anything else, is forming the character of the new region. Since the official policies of switching the fuel emphasis from coal to oil and gas on the one hand and the industrial emphasis from metals to chemicals (largely petro-chemicals) on the other hand, this region, possessing most of the country's oil and a sizable part of its gas, has been the obvious beneficiary. Very large hydro-stations commissioned in the late fifties have further attracted power-intensive industries. One must add to these geological and governmental factors the pure factor of location, so important in a vast country like Russia—the Volga–Ural is near the centre of the Soviet population and effectively connected with its neighbours. Thus it is not surprising that this area experienced the fastest rate of industrial growth in the country between 1940 and 1960 (Fig. 12).

3B. Yenisey–Baykal. This region is in an even earlier embryonic stage than Volga–Ural and, although its resources are vast, its future is not so well assured. This is partly because its exceptionally cheap energy resources do not include oil or gas but mainly because of its great distance from European Russia. Its hydro-resources are only beginning to be tapped and there is official doubt about the wisdom of the initial capital investment involved and also about how the power is to be consumed. Another recent policy change has resulted in considerable development of the region's very cheap open-cast brown coal for electrical generation and in addition oil is now piped into the region from the Volga. Various industries, including power-intensive metal-processing, timber-working and chemicals have in fact been introduced, and high-voltage transmission lines now connect such centres as Irkutsk, Bratsk and Krasnoyarsk. The ground work for a major industrial region has been irrevocably laid, but the rate and direction of future growth is dependent on such broad technical problems as the very long transmission of very high-voltage electricity, and governmental policy decisions such as whether the drive to the east in capital investment and population of the last three decades is to be a permanent feature of Soviet geography.

3C. Karaganda and its environs. Although this is altogether more confined in area and scope than the above two regions, its industrial development has gone far enough to ensure that it is no longer an ephemeral or pioneer venture. Before the war it was merely a supplier of coal to the Urals, but in the post-war period it has been built up into a metropolis of half-a-million with large steel enterprises, chemicals and a varied industrial structure. Although somewhat isolated, its accessibility to the many mineral deposits of northern Kazakhstan, and connections with the burgeoning areas of the southern Urals and Central Siberia, are making it a notable nucleus for an eventual secondary industrial region.

Group 4. Outlying resource-oriented industries

Outside the broadly settled triangle, or 'effective national territory' of the U.S.S.R. (i.e. Leningrad—Lake Baykal—Black Sea) there are a number of islands of national significance amid an ocean of negativity and emptiness. These settlements are mainly concerned with exploiting minerals valuable enough to stand the extra costs of transport to the market and to provide for the daily needs of a somewhat marooned community. They are likely to be ephemeral, either because of exhaustion of deposits or because of changing government policy with regard to transport costs or substitution of materials. The wherewithal for the setting up of a sizable well-established industrial region is just not present. They are typically pioneer settlements or, as the Russians would say in other contexts, colonial-type. The most notable mining areas of this type are the nickel centres of the Kola peninsula and Norilsk within the Arctic circle and the copper producers in the desert of Kazakhstan. Others are the lead-zinc of the upper Irtysh, the oil and salt of the eastern shore of the Caspian and the gold and diamonds of Yakutia.

Much more durable are the timber- and fish-based industrial settlements of north-west European Russia (Archangel and Karelia) and of the Soviet Far East, including Sakhalin. The isolation of the latter region is even worse in terms of the national economy and less conducive to a large industrial build-up, than the former, in the absence of fruitful links with China or Japan.

TRENDS AND PROSPECTS

Soviet industry is obviously in a state of flux. The decade following the death of Stalin has been an active transitional stage from a country whose industry was heavily based, like pre-1914 Britain, on coal and steel, towards one which aims at something more like present-day America, with oil and gas providing most of the energy and also the chief basis for a vast complex of chemical industries. The inflexibility and heavy capital and labour investment of the giant hydro-electricity dams has been superseded to a large degree by thermal power stations in smaller, more manoeuvrable units which pay better dividends in the short run. During this period the Soviet Union has also become virtually self-sufficient in industrial raw materials and has become an exporter of metals previously in short supply. Industry has been greatly diversified and, for the first time in the history of Russia, consumer-goods on a mass scale, though not yet the American scale, have become a significant sector of the industrial economy.

The map of industrial growth between 1940 and 1960 shows striking regional contrasts (Fig. 12). Almost all the areas showing more than a six-fold increase in industrial output are packed into the territory between the Middle Volga and Lake Baykal, and many of these areas have shown an increase more than ten-fold. On the other hand European Russia west of the Volga, with the possible exception of the annexed Baltic republics, have shown a much slower increase, as also have most of the marginal areas like Caucasia, Middle Asia, the Far East and the North.

Though undoubtedly accelerated by the war, this regional trend in favour of the Volga–Baykal zone has the support of a new axis of accessible and cheap energy resources and also major concentrations of industrial raw materials, while communications have greatly improved.

However, we cannot lose sight of the fact that at least half of Soviet industry is still located west of the Volga. Further, if one includes the

Volga–Ural region, the Eastern Urals and the Caucasus with European Russia, the proportion is more like three-quarters and forms a dominant industrial corner similar to the north-eastern manufacturing belt in the United States.

Moreover, it seems that the shift of the industrial centre of gravity to the east in the Soviet planned period has come to an end for the time being. The advantages of the European 'core' in the present phase of oil and gas, skilled labour and the market, and in respect of climate and 'amenities', are irresistible. While the regions to the east of the Urals should continue to develop their energy and raw material-intensive industries, and become increasingly vital to the country's energy needs as the European supplies become exhausted or too expensive, they do suffer from chronic problems of labour recruitment and distance from the major market, which can only be overcome at a cost. This cost may well be considered worth paying for ideological, strategic or other reasons. In the meantime, the outstanding new feature of the redistribution of industry since 1930 has been its easterly extension along the Trans-Siberian axis between the Volga and Lake Baykal—an extension of the national industrial framework which may well be permanent.

CHAPTER FIVE

Transport

THE transport system of the Soviet Union is probably more hard-worked than that of any other important country. The ton-mileage of freight has increased more than fifteen times since the Revolution, while the rail mileage has scarcely doubled. Transport inadequacy has often proved the critical factor limiting economic development, and yet, as with agriculture, there has been, during most of the Soviet period, a curious reluctance to invest enough to provide flexibility for economic expansion. Capacity has been stretched to the limit.

However, the post-Stalin economic revolution in the fuel balance and in the character of industry is effecting fundamental changes in the nature of the transport system. The advent of the pipeline age in the Soviet Union, and also that of the national electrical grid, should increasingly give respite to the well-worn railways.

But the transport network remains the crucial link—still a weak one—in the chain of regional and national economic development. The map of freight flows faithfully reflects the relative intensity of economic activity, revealing the main arteries of the nation, running from Ukrainia, through Moscow and the Middle Volga to Central Siberia (Fig. 15).

NATURAL HAZARDS

A superficial glance at the relief map of the Soviet Union suggests that, although distances are immense, there are few physical impediments to the laying out of lines of communication. While this is true in some important areas, such as the Siberian wooded steppe, climate and relief combine to cripple transport over much of the country. The presence of permafrost in the eastern half of the country has placed costly difficulties in the way of the building and maintenance of railways, roads and bridges. Apart from these terrain problems, the prolonged intense cold causes great difficulties with lubrication and freight-handling. The rivers are closed by ice for at least half the year, while the vast flooded lands of the Ob present almost insuperable problems to the builder of permanent ways.

The fact is, of course, that most of the territory just mentioned is ruled out on other grounds for the degree of density of settlement needed to warrant profitable transport operations. Still, it does contain valuable resources and the critical factor in deciding whether they can be competitively exploited is usually the transport situation.

Moreover, even south of the coniferous forests, there are considerable natural hazards, apart from the effects of the continuing, though somewhat moderated, winter cold. Shortage of water was a serious problem, especially in Middle Asia, although the introduction of diesel fuel is rapidly solving it, while sand drifting across the track is another troublesome hazard in this area. Even in the Ukraine widespread gullying has necessitated expensive remedial measures on the railway foundations, and alternating frost, mud and dust have traditionally inhibited road development in Russia. Thus, taken all round, the Soviet Union has some formidable natural obstacles to the formation of an adequate transport network, compared with the United States, even apart from the overriding necessity of overcoming great distances.

EVOLUTION OF THE NETWORK

Until about a century ago, the great bulk of Russian traffic, other than local everyday hauls, was on the rivers. But, although the Russian state was born and grew rich on its rivers in the days of Novgorod and Kiev, hardly any of the trade could be regarded as inter-regional in the modern sense. Most of the Russian people, living circumscribed, self-supporting lives, would be only dimly aware of the river traffic. The Volga system has been pre-eminent ever since the early days of Muscovy, eventually opening the way to the riches of the Near East and China. It also led to the Urals—gateway to Siberian furs and site of Russia's first major ironworks, the development of which depended absolutely on the river and its left bank tributaries. When Russia turned west with the founding of St Petersburg, the major effort (in the eighteenth and early nineteenth centuries) in the transport field was devoted to the cutting of water-links between the Volga and the Baltic. There was also some road-building—the Great Siberian Highway as well as those of European Russia—which was considerably more advanced in relation to contemporary world standards than its Soviet equivalent is today.

But the backbone of the present Soviet transport system was created in the last half-century of Tsarism, both in response to and as a necessary condition for, the tremendous growth of agriculture, industry and trade. By 1890 Russia west of the Volga had acquired a considerable railway net, linking the new wheatlands and heavy industry of the Ukraine with Moscow, St Petersburg and Western Europe. In the south, the Black and

Caspian Seas were linked by rail through the Transcaucasus and the strategic Trans-Caspian railway was being driven into newly conquered Middle Asian territories.

Between 1890 and the Revolution the Trans-Siberian railway reached Vladivostok and the Turkestan railway reached Tashkent, while Moscow and St Petersburg were linked with Archangel and Murmansk respectively. Under the guiding hand of Count Witte, investment in railways was very liberal in relation to the general level of economic development. All the important parts of the Empire were linked with Moscow by 1917—an exceptionally valuable bequest to the Bolsheviks. The railways were by then accounting for over half of the national ton-mileage. Grain movements, formerly the mainstay of the traffic north and south from the wooded steppe, declined relatively, although the flow of wheat and butter from Siberia had become notable. Coal had become the chief northward-moving commodity, and Baku oil became the main upstream product on the Volga, with timber the chief downstream item. Cotton was being shipped from Middle Asia to Moscow. Altogether the variety of products and the haulage distances increased remarkably in the last quarter-century of Tsarist rule.

The rivers had lost their traditional place, but still accounted for a quarter of the ton-mileage. After an initial setback from the railway age, the Volga fleet underwent considerable expansion and renovation around the turn of the century and the Volga system alone still handled about one-sixth of the total Russian ton-mileage in 1913. Sea traffic was also relatively much more important than it has been since, but road transport had sunk very low.

Soviet extensions and trends

The effect of the Stalin period was to maximize to an extraordinary degree the use of the railway system constructed before the Revolution. By 1940 the ton-mileage of the Soviet railways was about six times as great as it had been in 1913, while the track-mileage had only increased by about 30%. Much of the latter was accounted for by double-tracking (e.g. of the Trans-Siberian) or the provision of north–south cross-links, as in the Urals. Apart from this, the major Soviet effort was the building of the Turk-Sib railway, linking Middle Asia and Western Siberia, and even this had been planned and begun before the Revolution. During the Second World War there was feverish activity on certain strategic connections, such as along the right bank of the Volga, joining up the Murmansk and Archangel lines, and building the long sub-arctic line to the Vorkuta coalfields. There was also considerable construction in the steppe between the Urals, the Kuznetsk basin and Karaganda in the 1930s and 1940s. Taken all round, in conjunction with the course of regional development, the transport pattern and nature of freight in European Russia west of the Volga, though much intensified, had not changed fundamentally when Stalin died. The most radical changes, specifically set in motion by the Ural–Kuznetsk combine, have taken place in the zone between the Volga and Lake Baykal, and even today this is where most of the new railway-building is taking place.

Several canals were cut during the Stalin era, notably those connecting the Baltic with the White Sea, Moscow with the upper Volga and the lower Volga with the Don. However, although the absolute ton-mileage on the rivers increased slowly and the Volga remained the great carrier of petroleum, timber etc., the relative place of rivers slipped sharply from 1913, when they accounted for a quarter of the national ton-mileage, to 1950, when it was only 6%. By comparison, railways increased their share of the ton-mileage until the late forties, when they accounted for nearly nine-tenths, probably about the same as the share of the rivers a century earlier.

CONTEMPORARY TRENDS

In the post-Stalin era and particularly in the Seven Year Plan, far-reaching policy changes have been inaugurated. These were long overdue by comparison with the United States. They have been closely bound up with radical changes in the fuel balance and with the need to reduce the excessive strain on the railways. The latter's total track-mileage is less than a third that of the United States, and yet carries more freight, so that the Soviet Union is not yet able to stop building railways, still less close down lines as most Western countries have been doing since the war. Moreover, the relief of the railways is closely bound up with reduction in the demand for coal, still the chief commodity carried by rail, and particularly on the most over-loaded stretches of line, such as between the Urals and the Kuznetsk basin, or in the Eastern Ukraine. The railway locomotives themselves were voracious consumers of coal, and during the Seven Year Plan a massive change-over from steam to diesel and electrical traction has taken place.

The new and probably the most powerful factor which has been revolutionizing the transport structure since 1958 is the change-over to oil and gas for industrial and domestic purposes. Since pipelines are clearly the most economical and convenient carriers for these fuels the demand for rail-borne coal is inevitably decreasing. Even in the metallurgical regions the demand for coke is being reduced by the increased gas input.

In addition to this, the development of electricity grid systems and the constantly improved efficiency of transmission without much loss by long-distance, very high voltage lines, offer great prospects of saving railway coal-freights. Cheap open-cast brown coal in Central Siberia, for instance, can thus be converted into electricity on the spot and transferred by a series of steps to the demand points further west, whereas the coal itself could not stand the cost of conventional transport. Already most of European Russia, including the Urals, is covered by a grid, and so is Central Siberia, including the Kuznetsk basin. A gap remains between them but with the development of Direct Current, very high voltage transmission, it should eventually be liquidated by the projected national grid, which would embrace the great majority of the population and accessible resources of the country.

Compared with the United States or any Western European country, freight transport by road is still of minor importance in ton-mileage terms. Most of the trucking consists of short-distance hauls to and from railways and rivers and therefore does in fact play a more important role in the economy than might appear from the ton-mileage figures. Long distance 'coast-to-coast' road-hauling—such a familiar feature of the U.S. transport system, is almost unheard of in the Soviet Union and traffic is very light on the arterial roads outside the city environs. Also some areas, such as Eastern Siberia or the Caucasus mountains, depend heavily on the roads for local contact with the railway network. The same could be said about river and air transport in northern Siberia—which hardly show up at all on a national ton-mileage scale, but afford the cheapest and most convenient transport arrangement for certain important but isolated regions.

River-transport as a whole continues to diminish in relative importance, in spite of persistent efforts to boost its competitive position by tariffs, and considerable investment in facilities such as the recent modernization of the Baltic–Volga waterway. In spite of the decline in the previously all-important shipments of Caspian oil, the Volga system continues to be by far the most important of the rivers, accounting for over half of all the ton-mileage carried on the Soviet inland waterways (which however amounts to only 3% of the total Soviet ton-mileage of all freight). Sea-transport has been steadily growing in relative importance in the last decade, with the expansion of Soviet trade, particularly with Europe. Black Sea ports now handle over half of the Soviet overseas trade, with oil becoming an increasingly significant cargo.

In spite of the new trends, the railways still account for between two-

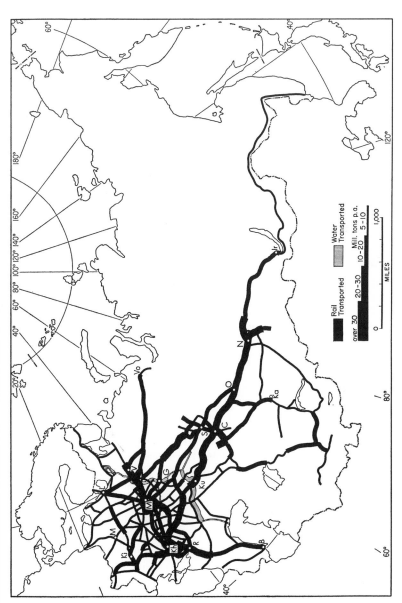

FIG. 15—The general pattern of freight flows. (Based largely on Nikolsky and recent estimates, ignoring lines of communication where annual freight seems to be less than 5 million tons.)

thirds and three-quarters of the ton-mileage of freight carried in the country, and will continue to bear the brunt for the foreseeable future. At the same time they are rapidly being made more efficient and the days when Ural–Kuzbas coal trains consumed a quarter of their cargo in the locomotives have virtually gone. But pipelines and electricity transmission lines may be expected to replace quite rapidly many of the simple long-distance fuel shipments which have always figured so prominently in the railway work-load. The most glaring contrast between the character of the trans-port networks of the U.S.S.R. and the U.S.A. concerns the roads. Nearly a quarter of the U.S. ton-mileage of freight is taken by road, compared with one-twentieth in the U.S.S.R. But the greatest discrepancy lies in the realm of passenger cars—the U.S.A. has a hundred times as many cars as the Soviet Union and probably fifty times the mileage of hard-surfaced roads, although the significance of such comparisons, in economic terms, can be exaggerated. Air transport has been made competitive with other forms of long-distance travel for passengers and, as in North America or Australia, the population, at least the urban population, is becoming quite air-minded.

THE EMERGING REGIONAL PATTERN

Generally speaking, the greatest density of freight flows—essentially on the railways—follows what may be called the economic spine of the country, from the eastern Ukraine to Moscow and thence eastward, through the Middle Volga and the Urals to Central Siberia. Moscow stands at the incoming centre of the network, dominant directions of movement being northbound from the Ukraine and westbound from Siberia and the Urals. But Moscow is also by-passed to some extent by direct flowlines between the Ukraine and Volga–Ural. By and large the pipelines—gas from the Kuban and Ukraine and oil from the Middle Volga—reinforce this pattern, but oil also flows, in smaller quantities, the other way from the Volga to Irkutsk, revealing the absence, until recently, of native strikes in Siberia.

The Ukraine stands out as the region with the greatest tonnage origina-ting and terminating, followed by the Moscow region—heavily un-balanced in favour of incoming shipments. Within the Ukraine there is also a very important east-west flow between Krivoy Rog and the Donbas. The share of the regions east of the Volga has greatly increased since the War—the main commodities consisting of coal, grain, lumber and oil.

Outside this economic spine there are several limbs which are worthy of note: (a) leading to Baku by railway or via the Volga—much less vital than formerly; (b) to the great consuming centres of the Baltic, particularly

Leningrad; (c) timber from the north, especially via the Dvina from Archangel; (d) coal from Vorkuta, which has an uncertain future; and (e) cotton from Middle Asia. The Trans-Siberian railway beyond Lake Baykal has become largely negative in the national context, apart from possessing considerable strategic importance.

The very being and character of such outlying regions as Middle Asia, Caucasia or the Far East are bound up with the transport links which connect them with the effective national territory. The perennial question about how they should balance the relative claims of regional specialization and regional self-sufficiency hinges to a large extent on the actual capacity and character of the transport facilities and the cost-distances involved. Long hauls have always been the bane of the Soviet transport planners, and it may be that the arguments for concentrating on the perfection of a closely integrated network within the bounds of the prospective National Electricity Grid, i.e. where the majority of the people live, will prove, as in the case of agriculture, more and more persuasive. Unlike North America, the deliberate laying down of lines of communication as trail-blazers through virgin territory to encourage settlement, and the exploitation of resources, has rarely been a feature of the Russian experience. Railways have, in general come, belatedly, in response to a previously pent-up demand, and have promptly become over-used. But east of the Yenisey some recent railways, notably the branch from Tayshet to Ust-Kut, do possess something of the trail-blazing character, beyond the limits of normally attractive agricultural settlement, and yet not quite beyond the pale, as in the far North. The importance of liberal investment in transport facilities, as a prime stimulus to economic development within the limits of the country's promising and accessible territory, may once again be becoming fully recognized.

CHAPTER SIX

Growth and Distribution of Population

THE map of population speaks volumes about the essential character of any country. To attempt to understand the present distribution of population in the Soviet Union, preferably through tracing its evolution, leads one automatically into the full range of geographical enquiry. Thus it is a convenient way of summarizing, and presenting synthetically, the geography of the country.

The population on the land now comprising the Soviet Union has more than doubled in the present century. The North American experience has been broadly similar, in both relative and absolute terms. But, whereas everyone knows that this has been the American Century, for the Russians it must rank as one of the most catastrophic in their history, or indeed that of most nations. Where America has been enriched by the immigration of people of initiative and skill from Europe, Russia has been impoverished by the loss of such people (often to America) by emigration (and its later designation—defection). Whereas for America the World Wars may be regarded, from one viewpoint, as massive economic boosters, involving relatively light human losses and no ravaging of the homeland, for Russia they have, especially the last one, involved unparalleled destruction and loss of life. Whereas America has been blessed with a generally affluent, peaceful and open society, Russia has been cursed with famines, revolutions, forced labour camps and a generally depressed standard of living.

In the early 1960s these differences between the superstates have, to a substantial degree, been narrowed, but the record of the past in the U.S.S.R. is dramatically revealed in the demographic structure. Whereas the United States has a surplus of some 2 million females, in the U.S.S.R. it amounts to 20 million. The effect of this on the next generation is also clear. However it should be noted that there is no disparity between the sexes in the age-groups below 35, i.e. those who were below the age of 18 at the end of the war. Moreover two out of every three residents of the Soviet Union are younger than 35. The average annual rate of population increase is almost identical with the North American rate and double that of most of Europe.

It is vital also to realize that the Soviet Union is still in the throes of carrying through the fundamental changeover from a rural to an urban society, which has virtually been completed in North America and most of the countries of Western Europe. Before 1928 at least 4 out of every 5 Russians had always been tied to the soil, comparable with the situation in much of Southern Asia today. However, in 1962, for the first time in Russian history, the urban population outnumbered the rural (North America reached this stage around 1920, Britain around 1860). Since the rural segment is now a notably ageing population, in comparison with that of the cities, its further decline can be expected to be rapid in the next decade.

THE ETHNIC MAP

The official Federal structure of the U.S.S.R. draws attention to the fact that the population is made up culturally of heterogeneous groups. However, although it is certainly true that one can find people closely related to the Persians, the Mongols, the Finns, even the North American Indians, their national significance can be greatly exaggerated. The overriding fact is that more than three-quarters of the total population comprises that Slavic-speaking amalgam which has spread across the continent and which holds key positions even in those areas in which it is in the minority. Undoubtedly in these areas, notably Middle Asia, Transcaucasia and the Baltic republics, the regional personality is largely formed by the nature of these nationalities, but it so happens that they are regions which have become marginal in national significance as well as geographical location. Throughout the economic core of the country, from the Ukraine and the Moscow region to Lake Baykal, the Slavic character is all-pervading and the few non-Russian nationalities that are in this main stream, like the Tatars, and some of the Kazakhs, are inevitably being absorbed and Russified. Moreover, even in the marginal republics, although the native languages are encouraged, Russian is inevitably the essential second language for the more ambitious and potentially influential of the population, and the *lingua franca* of the cities.

THE EVOLUTION OF THE PRESENT DISTRIBUTION

The dashing Russian victories and adventurous journeys in the sixteenth and seventeenth centuries made a hardly perceptible mark on the population map of Eurasia, however important they may have been for increasing national prestige and as a pointer to future settlement possibilities. By the time of Peter the Great (early eighteenth century) about two-thirds of the population were still crowded into the relatively unproductive mixed forests of Central European Russia and almost all the remainder were in neighbouring parts of the 'wooded steppe', which had been gradually infiltrated during the previous two centuries.

Throughout most of the eighteenth and nineteenth centuries the dominant set of the migratory tide was southward into the superior black-earth of what is now the Ukraine and North Caucasus (Kuban) which by the mid-nineteenth century claimed two-thirds of the Russian population. The European wooded-steppe had become, and remains today, the most crowded part of rural Russia, and the reservoir for most of the subsequent migration to the newer farmlands of the east and eventually, the cities. It was indeed only after the third quarter of the nineteenth century that the eyes of the land-hungry peasantry turned to the open spaces east of the Volga and built up enough pressure to induce a railway to cross a continent.

Thus the lifetime of an old man today spans the period of dominance of the easterly population movement—a movement which is apparently now drawing to a close. The scale of the easterly displacement can be roughly measured if we compare European Russia (north of the Caucasus and west of the Volga) with the main eastern reception area, the Volga–Baykal zone. During the half-century before 1911 the Volga–Baykal zone probably acquired about 10 million new inhabitants (almost half of them after 1897) but the European zone gained over 40 millions, no doubt largely through natural increase. However during the half-century following 1911 the East (Volga–Baykal zone) has added about 25 millions, which is more than double the contemporary gains of the European zone. Of course the catastrophic warfare over much of the European zone, with the corollary of the easterly evacuation, was most immediately responsible, but the scale of the net redistribution is still remarkable, considering that the European zone had four times the population of Volga–Baykal in 1911. Further, we may assume that flash-in-the-pan wartime movements, not in line with long-term policies, would have left little trace by now.

While the spectacular easterly migration in the quarter-century preceding the First World War was almost entirely agricultural, the even more remarkable second wave since 1928 has been mainly industrial and urban, reflecting the lateral dispersion of the country's industrial base, as outlined in earlier chapters.

THE GROWTH OF CITIES

The geographical course of the more positive economic developments of the Soviet period can be followed most surely through the comparative study of the growth of cities. Only cities of over 50,000 will be considered here. There are now over 300 of these, housing one-third of the Soviet population, compared with about 50, containing one-twentieth of the Russian population, at the outset of this century. Whereas the rural population has declined absolutely since 1926 the city population, so defined, has increased over five times in the same period, involving a net addition of 55 million (the population of Britain today) to the Soviet cities. This combination of speed and volume in city growth is probably unparalleled in the history of the urbanization of a nation.

Before 1939

Russian cities, even the large ones, were slow to get off the mark in the nineteenth century, in comparison with those in Western Europe. However, St Petersburg, the western showcase of Russia, had the special favours of the Tsars lavished on it and became the largest city in the last century of Imperial Russia. In 1870 it was (with half a million), 50% larger than Moscow, but the latter has gained ground since then, although St Petersburg remained slightly ahead right up to the Revolution. The growth of these cities was rapid by any standards, each of them reaching the million-mark by the end of the century and doubling again by 1915. In 1897, after the twin million-cities, came the wheat export port of Odessa, followed by Riga and Kiev, all near the European border. Tashkent was the only city east of the Volga with more than 100,000.

A considerable momentum of city growth, resulting from the belated industrial revolution and the newly found continental mobility of the late nineteenth century, carried over into the first decade of Soviet control. However, all this paled beside the uprush of cities which characterized the first Five Year Plans. Between the census years of 1926 and 1939 the number of city-dwellers (over 50,000) almost trebled. About half of the net additions, though, accrued to the Moscow region and the greater Ukraine together—each of these regions gained more than the whole of the Volga–Baykal zone, spectacular though the latter's rate of growth was. The Soviet Union was first and foremost building on the foundations bequeathed by the last decade of Tsarism, with the important, but somewhat unique, exception of the Ural–Kuzbas Combine. This was, to be sure, the era of the mushroom towns, symbolic prototypes of the All-Soviet City, such as Magnitogorsk, Karaganda and Komsomolsk. They blazed a trail which was to be well-travelled later. But still, it is well to remember that two-thirds of the boom cities (defined as those over 50,000, which had doubled during this period) were situated *west* of the Volga.

Since 1939

Thenceforth, however, the tables were turned. Two-thirds of the cities which doubled in the two decades since 1939 are situated east of the Volga, and over half within the Volga–Baykal zone. Moreover, even in absolute terms the Volga–Baykal zone acquired more new city-dwellers in this period than did the whole of European Russia, west of the Volga and north of the Caucasus. Further the six largest of the Soviet cities which doubled in this period (Novosibirsk, Kuybyshev, Chelyabinsk, Perm, Omsk and Ufa) are all in the Volga–Baykal zone.

There is a curiously close parallel here with the geographical behaviour of the cities of the United States during the same period. Some three-fifths of the cities (over 50,000) which doubled in the United States are situated west of the Mississippi (cf. Volga). In no other previous comparable period had these vast 'new' lands claimed a majority of the boom cities of either Russia or America. Possibly this indicates that the two giants are coming of age geographically rather more closely together in time than might have been imagined.

The map of regional rates of city growth (Fig. 16) shows that all the groups of cities within the Volga–Baykal zone, but none outside, increased more quickly than the comparable cities of California during this period—and anyone who has lived through this will appreciate the speed involved. If we may use a further U.S. measure of comparison, the Volga–Baykal zone in that time acquired more new city population than did California *plus* the great block of industrial states between New England and Illinois.

The Spread of Large Cities

At the outset of the present century St Petersburg and Moscow were the only two cities of over half a million inhabitants in Russia, and even by 1926 the only addition to this class was Kiev. There are now some thirty cities of this size in the Soviet Union (nearly half of them east of the Volga) and a whole phalanx of others approaching that category. Moreover that supreme symbol of mature urbanization in the modern world, the metropolitan area of over a million, now counts nine representatives in the Soviet Union, with two or three others likely to be added in the near future. This was about as many as North America had during the Second World War—it now has two or three times as many.

Moscow and Leningrad are still head and shoulders above the others, of course, and it is remarkable how Moscow, on resuming its capital status after two centuries, has grown much more quickly than Leningrad, so that it is

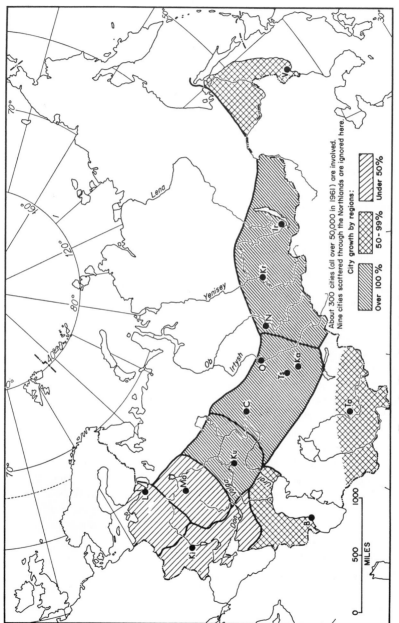

About 300 cities (all over 50,000 in 1961) are involved. Nine cities scattered through the Northlands are ignored here.

City growth by regions:

Over 100%

50–99%

Under 50%

Fig. 16—Growth of cities, by regions, 1939–61

now more than twice as large. With seven or eight million people, depending on where one puts the boundaries, it now takes its place as the most northerly of the half-dozen mammoth cities of the world. Of these million-cities of the Soviet Union, five are in the older parts of European Russia, west of the Volga (Moscow, Leningrad, Kiev, Gorky and Kharkov), two are in the Volga–Baykal zone (Kuybyshev and Novosibirsk, which should be joined soon by Sverdlovsk and Chelyabinsk) and two on the southern margins (Baku and Tashkent). The dispersion of the large city, with all the regional decentralization which it denotes, is one of the most significant geographical legacies of the last two or three decades of Soviet rule.

PROSPECT

The easterly displacement of the Russian people seems to have come to an end for the time being, particularly east of the Urals. There have recently been persistent reports of an outflow of people from Siberia for climatic, cultural and other 'amenity' reasons, a process which, as in similar regions of Canada, can now only be reversed by unusual incentives and general subsidization. The government has long shown a willingness to allocate disproportionate amounts of capital to the East, which has been justified by resource, strategic and other factors, but it is probable that industries other than labour-intensive ones will now be favoured, reducing population growth. Sheer location is very important, though there are likely to be special cases, like Novosibirsk. The centre of gravity of the Soviet population is not far from Kuybyshev in the Middle Volga, but the fastest growing of the large towns over the last two decades, and also in the latest two or three years, has been Novosibirsk, fifteen hundred miles further east. There are many imponderables which make it risky to attempt a long-term forecast of the nature of the national location policy for industry, on which the fortunes of any particular city or group of cities will inevitably depend. For instance, what effect would a lasting estrangement from China have—would industry and population be encouraged to retreat from the borderlands or would development be redoubled to stake out the claim, as it were? On the other hand, if Eastern Europe with its hundred millions, becomes integrated economically with the U.S.S.R., would not cities like Moscow or Kharkov be the best placed for the whole Soviet bloc market? The most likely course would seem to be a balanced development, which in any case would be doctrinally and strategically most acceptable, throughout the cities of the national triangle, but there would appear to be considerable difficulties in its eastern parts for quite a long time to come. Whatever happens, and taking into account the higher rate of natural increase characteristic of the newly developing regions, it is still difficult to foresee a time when the European zone, west of the Volga, will have less than half the total population, or the Volga–Baykal zone more than a third. Discounting then all thoughts of a revolutionary alteration of the familiar Soviet population map, there is no doubt that the character, direction and volume of such marginal redistributions of the Soviet people as do occur will always have relevance to the understanding and assessment of the country's development and future as a world power.

PART II: REGIONAL

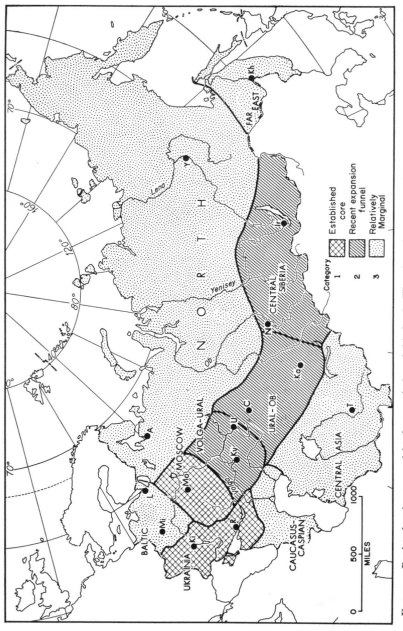

FIG. 17—Regional units, as used in the remainder of this book. They have been grouped into three general categories, the criteria for which are discussed in this chapter

Introduction

A SCHEME OF REGIONS

PERHAPS the most difficult task which has to be faced by a regional geographer is that of choosing his regions. This is especially so when one is concerned with very large, centralized super-states like the United States and the Soviet Union. However, the effort is necessary and worth-while, and involves a searching investigation into the really significant aspects of the geography of the country.

No particular scheme of regional divisions can ever hope to please everybody and none can be expected to provide a correct framework for analysing all regional problems. Moreover, it is well to realize that, within a sovereign state, it is fruitless to expect to draw thin-line regional boundaries, except in rare cases, and that we must accept thick lines as inevitable. The typical geographical boundary is a zone of transition and our attention should be fixed on the cores of regions rather than their edges.

The actual division made will necessarily reflect the author's geographical philosophy. Regional geography is a way of looking at a part of the earth synthetically, bringing out the links rather than the differences between such things as nature and man, city and country, quantities and qualities, past and present. The aim should be to paint as complete a portrait of a region as possible but, as in any portrait, careful selection of detail and the building up of a theme are essential.

Why people have come to be just *where* they are is taken here to be the most all-embracing question posed in the geography of a region. This kind of specific investigation of the factor of location in human affairs involves a thorough knowledge of the workings of the natural environment and the character of the natural resources, but also of the changing notions which people have about these things and about distance itself—in other words changing geographical values. In new lands like Russia and America it is especially important to understand the peopling process which has gone into the making of the population map and also to take account of stages of development and different rates of growth.

Most of the schemes of division used in regional geographies of the Soviet Union are unsatisfactory from the point of view of defining and interpreting these kinds of problem. For instance the natural zones (forest, steppe, etc.) are commonly employed, with some justification in view of their impact on the course of Russian history. However, as cities and industry loom ever larger than agriculture, these zones become less and less coincident with the real human regions, and the reader is condemned to grasshop over several chapters in order to find out what is really going on in one of the fast-developing economic regions. More commonly, in recent regional treatments, the tendency has been to use the official Soviet administrative or economic regions. Although this has much to commend it from the statistical standpoint, it can be very cramping to anyone searching for the geographical realities (cf. using the States as units for the U.S.A.). Some of these governmental divisions may serve quite well but, as in any country, many tend to be anachronistic and irrational, blurring rather than heightening the reality of the human regions. For instance, the republic and economic region of Kazakhstan manages to break up the homogeneous wheat and metal area of the Western Siberian plains and also the very different area of ancient agricultural districts in Middle Asia, while its centre is a desert. And this geographical violence is done on ethnic grounds which are now quite invalid, since the Kazakhs are only a small minority in the northern, most vital part of the republic. Similarly reality is blurred by including in the Soviet official regions enormous under-developed areas, say in Siberia, with rich contiguous areas which are developing rapidly. Many other examples of this kind of administrative distortion of reality could be cited, as they could for almost any country.

It seems unnecessarily timid for geographers to cling to such administrative units just on statistical pretexts. By so doing one sacrifices true accuracy, which depends so much on the unit used, in favour of a formal kind of precision. In other words a generalization beginning 'about two-thirds . . .' of a meaningful unit of area is more accurate than '68·2% . . .' of a relatively meaningless one.

THE RELEVANT CRITERIA

The selection of the scheme of regional units used here has arisen out of a rather close examination of the Soviet Union from the particular point of view outlined above—that is, the changing location of people and their activities as an all-embracing problem. In turn the regional scheme has entered into the generalizations and indeed been inextricably bound up with the selection of subject matter and conclusions of this book. Thus, before listing the regions, the various criteria which have lain behind their selection will be discussed.

These are: (1) scale of contribution to the national economy as a whole; (2) rate of population (especially city) growth; (3) relative importance of *accessible* resources; (4) economic specialization which will necessarily, in many cases, involve a combination of agricultural and industrial specialisms; (5) a certain community of historical associations; (6) ethnic considerations where they actually loom large in the distinctiveness of a region.

These criteria are of course very heterogeneous and it is well-nigh impossible to accommodate them all adequately in any given area. It is obviously much easier to delimit specialist regions with one criterion, such as agriculture or vegetation, in mind. A good deal of subjectivity and compromise necessarily enters into the delimitation of composite human regions, and this has to be accepted if it is felt that there is something to be gained from looking at functional regions 'in all their aspects interlocked', in Mackinder's phrase. In the United States, the South, the Mid-West or New England are geographical regions composed of a variable mixture of historical, economic, physical and cultural ingredients, but none the less real or vital for all that. Many of the regions of the Soviet Union are as yet rather less coherent and less fully crystallized, but this only makes attempts to capture the essential character and to assess the prospects of a region all the more an intellectual adventure and challenge.

THE SCHEME

In the process of analysing the broad range of subject matter of Soviet geography, as outlined in the earlier chapters, with the foregoing principles in mind, the following general regional categories have been made (Fig. 17).

(1) *The established European Core.* This is composed of two main regions—the Moscow region and the greater Ukraine. Accounting for at least 40% of the Soviet population and industrial and agricultural output, this is the solid base of the main inhabited triangle of the country, comparable in national significance with the North-East of the United States. It was established in this role in pre-Soviet times, with a much greater dominance on the national scene than it has today. It is still vitally important to the country as a whole, but has grown at a slower pace than the regions in the next category in most of the Soviet period.

(2) *The Volga–Baykal Zone.* This is the tapering end of the triangle, with its apex at Lake Baykal. It may be called 'American Russia'—the effective, viable part of the vast 'eastern regions', characterized by a raw pioneering 'frontier' character, and by a more American mobility and scale of agricultural and industrial activity. Its character is, in contrast to that of category 1, largely a creation of the Soviet period. It contains a major portion of the country's accessible industrial resources. It is divided here into three sections, with the Ural crest and the Ob river as the break-points.

These two categories comprise more than two-thirds of the Soviet population, at least three-quarters of its industrial and agricultural output and some four-fifths of the accessible industrial energy and raw materials.

(3) *The marginal zones.* Around the edges of the inner heartland represented by categories 1 and 2 there is a heterogeneous collection of regions, spread over about two-thirds of the Soviet area but possessing less than a third of its population, and a much smaller proportion of the national production and resources. The majority of the population is non-Slavic, in marked contrast to the regions in the first two categories. Except for some rare metals, timber and sub-tropical crops like cotton and tea, these widely-scattered regions make a limited contribution to the national economy. With the exception of Leningrad and some other cities in the Baltic zone, which have some high-value, labour-intensive industries, they are essentially outside the main stream of Soviet industrial activity. These regions are thus largely marginal in the economic as well as the purely locational sense. They are the Baltic, the Northlands (containing nearly half the country's area), Caucasus–Caspia, Middle Asia and the Far East.

In the broadest terms, then, the Soviet Union seems to comprehend three or four 'worlds'—the European world west of the Volga, and the 'American' world of the Volga-Baykal—comprising together the Slavic Effective National Territory—flanked to the south by the more truly Asian world of Caucasia and Turkestan and on the north by the 'Canadian' world of the North and Far East. Put in this way, the Soviet Union is seen to possess as great a variety as any country of the significant cultural groupings of today's world.

A NOTE ON THE REGIONAL MAPS

The following chapters on regional geography inevitably presume the need to 'see things together'. Therefore it has been considered desirable to forego the undoubted advantages of a more spacious design and scale, and to place all four basic regional maps on facing-pages. The effectiveness of this system, however, depends on the reader. He is strongly advised to take a good comparative look at the double-page spread, and get a working sketch-map in his mind, before proceeding with the chapter. Thereafter he should keep his marker at the maps and turn back to them frequently, acquiring the habit of referring not only to the single feature in question, but to its possible connections with others on the page. Needless to say, these maps are no substitute for a good atlas, which should always be at hand.

CHAPTER SEVEN

The Moscow Region

UNLIKE most Soviet regions, this one owes its basic importance to legacies of the distant past. Poor in resources and transitional in nature, it derives whatever coherence it possesses from the dominating presence in its midst of the national capital—like London or Peking, a Heart of Empire.

Its original start in life owed a good deal to the demise of the much more attractive Kiev, to the stultifying influence of the nomads of the steppe, and to its early attribute as a remote, unprepossessing and therefore fairly secure haven in the forests. But, though dimly recognized at first, its position at the hub of the great water-system of the East European plain proved to be its fortune. Moscow had, by one means or another, prevailed over its rivals in this crucial region between the Volga and the Oka and become truly independent by the end of the fifteenth century. Henceforth the whole story of the spreading of the Russian people and the growth of Russian power becomes closely relevant to the rise of the city and its region.

The region itself remained depressingly unrewarding to the overwhelming majority of the Russian population who were tied to the land,

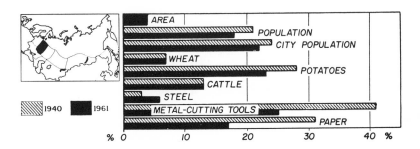

FIG. 18—Location and importance of the Moscow Region in relation to the Soviet Union as a whole, for certain selected items

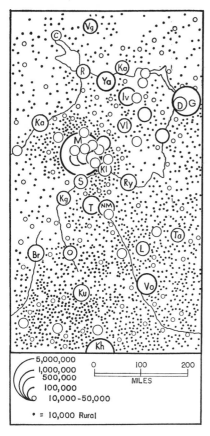

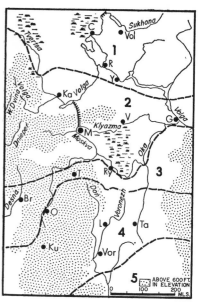

FIG. 20—The Moscow Region: nature.
Vegetation zones: 1=tayga, 2=mixed
forest, 3=deciduous forest, 4=wooded
steppe, 5=steppe

FIG. 19—The Moscow Region: popula-
tion. Key to cities: Br=Bryansk, C=
Cherepovets, D=Dzerzhinsk, G=Gorky,
Iv=Ivanovo, Ka=Kalinin, Kg=Kaluga,
Kh=Kharkov, Kl=Kolomna, Ko=Kos-
troma, Ku=Kursk, L=Lipetsk, M=
Moscow, NM=Novomoskovsk, O=Orël,
R=Rybinsk, Ry=Ryazan, S=Serpu-
khov, Ta=Tambov, T=Tula, Vg=
Vologda, Vl=Vladimir, Vo=Voronezh,
Ya=Yaroslavl

126

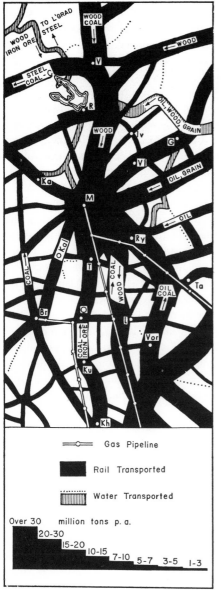

FIG. 21—The Moscow Region: movements

FIG. 22—The Moscow Region: economy

although it was virtually all they knew until the late seventeenth century. However, since then the really significant period of expansion of the Empire and the peopling of it has inevitably involved the diminution of the relative importance of the Moscow region within the Russian State. Then the home of some three out of four of the State's citizens, it now houses less than one in five. The establishment of a powerful rival, St Petersburg, the planting of industry in the Urals, the conquests on the Baltic, and above all the colonizing of the long-prohibited black-earth lands of the south and later of Siberia—all this announced a final breaking out by the Russian people from the unsmiling and increasingly crowded and exhausted forest compound which had been their refuge several centuries before.

On the other hand, it was equally certain that the controlling centre of the Russian state had become irrevocably established, St Petersburg notwithstanding, with the political, financial and cultural centralization, the convergence of communications, the skilled labour pool and other fundamental components of a national nucleus. These attributes have subsequently become accentuated and remain today those which characterize the region in the scheme of things and enable it to transcend a rather meagre natural environment and resource endowment.

The momentum or inertia of this centripetal force has induced the inflow of the economic necessities—energy, raw materials and food from all parts of the country—the converging gas and oil pipelines and high-voltage electricity transmission lines being its latest expression. In addition the presence of the urban agglomerations promotes a much more intensive agricultural use of land than would be justified on grounds of natural endowments alone.

Because of the national as well as merely regional influence of Moscow, and the lack of any notable homogeneity of the natural landscape, it is particularly difficult to arrive at definitive borders for the present region. Nevertheless, there is obviously a special, all-pervading metropolitan orientation within a distance of, say, 250 miles of the capital (cf. London and south-east England) which outweighs any other regional coherence or power of attraction. In terms of meaningful quantitative economic and demographic indices, however, the region is not a simple circle, but has been clearly weighted towards the east and the south, in relation to the metropolis, i.e. along the two main axes of national development. The area immediately to the west of Moscow is thus negative in a relative sense, and in character belongs more to the Baltic region, with which it is included in this book, while on the east the counter-attraction and character of the next regional focus, the Middle Volga, is only felt beyond the large city of Gorky. On the north the edge of the region about Vologda is the edge of the broadly settled belt, while on the south the region extends to the borders of the Ukraine, taking in territory which is physically and agriculturally akin to the latter but which is distinguished largely by its stronger traditional and also actual orientation towards Moscow.

The pull of Moscow is the overriding common denominator which justifies the combination in one region of its northern and southern halves, which are in fact commonly and justly characterized separately in Russian tradition as the Central Industrial and Central Black-earth districts. Broadly speaking, a line from Orël to Gorky marks off these two landscapes—to the north one of industrial cities, pine forests and niggardly agriculture and to the south more humus-rich soils, warmer climate, dense rural populations and, until the recent and highly promising iron and steel developments, a lack of non-agricultural industry.

In some ways these two divisions, though traditionally set apart, are growing together even more securely and a true metropolitan region, with its counterparts in other parts of the urbanizing world, is actively in the making.

THE NATURAL HABITAT (Fig. 20)

The Volga's major right bank tributary, the Oka, which cuts through the heart of this region, follows the zone in which precipitation and evaporation are in equilibrium. It is the most fundamental dividing line in the region and also epitomizes the most characteristic quality of its natural environment—transition. The northern and southern fringes are tayga and steppe respectively but most of the land is covered by mixed forests or wooded steppe—both typically transitional biogeographical zones (Plate II). The Oka marks off the predominantly podzolic coniferous and birch forests to the north from the largely black-earth (if 'degraded') broadleaved forest and half-open steppe to the south. Annual precipitation does fall off gradually from north-west to south-east but the more critical change in the equation of effective moisture is induced by differences in the provision of heat. The effective accumulated temperature values are half as high again in Voronezh as in Vologda, while snow lies for four months as compared with nearly six. Needless to say, these climatic factors have produced not only north-south differences in the soil and vegetation cover, but also in the prevalence of waterlogged ground.

These climatic distinctions between the north and the south are exacerbated by the results of the recent glaciation, the main southern limit of which is commemorated by the terminal moraine known as the Smolensk-

Moscow ridge. North of this ridge and also of the lower reaches of the Oka the drainage has been greatly disrupted, with extensive marshy areas which can easily be converted into lakes, as in the case of the Rybinsk reservoir. To the south, on the other hand, the drainage is largely undisturbed and marshes are rare.

The actual relief is of only minor significance. Apart from the Smolensk–Moscow ridge, already noted, the main division is longitudinal, the western half of the region being taken up by the Central Russian upland and the eastern half by the Volga–Oka–Don plain. The general level of the former is about 800 feet, deeply dissected by rivers and gullies, while the latter lies at about 400 feet, with gentler gradients. The iron-bearing quartzites of the Kursk Magnetic Anomaly come close enough to the surface in several places to be economically exploited on a large scale. The sandstones and marly clays overlying the hard rocks are coated with coarse fluvio-glacial debris in the north and finer silty *löss* in the south.

Finally we return to the river network, perhaps the most influential of the natural features in the formation of the regional character and function. Most of the territory is drained by the Volga system including particularly its main tributary the Oka. The southern black-earth region, however, is largely within the Don system, while the Dnieper and Western Dvina systems lead off from the western edge of the region to the Baltic and Black Seas and the Northern Dvina towards the distant Arctic. Short distances and low ground characterize the watersheds between these rivers and herein lies, in considerable part, the secret of the rise to power of the Moscow region.

THE PEOPLING OF THE REGION

The first effective occupation of the forests between the Oka and the Volga by Slavic-speaking peoples probably occurred about A.D. 1000. They did not encounter an entirely empty land, but the incumbent Finnish tribes of hunters and fishers did not prove a serious obstacle, and were either driven further to the north-east or assimilated. The Slavs were constricted by the presence of the Tatars and also the Moslem Bulgars to the east and for some time treated the region as a refuge, settling in scattered family groups rather than gathering in villages or towns. In a somewhat waterlogged environment tolerably well-drained sites were sought after, but shifting agriculture was by no means the sole activity. Fishing, hunting (specially for furs) and bee-keeping were also vital, and dry sites, easily accessible to a navigable river, were at a premium. After the Mongol invasion of the mid-thirteenth century and the blotting out of Kiev and the wooded steppe generally from the Russian world, the Volga–Oka lands experienced an influx of population and became fragmented into rival principalities. Moscow, in the centre of the mesopotamian region, began to show a regional supremacy in the early fourteenth century and by the late fifteenth had finally established its control not only over Volga–Oka but over the rich forest dominions long held by Novgorod. Furthermore it had, by various stratagems, become strong enough to refuse payment of tribute to the Tatars. Thus after many centuries of Russian subservience to the nomads, the tide had at last been turned, and turned by Moscow, thenceforth the established leader of all the Russians.

Farming settlement then became feasible on the better lands south of the Oka; people in favour with the Tsar were granted land and recruited labour from the increasingly crowded and impoverished north, and the fortified lines crept inexorably southwards into the wooded steppe. Improved methods of farming and the inherently better fertility of this almost virgin land made the Central Black-earth region the new granary of Russia. A notable division appeared within an enlarged Moscow region in which the growing cities of the Volga–Oka came to depend heavily on grain shipments from the south. These cities were thus enabled to exploit their good locations with regard to assembly, distribution and political control to develop a wide range of industries, laying the foundations of the dominant regional character of today. The earliest industries were concerned with processing local products—wood, flax, hemp, hides and fur—as well as food. But the capital accumulation associated with the general expansion of the Russian state made possible the growth of others, such as the iron-working of Tula, using local ore and charcoal, in the seventeenth century. In the late eighteenth century cotton began to be imported and thenceforth steadily replaced the indigenous textiles. By then the rise of St Petersburg had challenged the dominance of Moscow, but only reduced rather than supplanted the Moscow region's primacy in both industrial and agricultural matters in a period of continuous territorial expansion of the State.

The scene about 1900

The established nodality of the Moscow region was greatly enhanced by the emergence of a network of railways radiating from it during the second half of the nineteenth century. However, this was by no means an unmixed blessing for many parts of the central region. Food, energy and industrial materials flowed in as never before, and the sharpened competition proved fatal to many enterprises in the region which had hitherto enjoyed a natural protection.

The greatest decline took place in agriculture. The rapid exploitation of the virgin fertility of the southern steppes, resulting in the northward flow of cheap grain, especially wheat, dealt a heavy blow to the farms of the Centre, even south of the Oka, which were by then impoverished, over-crowded and in a somewhat chaotic state following the end of serfdom. The effect was comparable to that of the opening up of the North American prairies on the wheat producers of Western Europe. Much of the poorer land north of the Oka was abandoned altogether, while the regional centres south of that river turned into overgrown villages, choked with redundant peasants, many of whom were on the point of migrating to the newer lands of the Ukraine and Kuban, and across the Volga.

The newly exploited brown coal basin to the west and south of Moscow was subjected to the competition of Donets black coal and Baku oil in the last quarter of the nineteenth century. Foreign capital was attracted to these newly emerging regions and to St Petersburg rather than to the Moscow region, so that the latter's industries became technically less advanced and widely scattered in small units, often in the countryside, where cheap part-time labour was available. All the same, industry did expand rapidly in this Volga–Oka region during the last fifty years of Tsarist rule. In the early twentieth century the region still accounted for over a third of the Russian industrial production and labour force (excluding Poland) while in the textile group of industries, still the most important national industrial category, the proportion was more like nine-tenths. Well over half of the whole region's industry (by value and employment) was accounted for by textiles (mainly cotton). The general pattern of industrial concentration, largely to the east and north-east of Moscow, was remarkably similar to that of today.

There were over 25 million people in the region in 1897, the great majority of them country folk. However, Moscow had a million people, having trebled its population in forty years, while by the eve of revolution it had risen to nearly two millions. There were about eight other cities of over 50,000 in 1897—mainly old Volga–Oka cities like Nizhnii Novgorod (Gorky), Tula, Yaroslavl, Tver (Kalinin) and Ivanovo, but including also southern agricultural centres like Voronezh and Orël. The Russian empire had expanded to its limits and in spite of St Petersburg and the competition of the new-rich lands, this national glory was inevitably reflected to a considerable degree in the founding nucleus of the Empire itself.

Eve of the Second World War

By 1939 the region's population had grown to some 40 millions and the rural component had been reduced to little more than half. Textiles had lost their dominance in the greatly enlarged scale and variegated structure of industry. The skilled labour pool, coupled with the special demands of the Soviet government, had made engineering the major industrial component of all but the old textile towns grouped about Ivanovo. Gorky in particular had become the main centre for motor vehicles and had grown to 650,000. This was twice as large as any other city of the region except Moscow, whereas in 1900 Gorky had just been one of several, and not the largest. Moscow itself, 4½ millions in 1939, had doubled itself in the period of the Five Year Plans—a clear consequence of the resumption of its status as capital of a centralized and authoritarian state, and the inertia value of its traditional pool of scarce skilled labour. Its physical centrality was enhanced by the cutting of a deep waterway directly north of the Volga in 1937. Following this the first three hydro-dams of the Great Volga scheme were constructed, contributing some half-million kilowatts of electricity to the Moscow region. The energy deficiency was still acute, and heavy imports of coal, as well as exploitation of the poor local lignite and peat, were necessary.

The chemical industry, in particular synthetic rubber, began to be developed, Voronezh and Yaroslavl, the next largest cities in the region after Moscow and Gorky, becoming the main centres. Potatoes were widely used as a raw material—but one indication of the changes in the structure of agriculture in the pre-war Soviet period. The rapid growth of the urban population, from 7 to 13 millions, between 1926 and 1939, stimulated a shift towards livestock and vegetable products, whilst wheat acreage was also increased in the podzolic Volga–Oka zone, though, it appears, for doctrinaire reasons rather than those of agricultural economics.

THE PRESENT ECONOMY (Fig. 22)

Although the broad patterns of the economic landscape remain recognizably those evolved in Tsarist times, it would be far from correct to create an image of stagnation. In spite of the war—the industrial core from Moscow to Gorky was not actually fought over but the agricultural south was—the region has notably expanded the scale of its economic activities. Since about 1959 the basic economy has been injected with some significant new elements which bid fair to alter fundamentally the traditional structure. These are the increasingly prominent place of gas in industry, the inauguration of the long-postponed build-up of large-scale heavy industry based on the Kursk Magnetic Anomaly and the new chemical and agricultural revolutions. However, the presence of the capital and the centrality of the region as a whole remain the chief economic spur to this kind of expansion.

The inflow of energy

Of all the sizable industrial regions of the country, this one is the most completely dependent on others for its basic material needs. Probably three-quarters of the energy requirements have to be imported and this proportion is steadily increasing, as comparative costs come to the fore. Wood and peat are ancient energy sources which still play some part but the lignite basin, chiefly around Tula, has been the chief indigenous supplier for some time. However, it is very poor quality, compared with other Soviet brown coals, suffers from waterlogging and the presence of gas, and would have been plainly uneconomic were it not for the local demands and shortages and the need to avoid overloading the railways. It accounted for nearly a tenth of the Soviet coal output in the 1950s.

The days of this coal basin's life are clearly numbered, since gas now comes in to Moscow by pipeline from the very large sources in the North Caucasus, Ukraine and Volga. This is the most significant inflow and should soon account for most of the region's industrial and domestic fuel demands. But in addition oil is piped from the Middle Volga and electricity sent by 500 kilovolt lines from the big Volga dams. These economical inflows are designed to substitute not only for costly local fuels but also for black coal imports from the Donets basin and even further afield. Atomic power stations have also been built in this region, but so far are not major power contributors.

Industrial raw materials

Similarly, until about 1960 there were no really important developed natural resources in the region. Timber was the chief one, but even here long depletion of the forests had taken its toll and there was a net import even of this commodity. Flax and hemp, traditional industrial raw materials, had declined in importance, and the exploitation of phosphates, iron ore (around Tula and Lipetsk) and some building stones was relatively insignificant.

However, this dismal picture of natural resources was greatly brightened by the news that large-scale exploitation of the Kursk Magnetic Anomaly, a well-nigh inexhaustible reserve of iron ore—one of the world's largest—had begun in 1959. Its existence had been known since the eighteenth century, but periodic intentions of exploiting it were frustrated by unfavourable hydro-geological conditions. Most of the high-grade ore is buried under several hundred feet of waterlogged sedimentary strata, and the lower-grade ore, nearer the surface, requires much investment in modern crushing machinery. The technological and economic pre-requisites have only just materialized, and the decision has been made to develop this great resource, mainly to the south-west of Kursk.

The industrial pattern

Clearly, then, the K.M.A. is beginning to effect a fundamental alteration in the industrial emphasis of the region. Ore is being sent to Tula and Lipetsk, pre-existing minor steel centres which are being greatly expanded into large integrated plants. The iron ore is destined for the Donets basin, Eastern Europe and perhaps Cherepovets as well. A drawback to the development of large scale ferrous metallurgy in this region in comparison with Siberia is the increasingly high cost of Donets coking coal, and water shortage may also be a limiting factor. However, the availability of gas should considerably reduce the amount of coke needed and the central location of Kursk–Lipetsk between Moscow and the Donets basin is a very considerable asset.

The industrial pattern, though, still shows an overwhelming concentra-tion north of a line from Gorky to Tula, in the area long known in Russia as the Industrial Centre. The most valuable and widespread sector is engineering, but the most rapidly growing is chemicals, while the most traditional and still very important is textiles. Greater Moscow with its satellite towns is important for all three groups and continues to expand industrially, in spite of apparent official policy to the contrary. This extended metropolitan area probably accounts for nearly half of the in-dustrial output of the whole region and over a tenth of that of the country as a whole. The second engineering cluster and a much more specialized one (cars, ships, etc.) is that of Gorky, while the specialized textile cluster is centred around Ivanovo. Chemicals are more scattered over the whole region; from the north, e.g. Yaroslavl and Gorky, where it is associated with wood and paper industries and Volga oil, to the south, e.g. Voronezh and Novomoskovsk, where an early dependence on potatoes and grain has given way rapidly to one on gas.

Taken all round, and excepting the new K.M.A. developments, the whole region's industrial output is characterized by a higher ratio of value to bulk than the national average. This is a natural consequence not only of the scarcity of indigenous raw materials and the skill of the traditional labour pool, but the unrivalled function of the capital as a centre of educational and research institutions, political influence and market leadership.

Farming

While the industrial output of the region makes its contribution felt in all corners of the country, its agriculture is unspecialized and preoccupied with the difficult assignment of coping with the basic food needs of its own multiplying urban millions. The natural agricultural dividing zone lies along the Oka river, but it is increasingly being blurred by the all-pervading influence of the metropolitan area, which gives every incentive for heavy investment in the improvement of naturally poor but accessible land.

In the cold damp fringe-lands north of the Volga, less than a tenth of the land is normally cultivated, and the forest and the marsh is ever present. In the relatively warm southern fringes, on the other hand, at least two-thirds of the land is sown and droughts are a common problem. Between these extremes types and combinations of mixed farming vary widely.

North of the Oka, fodder-crops (mainly for dairy cows) and vegetables—above all potatoes—predominate. Grain crops, mainly rye, oats and barley are now distinctly secondary, though serious attempts have been made in the Soviet era to increase the wheat acreage. Flax is the only non-food crop of any consequence, and its traditional importance along the upper Volga is declining.

In the south grain is still the main component of agriculture. Winter wheat has traditionally dominated, but maize and other fodder-crops are on the increase, while livestock products other than milk are more important than in the north. Sugar beet, sunflowers, hemp and tobacco also make their appearance on the southern fringes of the region.

To sum up, the southern half of this region is a part of the belt of European black-earth which constitutes the Soviet Union's main block of good farmland. The north, on the other hand, in the damp podzolic belt, is mainly second or third-rate land, much of which would not be farmed at all were it not for the immense demands of the growing urban market. There is thus a constant movement of food from south to north, but generally speaking the whole region is probably a net importer of food.

Transport (Fig. 21)

Moscow is the hub of a remarkable network of communications—a system which has been many centuries in the making. As in the case of London or Paris, the tonnage of incoming freights exceeds the outgoing, but if value is substituted the reverse is almost certainly the case. However, with the recent rapid substitution of gas intake for coal, the weight factor is becoming less meaningful.

The dominant flow pattern of both the railways and pipelines reflects the lopsided economic orientation of the region. The first is to the south—to the Donbas industrial region, the natural gas of the north Caucasus and the food of the black-earth. The second is east-north-east to the oil and electricity of the Middle Volga, the timber of the Upper Volga and Urals and the region's own industrial towns. The meeting of these major currents in Moscow epitomizes the dynamic economic realities of today's Soviet Union, superimposed on the Imperial history of Russia. By contrast the west and north-west is strikingly unresponsive, except for the single historical link with Leningrad.

Though inland waterways are now of secondary importance, they still continue to expand in absolute terms. Moscow's water position has been greatly enhanced by the building of the Moscow–Volga canal and by the modernization of the Volga–Baltic waterway. On the Moskva river itself, the main freight consists of heavy building materials, but on the Volga and its connections to the north, timber is the chief item.

With the increasing complexity of industry in the Greater Moscow region, and the obvious need for a more flexible mobility, road transport is, at long last, rapidly increasing in importance, while the building of several more airports was indicative of the immense rise of this form of passenger carriage.

THE PRESENT POPULATION (Fig. 19)

The central fact about this region today is the presence of the great metropolitan area of some eight million persons in its midst, where there had only been one million at the beginning of the century. Further, there are now some fifteen million city dwellers (in cities of over 50,000) in the region compared with little more than three million before the Soviet planned era (1926). However, in spite of such impressive figures, the fact remains that, whereas roughly one in four of the Soviet total and city populations lived in this region in 1926, it is now one in five in each case.

The heart and nucleus of the Empire, this region is almost entirely Russian in ethnic composition. There are small numbers of Finnish language groups, particularly the Mordva, who are found in rural communities on the eastern margins of the region.

With some forty million inhabitants it approaches the population and area of France, or perhaps more meaningfully, of the block of states along the Eastern Seaboard of the U.S.A. from Massachusetts to Pennsylvania (including New York)—also the nucleus and present 'Main Street' of a continental nation.

The rural distribution

However, one of the features which contrasts with these two foreign areas, especially the U.S.A., is the enduringly larger rural component in the population. The urban areas are relatively concentrated and most of the region still has a dominantly rural composition.

The line of the Oka does mark off, though, a relatively high rural density to the south from a notably less dense area to the north and west. The greater Moscow district itself, although north of the Oka, forms a special extension of high rural density, related to the intensive market garden 'urban farming'. North of the Volga the true rural population, excluding foresters, becomes very thin.

The cities

This is a region of cities, by Soviet standards, with well over a third of its people resident in centres of more than 50,000. There are now over fourteen million people in them, compared with nine million before the war. However, as in the Ukraine most of these cities are concentrated into one zone—four-fifths of the city population is enclosed inside a line joining Gorky, Tula, Kalinin and Yaroslavl, while over half is in Greater Moscow itself.

Moscow stands in a class of its own, both in the region and in the whole country (Plate I). Within 20 miles of the Kremlin there are probably about 8 million people, and metropolitan Moscow may only be exceeded in size by New York, Tokyo and London. It is the most northerly of the giant cities of the world and in the least prepossessing natural environment. Its closest latitudinal counterpart in North America is Edmonton, the most northerly city of any size on the continent.

Since the story of the region as a whole is bound up with the rise of Moscow, the latter has been outlined in several parts of this chapter already. The lands between the Volga and the Oka, with their comparative security in the age of the nomads, their just tolerable agricultural potentials, and above all their position at the hub of the East European waterways, were clearly destined to lead Greater Russia. If this is granted, the question here is—but why Moscow, rather than some other point between the two rivers? While we must not discount the considerable tactical skill displayed by the Princes of Muscovy, particularly in their dealings with the Tatars, we cannot leave it at that. The site on which the original Moscow Kremlin was built in the middle of the twelfth century had indeed substantial locational advantages in the Russian river-world of the time. On a flood-free, defensible bank of the navigable Moscow river, it was midway between the Volga and the Oka at the point where they come closest together (other than in the east where they join, which was neither as central nor as secure). In addition to this centrality with regard to the northern and southern waterways—extended later to the Northern Dvina and the Don— Moscow was also equidistant from the confluence of the Oka and the Volga on the east and the upper reaches of the Dnieper and the Western Dvina on the west. The river Klyazma and the upper Moskva river together provided an additional east-west route through the middle of the mesopotamian region. Thus it seems clear that the early Muscovites were blessed with significant locational assets in relation to their world and, with good political timing and a measure of luck, were able to turn them to lasting advantage. Centrality, with respect to the distribution of the Russian people from the thirteenth century on, coupled with a maximum sanctuary-like quality, must have counted a good deal. To emphasize, as one must, important factors such as the decision to make Moscow the ecclesiastical capital of Russia in 1326, or the favoured position of Moscow princes as tax-collectors to the Tatars, does not necessarily make the hypothesis of the fundamental significance of location invalid as an explanation of why Moscow, and not some other place, came to inherit supreme imperial power.

When Peter the Great assumed control of Russia in the late seventeenth century, Moscow had reigned supreme over an independent and expansionist state for several centuries, but it was a state still largely confined to the forests and its only sea-outlet was the Arctic. The city probably contained little more than 100,000 inhabitants. The period of really significant imperial expansion was yet to come, in the eighteenth and nineteenth centuries, during which the helm of affairs of state was St Petersburg, not Moscow. In little more than half a century the great Moscow had been overtaken in population by its upstart rival and throughout the nineteenth century continued to lag behind.

All the same its region remained, as it had been for centuries, the hub of Russia's industry and, between the end of serfdom in 1861 and the First World War, Moscow's expansion was rapid by any reasonable standards. The population grew from 350,000 to one million by the end of the century and nearly two million in 1915. Some two-thirds of the inhabitants of the city in 1900 were said to be peasants, comparable to early nineteenth-century situations in England. Nearly half the industrial employment in the city was in textiles, the remainder encompassing a traditional variety of food-processing and engineering industries.

Moscow having been proclaimed the national capital again in 1918, the population of its metropolitan area more than doubled by the eve of the

Second World War and has probably doubled again since. It is now more than twice as large as Leningrad and growing at a much faster rate. Specialized engineering and chemical products have overshadowed textiles, although Moscow is still one of the country's chief manufacturers of the latter. The city's industrial and domestic fuel is now natural gas and the network of pipelines converging on the city provides a new look to its nodality, earlier expressed by the rivers and the railways.

Moscow is showing many of the features associated elsewhere with metropolitan areas, such as ribbon development along routes served by suburban electric trains, green belts, satellite towns, ring-roads, etc. As in London, there is official disapproval of further growth, including a system of residence and industrial permits. However, it should be noted that less than one in twenty of the Soviet people live in Greater Moscow, compared with about one in five for London, Paris or Tokyo and one in eleven for New York. Whatever the planners say, the growth of the metropolis seems likely to go on for the foreseeable future.

At the far end of the cluster of industrial cities which fans out eastwards and north-eastwards from Moscow, is the city of *Gorky* (formerly Nizhnii Novgorod) which, with its satellites, notably *Dzerzhinsk*, has a population of more than $1\frac{1}{4}$ million, probably the third largest metropolitan area in the country. It is clearly a great city in its own right—and not a mere satellite of Moscow—but it does have close and long-standing contacts with Moscow and a rather similar industrial character. At the confluence of the Volga and the Oka, the twin highways of early Muscovy, a town was almost bound to arise, and a fortified one at that. Being situated between Russian Moscow and Tatar Kazan had its hazards as well as advantages, but in relatively peaceful times it became a natural interceptor for Eurasian trade. The annual Fair, at which European metal wares jostled Persian carpets and Chinese tea, had the greatest turnover of any in Russia in its heyday in the mid-nineteenth century. Thereafter the opening of the Suez Canal and the unequivocal spreading of Russia into Asia caused a decline, and the population was less than 100,000 in 1900. In the Soviet era, however, it grew rapidly, to 650,000 in 1939, and it is now more than twice the size of any other city in the region except Moscow. It is an engineering city, specializing in motor vehicles, ships and aircraft, but pipeline and river connections with the oil and gas sources to the east have also stimulated chemical industries. In addition a hydro-station upstream on the Volga was recently completed and nearby is one of the largest newsprint mills in the country at Pravdinsk (for the Moscow daily newspaper, *Pravda*). Gorky's favourable position in respect to routes and fuel supplies and the fact that it is on the main industrial axis from Moscow to the Urals and Siberia augur well for its future growth.

Of the ancient cities along the upper Volga, *Yaroslavl* (440,000) is probably the oldest and the most important today. It was founded in the early eleventh century as a suitable crossing point on the way from the south to the furs of the northern forests and it retained this function since the main route from Moscow to Archangel crossed the Volga there. The seventeenth century was perhaps its heyday (when many of its most famous churches were built by its wealthy merchants), just before Peter the Great opened the rival route to the Baltic. The main railway to Archangel later also passed through the city. The wood and textile manufacturers of Tsarist times have largely been superseded by the manufacture of synthetic rubber and secondarily motor vehicles.

Ivanovo (360,000), away from the Volga itself, is the centre of the most specialized group of cotton textile towns in the country—and has indeed been nicknamed on occasion the Russian Manchester. It also makes a variety of textile machinery for the region. *Kostroma* (190,000) an old town on the Volga is the centre of the linen industry, but this industry, and therefore the town itself, are growing relatively slowly.

On the Klyazma, south of Ivanovo, is the very old city of *Vladimir* (170,000) which in the early fourteenth century looked as if it was a serious rival to Moscow (the Orthodox Church Metropolitan resided there for a time). But after Moscow had triumphed over it, Vladimir sank into oblivion and indeed until the 1930s, when some tractor and other engineering industries were planted there, it was insignificant. Another city which was an early contender for Russian leadership, now also slow-growing and rather isolated on the wrong side of Moscow, is *Kalinin* (290,000), formerly called Tver. Its position in its early days was a strong one, near the head of navigation on the Volga, at the point where the almost continuous water-road to Novgorod (initially the Tvertsa river) joined it. Novgorod's demise brought also the demise of Tver. Now on the railway between Moscow and Leningrad, it is the centre of a poor farming district and makes textiles and rail equipment.

Other somewhat marginal cities to the north of Moscow are *Rybinsk*, for a time called Shcherbakov (190,000) a timber centre on the upper Volga with a pre-war hydro-station which has created a very large reservoir, and *Vologda* (150,000) the centre of a dairying and timber district. The latter is situated quite deep in the coniferous forest zone but is a major route junction, where the Moscow–Archangel and Leningrad–Ural railways intersect, and also situated on a navigable part of the Northern Dvina system, linked with the Volga. Also in this region at the northern tip of the Rybinsk reservoir is the new steel town of *Cherepovets* (120,000). It was built specifically to supply Leningrad, with which it is connected by rail and by the Volga–Baltic canal system, and uses ore shipped from the Kola peninsula and coal from Vorkuta, both very far away. The enterprise has of late been branded as uneconomic, and alternative fuel and ore sources are being considered.

South of Moscow, along the Oka river, there is a string of second-rank industrial cities, of which the largest is *Ryazan* (250,000). Founded in the eleventh century, it lay on the track of marauding nomads and often became, willy-nilly, a shield for Moscow. It was a small town at the end of the Tsarist period, but since the Second World War particularly, with the arrival of gas and oil pipelines from the Volga and electrification of the railway from Moscow, it has grown very rapidly as a centre of diversified engineering and chemical industries. Where the Moskva river joins the Oka is the long-standing locomotive-building city of *Kolomna* (120,000) while further up the Oka are the textile city of *Serpukhov* (110,000) and the city of *Kaluga* (150,000) which makes matches and rail equipment.

But the most important of the industrial cities to the south of Moscow is *Tula* (340,000), an iron-working city of Russia with the oldest traditions, and a Sheffield-like reputation which even today makes it the major centre for ornamental metal articles such as samovars. Although founded on local deposits of iron ore and situated on the most productive part of the Moscow lignite field these factors are no longer at all significant. In the production of basic metal (iron or steel) it was severely hit in the eighteenth century by the competition of the Urals and in the following centuries by the Ukraine. However in 1897 it was more populous than Nizhnii Novgorod and second only to Moscow in the whole of this region. It is having a new lease of life in this respect since the beginning of large scale iron-mining at Kursk to the south, with which it is increasingly linked, and the arrival of piped gas from the North Caucasus. It is still an important agricultural centre and nearby is the all-Soviet chemical complex of *Novomoskovsk* (110,000), formerly called Stalinogorsk, a major manufacturer of fertilizers.

South of Tula and what is commonly called the Central Industrial District, a number of well-spaced cities have traditionally been agricultural centres for their surrounding regions. While this is still an evident characteristic of most of them, changes have been coming in very quickly in recent years. The most significant development in this century has been the emergence of *Voronezh* (520,000) as a city twice as large as any of the others—in 1900 it was just one of several of about the same moderate size.

On a navigable tributary of the Don, near the main river and near the edge of the steppe, Voronezh was founded as one of the southern outposts of Muscovy against the Tatars, and Peter the Great built his fleet there to send down river against the Turks. The city now has a remarkable variety of engineering industries, reflecting its regional responsibilities in relation to agriculture, mining and chemicals particularly. It has a long-standing synthetic rubber industry, formerly based on grain and potatoes but now on gas piped from the south. It might easily become another Kharkov, placed midway between the two main industrial concentrations of European Russia.

A contrast is provided by *Orël* (170,000) and *Tambov* (190,000), which were not much smaller than Voronezh earlier this century; they have grown much more slowly and remain, especially the former, primarily agriculturally focused centres. *Bryansk* (240,000) with a similar background but right on the margins of the good land, on a tributary of the Dnieper, has made use of local resources of phosphates, chalk, peat, sands and timber, to become the centre of a minor cluster of varied industries such as cement, glass and fertilizers, as well as rail and other equipment.

But the greatest changes in this region's urban growth today are to be laid at the door of the recent decision to exploit the immense iron ore reserves of the region. *Kursk* itself (230,000) has long been primarily a regional market town of some importance. So far it has been affected less intensely than *Lipetsk* (190,000) which is being marked out as the chief iron and steel centre of this part of European Russia, and consequently growing more quickly than any other city in the region. It may well become another Magnitogorsk.

PROSPECT

This region is fundamentally a composite of two, traditionally distinguishable from each other but joined in a symbiotic relationship under the aegis of the powerful unifying force of a great metropolis. The North— the Central Industrial District—with three out of four people classified as urban, and the relatively poor farmland also urban-oriented, displays basically the same pattern, though writ larger, as in the nineteenth century. The South—the Central Black-earth—with two out of three of its people rural, is still solidly dependent on relatively favourable natural conditions for agriculture.

Both of these regions are, however, undergoing rapid qualitative changes. The industrial cities of the north, still, as always, concentrating on brain rather than brawn, are shifting to even more complicated precision engineering and chemical industries making use of scientific and technical knowledge, which the region possesses in such abundance. The former dominance of textiles has been steadily reduced. The farmlands of the south are moving away from their former over-dependence on bread-grains to a more diversified farming in which feed crops for animals loom large and the production and use of fertilizers is growing rapidly. But an even more radical change is the current rejuvenation of the iron and steel industry in the region, so that it bids fair to become a major national contributor in this respect.

All of these developments are being influenced fundamentally by the revolutionary changes in the structure of fuel consumption. Natural gas is much the most significant new transfusion into this perennially fuel-deficient region. Already it is much the most widely used type of fuel in the city and it seems only a matter of time until the same becomes true of the region as a whole. Gas is likely before long to have ousted brown coal and peat in the power stations, and food crops at last from the chemical industry. It will also enable synthetic fibres to compete more readily with traditional textiles and to have reduced drastically the amount of expensive Donbas coal needed in the steel industry. The latter would mitigate the hitherto most important objection to establishing large-scale steel-making in the Central Region.

Not all parts of the region, clearly, will participate equally in the general expansion. Greater Moscow itself, Greater Gorky and the Voronezh–Lipetsk region, for instance, seem bound to experience steady and rapid growth, but the same cannot be said with such assurance of, say, Orël, Kalinin, Tambov, or even Ivanovo and its satellites.

But we have now to return to the theme which has run through this chapter—the nature and extent of the metropolitan influence and its changing place within the entire national scheme of things. We have seen that the Moscow region housed three in four of the citizens of Russia at the end of the seventeenth century, one in four earlier this century and now fewer than one in five. Is this relative decline likely to continue indefinitely or can it be likened, say, to the temporary relative decline in the importance of the London region within Britain in the nineteenth century? When the new lands have been developed and when heavy industry has become relatively less important, will the manifold attractions of the metropolitan area, the market, the educational, political and scientific advantages, with the ever-increasing emphasis on skills rather than bulk, make the Moscow region the fastest growing in the country? This does not seem to be happening now but he would be sanguine indeed who would

I. Red Square in Moscow, with the Kremlin walls and Lenin's tomb in the foreground and St. Basil's cathedral and the Moskva river in the distance.

II. A herd of aurochs in a reservation in typical mixed forest country near the river Oka.

III. The Dnieper river at Kiev, looking from the cliff-like right bank, largely laid out as a public park, to the low, sandy left bank. The statue is of St. Vladimir.

rule out such a development later on in the century. We have seen that, compared with London, Tokyo and New York, its peers on the world urban scene, Moscow so far has a modest degree of national concentration of people. What of the official protestations about the need for decentralization, which presumably could be expected to have much sharper teeth in them than in the 'free enterprise' countries? What of a possible future climatic drift, similar to that to California or, to a lesser extent, south-east England, which might, other things being equal, favour the Ukraine or the Caucasus over Moscow, but Moscow over most of the East?

The degree of qualitative, if not quantitative concentration in Moscow is remarkable. Moscow University, for example, has been raised far above all the others in a way which has no parallel anywhere (with the possible exception of Paris). A map of air-routes for the Soviet Union, gives a striking 'all lanes lead to Moscow' impression. The examples could be multiplied. But it is still by no means a foregone conclusion that Russia will follow Western rules and experience in such matters as the tendency to metropolitan concentration.

Whether Moscow, with its region, expands or shrinks in relation to the other regions of the country will, in any case, be of only marginal importance. This metropolitan region will remain an outstanding feature of the Soviet Union, with its roots in the peculiar geographical and historical contexts of the early Middle Ages in the forests of the East European plain, and in the subsequent growth of an Empire.

CHAPTER EIGHT

Ukrainia

TAKEN all round this is the best endowed and most productive of all the
Soviet regions—the one the Union could least afford to lose. Conversely
it is the only region which on its own could hope to measure up, in wealth
and viability, to the great nation-states of Western Europe. With well over
fifty million people, it has the numbers and industrial might of the German
Federal Republic, and the farmland and population density of France.
Its general location is good, not only from the point of view of climate
and access to the sea, but also in relation to other important population
concentrations, especially the Moscow region and the richest parts of
Communist East Europe. For the German invaders in 1941 it was the most
glittering prize, and they succeeded in seizing all of it for a time. Since it
then accounted for a major part of the nation's food, energy and heavy
industry capacity, the wonder is that the Soviet Union was able not only
to survive but strike back as decisively as it did.

At first glance this region seems remarkably homogeneous both physically, since it is almost all black-earth country with a distinctive type of

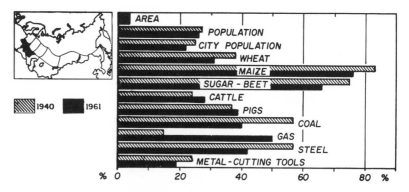

FIG. 23—Location and importance of Ukrainia in relation to the Soviet Union as a
whole, for certain selected items

agriculture, and culturally, since most of the people classify themselves as Ukrainians. However in terms of age of colonization it displays remarkable contrasts. A thousand-year-old city like Kiev (the Mother of Russia) in the crowded peasant northern fringe coexists in the region with the broad prairies and industrial cities of New Russia to the south—as youthful as their North American counterparts. The nineteenth century witnessed the transformation of the region from a Cossack frontier zone (Ukraine means 'border region') into the agricultural and industrial heart of a vast Empire. Alongside this massive economic growth came the first real flowering of Ukrainian nationalism, which found formal but fleeting expression as a nominally independent state in 1918.

Nevertheless, this marked the peak of the region's strength in relation to the rest of Russia. During the Soviet period, population and production has continued to show substantial growth and, even now, taken all round, it probably leads all the other regions treated in this book. However, it has lost the overwhelming dominance which it held on the eve of the Bolshevik Revolution, most notably on the industrial scene. Then it contributed nearly nine-tenths of the coal and over two-thirds of the iron and steel, whereas now this is less than half in each case. One in five of the Soviet city-dwellers are still located in the region, but it was two in seven at the turn of the century (Fig. 23).

Although the whole traditional group of Ukrainian-speaking people was united in one political unit for the first time in 1945, Ukrainian nationalism has probably receded within the region until there is now very little question of an independent Ukraine. The republic is closely woven into the whole Soviet economic and social fabric and Ukrainians have long converged with Russians in the easterly and southerly migrations. Therefore the Ukrainian administrative Republic makes up the main but not the only part of the region treated in this chapter. The Kuban lowlands of the North Caucasus and the lower Don valley have been added as being very similar to the southern Ukraine in physical conditions, agriculture and settlement history, and Moldavia must obviously be included on physical and economic grounds. More debatable, perhaps, is the additional inclusion of the elbow of the Volga at Volgograd (Stalingrad). This has by tradition been included with the larger Volga river region. However, its important steel industry marks it off from all the other Volga towns, as does its military experience at the hands of the Germans. These bonds with the rest of the European south are strengthened by increasingly close transport links, by rail, then Volga–Don canal and finally through the first very high-voltage Direct Current transmission line in the Soviet Union, connecting Volgograd

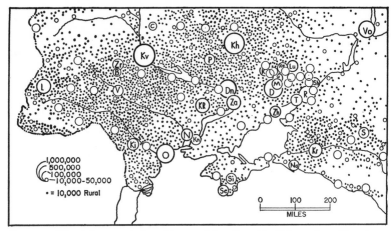

FIG. 24—Ukrainia: population. Key to cities: B = Berdichev, C = Chernigov, D = Donetsk, Dn = Dnepropetrovsk, G = Gorlovka, K = Kramatorsk, Ka = Kadiyevka, Kh = Kharkov, Ki = Kishinev, Kn = Kherson, Kr = Krasnodar, Kv = Kiev, Kr = Krivoy Rog, L = Lvov, Lu = Lugansk, M = Makeyevka, N = Nikolayev, No = Novorossisk, O = Odessa, P = Poltava, R = Rostov-on-Don, S = Stavropol, Se = Sevastopol, Sh = Shakhty, Si = Simferopol, T = Taganrog, V = Vinnitsa, Vo = Volgograd, Za = Zaporozhye, Zh = Zhdanov, Ze = Zhitomir

FIG. 25—Ukrainia: nature. Zones: 1 = podzol–wet forest, 2 = wooded steppe–partly black-earth, 3 = steppe–black-earth, 4 = semi-desert

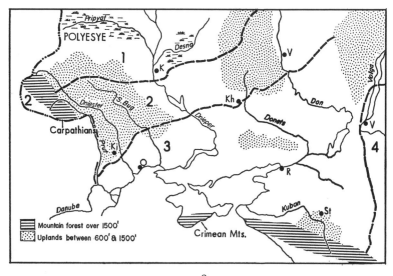

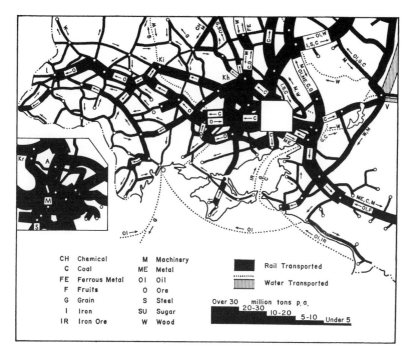

FIG. 26—Ukrainia: movements

FIG. 27—Ukrainia: economy. Da = Dashava, Ka = Kakhovka, Kr = Kremen-chug, M = Maykop, N = Nikopol, Sh = Shebelinka

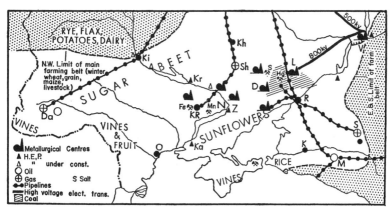

with the Donbas—industrial heart of the region. East of the Kuban plains the rapid falling-off of the rainfall and the dominantly non-Slavic character of peoples mark the boundary of the region. On the north-west of the Ukraine, similarly, the edge of the Belorussian marshlands forms a clear physical and human boundary, but on the north-east the boundary is less clear. There is some case for including the regions of Kursk and Voronezh in this region, from the physico-agricultural point of view, and because of the new iron-workings. However, they have been excluded here partly because of the already large size of the southern region, but mainly because they are traditionally oriented towards Moscow rather than to the eastern Ukraine, although this may not be so much longer.

By Soviet standards, almost all of this region is well-peopled and well-developed. However, two main axes of unusually dense population stand out (a) the old agricultural districts of the north and west (the wooded steppe), and (b) the new industrial belt between the Dnieper bend and the Volga bend. Away from the industrial concentrations, the southern and eastern fringes of the region, New Russia, are more sparsely peopled, but only by comparison with the rest of this unusually well-endowed and well-developed region (Fig. 24).

THE NATURAL HABITAT (Fig. 25)

Black-earth with steppe or wooded steppe vegetation characterize most typically the greater part of this region. However, there are significant internal variations, ranging from the edge of the forested marshes in the north-west to the margin of the semi-desert in the south-east. These differences reflect above all the distribution of effective moisture. North and west of a line from Odessa to Kharkov (roughly the 20-inch isohyet) precipitation amounts everywhere to at least two-thirds as much as the evaporation and is fairly reliable. Thus drought problems are rare and the natural vegetation is predominantly wooded steppe. South and east of this line precipitation is almost everywhere less than two-thirds the evaporation and fluctuates more from year to year—irrigation is a common phenomenon here. In the latter region the desiccating summer wind from the east—the *sukhovey*—aggravates the dryness, and has given rise to the planting of protective shelter-belts of trees.

The heat budget is everywhere adequate for most crops and shows an increase towards the south-east. The growing season at Kiev is the same as that of Chicago and the winter is much less severe and long than in the Canadian Prairie provinces, or most of the U.S.S.R., although two or three months with freezing temperatures are normally experienced. Climatically the closest analogue in North America seems to be the U.S. Winter Wheat belt and the drier parts of the Corn belt in Kansas, Nebraska and northern Iowa, but the Ukraine is more generally open to maritime influence.

A climatic anomaly is the southern coast of the Crimea, the only part of the region with no regular freezing in winter (although there may be quite heavy frosts even here on occasion), and with its rainfall maximum in winter—a régime which gives rise to a marginal growth of Mediterranean-type vegetation (Plate VII).

In general the relief features are unglaciated, unobtrusive and display a certain symmetry. The shield of ancient hard rock which underlies the Ukraine rarely appears at the surface, although when it does, as in the former rapids stretch of the Dnieper river, it makes itself felt. It is covered by sedimentary layers such as sandstones and limestones, which bear coal and iron and salt, and in turn these are blanketed by the fine silty *löss*—the basis for the best soil.

Rolling plateaux and escarpments alternate with river valleys. In the western extremity the Soviet Union now includes a 200-mile section of the Carpathians which rises occasionally to 6,000 feet but is deeply dissected and has several easy passes. This range presents a steep face to the west overlooking the small Soviet part of the Danubian plain, but leads off eastwards into the ramp-like Volyn–Podolian uplands, descending towards the Dnieper. Rivers have cut deep gorges in the limestone here and access to ground water is a crucial factor in village location. As elsewhere in the region the soft *löss* has been carved into gullies (*ovragi*), accelerated by unscientific farming practices. East of the Dnieper lies the low Donets ridge, mainly below 1,000 feet, the site of the Donbas coalfield. South of these uplands are more level plains fronting on to the low Black Sea coast with its sandbars, and including most of the Crimea and the Kuban lowlands. Finally, there are the Crimean mountains, with limestone cliffs facing the sea, up to 5,000 feet high, and the northern foothills of the much higher Caucasus ranges.

A remarkable pattern of rivers, following parallel courses from northwest to south-east, is etched across the relief, with typically a cliff-like right bank towards which the river has cut and a low left bank from which it has strayed (Plate III). The most notable is the Dnieper, a historic river long beset by the now submerged rapids—a river which, like the Volga, is fast becoming a string of lakes. The Prut and, for a short stretch, the Danube into which it flows, form the south-western frontier of the Soviet Union, while the Dniester and the Southern Bug drain the Podolian plateau. The Don drains the Central Russian uplands and, since the

Volga–Don canal was cut, forms the exit, in a human context, for the whole of the vast Volga basin. The snow and ice fields of Elbrus, the highest mountain in Europe, give rise to the Kuban, which makes its way to a coast spattered with marshes and lagoons.

PEOPLING OF THE REGION

The heart of the region, the steppe, has been until the last century or two a major through routeway between the Asian and the Euro-Mediteranean worlds, rather than a permanent home for human populations. But this is not to say that no agriculture was practised. The first historical glimpse of the land was provided by the Greeks who, around the eighth century B.C., established trading cities on the north shore of the Black Sea. Athens came to depend heavily on wheat obtained from the nomadic Scythians, who in turn extorted it from numerous agricultural communities who owed them allegiance. The Romans inherited this orderly arrangement but in the early centuries A.D. the peace was shattered by the advent of the wilder Sarmatians, Avars, Huns, and others from the east, dislodging the Mediterranean trading outposts and inaugurating the real hegemony of the nomads which was to last, off and on, for the next millennium and a half.

In this setting, in a comparative lull between the worst nomad incursions, from the ninth to the eleventh centuries, the river-state of Kiev, probably the first rallying centre of Russian nationality, blossomed with astonishing rapidity. Slavic-speaking agricultural peoples had infiltrated the wooded steppe and were organized by a merchant aristocracy, of which some of the key figures were from Scandinavia (the men of Rus). The water-road, tenuously linking the Baltic and Mediterranean worlds via the Dnieper and Novgorod, provided the means to assemble the riches of the northern forests and to trade with them. Contacts with Byzantium were strong and gave Russia its own Church through Kiev. However this early light of Russian nationhood was quickly snuffed out in 1240 by the Mongol hordes and the remnants of the Slavic peoples fled north into the forest. Thereafter, two or three centuries went by before infiltration of the wooded steppe from the north was resumed. Most prominent in this new colonization were the Cossacks or freebooters, some of whom, like the Zaporozhian host and the Cossacks of the Don, ventured south into the steppe proper, in uneasy coexistence with the nomad groups.

But regular settlement of the open steppe lands of the Ukraine, the Don and the Kuban had to wait until the late eighteenth century when the Crimean Tatars and their Turkish protectors were finally subdued and the writ of Russia ran along the northern Black Sea coast and the Caucasian foothills.

The European black-earth thus became fully available to the farmer and by the mid-nineteenth century had come to support a majority of the people of Russia. But the over-crowded wooded-steppe of the north, stronghold of serfdom and the Russian peasantry, contrasted strongly with the steppes of New Russia, where extensive estates were founded, devoted first to sheep and later to wheat for export. New Russia was also to become the venue for the Empire's major heavy industry base. For most of the region, the nineteenth century was the time of triumphant coming-of-age— the taking possession of the land after many centuries of lying fallow.

The scene about 1900

By the end of the nineteenth century the great southerly agricultural migration within European Russia had spent itself and the stream, which was still flowing strongly, had been deflected towards Siberia. The European South—the black-earth—had finally become established as the agricultural heart of the country. The headlong development of the steppes of New Russia, comparable to that of the American wheatlands, was reflected in the growth of Odessa. Only a century old, this port had over 400,000 inhabitants in 1897, was easily the largest city in the region and exceeded only by St Petersburg and Moscow in the entire Empire. It was a striking symbol not only of the new colonization of the Black Sea lands but of the new international position of Russia as a major exporter, especially of wheat. The older Ukrainian cities of Kiev and Kharkov, in the crowded rural belt of the north, had grown more slowly and had around 200,000 people each at the turn of the century.

After about 1880, as the agricultural spotlight was shifting to Siberia, the modern industrial revolution in Russia had its belated beginning in the southern Ukraine. It was fundamentally iron and steel, based on coke instead of charcoal, which soon enabled the Ukraine to send into eclipse the long-standing iron industry of the Urals. Several attempts had been made earlier to develop the known coal and iron resources of the region, but the emancipation of the serfs, the growth of the home market, the development of railways and the growing interest of foreign capital and technicians had finally created the right conditions by the 1880s. By 1913 the new industrial belt from the Donets to the Dnieper bend was producing nine-tenths of the coal, three-quarters of the iron and two-thirds of the steel of the country. The region had become the most populous and the most highly developed—agriculturally and industrially—in the Russian Empire.

On the eve of the Second World War

In the first four decades of the twentieth century the population of the region grew from 30 to 50 millions. The city population increased five-fold and there were some 50 cities with over 50,000 inhabitants. These figures betray a great economic expansion, but other regions of the country had been growing even more quickly, and there were signs that its domin-ance, though still considerable, was not what it had been at the end of the Tsarist period. Yet when the Germans invaded the region it still supplied over half of the Soviet output of coal, iron and steel and well over a third of the grain and livestock (Fig. 23). Building on the foundations laid down at the end of the Tsarist period, with Donets coal and Krivoy Rog iron, heavy industry had expanded rapidly and a dramatic addition to the energy base was the construction of the first large Soviet hydro-station on the Dnieper bend in 1933. Another development was the increase in oil extraction in the Kuban (Maikop), and the construction of a pipeline through this region from the Caspian to the Black Sea. However, the scale of this should not be exaggerated—it contributed 5% of Soviet oil in the late thirties. The steel industry had become less exclusively concentrated on the Donbas coalfield itself, and more on the Sea of Azov, and around the Dnieper bend.

Winter wheat remained the chief crop and grain was still much more prominent than fodder crops. Rice was successfully in-troduced in the Kuban, but an attempt to introduce unirrigated cotton into the region (a quarter of the Soviet acreage and a tenth of the output were attributed to the region in 1937) was quickly abandoned.

The rural population declined steeply in the northern wooded steppe zone (net loss of some 5 millions between 1926 and 1939) but actually increased in the Kuban, Crimea and Black Sea coastlands. Since the revolution Odessa had tended to stagnate and been overtaken by Kiev and Kharkov (with over 800,000 each). In 1939 there were in addition four cities of about half a million—Dnepropetrovsk, Donetsk (then Stalino), Volgograd (then Stalingrad) and Rostov-on-Don. Moreover there were 15 cities of over 50,000 which had trebled their populations between 1926 and 1939 in the industrial belt between the Don and the Dnieper bend—constituting a third of all such boom-cities in the Soviet Union in this period. Thus the region was unquestionably a prime growth-area and focus of productive capacity—so much so that one might reasonably have characterized it as indispensable to the national economy. However, it was dispensed with willy-nilly in 1942, the country survived, and it is doubtful whether the region will ever quite regain the national significance it had before the War, let alone before the Revolution.

THE PRESENT ECONOMY (Fig. 27)

However, in spite of the scorched-earth policy during the German invasion and the spectacular easterly shift of most forms of economic activity, this region is still the most valuable in the country from the combined agricultural and industrial points of view. While its relative position has declined, as outlined above, its basic locational and resource assets remain very favourable and will inevitably continue to be capitalized upon by the Soviet government. Into the established lines of the economy laid down earlier, some important new features have been injected recently, such as the maize-livestock drive and the exploitation of large deposits of natural gas. Farming as a whole probably looms larger in the region's relative contribution to the national economy than does industry so that it will be considered first here.

Farming

Virtually all the region is actually or potentially good crop land and stands out on a map of sown acreage in the Soviet Union as having an unusually high density. Only on the margins, such as the dry left bank of the Don, the Polyesie marshes or the Carpathian and Crimean mountains does the density become thinner, but these are relatively insignificant within the region.

Mixed farming, with grain, fodder crops, livestock, fruit and vegetables, has become steadily more typical throughout the region in the Soviet period, and particularly since 1954, with the intensified maize livestock drive and the emphasis on fertilizers. Grain accounted for nearly nine-tenths of the sown area in 1913 and fodder crops less than a twentieth. In 1960 the proportions were roughly a half and one-third respectively. Moreover, the ratios of the major grains have changed. Whereas wheat led maize by 9 : 1 in 1913 and 6 : 1 even in 1953 the present ratio is 3 : 2, though this may decrease now. As stated earlier the region is climatically quite closely analogous to the Winter Wheat and drier parts of the Corn belt in the U.S.A. and both these crops are distributed fairly evenly over it (Plate V).

The chief difference between the damper north and west and the drier east and south is that in the latter grain claims a greater share of the total sown area, while in the former other crops such as sugar-beet and fodders provide rather more variety (Plate IV). The whole region accounts for two-thirds of the country's sugar-beet, compared with over four-fifths in 1913. The absolute output has however gone up four-fold since that time and its contribution to animal fodder has grown rapidly in recent years, stimulated both by the domestic livestock drive and the sudden large imports of cane sugar from Cuba.

On the cooler, more humid northern fringes hemp and flax are still grown, though decreasingly, as well as rye, oats, potatoes, buckwheat and green maize. On the drier southern and eastern margins sunflowers grow in profusion and sheep and goats become more numerous. Vineyards are concentrated particularly in Moldavia (with one-third of the Soviet acreage), the Crimea and the lower valleys of the Don and the Dnieper, while fruits such as melons are common throughout the south (Plate VI).

The Kuban area merits special mention, since it is probably the nearest counterpart to the better lands of the American Mid-west in farming potential. Some of the best farms in pre-Soviet Russia were to be found there and it has recently become a Soviet showcase for maize, winter wheat and irrigated rice.

The region is still the main source of food for the nation. Its output of such commodities as maize, sugar-beet, wheat, vines, sunflowers, vegetables and even potatoes exceeds that of other regions, and it contains more cattle, pigs and poultry (though not sheep) (Fig. 23). While its relative contribution to the national output has declined in recent decades, its actual output has increased steadily. With the new policy of further intensifying agriculture on the better lands with greater fertilizer input and irrigation schemes (which on the Don, Dnieper and Kuban are coming to fruition) there seems no doubt that this region will continue to play a major part in effecting the desired improvement in variety and quantity of food on the Soviet tables.

INDUSTRY

While the densest rural population and more intensive agriculture is found to the north-west of a line from Kharkov to Odessa, almost all the industries of national significance lie to the south-east of this same line. The heart of this southern industrial zone is still the Donbas coalfield with its steel-based industry trending mainly westwards to the Dnieper bend, but also to the Sea of Azov and to the Volga bend. The neighbouring large cities of Kharkov and Rostov have become attached to this region and the increasing diversification of industry, in particular the rapid growth of chemicals, should lead to further dispersion towards the north-west and extreme south (Crimea–Kuban) where at present the industrial concern is largely with food processing and miscellaneous commodities for the local market.

Energy resources

The Donbas coalfield still supplies most of the energy of the region but other sources are increasing more rapidly, just as on the national scene other coalfields have steadily reduced the degree of dominance the Donbas once had. Producing over a third of the Soviet coal and perhaps more meaningfully, over half of its coking coal, it remains one of the world's great coalfields, exceeding in output the Ruhr or the northern Appalachian fields. Like the latter, and South Wales, it contains both high-quality coking coal and (in the eastern part) anthracite. The coal-workings are scattered among the many valleys which radiate from the Donets ridge.

Having undergone a relatively long and intensive period of exploitation, the more accessible, thick and therefore economical seams have been worked out and mechanization of the mining process has been limited. Thus, just as West Virginian coal can be delivered competitively in Europe in spite of higher labour costs, coal from Central Siberia costs barely a third of that of the Donbas, and could compete in, say, Moscow. However, the general location of the Donbas with reference to the greater East European market and also to iron ore resources, together with the urgent need to relieve the overloaded transport system ('irrational shipments') ensures its continued production. Small quantities of lignite are also mined in the Dnieper region and peat is cut in the northern edge of the Ukraine.

The most spectacular addition to the resources of energy in the last decade has been natural gas and this promises to loom even larger in the fuel balance and also as a basis for the chemical industry. The chief deposits are in the upper Kuban around Stavropol, and at Shebelinka, south of Kharkov, both of which send gas by pipe to Moscow and to power stations in the Donbas and on the Dnieper respectively. A third, relatively minor source in the Carpathian foothills (Dashava) supplies the large cities of the western Ukraine as well as Moscow. Altogether this region could become the chief Soviet source of natural gas. There is also some oil in the Carpathian foothills but, although output has rapidly increased in recent years, it is still much less important than that of the Kuban–Caucasian foothills which is piped to the Black Sea. In a relative sense, oil is not of major significance in the region as a whole.

Hydro-electric development is also worthy of note, although much of it may be said to be somewhat incidental to the needs of irrigation and navigation. The Dnieper 'cascade' project designed to make the river a continuous string of lakes from its confluence with the Pripyat almost to the Black Sea is well under way. Three stations are fully operating and the remaining three are being constructed. About three-quarters of the planned power capacity of the whole scheme is already installed—however, it should be noted that this (some 2 million kilowatts) will be less than the present capacity of the station at Volgograd (Stalingrad) on the Volga bend, and less than that of two of the larger Ukrainian thermal power-stations. The Volgograd Station began to feed power in to the Donbas through an 800 kilovolt transmission line in 1962. There are also smaller, individual hydro-stations on the Don, Dniester and Kuban rivers.

The present evidence points to the conclusion that, while coal will continue to be the main source of energy, and output of oil and hydro-power will also rise, natural gas seems likely to set in train the most fundamental changes in the fuel balance of the region in the foreseeable future.

Raw materials

Where the crystalline basement rock comes closest to the surface, from the Dnieper bend to the Don, there is a wealth of accessible mineral resources. The iron ore of Krivoy Rog takes pride of place and still accounts for nearly half of the Soviet output. The ores so far used have been high-grade (about 60%) and there are still substantial reserves of this left, but rising costs have, as elsewhere in the Soviet Union (and Minnesota), caused a steady shift towards use of lower grade quartzites which are present in great quantity. In addition to Krivoy Rog there are large reserves of lower-grade ores at Kerch in the Crimea which, though not entirely satisfactory, are well placed for transport to the steel mills across the Sea of Azov. Further, the existence of the Kursk Magnetic Anomaly and other large reserves to the north makes it quite clear that there will be ample iron for the future needs of Soviet Europe.

Just south of Krivoy Rog, at Nikopol, are the most important and best located deposits of manganese, the chief alloy for steel, in the world. In the Donbas area (Artemovsk) virtually unlimited supplies of common salt exist and nearby (Nikitovka) is the chief Soviet source of mercury. Other salts, graphite, kaolin, sands suitable for glass making and plenty of limestone and fireclays for the steel industry are found in the neighbourhood of the Donets ridge. Probably the most prominent major industrial raw material in short supply in the region is timber, brought down by river and rail from the north.

The developing industrial pattern

The chief concentration of steel production is on the western side of the Donbas field in Donetsk (Stalino) and its satellite Makeyevka. This is in the best coking coal part of the field and nearest to the iron ore sources. Other expanding centres are at the sources of iron and manganese (Krivoy Rog and Nikopol) on the Dnieper bend, midway between coal and iron (and with hydro-power and piped-in gas) and on the Sea of Azov (cf. the Lake Erie mills in the U.S.A.). The steel works at Volgograd (Stalingrad), the only one on the Volga, is fed mainly by scrap, while aluminium is also smelted there and at the other main hydro-centre of Zaporozhye on the Dnieper.

The chemical industries are also concentrated in the Donbas area with its coking by-products and salt deposits, but the advent of gas is leading to rapid developments in other areas, especially the Kuban. This group of industries is likely to grow more quickly than the metal group and to decentralize somewhat, as engineering industries have spread to surrounding cities, like Rostov and Volgograd (tractors), Kharkov (transport and electrical equipment) and Nikolayev (ships). However it seems likely that the hard core of nationally significant industry will remain for some time within the triangle Odessa–Kharkov–Rostov, with the remainder of the region still largely occupied with food processing, some textiles and locally oriented light industries.

Transport (Fig. 26)

The hub of the region's transport system is the Donbas coalfield and the freight-flow map reflects the fact that here, as elsewhere in the Soviet Union, railways are dominant (80%) and that the chief items transported, by weight, are coal, iron ore and steel. Intersecting at the Donbas are the two main flow lines which epitomize the geographical orientations of the region: (1) east-west, primarily from Krivoy Rog to the Donbas (electrified), but also extending less intensively from Volgograd to Kiev, Lvov and the industrial centres of Communist East Europe; and (2) north-south from the Moscow region, through Kharkov and Rostov to the Caucasus. The gas pipelines are tending to reinforce this pattern.

The Volga at Volgograd carries much more freight than does the Dnieper. Timber is the main westbound item on the Volga–Don canal (completed in 1952) while coal brought down the Northern Donets river is the chief commodity going the other way, although traffic in the canal is unexpectedly light. Since the first Dnieper dam was built the river has been fully navigable, and the eventual completion of the whole series of six dams will herald the advent of a deep waterway from the Baltic to the Black Sea.

Marine transport plays an important part in the economic life of the region, and exports account for about half the traffic. Oil is now the chief commodity, and important loading ports for it are Novorossisk and Tuapse in the Caucasian region, while Odessa has long been the chief receiving point and the chief port of the whole region. Coal and iron ore especially cross the Sea of Azov and there are plans for a deep waterway directly from the lower Dnieper to this sea via the Crimea. Recent imports of grain and sugar from the New World have largely been destined for the Black Sea ports. The Danube, now partly a Soviet river, offers a valuable route of entry to South-East and Central Europe.

As in other parts of the country future developments will probably be largely in the realm of pipelines, especially gas, electrification of railways, and the extension of road transport. As a curiosity, it may be mentioned that there is a trolleybus route over the Crimean mountains from Simferopol to Yalta and other resorts, probably the only lengthy trolley route in the world in which most of the mileage runs through uninhabited territory.

THE PRESENT POPULATION

This region contains slightly more than a quarter of the population of the Soviet Union, much the same as it did at the end of last century. However, this bald comparison conceals much. The fact that the rural sector is markedly top-heavy with old people is bound to accelerate the decline in population, especially in the north where most of the *oblasts* are more than three-quarters rural. Then there is the effect of the war, in which the whole population was involved. Between 1939 and 1959 the region's total population grew by only some two millions, to 53 millions, compared, say, with the Ural–Ob region which added five millions, to reach a total of 15 millions.

A more realistic indicator of the changed relative position of the region is the fact that, whereas it claimed two out of every seven city-dwellers (over 50,000) at the end of last century, it now has hardly more than one in five. Nevertheless, there are not far short of twice as many people living in the region as there were then and nearly eight times as many residents of cities of more than 50,000.

The whole region is almost exclusively European, Slavic-speaking and within the traditions of Orthodox Christianity. About two-thirds of the population is classified as Ukrainian, but many of these use Russian as their

IV. Sugar-beet harvesting near Vinnitsa in the rolling wooded steppe of the Western Ukraine. A typical Ukrainian collective farm village.

V. A field of maize in a collective farm near Odessa. The two people on the left are natives of Odessa, the other woman being a Muscovite.

VI. A wine producing collective farm village, with private plots, on the right bank of the lower Don.

VII. The Crimean coast south of Yalta with its Mediterranean vegetation and Sanatoria.

main language. The two languages are in fact very similar and mutually intelligible, and a fifth of the inhabitants of the Ukrainian Republic are in fact Russians. It seems inevitable that as urbanization becomes more and more the rule, the distinctions between the two Slavic peoples who have together colonized much of the Soviet Union will become even more blurred.

The only people of any significance who may be said to be non-Slavic (although they use the Cyrillic script and are Orthodox) are some two million Moldavians who speak a Romanian language and were in fact included in Romania between the wars. They were in the Russian Empire for over a century before 1917 and there seems to be no appreciable movement in favour of reunion with the Romanians, from whom they are in many ways distinct.

There is a sprinkling of other peoples such as Greeks, Bulgars and Armenians in the southern Ukraine, and of several Caucasian peoples in the Kuban, but nowhere are these notably concentrated in one location and the numbers are small. The largest non-European group in this region before the Second World War was some quarter of a million Crimean Tatars. They were, however, like some smaller groups in the Caucasus, accused of collaboration with the enemy and were deported permanently from their homeland by the Soviet authorities.

The rural distribution (Fig. 24)

In the whole region rural population probably still outnumbers urban, and in the northern and western segments the disproportion is great. The latter regions indeed, particularly the right-bank lands west of the Dnieper in the better watered wooded steppe, have long been the most densely populated (very frequently over-populated) rural areas in Russia, as well as being the main reservoir of migrants for settling Siberia and the new cities.

In the steppe proper (New Russia) south and east of the Odessa–Kharkov line rural densities are generally lower, but it should be noted that the Kuban area now has as dense a rural population as the old right-bank lands, or the prevailing density in peasant Central Europe. Only in the dry margins of the middle Don–Volga and the wet margins of the Polyesie do the rural densities become really light (less than 10 to the square kilometre). Moreover, irrigation and drainage schemes are well on the way to bringing these areas more nearly up to the regional average. No appreciable part of the region is really negative from the farming point of view.

The cities

One in four of the people in the region live in cities of over 50,000, compared with less than one in five in 1939, but this proportion is still lower than the national average. The city population involved here amounts to over 14 million in some seventy cities—about 50% more than the pre-war figures.

The area of greatest concentration of cities may be defined as enclosed by a line joining Odessa, Kharkov, Volgograd (Stalingrad) and Rostov. Of the sixteen cities of over a quarter of a million in 1962 in the whole region, all but three were within this zone. This was the zone which emerged clearly in the earlier discussions of industrial development.

However, the largest city in the region is outside this industrial core zone and deserves pride of place in any discussion of Ukrainian cities. With a population of about one and a quarter million, *Kiev* is now second only to Moscow and Leningrad in the Soviet Union, and unmistakably the regional and cultural capital of the Ukrainian people. However, it has experienced many vicissitudes in its long history—it was not the largest city in the Ukraine in 1900 and was not the capital of the Republic for the first decade and a half of Soviet rule.

Kiev is probably the oldest Russian city of any importance, and deserves to be called 'Mother of Russia'. Its foundation, probably in the eighth century, is to be seen in the context of the time. It was situated on the northern edge of the wooded steppe, providing more fertile and more easily cleared soil than in the marshy forests to the north, while at the same time granting a measure of security from the then predatory nomads of the open steppe to the north. The cliff-like right bank of the river on which the settlement was planted enhanced this security from attack as well as from floods (Plate III) Although primitive farming occupied most of the tributary population, trade gave the impetus to create the large and properous city and capital of the sprawling domain of early Kievan Rus. The main water routes between the Baltic and the Mediterranean converged on the Dnieper, and Kiev happens to be situated just below its confluence with the Desna, Pripyat and other tributaries and was therefore in a pre-eminent position to collect and control people and goods. However, all these locational advantages depended on a certain balance of power between the settlers and the nomads and, after several centuries of Kievan prosperity and civilization, this balance was rudely upset by Batu's Mongol hordes who laid waste the city in the mid-thirteenth century. Kiev's mantle fell upon Moscow and three or four centuries later the city was resurrected under the aegis of an expanding Muscovite empire, as one of several outposts in the slow agricultural re-colonization of the wooded steppe.

In the late eighteenth century the conquest of the steppes and the Black Sea coast, setting the stage for the first permanent colonization in these southern regions, transformed Kiev's relative position. It was thenceforth no longer on the frontier but, like Chicago, the heir to a new, rich hinterland. The opening up agriculturally and industrially of the greater Ukraine clearly enriched Kiev, which had grown to a quarter-million by the late nineteenth century. However, the wealth was far from being funnelled exclusively through Kiev—the new international orientation was reflected in the even more rapid growth of Odessa, while Kharkov was much better placed to capitalize on the Donbas coal and steel developments.

The regaining of Kiev's capital function in 1934 has ensured a steady growth, in spite of its destruction during the War. It is a minor edition of Moscow in some ways, in that it has few non-agricultural resources at hand and streams of fuel and raw materials converge upon it from some distance. Its industrial structure is well balanced, with varied engineering industries, textiles, food-processing and chemicals, and it is centrally placed in regard to the richest and most intensively farmed part of the country. Its historical significance in the Russian nationality, State and Church make it something more than a politico-regional centre for the Ukraine. Kharkov may conceivably grow larger, but cannot now challenge Kiev's pre-eminent position, any more than Milan can supplant Rome as capital of the Italian State.

The other million-city of the region, *Kharkov*, has none of Kiev's aura of ancient greatness nor an imposing site. It was founded in the mid-seventeenth century as a military post against the Tatars and a focus of colonization in that part of the wooded steppe. It was unusual in not being located on a navigable river (merely an insignificant tributary of the Northern Donets) and it grew only slowly in the eighteenth and most of the nineteenth century as a minor agricultural and commercial centre.

The rise of Kharkov dates from the latter part of the nineteenth century, when it found itself on the direct railway line between Moscow, the Dnieper and the Black Sea and also at the main junction for the Donbas, which was at that time fast becoming Russia's prime industrial base. Thenceforth Kharkov's fortunes have been tied up with the Donbas (like Düsseldorf with the Ruhr, or Novosibirsk with the Kuzbas). The population grew from some 50,000 in 1870 to 350,000 in 1916 and in the early Soviet period, apart from a massive industrial development, it also became the administrative centre of the whole of the Ukraine. Thus by 1939 it was almost as large as Kiev and had far surpassed Odessa which had been more than twice its size in 1900. Deprived of its erstwhile administrative status and battered in the war, it has grown relatively slowly and has fallen behind Kiev again.

Kharkov still has a basically favourable situation and potential for further growth. Its position between the Donbas and Moscow along a major axis of Soviet development and as an unexcelled railway junction remains. Further, if one can consider the Comecon grouping of countries as a potential economic unit, Kharkov might prove to be more centrally placed with reference to the population of such a unit than any other large city. Although it is a major regional centre and has a number of varied industries like Kiev, it specializes primarily in engineering, building, transport and agricultural machinery, coal and oil mining machinery, electrical equipment, etc. It is well placed to take advantage of the current shift to chemicals, with the large Shebelinka gas reserves nearby. But above all its prospects are tied closely, as before, to those of the belt of southern heavy industry from the Dnieper to the Don, which seem fairly bright.

Odessa (700,000) is a monument to the nineteenth century—to the headlong growth and international connections of New Russia. In 1897 it was easily the largest city in the whole region and the third largest in the Empire. By 1962 it had dropped to fifth place in the region and sixteenth in the Soviet Union. However, it cannot quite be said to be moribund by ordinary standards and has recently shown evidence of substantial growth.

Following the capture of the Black Sea coast in the late eighteenth century various attempts were made to establish ports. Kherson on the Dnieper estuary and Nikolayev on the Bug proved to be rather unsatisfactory from the point of view of ice and silting conditions, and the Odessa site between the Dnieper–Bug and the Dniester outlets, with negligible problems of silting and only about a month when ice tends to be troublesome, was selected in 1794. Its westerly situation was to some extent an earnest of Russia's intentions of pressing on towards the Danube, and this materialized soon afterwards. When wheat began to be grown on a large scale in the newly opened hinterland, Odessa became the dominant export port, fed at first by boats descending the Dnieper, Bug and Dniester and by caravans of oxcarts and, after 1866, by the railways. It was the advent of railways, coupled with the opening of the Suez Canal (1869) which really inaugurated Odessa's hectic growth-phase. Immigrants poured in on an American scale and the population rose from 100,000 in 1870 to some 600,000 on the eve of the Bolshevik Revolution. But already by 1900 the competition of foreign wheat producers and of some other Black Sea ports had reduced the dominance of wheat in Odessa's trade. Oil from the

Caucasus henceforth became increasingly important and the petroleum section of the port looms large today.

The drastic reduction of international trade after the Revolution and the dominant easterly movements of industry, tended to depress Odessa, and the loss of Moldavia had put it, like Leningrad—which suffered a similar relative eclipse—right up against the frontier. Like Leningrad too the city was subjected to a long siege during the Second World War and it is only in recent years with the revival of Soviet trade, especially with the Mediterranean and Afro-Asian countries and Cuba, that it has again shown signs of real growth. It has a balanced industrial structure with the traditional food processing industries, alongside chemicals, light engineering and textiles. It is also no mean cultural centre and retains a relatively cosmopolitan flavour. A new port is being built south of the main city, on a sheltered, virtually ice-free site and with the projected Baltic–Black Sea deep waterway, the steady growth of the Ukraine and the integration of the Comecon countries, Odessa's prospects are clearly more promising than they were in the inter-war years (Plate IX).

On the other hand a comparison with the case of *Rostov-on-Don* (660,000) gives more of a sense of proportion to a discussion of the twentieth-century progress and prospects of Odessa. They are now both much the same size, whereas Odessa was more than three times as large in 1900. Rostov, at the head of the Don delta, on the high right bank, was founded as an outpost against the Turks in 1761, but grew slowly for the first century of its life. In the late nineteenth century the development of the Donbas and the rail connections with Baku enabled Rostov to begin to make use of its good situation between the Caucasus, Central Russia, Ukraine and Volga, and its favourable site at the lowest practicable bridging point of the Don. It began to wrest an increasing share of the Black Sea trade from Odessa and has grown rapidly during the present century. The opening of the Volga–Don canal in 1952, making Rostov the sea outlet for the whole Volga basin (while also providing for irrigation) and the recent developments in the Kuban, in natural gas (the pipeline goes through Rostov) and agriculture, have all enhanced Rostov's potential as a nodal centre. Agricultural machinery is its chief speciality (even the City Hall is shaped like a tractor! [Plate VIII]), but there are also many other engineering, food and chemical industries, which the city is well suited to expand. Provided industrial and agricultural development continues to expand in the south-east Ukraine, the Kuban and Volgograd, Rostov seems bound to benefit and to gain further stature as a regional focus.

At the other end of the Volga–Don link, *Volgograd* (650,000, formerly called Tsaritsyn and later Stalingrad) has grown even faster than Rostov this century, being half the size of the latter in 1897, and this despite the fact that it was probably more completely wrecked during the Second World War than any other large Soviet city. Although it was founded in the sixteenth century, it remained very small and retained a fortress and local character until the nineteenth century. In 1862 a railway linked it with the Don and trans-shipments of lumber, wheat and fish began to take place. Later the development of the Donbas industrial region and, still more, Baku oil, greatly enhanced the strategic position of the city. In the Civil War period it was a key point, and its retention by the Bolsheviks not only ensured the oil supply to them, but separated the Whites in the North Caucasus from those in Siberia. In the Second World War its strategic value was dramatically demonstrated in the battle of Stalingrad, which became the turning point of the whole war. At that time petroleum was even more crucial, as almost all the Soviet output still came from Baku and its availability was vital to the conduct of the war.

Rebuilt after the war, its real situation and orientation have fundamentally changed. Baku oil, and the Caspian generally, are now of minor national importance, while the building of the Volga–Don canal has set the seal on this relative decline and symbolized the increasing connections of Volgograd with the Donbas. Oil now comes down the Volga rather than up it, and the recent completion of the giant hydro-station has given the city a considerable surplus of power, one spectacular disposal of which is through the new 800 kilovolt line to the Donbas. Like the latter region, but unlike any other Volga city, Volgograd has a steel works, based on scrap and Donbas coal and, like Rostov, has a large tractor works. Aluminium smelting, chemicals, timber working, oil refining and miscellaneous engineering and processing industries occupy the city today. Five railways, mainly from the west, converge on the city, rail-water contacts are very important, and the city's position at the point where the Volga comes nearest to the industrial Ukraine and to the open sea now seems likely at last to have its latent value fully realized.

Inside the line joining up the four cities last considered lies the most urbanized and specialized industrial part of the region. There are many cities, the two main groups of which may be called the Donets and the Dnieper groups, respectively. The former, with nearly 6 million people classified as urban, is at least twice as important as the latter, and of the same order of magnitude as the Ruhr.

The chief centre of the Donets group is *Donetsk* (formerly called Yuzovka, later Stalino) which, including its nearby satellite *Makeyevka*, has a population of well over a million. It was founded in 1870 and named after the Welsh industrialist John Hughes, who directed the setting up of the first blast furnaces, but by 1914 there were still less than 50,000 inhabitants. Probably at least half of the steel smelted in the Donbas originates in Donetsk–Makeyevka. In addition there are coal-mining and chemical activities. Donetsk is unquestionably the capital of the whole Donbas industrial region—the 'Pittsburgh of the Donets'—and other large cities like *Gorlovka* (with its satellites, about half a million) may before long be physically merged with it, as Makeyevka has been.

The chief city of the eastern half of the Donets cluster is *Lugansk* (for a time called Voroshilovgrad—over 300,000) which is important for heavy engineering, especially locomotives. Other Donbas centres, mainly concerned with coal-mining and chemicals and with at least 200,000 inhabitants each, are *Shakhty* and *Kadiyevka*. On the Sea of Azov, directly south of the Donbas, are *Zhdanov* (formerly called Mariupol—320,000), and *Taganrog* (220,000) which, like the Lake Erie steel cities, are rapidly expanding.

The counterpart to Donetsk in the Dnieper bend group of cities is *Dnepropetrovsk* (formerly called Yekaterinoslav) which with its satellites (including Dneprodzerzhinsk but not Zaporozhye) has a population of about a million. Founded in the late eighteenth century, above the rapids and at the confluence of the Samara river which used to be quite an important east–west route, it later became the bridging point of the main railway line between the Donbas and Krivoy Rog. Farther south is *Zaporozhye* (formerly called Alexandrovsk), with half a million people, at the site of the original Dnieper hydro-dam. Because of the latter it became one of the first aluminium smelting places in Russia, and like Dnepropetrovsk has also developed steel, heavy engineering and chemical industries. *Krivoy Rog* (450,000), the site of the great iron mining enterprises, on a tributary of the Dnieper, is also a steel and engineering centre. Farther south *Nikolayev* (250,000) at the mouth of the Bug is a major shipbuilding centre and *Kherson* (180,000) at the mouth of the Dnieper makes agricultural machinery and textiles. These cities in some ways are more akin to Odessa than to the cities of the main industrialized belt. They have each trebled their population during this century which puts them somewhere between Odessa, which has not yet doubled, and Rostov, which has increased five-fold.

Almost all the cities so far considered have been either in the main industrialized zone or on the fringes of it. There are also, however, a number of cities in the region which are primarily service centres for predominantly agricultural hinterlands. The largest of these (if we except

Kiev which has already been treated, and whose significance is felt far outside its immediate district) is *Lvov* (450,000). This ancient city, founded in the thirteenth century, is in the peculiar position of having been, along with its largely Ukrainian-speaking region (Galicia), under foreign control during almost the whole of its history. Its region was under Polish rule until the eighteenth century, after which its was incorporated in the Austro–Hungarian empire (as Lemberg) and was returned to Poland after the empire's demise in 1918. Thus it has only been associated with Russia, as part of the Ukraine, since the Second World War. Naturally enough it is in many ways a Polish city and lies traditionally within the Catholic rather than the Orthodox sphere. At present it is essentially a regional centre with varied engineering (especially electrical), food and textile industries—a Kiev in miniature. There are modest reserves of gas and oil in its Carpathian neighbourhood, which are piped to the city and form the basis of an incipient chemical industry. It is a notable railway-hub and is the main link between the industrial Ukraine and the countries of Eastern Europe. Near it are the boundaries of Poland, Czechoslovakia, Hungary and Romania, and it thus has a certain strategic significance. However, its growth has been relatively slow and its agricultural-regional functions, with more chemicals subserving these functions, are liable to remain.

Similar to Lvov, though half its size (240,000) is *Kishinev*, the capital of the Moldavian Republic. It was part of Romania between the wars but previously had been in the Russian Empire for over a century and was indeed one of the four or five largest cities in the whole Empire about 1860 (it is now sixty-seventh among the Soviet cities). On a tributary of the Dniester, it is centrally situated within its intensively farmed republic, and its industries are mainly concerned with food and wine processing, leather and other locally oriented activities. There is little in the way of industrial resources in the vicinity to encourage much else.

Expressing the more buoyant and varied developing economy of the Kuban region, *Krasnodar* (formerly called Yekaterinodar—350,000) has had a rapid growth this century. Founded in 1794 on the right bank of the Kuban at the main crossing point on the river between the Volga, Don and Caucasian Black Sea coast, it became the capital of the Kuban Cossacks and the undisputed centre for a rich and well-organized farming area. It is still primarily a food processing centre but the oil and, still more, gas in the immediate hinterland have become the basis for an expanding chemical industry. Its ice-free port on the Black Sea is *Novorossisk* (100,000) which ships out food and oil products as well as being one of the chief producers of cement in the whole Union.

The equivalent all-purpose regional centre of the Crimea is *Simferopol* (200,000) on the northern foothills of the mountains, controlling routes with the northern wheatlands, with the main Black Sea naval base of *Sevastopol* (170,000) and, by trolley-bus, with the row of well-patronized south coast resorts centred on *Yalta*.

Finally there are a number of third-rank regional centres, with 100–150,000 people each, in the older agricultural belt of the north and west. Some of them are historically distinguished such as *Poltava* or *Chernigov* while others like *Kremenchug* are getting a new injection of energy and industry. But there are several smaller cities, like *Berdichev*, the same size as it was at the beginning of the century, which have been left by the wayside during the urban revolution and rural exodus of the Soviet era.

THE PROSPECT

This region is unusually well endowed and highly developed by Soviet standards, but its place in the Soviet sun is less prominent than it was.

The main foundations for the development in Soviet times of this region's character—agricultural, industrial and even ethno-cultural—were laid down in the last century or so of the Tsarist era, which cannot be said, for instance, for most of the more easterly regions of the country. In other words the Greater Ukraine had come of age by the early twentieth century, and this process had primarily involved the taking possession and development of the steppelands of New Russia. This reversed the relationship between the two main parts of the region—north-by-west and south-by-east respectively of a line from Odessa to Kharkov. Before the nineteenth century the former—the wooded steppe—was incomparably the more valuable and developed, but afterwards the emphasis has been placed more and more on the latter, and this trend is still evident. Thus the dividing line—a rainfall-vegetation line and a long 'frontier', in the American sense, between the settled and the wild lands, has come instead to separate the predominantly agricultural and comparatively slowly growing north-west, with few non-agricultural industries of national significance, from the highly industrialized, mobile and expanding south-east, a major bulwark of Soviet power.

One can therefore point to a region of wealth, power and growth potential in the south-east, with its long-established core in the Dnieper–Donbas, but beginning to disperse from this core under the influence of new factors such as natural gas and chemicals, to Kharkov, the Kuban, Volgograd and the Sea of Azov. These dispersing forces may be expected to favour particularly the growth of Rostov on the one hand and Kharkov on the other, on the major axis from the Kuban to Moscow via the Donbas. The western and especially the north-western Ukraine (probably including Odessa) suffers a relative locational disadvantage in this situation and may be expected to continue to expand less vigorously, but much depends on the degree of economic integration between the Soviet Union and the other Communist countries of Eastern Europe.

It would not be correct to leave an impression of one part of the region as impoverished, stagnant and of little use. By any reasonable standards almost the whole of this greater Ukrainian region is composed of positive, contributing country and, with the current projects for drainage and especially irrigation, even the few weak spots are liable to disappear. By Soviet standards this region contains consistently good farmlands and highly developed industry and thus stands in much the same relative position in the U.S.S.R. as much of the Mid-West does within the United States. Its location, in respect to population, international connections and climatic advantage, is most favourable. In agricultural potential it is without peer among Soviet regions, and the new policy of intensive agricultural investment (chemicals, irrigation, and emphasis on livestock) is making it even more competitive for the available investment. In a relative sense its national contribution in agriculture will probably be more indispensable than that in industry. However, its industrial resources, especially in ferrous metals and coal are also impressive. A question does arise whether the new policy of de-emphasizing coal and also steel in the scale of industrial priorities would be bound to act as a depressant to a region whose industry has been traditionally based on these things. This may prove to be true to some degree but the region does have many of the ingredients for success in the new chemistry-oriented industries too, such as a large market (especially for fertilizers), rich resources of gas, salt and coal, and a legacy of past investment in industrial and transport installations. Whether, without much oil, it will be able to compete with the Volga–Ural region in petrochemicals, remains to be seen. Here is a region then, rich in the wherewithal for agriculture and industry, with a large, culturally homogeneous, enterprising population, and with climate and amenities which are among the most attractive in the country—increasingly important considerations these days. Although it has lost the degree of dominance it once had on the national scene, it is still, all in all, probably the most valuable of the Soviet regions, and has considerable potential for still further development. Such far-reaching innovations as the maize-livestock and the gas-chemical drives in recent years have demonstrated the flexibility and many-sided possibilities still latent in this basically rich region.

CHAPTER NINE

The Volga–Ural Region

BETWEEN the closely-knit, Moscow-dominated, central region of European Russia and the homogeneous metallurgical strip on the eastern flank of the Urals is an area, twice as large as Britain but with half its population, which is now having the foundations of its whole regional structure transformed.

For several centuries the great river, with its far-reaching tributaries, has created a region and stamped it in the image of its dominant personality. It became one of the historic highways of Russia, pervaded its history and at the same time became the effective symbol of the 'frontier' in the American sense. The left and right banks, until very recently, have represented Asia and Europe, barbarism and civilization, anarchy and order, freedom and bondage, the desert and the sown. At the same time people and their economic activities gravitated inevitably to the river-banks.

But over the last seventy years or so the ferment of change has slowly but surely set in. The spreading of railways to open up, exploit and settle the vast back country of the continental state has made the Volga, like the Mississippi, a bridge and a hub rather than a frontier. Now the most beaten tracks are at right angles to the great river. On top of this, largely since the war, has come the uncovering and harnessing of great

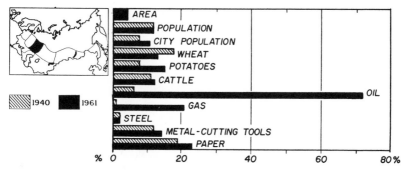

FIG. 28—Location and importance of the Volga-Ural region in relation to the Soviet Union as a whole, for certain selected items

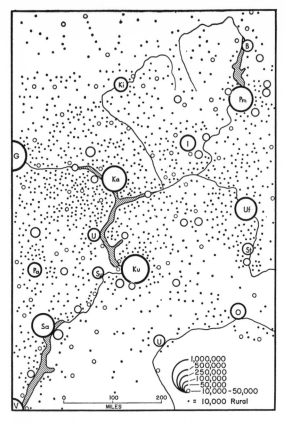

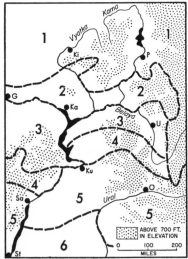

FIG. 29—Volga-Ural: population. Key to cities: B=Berezniki, G=Gorky, I=Izhevsk, Ka=Kazan, Ki=Kirov, Ku=Kuybyshev, O=Orenburg, Pa=Penza, Pm=Perm, Sa=Saratov, St=Sterlitamak, Sy=Syzran, U=Uralsk, Uf=Ufa, V=Volgograd

FIG. 30—Volga-Ural: nature. 1=tayga, 2=mixed forest, 3=deciduous forest, 4=wooded steppe, 5=steppe, 6=semidesert

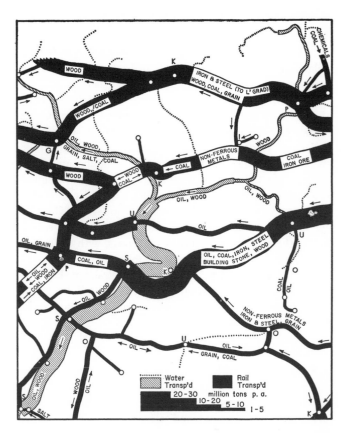

FIG. 31—Volga-Ural: movements

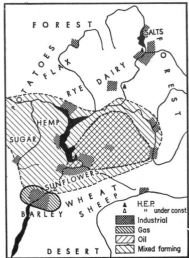

FIG. 32—Volga-Ural: economy

riches of oil and secondarily water-power and gas, which have set off a belated industrial revolution and made the region a national powerhouse.

Therefore this region has been defined here as that part of the Volga basin in which oil and its derivative industries are increasingly dominating the economy and landscape. On the west the line has been drawn below Gorky which is essentially bound up with the Moscow industrial region, and above Volgograd (Stalingrad) which, although the other great gateway to the Volga–Ural region, is increasingly bound up with the Donets steel region. On the east the crest of the Urals is a rough dividing line, as satisfactory as the Pennines, leaving such oil-chemical-timber towns as Perm and Ufa well within the orbit of the region. On the north and south the region fades to the edge of effective, climatically-sanctioned settlement before the cold forests and the dry steppes, with the population clusters of Kirov, Perm, Saratov and Orenburg included.

The Lower Volga Valley, north of Astrakhan, has no longer an overriding functional connection with the Middle Volga and its fortunes have only too obviously declined in inverse proportion to the rise of those of the lands included in this chapter.

THE NATURAL HABITAT (Fig. 30)

Physically this region is Russia in microcosm, with great rivers weaving south through the latitudinal warp of the natural zones, set in their asymmetrical valleys, emerging from acid soils and coniferous forests and descending into the scrub and salt-tinged soils of the dry steppe and semi-desert. Between these two marginal soil-vegetation zones is an agriculturally quite attractive belt of varied soils in which the wooded steppe and a type of black-earth predominates.

However, the Volga itself is a very real climatic frontier in its middle and lower reaches, and this is strikingly reflected in the unconformity of the vegetation belts on the left and right banks respectively. Rain-bearing air comes from the west, so that the higher lands of the right bank can intercept the moisture and disastrously reduce the relative humidity which descends to the left bank. Thus the deficiency and variability of the rainfall vitiates the usefulness of many of the potentially productive lands south of the Kuybyshev bend—the mean annual precipitation declines quickly from about 16 inches at Kuybyshev to 8 inches 200 miles due south of it, while the intensity of evaporation increases and is exacerbated by the desiccating *sukhovey* which blows out from Central Asia. It should be noted, though, that precipitation increases significantly as the Ural foothills are reached. Periodic famines have been endemic in the Middle and Lower Volga lands and irrigation is not the least important of the long-term benefits which should result from the present river control projects.

Temperature conditions are typically continental with a frozen period ranging from three to five months and July temperatures everywhere higher than those of London. But length of growing season and heat intensity vary considerably. The southern fringes of the region have twice the accumulated temperature budget (over 50° F.) experienced on the northern fringes. On the other hand, north of Kazan precipitation everywhere exceeds evaporation, whereas on the southern fringes of the dry steppe effectiveness is less than a third. Hence the basic Soviet agricultural tragedy of lack of correspondence of heat and moisture.

The physical landscape is gentle and subdued, but not monotonous. Nowhere does the crystalline basement rock obtrude at the surface and the overlying sedimentary formations, chiefly sandstones and limestones, have proved exceptionally favourable to the occurrence of petroleum, though not so ideal for building dams for water-power.

The main relief feature is the asymmetrical valley typical of South Russia: the high right bank of the river forms the eastern edge of the Volga uplands, a dissected plateau whose ridges occasionally rise to about 1,000 feet, while the left bank is low, bearing the footprints of the river's westward trek until the land rises gradually eastwards towards the Ural foreland. Only east of the Kama and Belaya rivers does the dissected plateau character of the foreland give way to the more steeply rising foothills of the Urals itself.

The Volga, with the Kama, is in the process of being tamed and put to work. Its natural régime is highly irregular, with flood levels in April and May followed by quickly subsiding levels and eventually four or five months paralysis by ice. As the Great Volga scheme gets under way, and the river becomes a T.V.A.-like string of lakes, floods, soil erosion and navigation snags are being ironed out and electricity and irrigation water provided. On the negative side should be mentioned the submergence of much good alluvial garden land, and the aggravation of the already serious fall in the water-level of the Caspian Sea by increased evaporation from the spreading water-bodies in the middle reaches of the river.

THE PEOPLING OF THE REGION

Although Mother Volga has become almost a symbol of Russian nationality, the Russians are actually the most recent ingredients in the ethnic melting-pot which characterizes the Volga lands today.

From the ninth to the twelfth centuries, when the first seeds of Russian nationality were germinating about Kiev and Novgorod, the Middle Volga lands were settled by the Bulgars, whose centre was just south of the Kama–Volga confluence. These people, speaking a Turkish language and newly converted to Islam, were farmers and traders, and had earlier subdued several Finnish-speaking tribes in the area. All these peoples succumbed in the early thirteenth century to the Tatar Golden Horde whose capital was established at Sarai on the lower Volga. While most of the Tatars continued to be nomadically inclined, those in the Middle Volga adopted the sedentary existence and culture of the Bulgars and established the break-away Khanate of Kazan. But they did not penetrate far into the forests and in the late fourteenth century men of Novgorod came into the upper Kama country and even across the Urals in quest of furs and the forest riches for their Baltic trade. The native hunters of the forest, like the Komi, were no serious obstacle, so that Muscovy, later the heirs of Novgorod, continued the activities and also began to mine the precious salt of Solikamsk.

But the crucial Russian breakthrough in the Volga lands came in the mid-sixteenth century, when the Tatar Kazan fell to Ivan the Terrible. Within a few years the entire river was Russian and the large cities of today, like Kuybyshev, Saratov and Volgograd were founded in this period. They sailed up the Belaya river and subjugated the Bashkirs, who were largely steppeland cattle herders, and built the fort at Ufa in 1586. The way was opened to the Urals and Siberia for the merchant adventuring of the following century. But although scattered Russian farming colonies were established on the Volga they had long to be fortified against Asian invaders such as the Mongol Kalmucks and there were also persistent revolts against the central government in which the subject Moslem peoples and Russian serfs frequently made common cause. Russian political control was finally made effective only at the end of the eighteenth century when, under Catherine the Great, the Turks were driven from the Crimea, thus cutting the links between the Volga Moslems and Constantinople, and colonists from Germany and other parts of Central Europe were planted on the right bank of the Volga. The subsequent Russian incorporation of Central Asia and Caucasia created a new position for the Volga lands as part of the inner territories of the Russian empire.

The scene about 1900

The southward-flowing Volga, although a great traffic artery, was still very much a frontier of settlement less than a century ago. The right and left banks were two different worlds, both physically and socially. On the right bank, with better soils and more reliable rainfall there was a steadily worsening condition of rural over-population during the period following the end of serfdom, with famine not uncommon. But the left bank was still 'Siberia', with all that that had come to mean in terms of lack of social cohesion, sedentary living and communications.

The upper Kama region about Perm had been rather less of a frontier since it was, from the eighteenth century, on the main road to the metal-works across the Urals. Similarly there had been sporadic contacts between the Volga lands and Middle Asia for centuries, first by the Tatars as between kinsmen and later by the conquering Russians who built outposts such as Orenburg for trading as well as military ends. The great fair at Gorky (Nizhnii Novgorod), where Sheffield steel met Persian carpets and Chinese tea, was the most spectacular demonstration of this age-old func-tion of the Volga as a link between Europe and Asia. However, movements of both people and goods eastward and south-eastwards from the Volga had necessarily been kept down to a trickle by the lack of proper com-munications. It was only about the turn of the century that the railways began to push on from the Volga lands to the 'wide open spaces' of Siberia and Middle Asia, at least a generation after the American railways had struck out beyond the Mississippi. Thenceforth the locational assets of the Volga region in the context of the new and vast Russian Empire became endowed with real meaning. Among the more important consequences of the railway age in Russian Asia were the increasing geographical division of labour leading to exports like cotton and wheat, and also the flood of peasant migration from the Volga lands along the newly blazed trail to the east.

The industrial revolution which had come, belatedly, to the Moscow region and the Ukraine during the latter part of the nineteenth century, had all but smothered the previously flourishing metal industries of the Urals, but had passed the Middle Volga by. Except for a small amount of non-agricultural industry at Saratov, a centre for the Volga German community, and Perm, with its salts and Ural associations, those in-dustries which did exist in the region about 1900 were based on farm and forest and were moreover mainly of the *kustarny* or cottage type.

There was no source of power in sight—no coal, only slow-flowing but erratic rivers and, at a time when Baku was the world's most productive oilfield, no knowledge of the immense reserves of energy stretching from the Volga to the Urals.

On the eve of the Second World War

During the twenty years following the Bolshevik Revolution the Volga–Ural was something of a Cinderella among the Soviet regions. Although some growth did take place it lagged well behind the other regions with comparable resources and locational advantages, such as the Moscow region, the Eastern Ukraine, the Eastern Urals or the new industrial regions of Siberia. In fact it was one of the very few regions of the Soviet Union to show a net loss of population between 1926 and 1939, while the growth of its cities was much slower than the average, even for European Russia.

The region remained solidly agricultural in character well into the 1930s and had moreover been hit very hard by the post-war famines. Even at the end of the second Five Year Plan (1937) it had virtually no power supply of its own. Although the great oil-bearing region had been discovered and exploited at scattered points it only contributed 3% of the Soviet output and there was almost no refining in the area. None of the schemes for hydro-electric power and canal building had begun to be implemented and north–south communications were virtually non-existent when the rivers were frozen or at a low level.

As the forebodings of war grew in Central Europe, there was a sudden acceleration in the Soviet policy of moving industry and population to the east which, amongst other things, inaugurated for the Volga–Ural region the modern phase of development in which the region has increasingly been 'found' in a geographical sense and its relative importance in the Soviet Union as a whole greatly enhanced.

THE PRESENT ECONOMY (Fig. 32)

By the middle of the present century it suddenly became clear that this region was undergoing a radical change in its basic economy. Although several Soviet regions underwent such a metamorphosis in the thirties, the experience of the Volga–Ural in the last two decades has been virtually unique. The tempo of economic development has been steadily quickening, and has shown no sign that it is likely to slow down in the foreseeable future.

The region has only just begun to emerge from the transitional stage between its pre-war character as a largely agrarian backwater, with a serious shortage of industrial power, and its new function as an industrial focus and a national source of power.

The power base

In the early 1950s, coal still accounted for well over half of the energy consumed in the region and furthermore most of this coal was apparently hauled from the east of the Urals. Since then the great new sources of power have steadily taken over.

Petroleum takes pride of place. The late war, which highlighted both the approaching exhaustion and the strategic vulnerability of the Caucasus fields, made urgent the need for exploring the known Volga–Ural province, but in spite of much drilling, the latter accounted for little more than a quarter of the Soviet oil even in 1950. However, production had risen almost ten-fold by 1960 and over two-thirds of Soviet oil is now Volga–Ural in origin (Fig. 28). Moreover, this preponderance is likely to increase still further, since it is now calculated that the region contains over four-fifths of the Soviet reserves, the same proportion as was credited to the Caucasus fields in 1939.

These basic facts are especially significant in view of the recent major change in fuel policy which calls for the substitution of oil (with gas) for coal as the dominant Soviet source of power during the present decade. While the Volga region is less important nationally in the case of gas (with about one-sixth of the Soviet production and reserves), it plays a significant part in the industrial plans of the region and its neighbours.

The Volga–Ural oil-bearing region covers an area similar to that of the great Mid-Continent province in the United States and bears comparison with the latter in its dominance within the country and in potential volume of output, though it is at a much younger stage of development. The earliest oil strikes were made in the upper Kama region, and it is a thousand miles to some of the newer fields around Volgograd. However, the great bulk of Volga–Ural oil (and indeed the majority of all Soviet oil) is now being obtained from an area within 150 miles or so of Almetyevsk, with its axis stretching from the great bend of the Volga at Kuybyshev to the middle reaches of the Belaya river. The oil here is also the cheapest in the country and the only brake on its exploitation in the last few years has been the inevitable lag in provision of refineries and pipelines (Plate X).

Most of the gas exploited has been in the region of Saratov and it has been piped to Moscow since 1946, but much gas formerly wasted in the main oil region is now being put to industrial use.

Although oil is providing the main stimulus behind the present boom in the Volga–Ural and looks like determining the salient character of the region's industrial development and national role for the rest of this century it should be remembered that this is a notoriously expendable power resource. Therefore in the long run the remarkable projects for hydro-electric power which have come to fruition in the late 1950s as one facet of the Great Volga scheme, may prove to be the most solid foundation for regional development.

The Volga–Kama system is so far much the greatest power producer of any Soviet river system and boasts two of the most powerful hydro-stations in the world at Kuybyshev and Volgograd (Stalingrad). The Kuybyshev station is of particular importance because of its massive contribution (over 2 million kw), alongside oil, gas and shale, to making the district around the Volga hairpin bend a Mecca for power-hungry industries and the point of origin for power needed in the Urals, Siberia and the Moscow region.

The station above Perm on the Kama has barely a quarter of Kuybyshev's capacity, but a much larger station further down the river at Votkinsk has recently been completed. Other dams in the eventual chain will be constructed in the more distant future.

The only 'native' source of power dating back before the Soviet Five Year Plans is oil shale which is still mined on the right bank of the Volga near Syzran and used in a local power plant. However the cost is now so exorbitant in comparison with the new local sources of power that its days are undoubtedly numbered.

Transport (Fig. 31)

The region is much more closely knit by lines of communication both internally and externally than it was before the war. The value of the Volga river system, which carries nearly half the inland water transport tonnage of the country, was greatly enhanced when the opening of the Volga–Don canal in 1952 realized an old Russian dream. Further, the construction of the power dams is leading to a more uniform depth of water in the navigation season and even a reduction of effective sailing distance, but the situation with regard to the length of the freezing season has notably deteriorated. No longer has the river a monopoly of north-south communication. During the war a railway was laid parallel to the river along the right bank and several important longitudinal lines have been built in the Belaya and Kama valley areas.

In spite of the age-old importance of the Volga as an artery and its dominant position among the Soviet waterways, water-borne freight even in this region is smaller than that handled by the railways. Gone are the days when little of consequence lay east of the Volga and when the river was *the* trading link between Russia and Asia. The region is now inescapably a transit zone between the recently developing eastern regions and the established control-point of this development in the Moscow region. Thus the railways which carry the most freight trend east–west, and the predominant direction of flow is westwards towards Moscow and also Leningrad with coal, oil, iron and steel as the major commodities. The busiest traffic of all is found on the Trans-Siberian passing through Kuybyshev and Syzran, which has recently been electrified. In the case of oil, which is by far the most important item loaded on railways in the region for other regions, the flow goes to an increasing extent eastwards to Siberia, and the recent pipeline revolution is intensifying this east–west oil axis. Until recently the main oil flow was up the Volga from the Caspian fields to Central Russia, but the relative demise of these fields sends oil mostly downstream nowadays, from the Volga–Ural fields to the under-utilized Caspian refineries. But Caucasus oil, which is generally freer of sulphur than that from the Volga–Ural and still very much in demand, is still a significant upstream commodity on the Volga.

Traditionally the most important product coming down the Volga and its tributaries the Kama and Vyatka is wood and this is still today the largest item on the river, by raft and ship. The large cities of the region are all trans-shipment points between rail and water, and the great Volga system is still a galvanizing force in the region. It is easily the chief north–south artery and cheaper per ton-mile, if slower, than the parallel railways. Moreover, the booming economic activity along its banks should prevent the loss of its long-standing role as one of the world's busiest waterways, although river transport is generally ailing and subject to subsidy.

The industrial revolution

The industrial personality of the region is being transformed in response to the rapid transition from poverty to affluence in power-supply. Several distinct groups of industry have resulted. First, there were the vital precursors such as cement, hydro-turbines, excavators and oil-boring and pumping equipment, and the region is becoming steadily more important as a supplier of these things for projects in other parts of the country. Secondly, the plentiful power in itself has attracted a variety of industries not associated with Volga enterprises or raw materials, particularly in the engineering group. Finally, perhaps the most spectacular industrial process at present is the blossoming of a wide range of petrochemical industries dependent on oil and gas as raw materials, such as synthetic rubber and other fibres, fertilizers and alcohol. This represents one of the major industrial trends and will have a radical effect not only on the character of consumer goods industry but also on farming, through the extension of fertilizers and also diversion of large quantities of potatoes, beet and grain from industrial purposes to food.

These new industries have overshadowed the long established agriculturally-oriented industries in the region, and are concentrating particularly in the Kuybyshev district, where the industrial growth rate has been as fast as any comparable spot in the country since 1939, the cities of the Belaya valley and in the area between. In the Kama valley above Perm long-used local resources do still form a solid basis for nationally important industry— timber primarily for paper-making and the great deposits of potash and common salt for the chemical industry.

The Volga–Ural is the Soviet region most recently converted to a positively industrial bias. With about one-ninth of the total Soviet population, it contributes about one-eighth of the manufacturing, and its relative importance in this field is bound to be steadily enhanced in the foreseeable future.

Farming

As in many things, so in farming this region is transitional and represents a microcosm of Russia. It lies squarely astride the great grain belt which follows the black-earth. Its grain production, although substantial, is only about half that of either of the two giant areas, the Ukraine or Western Siberia–Kazakhstan.

The Volga river still noticeably retains its border character in agriculture. The left-bank lands, generally to the south of Kuybyshev, form the western extremity of the Virgin Lands zone, which have experienced a massive expansion of wheat growing in recent years. In fact in some aspects these Volga lands, which were successfully practising dry farming and using *durum* wheat before the Virgin Lands Project was launched, can be regarded as a 'pilot' area for the main scheme.

The right-bank lands, more reliably watered and longer farmed, are really an extension of the northern Ukraine and the Central Black-earth districts, and are moving towards something of a Corn Belt emphasis on milk and meat production. Sugar-beet is also becoming a part of this economy and potatoes released from industrial uses are contributing towards pig production.

In the Vyatka and Kama valleys the 'mixed forest' farming—rye, oats, potatoes, flax and dairying—becomes characteristic, while on the southern dry margin of the agricultural core of the Volga–Ural region extensive ranching activities predominate, in which sheep-rearing is increasingly important.

The building of the hydro-dams on the river is having profound agricultural consequences. The new reservoirs have flooded much alluvial garden land, but are increasing the rainfall in nearby areas and also the supply of water-meadow hay, and they are being stocked with fish. The stage is now set for implementing some of the long-laid irrigation plans in the Trans-Volga lands, in which it is planned to grow such crops as maize, rice and sugar-beet, as well as fruits and vegetables.

The diversification and intensification of agricultural activities in this region may be regarded as closely tied up with, if not responding to, the far-reaching industrial and urban expansion.

THE PRESENT POPULATION

In 1959 there were about 23 million people in this region compared with about 20 million in 1939. This indicates a rate of growth nearly twice the national rate for the period. The block of American Mid-West States astride the Mississippi (Illinois—including Chicago—Missouri, Iowa, Wisconsin and Minnesota) has roughly the same population and covers roughly the same area. But it should be noted that the Volga–Ural region is entirely north of the 49th parallel of latitude and that the Canadian prairie provinces have barely three million inhabitants.

The region is ethnographically interesting in that it contains much the most sizable concentration of non-Slavic-speaking peoples within the vast Russian Federated Republic—a living testimony to the rich succession of human cultures which had taken root here before the relatively recent invasion of the now dominant Russian groups. These minorities can be conveniently grouped into those living east of the Volga—the Tatars and the related Bashkirs, and those living west and north of the Volga—the Chuvash (possibly descendants of the original Volga Bulgars) and the Mordva, Udmurt, Mari and Permyak who speak Finnic languages.

However, even before the war these people numbered only about a quarter of the total population of the region and it may be assumed that the proportion has been appreciably reduced by recent Russian immigration. More important than ethnic statistics, however, is the inexorable process of assimilation brought about by the use of the Russian *lingua franca* and the urban, industrial and scientific revolutions. Thus although there is an ethnic foundation for most of the administrative boundaries in the region, the melting-pot process has recently deprived the ethnic map here of most of the geographical significance it may once have had.

The rural distribution (Fig. 29)

While the cities have, of course, set the pace in population growth in the Soviet period, alongside the dwindling of the rural population, rather more than half the people in this region are still classified as rural. Moreover, the cities of any consequence remain within the effectively farmed area or on its edges.

For in the first place, as always, climatic limits on settlement have been set on the northern and southern edges of the region by lack of effective heat and reliable moisture respectively, and farming settlement has, in general, reached its economic frontiers north of Kirov or Perm and south of Saratov and Orenburg.

Superimposed on these formidable east–west frontiers is the historical and psychological one of the north–south flowing Volga, which from the first Russian incursions into this region symbolized the break between order and anarchy (and for some between bondage and freedom), civilized Europe and barbarian Asia. Crossing the river was long a perilous undertaking in itself at some seasons, which lent credence to its Rubicon-like reputation.

South of the great bend at Kuybyshev the river is in itself a very real climatic dividing line, with the low left bank lands deprived of eastward-moving moisture but wide open to the dry northward-blowing *sukhovey*. North of Kuybyshev on the other hand, this difference is much less noticeable; from the point of view of the Russians this left bank was Tatar-Bashkir country with alien traditions of land use. North of the Volga in the less attractive but more familiar forest margins of the Vyatka and Kama there were no such barriers, and from the early Novgorod days Russians came for furs and later salt and timber, or to open the first gateway to the Urals and beyond.

During the past century, which has seen the extension of effective Russian control over Siberia and Central Asia, the end of the age-old struggle between settler and nomad, and the taming of the great river itself, the significance of the Volga as a historical–psychological–ethnic divide has almost been eroded away.

Only where climate has the last word and is in league with the Volga, as it is south of Kuybyshev, is the river a frontier of settlement. But the greatest density of rural population in the region and the only area comparable to the northern Ukraine or Central Europe, is still the right bank of the Volga north-west of Ulyanovsk. This district is part of the long-settled zone which experienced severe rural overpopulation after the abolition of serfdom; physically it is lower and less broken than the other right-bank plateau-lands to the south and it occupies part of the inner zone of the region which is the most favourable climatically for agriculture.

The cities

Nearly one-third of the population of the Volga–Ural is now concentrated in cities of over 50,000, compared with one-sixth in 1939. The cities here have grown at a faster rate than those of any other regions of European Russia and more than twice as fast as those of the Moscow region or the Ukraine. In fact even the well-known burgeoning cities of California have grown no faster during this period.

There are now five cities of over half a million people, while there were none before the war. These great cities, with several others of more than a quarter-million, are increasingly directing all that is most dynamic in the geographical progress of the region, and at the same time accurately reflecting the changing geographical values within the region.

Kuybyshev (880,000), formerly called Samara, is now clearly the most important city in the region and one of the nine largest in the Soviet Union. Of the big Soviet cities (with over three-quarters of a million people today) only Kuybyshev and Novosibirsk have doubled since 1939 and they are similar in that they represent the recent headlong economic growth of their fuel-rich regions. The city with the most closely comparable record of growth in the U.S.A. over this period has been Dallas, Texas.

Kuybyshev's rise to pre-eminence is a very recent phenomenon and some of its success must be attributed to a national role as a link between Europe and Asia. The seeds for this were planted in the late sixteenth century when, shortly after Ivan the Terrible swept victoriously down the Volga, it became the first Russian city on the left bank of the river. The site chosen was the easternmost tip of the river at a point where its tributary, the Samara (which gave the new city its name), enters the Volga from the direction of Central Asia. Jutting in between the rivers is a spur of slightly raised flood-safe ground such as is rarely found on the left bank. For the next three centuries it functioned primarily as an entrepôt between the Central Asian caravans and the Volga boats, but in the late eighteenth century it also took on flour-milling and other food-processing functions. In the late nineteenth century two railways struck east from the city to become, after much delay, the Trans-Siberian and Turkestan lines.

However, the other two Volga cities, Kazan and Saratov, were each 50% larger in 1897 and, even by 1939, Kuybyshev had hardly drawn level with them. Non-agricultural industries had become significant by the late thirties and war brought a great acceleration, but the really secure foundations for the city's current industrial growth have materialized in the last decade with the Tatar oil-boom and the completion of the giant hydro-station. The developing industrial structure is now very diversified and is closely connected with oil or electricity from the producer and consumer angle. There is a many-sided engineering group, and also a large food-producing group—for which the city's traditions and its easy communications with a wide range of agricultural surplus areas fit it well. A number of industrial satellite towns have sprung up recently and there must now be at least a million people within 30 miles of the city-centre, without including *Syzran* (160,000), a rail-centre on the right bank, which is certainly within Kuybyshev's orbit now, and reflects its economic character.

The rise of Kuybyshev must be looked at not only in the context of its historical origins, site and present wealth in fuel, but in its position within its region and in the developing nation as a whole, and in the light of the recently established communications by rail, water, air, power line and pipeline with the places that matter. The city was selected as a temporary capital during the war and, if geographers were kings, it might well be decreed the ideal capital for the Soviet Union of today and tomorrow.

Below Kuybyshev in the current urban hierarchy of the region, and ranged about it geographically, are the other four cities with over half a million people. Two of them, Saratov and Kazan, were each three times as populous as the other two, Perm and Ufa, in 1897.

Saratov (including Engels, 730,000) was the largest town in the whole region until the 1930s. In the heart of the steppes, and for long the only bridge-point on the river south of the Samara loop, it has been intimately bound up with industry and trade dependent on agriculture and particularly wheat. It was more open and exposed than the Russian towns further north, and its tentative foundation on the left bank was abandoned during the seventeenth-century revolts for its present site on the high right bank. A sizable German colony was planted in this region by Catherine the Great, and seems to have contributed much towards the relative eminence in industry and agriculture in the Volga region enjoyed by Saratov before the revolution. (The Volga Germans were expelled from this region in 1942 and their autonomous republic abolished—although they have since been absolved of collaboration charges, they will not be resettled in their former homeland, which has been occupied by Russians.)

During the War large deposits of natural gas were found, a pipeline was laid to Moscow and the region has since proved to have one of the country's greatest stores of gas. An oil pipeline was also built to by-pass Volgograd from Baku, which has made Saratov an oil trans-shipment point as well. A large hydro-station about 100 miles upstream, part of the Volga scheme, was being constructed but may have been indefinitely delayed as a result of the recent retrenchment of hydro-electricity and the local availability of cheaper fuel. These developments, added to the rail linkage with the salt-bearing regions east of the Lower Volga and the substantial rise in water depth due to the Volgograd reservoir which has backed up beyond the city, mean that Saratov (including *Engels* on the opposite bank) has a very good basis for the new petrochemical industries and others requiring bulky raw materials or plentiful power. On the other hand the proximity of the Virgin Lands wheat country will ensure the continued importance of the older industries like combine-harvester making and flour milling.

Kazan (710,000) occupies a valuable corner lot at the point where the Volga makes its right-angled turn towards the Caspian. As a matter of fact, although in the last few years the backing up of the Kuybyshev reservoir has caused the Volga to lap against the Kazan Kremlin itself, the city was planted three miles up a small tributary, the Kazanka. The Tatars, when they defeated the Bulgars in the thirteenth century and absorbed their civilization, did not take over their capital, which was situated just below the Kama confluence at a constricted high point on the Volga. As their eyes were on the northern forests and particularly on the young Muscovite settlements, Kazan was clearly the best spot from which to control the Volga without having to cross it. Later when, after a century of abortive attempts, the Russians finally took Kazan, the doors to the Caspian and Siberia were flung wide for them.

In the nineteenth century Kazan became a considerable centre for making such things as soap, candles, leather and fur goods. It is still a major centre for the latter but the recent growth of the chemical and engineering groups has relatively overshadowed them.

Its links with the eastern regions are less substantial than those of Kuybyshev—not until 1924 was a rail connection made with the Urals. Nevertheless, although it has grown only half as fast as Kuybyshev since 1939 (when Kazan was still the larger city), it obviously has the basis for substantial industrial growth in the future.

Perm (for a time called Molotov) (700,000), the focus of the Upper Kama population cluster, has doubled its population since 1939. While the early centre of the region's operations was much further north, at Soli-kamsk, when salt and furs were the main preoccupation, it moved south when contact with the other side of the Urals became important. Yermak's famous expedition across the Urals in 1580 went east from Perm, and from then on its fortunes have been partly connected with those of the eastern Urals, although its functions and economy have remained distinct. In this respect its site is important, being on the Kama just below its confluence with the Chusovaya, a tributary which leads out of the Urals from near the present city of Sverdlovsk. A regular route, known as the New Siberian Highroad went through Perm in the eighteenth century, to be replaced by a railway in 1909.

Its phenomenal growth in this century is due to the development of a number of industries based on local resources of timber and salts—paper and mineral fertilizers especially; and on steel brought from the Urals— engineering, including shipbuilding. It is an important rail-water trans-shipment point and has easy contact with several cities which are within its economic orbit, like *Berezniki* (120,000). However, unlike Kuybyshev, its fuel supplies are by no means affluent. Although the first strike of the Volga–Ural oil region was made near Perm, local production is now unimportant and imports of gas and oil are now essential. The hydro-station just above the city has less than a quarter the capacity of the Kuybyshev station. Plans afoot to connect the upper Kama with the Pechora system, in order primarily to arrest the fall in the level of the Caspian Sea, would incidentally put Pechora coal within economical reach of Perm. But fuel may well be a limiting factor, which together with the rather peripheral position of the city, will probably prevent Perm from industrial expansion on the scale seemingly destined for Kuybyshev.

Ufa (610,000) has, like Perm, doubled its population since 1939 and each had less than 50,000 people at the end of last century. Their geographical situation is curiously similar too—Ufa being on the navigable Volga-bound Belaya, just where the Ufa river comes in from the Urals opposite Chelyabinsk. It was the first Russian fort on the Belaya following the sixteenth-century conquest, and became a collecting point for metal and timber products from the Urals and a centre for some industry. Then the infant Trans-Siberian railway crossed the river at Ufa and soon another line was laid from the Volga at Ulyanovsk connecting Ufa with what was later discovered to be the heart of the great oilfields. Therefore Ufa is rather more on the beaten track than Perm, more central as to population and closer to the source of the favoured fuels for the forseeable Soviet industrial future. It has a varied industrial structure, including ship-building, rail equipment and food processing, but it is clear that the chemical industries, including cellulose from Ural timber, but primarily based on oil and gas products, are increasingly dominating the picture. This applies to several oil-field towns in Ufa's orbit, such as *Sterlitamak*

(130,000) where a large synthetic rubber plant was opened in 1961, based on local butane and synthetic alcohol from Ufa.

There are five cities in the region with a population of around a quarter of a million, and oddly enough each is more different from the others than are the five larger cities already considered.

Izhevsk (320,000) midway between Perm and Kazan, is a curious outlier of the metallurgical Urals, being the only specialized steelmaking and engineering centre in the region. The ore is in fact brought mainly from the Urals down the Kama to *Votkinsk* (where there is a large hydro-station) and thence by rail. The rate of population growth has been markedly slower since 1939 than the average for the steel towns of the Eastern Urals.

Orenburg (for a time called Chkalov) (290,000) has grown up almost entirely because of its position as a link between other regions rather than because of any local resources. It was founded in the mid-eighteenth century as an advance base for Russian political and economic penetration into the Kazakh steppes and Middle Asia. The site chosen was on the Ural river at the closest point to the source of the Samara tributary of the Volga. It is on the direct route between Kuybyshev and Tashkent, and this has given it an advantage over *Uralsk* (110,000), further down river, which was founded about the same time. In 1877 it became a railway terminus in addition to a camel-train focus and a military base for the sub-jugation of Middle Asia. After the conquest in 1905 the cotton railway to Tashkent was built, and the subsequent connection with the nearby metal centres of the southern Urals have given it a focal position. These circumstances, plus the nearby oil and gas, form the basis for varied industries such as engineering, chemicals, textiles and milling. The town has grown steadily if more slowly than others in the Volga–Ural region, but the pace may be accelerated.

Kirov (formerly called Vyatka) (280,000) may be regarded as the antipode of Orenburg in the region, as deep within the cold forest as Orenburg is in the dry steppe, and an outpost of settlement also. It is probably the oldest town in the region, being only a few years younger than Moscow. Like Orenburg, its links and its in-between situation are more impressive than its local resources. Although sited on a navigable waterway of the Volga system, it has more direct rail connection with the Urals, Moscow, Leningrad and with the European northlands. Traditional industries based on fur, hides and timber are still very important, but miscellaneous engineering, and especially railway industries have been introduced. It is at an even greater distance from its fuel than is Perm, except for the local peat, has fewer raw materials and has grown at a slower rate.

Penza (290,000) and *Ulyanovsk* (240,000) are each situated at the junctions of important east–west and north–south routes, and are set in productive farming regions. When Lenin was growing up in Ulyanovsk (then Simbirsk), it had only the river, whereas Penza already had its railway. Penza has been in many ways within the orbit of the Moscow region, and its labour-oriented light industry structure today (e.g. watches, printing, calculating machines) testifies to this. Ulyanovsk, on the other hand, was primarily oriented towards river-borne timber and grain. However, several engineering industries were brought in during the war, and it is now well connected with nearby oil and hydro-power. Ulyanovsk has grown twice as fast as Penza since 1939.

In addition to the dozen or so cities mentioned above, which all have over 100,000 inhabitants, there are some two dozen smaller towns which still have more than 50,000 people. Most of these have at least doubled since 1939 and some, mostly oil towns, have been born since then. In this connection, it is of interest to note the current construction of an oil town (*Nizhnekamsk*) on the Kama, at the tip of the Kuybyshev reservoir, with an eventual planned population of a quarter of a million.

PROSPECT

Here is a region, then, which is emerging from the chrysalis stage between an existence of several centuries as a rather stationary agrarian frontier, ethnically fragmented by a long succession of human cultures, and that as a highly industrialized and urbanized melting-pot, strategically placed on the population map of a new super-state.

In some ways the development of this region since the war is reminiscent of the experience of Texas and its neighbours at a slightly earlier stage. As regards stage (and latitude), but not scale, Alberta might be more comparable. However, neither of these areas has as focal a situation in the developing geographical scene in North America as the Volga–Ural has in the developing Soviet state. Virtually all contact between the older controlling regions of the Soviet Union and the newer resource-rich eastern regions must inevitably be funnelled through this region.

One must keep in mind that the age of oil has only just been inaugurated in the Soviet Union, and it looks as if this region will become as much the geographical prototype of the new oil–chemical industrial revolution as the Donets basin was of the coal–steel revolution. The power-affluence of the region is first and foremost a case of oil, since it enjoys absolute dominance over the regions in this, whereas the considerable gas output is just one among several equally productive regions, and the hydro-electricity should eventually be overshadowed by the Angara–Yenisey region. The extension of the transport net and secondarily of the farming operations are most important, but the fundamental basis for the growth of the region in the foreseeable future is fuel and its associated chemical by-products.

Within the region it seems likely that the Kuybyshev district is on the threshold of a clear dominance in its affairs, but there will clearly be substantial growth of the other established large cities, as well as of new ones.

In the national context the crucial elements in the transformation of the region's relative significance are the overnight emergence of a former poverty-stricken area as the country's most valuable powerhouse and the assumption of a role as a bridge and a cross-roads instead of a frontier. In today's conditions it seems bound for an auspicious future, the zenith of which is not yet in sight.

CHAPTER TEN

The Ural–Ob Region

THE Ural mountains, although hardly more effective a physical obstacle than the Volga, long symbolized for Russians the edge of the civilized world. Therefore, despite the adventurers who crossed over early, lured by the riches of furs and metals, the eastern Urals with the boundless plain of Western Siberia beyond, is essentially a new land, whose present character has been created well within the last century. The gently folded Urals, reminiscent in many ways of the Appalachians, are now the gateway to a new Russian Mid-East—a rather more raw counterpart of the American Mid-West.

While there are obviously deep-seated differences between North American and Russian institutions and traditions, the epic of the settlement of Siberia has come much closer to the American or Canadian experience than has anything elsewhere in the Russian realm. This was where family homesteading and democratic attitudes had begun to develop the firmest roots. The land was empty of any previously established sedentary population groups, and only in the dry steppe margins of the south did the Kazakh nomads constitute a settlers' problem similar to the North American Plains Indians.

The region is bounded on the west by the Ural crest, which in general marks off the great metal-processing centres from the oil–timber–river

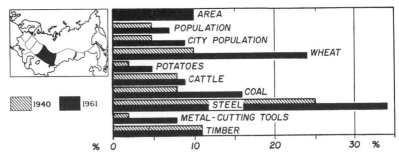

FIG. 33—Location and importance of the Ural-Ob Region in relation to the Soviet Union as a whole, for certain selected items

country of the Volga basin. The edge of the massive forested swamps of the middle Ob basin marks the northern boundary of the region and sets it apart from these northern wastelands, which are usually lumped in with it in the Soviet regionalization schemes. On the southern side the Kazakh uplands separate the extensive grain farming, metal industries and Russian ethnic preponderance to the north, from the desert of Middle Asia to the south. On the east the region has been made to fade out around the Ob, since most of the Siberian farmland is west of that river and to the east the great Kuznetsk coal basin begins to dominate the landscape. There was a time when the latter region and the Urals were so interdependent that to separate them would have been a difficult operation, but now the Kuznetsk region is quite self-contained and is looking increasingly eastward. The Karaganda coal basin, on the other hand, in spite of being loosely bracketed by Soviet planners with the so-called Third Metallurgical Base, is much more firmly linked with the Urals, and comes within our region.

In area, latitude and continental position this region is comparable with the northern Mid-West states of Minnesota, the Dakotas and Montana plus the Prairie Provinces of Canada, but has twice their population. Like this part of North America, metals (especially iron) and grain (especially wheat) provide the traditional bases of economic life and wealth.

The Ural–Ob region possesses a range of useful metals and minerals such as few, if any other parts of the world can equal, and it is a major focus for metallurgical industries in the Soviet Union. Although short of industrial energy and particularly coke, it is set between the two great power-surplus regions of the country, the Middle Volga and the Kuznetsk basin and transport facilities are fairly good. It is one of the two major bread-baskets of the U.S.S.R. and the seat of one of the most spectacular, if risky, extensions of grain-farming in this century.

The youth, wealth and industrializing pace are reflected in the fact that the cities of the region have grown faster than those of any other part of the Soviet Union in recent decades. The region also has more manufacturing per head of population than any other in the country. At the same time it is one of the few parts of the country where the rural population has also increased recently. Thus here we have a region in the heart of the continent which has developed rapidly since before the war but, in spite of its undoubted resources, has recently slowed down.

THE NATURAL HABITAT (Fig. 35)

Here, more than in any other part of the Soviet Union, the absence of relief has given the climate full rein to create a latitudinal succession of

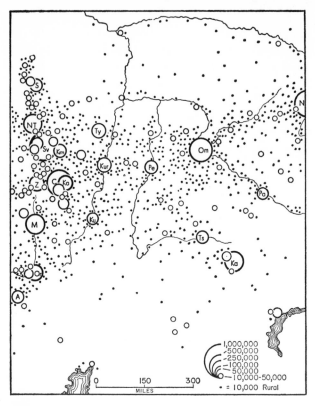

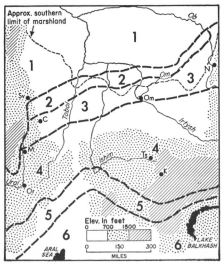

FIG. 34—Ural-Ob: population. Key to cities: A=Aktyubinsk, C=Chelyabinsk, Ka=Karaganda, Km=Kamensk, Ko=Kopeysk, Ku=Kustanay, Kur=Kurgan, M=Magnitogorsk, N=Novosibirsk, NT=Nizhnii Tagil, Om=Omsk, Or=Orsk, Pa=Pavlodar, Pe=Petropavlovsk, S=Serov, Sv=Sverdlovsk, Ts=Tselinograd, Ty=Tyumen, Z=Zlatoust

FIG. 35—Ural-Ob: nature. 1=tayga, 2=birch forest, 3=wooded steppe, 4=steppe, 5=semidesert, 6=desert

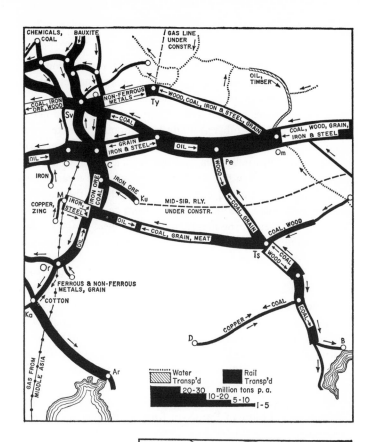

FIG. 36—Ural-Ob: movements

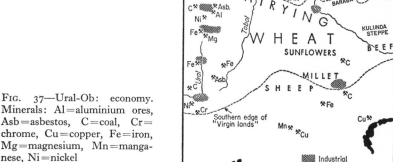

FIG. 37—Ural-Ob: economy.
Minerals: Al=aluminium ores,
Asb=asbestos, C=coal, Cr=
chrome, Cu=copper, Fe=iron,
Mg=magnesium, Mn=manga-
nese, Ni=nickel

195

natural zones, if we except the longitudinal intrusion of the Urals. Dryness and continentality are the keynotes to the natural characteristics of almost all the region. Only on the northern and north-western margins, in the forests, does precipitation exceed evaporation, and here the absence of relief enables an embarrassingly large amount of water to stand about. Over most of the region evaporation could devour over twice as much precipitation as actually falls, and ten times as much in the desert margins of the south. Even in the wooded steppe, where a mean annual precipitation of about 13 inches, concentrated largely in the growing season, is normally adequate, the total may vary from 23 inches to 7 inches. Further south, in the steppe, the increasing waywardness of the rainfall, alongside a decreasing mean expectation, makes farming a perpetual gamble, as on the dry grassland margins of North America or Australia.

In spite of the long and severe winters (the mean temperature hovers about 0° F. in January and snow lies for five months at Omsk) the summers are warm and the length of growing season (at least five months) and accumulated temperature budget are adequate for grain-farming everywhere south of the forest–swamp line, and comparable with conditions astride the Canadian–U.S. boundary area in the Great Plains. Although the heat budget quickly increases southwards from the main farming strip, a decline in effective moisture proceeds alongside it.

There are some differences to note between the various soil-vegetation zones here and those of European Russia. The deciduous mixed forest of Central European Russia does not cross the Urals, because of the winter cold. Instead, a narrow strip of birch forest is wedged between the tayga and the wooded steppe and the typical copses of the wooded steppe are also of birch, though the Scots pine actually extends further south into the steppe in places. The black-earth is usually shallower than its European counterpart but is often richer in humus. The soils of the wooded steppe range from *solonets* to *podzols* and only the northern part of the steppe zone proper is covered with black-earth, the southern part being typically the poorer chestnut-brown soil commonly associated with the semi-desert.

Although surfaces are frequently as flat as a table for hundreds of miles, a peculiar feature of the West Siberian plain is that it is spattered with several thousand lakes. They are especially numerous and large between the Ob and the Irtysh (Baraba and Kulunda steppes) and while some are salty and some fresh, all are shallow and are said to be the result of the settling and contracting of soils owing to heavy leaching of salts. These lakes often contain carp and other fish, and some of them are commercial sources of soda and Glauber's salts.

Another aspect of nature in the raw which, like the climate, makes this region harsher than corresponding parts of European Russia, are the plagues of mosquitoes, horseflies and grasshoppers.

This predominantly lowland region is framed by the Urals on the west and the Kazakh uplands on the south—both elderly ranges which have been worn down to a shadow of their former selves. The eastern side of the Urals consists of parallel longitudinal ridges, like the Appalachians, and a steeper and more fractured slope than is found on the western side. The central section between Sverdlovsk and Chelyabinsk is the most completely eroded, and latitudinal communication is much easier than it is in the northern or southern sections, where the mountains are higher and may reach 5,000 feet in places. Limestone topography is common in the south, and all along the eastern slopes are revealed igneous intrusions, rich in a variety of metals. The plateaux of the Kazakh uplands are even more subdued in relief than the Urals and are made of hard crystalline rocks like granite, with many intrusions of metals and minerals.

These two ranges are connected by a low ramp which is breached by the narrow Turgay gate, through which overflow water poured south into Middle Asia in the Glacial period from the Great Ob lake, which was blocked on the north by ice. If the Davydov Plan for recreating that situation with concrete instead of ice ever materializes, the Turgay gate will necessarily be the link between the waterlogged north and the parched south.

THE PEOPLING OF THE REGION

The first Russians to view the vast marshy plains of Western Siberia, no doubt 'with a wild surmise', apparently did so from the extreme north of the Urals astride the Arctic circle. They were men of Novgorod who, in the late thirteenth century, sailed up the Pechora river system and then down the Ob–Irtysh system as far as Tobolsk, in quest of fur. Although thenceforward the crossing points of the Urals moved steadily southward, the Russian activities were largely confined to the forest lands until the eighteenth century.

The real breakthrough into Siberia came in the late sixteenth century, with the expedition organized by Yermak, a legendary Cossack soldier of fortune, financed by the Stroganov family who had grown rich on salt and furs in the Kama valley. Within fifty years these counterparts of the *coureurs des bois* of French Canada had reached the Pacific, penetrating and plundering the great forests of Siberia with very little hindrance from the scattered native population. Their route over the Urals lay between Perm and Tyumen, and this remained the chief entry point into Siberia until the nineteenth century.

During the seventeenth century iron and other metals were discovered in the Urals and the beginnings of the great metallurgical base are to be seen in the peasant workshops. There was plenty of accessible timber for charcoal and the period of the Swedish wars and the reign of Peter the Great saw the establishment of the iron industry on the eastern slopes of the central Urals. Labour was at a premium, and the iron-masters were empowered to acquire serfs skilled in the trade and often concealed fugitives from European Russia. The late eighteenth century became the golden age of the Urals iron industry and put Russia in the forefront of the world's metal-producing countries—there were even notable iron exports to Britain. However, the nineteenth century saw Russia fall seriously behind Western Europe and the Urals stagnate and eventually collapse alongside the rise of the coke-rich Ukraine.

By the middle of the nineteenth century there was still only a sprinkling of true agricultural settlers along the strip of wooded steppe which would later be traversed by the Trans-Siberian railway. However, by all accounts, these old settlers were generally better off and more independent than their counterparts west of the Urals. Large numbers of deportees had passed this way but were mainly destined for Eastern Siberia. The Kazakhs still held their lands and lived their nomadic life in the steppelands proper, though this was beginning to break down owing to Russian commercial incursions and the use of their lands as a springboard for the conquest of Middle Asia.

The scene about 1900

The great stream of Russian migration into Siberia was coming into full spate at the turn of the century. In round figures, some seven million people crossed the Urals in the last century of Tsarism, half of them during the first fourteen years of the twentieth century.

The formal abolition of serfdom in 1861 had not immediately opened the flood-gates to Siberia, as the government was scared of vagabondage and a labour scarcity in the old regions and therefore hindered rather than encouraged movements to Siberia. Besides, the chief destination of migrating peasants was still the half-empty steppes of the Ukraine (New Russia) and the Kuban.

From the 1880s, however, the main current veered eastwards across the Urals and for the first time in the nineteenth century free settlers outnumbered convicts among the arrivals in Siberia. The government also began to frame a belated but positive migration policy, with subsidized travel, land survey, medical centres and above all the construction of the Trans-Siberian railway. The railway from Chelyabinsk reached the Ob in 1896 and the previous route of entry through Perm and Tyumen fell into abeyance. The new railway gave an immense fillip to settlement, especially in the steppe land to the south, which had hitherto been mainly the preserve of the Kazakhs.

The effect on exports of farm products was striking. During the first decade of the twentieth century wheat exports from Siberia increased five-fold and butter ten-fold, while half of the meat consumed by Moscow and St Petersburg in 1911 was supplied from Siberia. Large stretches of the Baraba steppe and the lake-strewn regions were drained. The epic of the opening up of the North America prairies was being repeated, and with comparable speed.

The boom in agriculture at the turn of the century was in sharp contrast to the depression in industry. The once dominant charcoal-based iron industry of the Urals had quickly become eclipsed by the new coke-based furnaces of the Ukraine, on which all capital investment was being concentrated. The Urals industry was tied to depleted forest reserves and handicapped by obsolete equipment and relative inaccessibility. Only the mining of precious metals, like gold and platinum, made headway, with foreign capital, during this period. The industries of the West Siberian plain were almost entirely tied to agriculture like flour-milling, distilling, tanning and butter-making, and were thus increasing. Most of the industrial units were of the *kustarny* or cottage type and they were mainly concentrated in the Tobol valley around Tyumen and Kurgan.

On the eve of the Second World War

After the civil war period, in which this region was particularly prominent, there was a stagnant condition for a time, owing to the scaling down of the former massive food export programme and the continued backwardness of the Urals iron industry.

However, a resurgence of regional development took place in the early thirties, with the decision to modernize the Urals metallurgical industries and to supply the missing coking coal for this by setting up the famous Ural–Kuznetsk Combine involving a thousand-mile shuttle service of coal —west—and iron—east—along the Trans-Siberian railway.

There was a net increase of some three million people between 1926 and 1939, most of it accruing to the Urals, in response to this development. This period had seen the mushroom growth of prototype Soviet industrial cities like Magnitogorsk, built on iron, and Karaganda, on coal. A notable feature of the changing industrial structure of the Urals was the great increase in the relative importance of engineering industries compared with crude metal reduction. At the same time the Urals greatly stepped up its output of long-exploited metals like iron and copper and became the chief Soviet source of new and vital ones like aluminium, nickel and chrome.

There was considerable railway building in the region between the wars, notably the longitudinal linking of the Urals metal centres, and the Karaganda–Magnitogorsk line. The Trans-Siberian was also double-tracked.

THE PRESENT ECONOMY (Fig. 37)

This region probably received a more powerful shot in the arm during the war than any other region, both through being a reception area for physically dismantled industrial plants from the west, and by attracting a disproportionate amount of new industrial investment on strategic grounds. In addition, great new metal resources, especially iron, have been uncovered here since the war, and there has been an extension of farmland unprecedented in this century. All in all, this region's diverse economy has bounded ahead at an unusually rapid rate since before the war, and has steadily enhanced its relative importance in the nation as a whole.

Metals for industry

The region is the richest treasure-house of metals in the Soviet Union and this fact underlies the character of industry and explains the region's unique industrial intensity.

Iron remains, as always, the basic metal, and there are scores of still productive deposits strategically placed throughout the inhabited Urals. The high-grade magnetite of Magnitogorsk and Tagil (Vysokaya), which was so crucial in the last war and is still going strong, is however destined for extinction within the next generation at the present rate of mining. Therefore other sources of ore are being earmarked and two in particular are destined to be the dominant suppliers for the Urals steel industry for the foreseeable future.

Pride of place goes to the enormous discoveries made recently in the Turgay region, astride the Tobol valley two hundred miles east of Magnitogorsk. These deposits of hematite, magnetite and limonite constitute one of the largest reserves in the country—if not in the world. Beneficiated ore from Turgay is already supplying the steel mills of Magnitogorsk and Chelyabinsk.

But the northern steel region of the Urals, about Tagil, is scheduled to depend more and more on the nearby low-grade but enormously large deposit of Kachkanar (which accounts for three-quarters of the proven iron ore reserves of the Urals). In addition the Atasuy group of hematite and magnetite deposits, south of Karaganda, is providing the basis for the recently constructed giant steel works near the latter city.

There are few non-ferrous or ferro-alloy metals not present in significant quantities in the region, and in most cases this region is the country's chief producer. Copper is particularly abundant in the southern desert margins (at Dzhezkazgan and Lake Balkhash) and in the southern Urals (Gay) and bauxite, for aluminium, in the northern Urals (Severouralsk). As for alloy metals, the southern Urals (Khrom Tau) contains one of the world's great chrome deposits while nickel and chrome are found in abundance in the central Urals (Ufaley). Even the rare alloys tungsten and molybdenum have recently been found in significant quantities in the semi-desert zone— they were until recently in short supply within the U.S.S.R. Manganese, the most widely used ferro-alloy, has recently been developed in the Karaganda region and the Urals, and it is said to be much less phosphoric than the large deposits of Georgia and the Ukraine. Zinc is found in association with copper, and sulphur is an important derivative from the plentiful pyrites of the Urals. Among other important metals produced are magnesium, titanium, platinum and gold (the two latter not as significant as they once were), and the region is also the chief Soviet source of such useful substances as arsenic and asbestos.

The problem of energy

Since the end of the charcoal days, the shadow of a fuel and power shortage has been cast across the rosy picture of metal resources.

The most troublesome shortage has been coking coal for the metallurgical industries. Four-fifths of the total coal reserves in the region of the Urals consists of lignite, which is used widely as a base for electric power-stations. Karaganda (and its neighbour Ekibastuz) alone sends to the Urals more hard coal than the latter produces itself. This Karaganda–Ural connection is gradually assuming a relatively greater significance than it had in the early days of the Kuznetsk–Ural Combine—the distance is considerably shorter. However, the Urals still receives, in absolute terms, more coal from Kuznetsk than it does from Karaganda. In addition to this import, there are plans for making a direct rail and/or water connection between the Urals and the Pechora coking coal basin of Arctic European Russia.

If the whole region has a chronic shortage of the right kind of coal, it has to import almost all its requirements of other forms of energy, notably oil and gas. A number of pipelines carrying oil and oil products now run between the Volga–Ural fields and Novosibirsk, and the south Urals is also connected with Caspian and Volga oil by pipeline. But the most spectacular project completed in the recent Seven Year Plan in this respect is the natural gas pipeline between the Middle Asian fields and the Ural, Turgay and Karaganda industrial regions. Apart from the cheapness of gas as power, the advent of plentiful gas to the iron and steel furnaces should have a marked effect on the quantities of coke required. Peat continues to be used in some of the Urals' electric power-stations and, at the other end of the scale, an atomic power-station has recently made its appearance near Sverdlovsk. Hydro-electric power is at present insignificant within the region.

The spectacle of streams of energy being pumped into this region from power-affluent neighbouring zones on all sides is eloquent testimony to its magnetic qualities as an indispensable industrial base.

The industrial pattern

This region is one of the two great concentrations of steel and rolled metal products in the U.S.S.R. and its output of these things is closely comparable with that of its rival, the Ukraine. By contrast, in 1940 it was less than half as productive as the Ukraine. The eastern flank of the Urals is more specialized than any other part of the Soviet Union in metal-working, at all stages. A rough grouping may be made into two industrial regions, based largely on raw material connections. The northern cluster, centred on Sverdlovsk, Nizhnii Tagil and Serov is to be based increasingly on local low-grade iron ore from Kachkanar and secondly the bauxite of Severouralsk, while for coking coal it looks to the Kuznetsk basin, to Kizel across the Urals and perhaps eventually to the Pechora basin. The southern cluster, centred on Chelyabinsk–Zlatoust, Magnitogorsk and Orsk is increasingly being oriented to the iron of Turgay and the coal of Kara-ganda, with gas injections from across the Urals and eventually from Middle Asia. The Karaganda region is the major outlier of the steel industry beyond the Urals itself, but scattered about the Kazakh upland, as in the Urals, are isolated oases of non-ferrous metal-working.

The industrial character of the towns which are spread across the farming belt of Western Siberia is totally different, the processing of farm and forest products and the making of machinery for these primary industries being the major activities.

Farming and forestry

This is the great bread-basket reserve of the Soviet Union. Over a quarter of the country's grain output comes from here and in recent years nearly half the country's wheat.

In its specialization on grain farming and its relative neglect of non-cereal crops, this region is as different from European Russia as are the North American prairies from the old farm-lands east of the Appalachians. But as in the American prairies the agriculture, at least in the better-watered belt of the wooded steppe, is becoming more diversified by the introduction of maize and other fodder crops for the livestock industry. The north-western part of this farm belt, between Tyumen and Omsk, has been a major dairy-farming area since the nineteenth century and has a substantial surplus of butter. In the drier areas to the south large-scale ranching activities are carried on for meat and wool, and here the Soviet state farm practices and the age-old nomadic herding of the Kazakhs have come into contact and not infrequently into collision. The northern half of the inhabited Urals, with the neighbouring lowlands towards Tyumen, is one of the most important parts of the country for lumbering and wood-processing.

The Virgin Lands

The frontier of farming settlement has been ever-present and restlessly advancing during the last two centuries. The most recent and perhaps the final act in this drama began in 1954 with the inauguration of the 'virgin and long-idle lands' plough-up campaign. In two years 90 million acres of virgin land were brought under the plough, at least two-thirds of which were in the Ural–Ob region. However, since then the area has been plagued with drought and a good deal of well-publicized mismanagement, and the net increase in production has been somewhat below expectations. At the same time the authorities recognized that they were gambling heavily with the rainfall, and claimed that the enterprise would be justified even if there were only two good years out of five. The chief aim of the scheme was to build up a wheat reserve area to enable the Ukraine and North Caucasus regions to switch over to maize and other fodder crops in the more urgent drive to increase meat and milk production (Plate XI). To a notable extent this has been done, but the danger still exists that, through insufficient attention to periodic fallowing and other essential conservation measures, a dust-bowl situation may develop, as it did in very similar country in the United States.

Transport (Fig. 36)

The dominant flow of freight in this region is east–west and the railway is King. Most of the new railway-building in the U.S.S.R. since the war has been in this region and most of the new construction in the recent Seven Year Plan has also been carried out here. The new developments have in general intensified the dominance of the easterly flow.

Until after the war the latitudinal traffic was inevitably confined to the fifty-year-old Trans-Siberian, and its offshoot from Omsk to Sverdlovsk. This line was sorely overloaded after the inauguration of the Second Metallurgical Base, founded entirely on the east–west shuttle-service of Urals iron and Kuzbas coking coal. Soon after the war the South Siberian railway was completed, linking the Kuzbas directly with Magnitogorsk in a broad sweep, passing through Tselinograd (then Akmolinsk), destined to be the hub of the Virgin Lands. This new line gave Karaganda a direct route to Magnitogorsk, thereby enabling Kuzbas coal to be channelled to the central and northern Urals. At present, to some extent through the conversion of narrow to broad gauge, another link, called the Middle Siberian, is being built to pass from Magnitogorsk to Barnaul, through the Turgay ironfields and the northern part of the Virgin Lands.

The most important goods moving westwards are coal and wheat, while oil is probably the chief eastbound item, by pipeline as well as rail. The loads of iron ore from Kustanay (Turgay) to the Urals are fast increasing and the longitudinal Ural railway, completed during the war, carries mainly metals and fuel.

The rivers act as useful north–south routes in Siberia, especially the Irtysh below Omsk, timber being the main item of freight.

The remarkable extension of the means of transport in this region is barely keeping pace with the demand. In addition to the railways, the actual and planned pipelines, principally for oil and gas products, can be expected to assume a growing significance in coping with the steady increase in ton-mileage, chiefly in heavy raw materials.

THE PRESENT POPULATION

This region is now the home of about 15 million people, nearly double the numbers at the beginning of this century. Since the eve of the Second World War, its city population has more than doubled, and since rural population has held its ground to an unusual degree, this region has probably experienced as fast a rate of overall population growth as any during this period.

Unlike the Volga–Ural region the ethnic picture is basically simple— a Slavic amalgam of the Russian, Ukrainian and Belorussian, the influx of which has all but swamped the scattered nomads who inhabited the area before. Although over half the area under review is in the Kazakh Republic, this is now an anachronism which will probably be rectified by an administrative change before long. Barely a quarter of the inhabitants of the Kazakh Republic are now Kazakhs and most of these are in its Middle Asian part. There can be no denying the fact that the interests of the Kazakhs of the northern steppe and that of the Russian settlers were long incompatible, as in the case of the Indians of the American Great Plains. They have fought bitterly both expropriation of their grazing routes and subsequently collectivization and many left for Sinkiang or other parts of non-Soviet Asia. At present, though, there seems little sign of conflict and most of those Kazakhs remaining in the north have entered the melting-pot of the industrial towns or the giant state farms.

The rural distribution (Fig. 34)

The majority of the people of the region are still classified as rural, and in some of the *oblasts*, like Tyumen or Pavlodar, the proportion rises to three-quarters. However, in those *oblasts* where industrial cities have grown and where the environment is unkind to farming, the rural proportion drops to a fifth. The Omsk *oblast*, in the heart of the agricultural belt but having varied industries as well, conforms to the regional average in this respect. Over much of the area, particularly the steppe country of northern Kazakhstan, the absolute increase in the rural population since 1939 has been notable, in contrast to the prevailing decrease over most of the country. However, in relative terms the rural component in the total population has been dropping steadily.

As in the Volga–Ural region, rural settlement meets climatic barriers on the north and the south—the cold, sodden forests and the arid, salt-ridden margins of the semi-desert. Drainage schemes here, irrigation and dry farming schemes there, have nibbled at the margins of this latitudinal farming belt, but have only modified in detail, not fundamentally altered, this basic picture.

However, unlike the Volga–Ural region, the prime historical axis of communication runs with the grain of the natural zones, not against it. The zone of greatest rural population density still follows the wooded steppe from Chelyabinsk through Omsk to Novosibirsk, never far from the

Trans-Siberian railway. However, even here the density nowhere equals that found in the farming lands west of the Volga, though it is appreciably greater than in the more comparable Canadian Prairies.

Aside from this main core of rural settlement, one should note the market-garden–dairying settlement around the urban centres of the Urals, the growing clusters associated with the state farms of the Virgin wheat lands around such centres as Tselinograd, Kustanay and Pavlodar, and also the more densely settled Altay wooded steppe on the eastern edge of the region.

There are large patches of land, such as the steppe between Tselinograd and Pavlodar, which are still essentially empty of rural population, owing to poor soils, brackish lakes and inadequate moisture. Although some of these areas will undoubtedly be claimed for farming eventually, it is possible to envisage also an eventual retreat from some marginal areas now being farmed.

The cities

At least one in every three people in this region now lives in a city of over 50,000, compared with one in five in 1939. In the aggregate, these cities have more than doubled their population since 1939, a much faster rate of growth than that of the cities of equivalent size in California over the period. The net addition of such city-dwellers since 1939 has amounted to some three millions.

There are now three cities of well over half a million people, while there were none before the war, and at least thirty cities with more than 50,000 inhabitants, at least double the number there were before the war. By investigating the details of just *where* this dynamic city growth has taken place, we can nail down and assess the character of the geographical revolution which has taken place.

The metal-based cities of the Urals represent nearly two-thirds of the city population of the region as a whole. Two giant cities, Sverdlovsk and Chelyabinsk, dominate the Urals and to some extent polarize the distinctive character of the north and southern clusters, each with its own particular orientation with regard to sources of the raw materials and energy on which they depend.

Sverdlovsk (formerly called Yekaterinburg) (850,000) is the largest city of the whole region and one of the ten largest in the U.S.S.R. Since the eighteenth century it has been the focal city of the Urals and is still today the strongest claimant for the position of regional capital. However Chelyabinsk has recently been hard on its heels, and Sverdlovsk's ultimate supremacy within its region is nothing like as assured as that of Kuybyshev or Novosibirsk within theirs.

The city was born during the metal rush to the Urals under the aegis of Peter the Great in the early eighteenth century, when rich copper deposits were discovered nearby. But the main routeway across the Urals lay well to the north and it was only later in the century when the Great Siberian Highway was laid from Perm via the long valley of the Chusovaya, tributary of the Kama, that the seal was set on the city's focal position. A century later the first railway across the Urals reached Sverdlovsk from Perm, fourteen years before the Trans-Siberian reached Chelyabinsk. At present seven railways lines converge on the city, but most of these enter from a northerly direction and it seems that Sverdlovsk will increasingly look to its northern hinterland for the ores (especially iron and bauxite) and energy (coal from Kizel and perhaps eventually from the Pechora, and gas from the lower Ob at Berezovo), on which its steel and engineering industries, which range from mining equipment to aircraft engines, depend.

Chelyabinsk (750,000) has grown at a much faster rate than Sverdlovsk during the period of the Soviet planned economy (population: 1926—60,000; 1939—270,000). In 1897 and again in 1926 it was less than half the size of Sverdlovsk, and no larger than several other Ural towns which have since sunk into relative obscurity, but at the present rate the two giant cities should draw level in a few years. (In fact if *Kopeysk* (170,000), the lignite mining city within ten miles of the centre of Chelyabinsk, were included, which it could well be, Chelyabinsk would even now be considerably larger than Sverdlovsk.)

Although dating back to Peter the Great's time, Chelyabinsk remained an obscure settlement, mainly engaged in flour-milling until 1892, when the arrival of the prospective Trans-Siberian from the west put it on the map as the gateway to Siberia. Like Sverdlovsk it is situated opposite a low pass and the valley-head of a convenient tributary (the Ufa) of the Volga system. Unlike Sverdlovsk, it is not in the forests but squarely in the fertile wooded steppe and on level land. It has made considerable use of its local lignite and of a variety of metals in its immediate hinterland to the west, especially Bakal iron. It is now becoming increasingly dependent on iron from the new Turgay fields to the south, and Karaganda coal, while it is on the oil pipeline axis from the Volga fields to Siberia and has gas piped to it from Middle Asia and from Saratov. The city was a prime wartime reception area for dismantled factories from the West; its industries today, mainly concerned with metals, range from steel and non-ferrous metal-working to tractors, aircraft and machine tools. In addition, the city's chemical industries benefit from its position on the oil pipelines, and its food-processing industries from the railway which serves the main farming regions of West Siberia.

The great industrial developments in the southern Urals since the 1930s have greatly enhanced the position of Chelyabinsk which is now the mid-way point between the most northerly metallurgical cluster around Serov and the southerly one around Orsk. This fact, together with its excellent railway links with all points of the compass and its position on the most beaten east–west track of the Soviet Union and in the centre of the agricultural axis, augurs very well for the future of the city and possibly for its regional pre-eminence in the long run.

Below these twin regional centres in the hierarchy are two steel-making cities with over a quarter of a million people each, and another which should soon be in the same rank. These cities contain three out of the four fully integrated iron and steel plants of the Urals—the other being at Chelyabinsk. The oldest is *Nizhnii Tagil* (360,000) which was founded in the early eighteenth century in the midst of a very rich group of iron ore deposits and good charcoal forests. As an iron town it shared in the general Urals decline of the later nineteenth century but the first Trans-Ural railway line from Perm to Sverdlovsk passed through it, and in 1897 it was second in size only to Sverdlovsk among the Ural towns. But it had less than a 40,000 population even in 1926 and its ten-fold growth since then has been tied up with steel and such heavy engineering industries as railway rolling stock, bridges, etc. It is easily accessible to plentiful reserve supplies of iron (notably Kachkanar), copper, bauxite and several alloys.

Magnitogorsk (330,000) is barely thirty years old and has become famous as the prototype of the All-Soviet planned industrial city. A few years after its foundation, next to a fabulous mountain of magnetite in the steppe on the banks of the Ural river, it had become the major metallurgical centre of the U.S.S.R. It is still said to turn out the cheapest steel in the country, but the local ore deposits are likely to be exhausted in the foreseeable future. Already the neighbouring Turgay mines are stepping into the breach and are destined to take over responsibility for a doubling of the Magnitogorsk steel output during this decade. Coking coal comes from Karaganda and the amount of this required has now been substantially reduced by the piping of gas from Middle Asia and the Volga–Ural fields.

Orsk (including Novotroitsk, 260,000), which was a small fortress town in the nineteenth century, on the edge of Kazakh country, is the newest of these fast-growing integrated metal complexes. Situated, like Magnitogorsk, in steppe country along the Ural river, it has, within a short range,

VIII. The City Hall at Rostov-on-Don, designed in the shape of a tractor to represent the city's major industry.

IX. A Black Sea beach in August, on the outskirts of Odessa.

X. An oil-field south-west of Ufa. Note the old strung-out village and the rolling landscape of the Ural foreland.

XI. A wheat-field in the Virgin Lands steppe country, a hundred miles west of Tselinograd.

rich iron ore and very plentiful supplies of copper, chrome and nickel, with bauxite and asbestos not far away. It is connected by oil pipeline with the Volga and the Caspian, and with gas from Middle Asia.

Coking coal comes from Karaganda. Orsk is specializing in high quality nickel and chrome alloy steels and it has a direct rail connection with the markets of European Russia and the central Urals. This group of towns is well-located and well endowed in a national context for what it is doing, and can be expected to continue to grow. It has all but quadrupled its population since 1939.

Other cities in the Urals area having 100,000 people or more include the old town of *Zlatoust* (170,000), west of Chelyabinsk on the Trans-Siberian, which makes special steel for the car industry and has miscellaneous engineering activities, and *Kamensk-Uralsky* (150,000) an aluminium processing city south-west of Sverdlovsk, which has almost trebled in size since 1939, and gets its bauxite from the northern Urals (Severouralsk).

The centre for the northernmost industrial cluster in the Urals, *Serov* (100,000) is another steel city. It has nearby not only iron ore, but also the bauxite mentioned above, manganese and lignite. (Charcoal is also still used here to some extent.) Surrounding it is one of the major wood-processing areas of the Soviet Union.

The antipode of Serov on the southern edge of the industrial Urals is *Aktyubinsk* (110,000), a nineteenth-century fort, like Orsk, and an agricul-rural centre in the Virgin Lands, which is being drawn into the economic orbit of the Orsk complex, and now processes alloy metals with the nearby nickel and chrome and makes specialized electrical equipment.

Most of the cities of the West Siberian lowland were little more than overgrown villages before the Trans-Siberian railway came through in the mid-nineties of the last century. Except for some mining towns, their characteristic location is at the junction of rail and river.

Omsk (650,000) is the only very large city, second only to Novosibirsk in all Siberia. It was founded as a frontier outpost on the right bank of the Irtysh in the early eighteenth century, and grew slowly as the Siberian agricultural migration gathered momentum. The Trans-Siberian railway reached it in 1895 and the population trebled between 1897 and 1911. It has more than doubled since 1939.

Omsk has, for such a big city, an unusually isolated situation, half-way between the urban clusters of the Urals and the Kuzbas. However, set in the middle of the fertile wooded-steppe belt, where the railway (and several oil pipelines) cross a great navigable stream, it is well-placed to focus much of its fast developing hinterland. Its industrial structure is very diverse, including the traditional processing of grain and livestock products, agricultural machinery and chemicals, the latter based on one of the largest oil refineries in the country. Looked at in the context of the increasing wealth and the industrial developments of the Soviet Union and the improving means of transport, not least by pipe, Omsk seems bound for a steady, if not a rapid growth in the foreseeable future.

There are several agriculturally oriented cities in the West Siberian lowlands, which were comparable in size with Omsk towards the end of the nineteenth century, but are now barely a quarter its size, in spite of having grown very rapidly since 1939. *Tyumen* (170,000) the oldest city in Siberia, was founded in the late sixteenth century by Yermak on the Tura river at the westernmost head of navigation of the Ob–Irtysh waterway system. It also became for a time the eastern terminus of the Siberian Highway and in 1885 of the first railway pushed beyond the Urals. Thus for three centuries before the building of the Trans-Siberian railway to Omsk, Tyumen was the real gateway to Siberia for settlers, adventurers and convicts alike. Even around 1900 it had more people employed in industry than any other Siberian city. Thereafter it stagnated rather until about 1940, since when it has almost doubled. Being on the border between good lumber-land and good dairy-land, its industries are still oriented mainly towards these products, but it continues to build ships as well. *Kurgan* (170,000) and *Petropavlovsk* (150,000), each an Omsk in miniature, are situated where the Trans-Siberian crosses the Tobol and Ishim respectively, rivers of a much lower scale of utility than Omsk's Irtysh. Kurgan is the more important railway junction; it makes agricultural machinery and has recently grown at a much faster rate than Petropavlovsk, trebling since 1939.

The development of the Virgin Lands Project has been reflected in the very rapid growth of a number of cities for processing, transport and the manufacture of agricultural equipment. The centre of this whole new area is *Tselinograd* ('City of the Virgin Lands', formerly called Akmolinsk, 130,000) at the junction of the South Siberian and Trans-Kazakhstan railways. Other cities in this region which have grown quickly are *Pavlodar* (110,000) where the South Siberian crosses the Irtysh, and *Kustanay* (100,000), also now the centre of the vast Turgay iron-mining region.

The enormous importance of the railways in the growth of all these Siberian farming towns is suggested by the fate of *Tobolsk*, one of the oldest towns in Siberia, at the confluence of the Tobol and Irtysh. It was still one of the two or three largest centres of Siberia in 1897, with 20,000 people, but thenceforth was stopped in its tracks, a monument to the forest-adventuring of a bygone day.

Of the non-agricultural urban settlements in the area, based on mining, the only one of any size in the great mining and metallurgical complex on the edge of the desert is *Karaganda* (with its satellites Temir Tau and Saran 550,000). With only a hundred or so people in 1926 this growth has been phenomenal, even by Soviet standards, and has been associated with the emergence of one of the three major sources of good coking coal in the U.S.S.R. In recent years Karaganda coal has become vital to the Urals, and half of the output found its way there in 1955. Karaganda is at present in the throes of a massive expansion in steel-making capacity. This expansion is based on local coking coal and nearby iron ore. The most serious long-term deficiency in a desert area—water—is being remedied by the construction of a 300-mile canal from the Irtysh. Also the nearby coalfields of *Ekibastuz* are now to be the base for massive electricity generation, to be transmitted to Voronezh in southern European Russia. Recent additional discoveries of iron and other metals in this semi-desert region, coupled with good coal and communications, make Karaganda's further development as a great coal and steel centre quite feasible. But compared with the clusters of Donbas or Ural, it is still a rather lonely outlier among steel towns, on the very edge of the inhabited agricultural triangle of the country.

THE PROSPECT

In a real sense the Ural–Ob region has become a vast heartland in reserve for the Soviet Union in the last two or three decades, and its relative importance in the national scheme of things is clearly growing. In the production of steel and grain, the twin staples and indicators of the modern Soviet economy, it is closely comparable in importance with the Ukraine, and no other Soviet region seriously competes with it. Until the Second World War the Ukraine stood unchallenged.

Although one might say that these developments had quite deep roots, going back to the Ural iron-workings of the eighteenth century and the agrarian homesteading of the nineteenth, this would be rather misleading in view of the catastrophic decline of the Ural industry in the late nineteenth century and the inter-war hiatus in Siberian farming. The building-up of the modern patterns of strength can more realistically be dated from the decision to set up the Ural–Kuzbas steel Combine in the thirties on the one hand and the inauguration of the Virgin Lands scheme and its wartime antecedents on the other.

In spite of the recent expansion of farming, the ratio of industrial employees to total population is greater here than in any other region and the phenomenal growth of the cities reflects the march of industry in the last two or three decades. What are the realistic prospects for future continuance of this growth? Thanks largely to major new discoveries of iron and other ores over the last decade, there is now looming up a surplus, rather than a shortage, of raw materials for the dominant metal-based industries, and indeed massive expansion in this field has been under way in the Seven Year Plan. Shortage of energy is likely to remain the chief industrial bottle-neck, but multiple pipeline transfusions of oil and gas from across the Urals and from Middle Asia, coupled with the well-established Karaganda–Ural coal movements, have done much to reduce the problem. Although it would be futile to forecast a further extension of the Virgin Lands plough-up campaign of the last few years, it is reasonable to expect a less spectacular but none the less real increase of farm production through intensification, conservation and increased productivity—though the possibility of an actual decline in acreage and output due to shortsighted mining of the Virgin Lands cannot be ruled out.

Although the Ural–Ob region has lately stolen a good deal of the Ukraine's thunder, it has done so largely under the initial stimulus of war or threat of war on the western borders, and this has counterbalanced its undoubted liability—distance from the major population concentrations. However, cheaper and more abundant raw materials, added to improved communications (most of the new Soviet railways are being laid in this region), and the still powerful but imponderable strategic factor, seem likely to continue to outweigh problems of distance and a small population (barely a third of the Ukraine's). With the neighbouring Middle Volga and Kuzbas regions, it is developing some of the characteristics and potentials of a continental Mid-East, as a counterpart (though much poorer agriculturally) to the American Mid-West. The future rate of development will depend heavily upon continuing government policy towards the 'eastern regions', and the increasingly acute problem of shortage of skilled labour in this rather unattractive environment.

Within the region there has been, since the thirties, a notable southerly shift of activity, accelerating trends which date back several centuries. This is reflected in the overhauling of Sverdlovsk by Chelyabinsk, the mushroom growth of giant steel complexes such as Orsk, Magnitogorsk and Karaganda, the farming cities of the Virgin Steppe, and the feverish railway building south of the Trans-Siberian. The forests of the early buccaneering days have receded still further from the geographical spotlights of today.

CHAPTER ELEVEN

Central Siberia

WITHIN this region of mountains and foothills, where all the great rivers of Siberia take their rise, is to be found the Soviet Union's greatest store of accessible industrial energy. This primary fact sets the region apart from its neighbours, and in particular from the Ural–Ob, in spite of their many historical, climatic and industrial continuities.

The two cores of the region are the Kuznetsk coal basin and the Yenisey–Angara–Baykal water-power zone, and they are growing together increasingly, becoming more interdependent. On the north the region fades away below Tomsk, taking in the entire course of the Angara and the rail-navigation head on the Lena, thus including all the broadly settled country and the sites for power and industrial projects. On the south the arbitrary limit is necessarily the frontier with Mongolia and China, and the distinct climatic and human break, just south of the Irtysh, with Middle Asia. The Ob river itself, with its cities, notably Novosibirsk, and the distinctive Altay Steppe are included in the region because of their close functional connection with the Kuznetsk area and because even the story of its agricultural settlement has been quite distinct from that of physically similar farmland further west. The Trans-Baykal lands have been included, in spite of considerable differences in

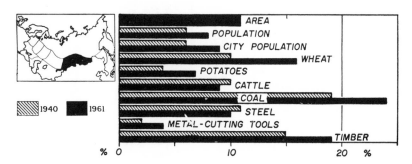

FIG. 38—Location and importance of Central Siberia in relation to the Soviet Union as a whole, for certain selected items

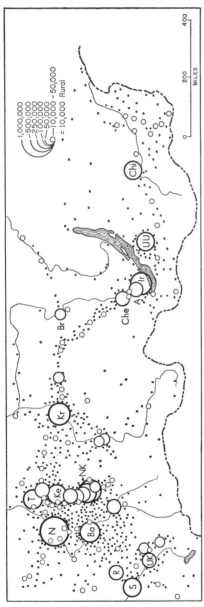

FIG. 39—Central Siberia: population. Key to cities: A=Angarsk, Ba=Barnaul, Br=Bratsk, Che=Cheremkhovo, Chi=Chita, Ir=Irkutsk, K=Kemerovo, Kr=Krasnoyarsk, N=Novosibirsk, NK=Novokuznetsk, R=Rubtsovsk, S=Semipalatinsk, T=Tomsk, UK=Ust-Kamenogorsk, UU=Ulan Ude

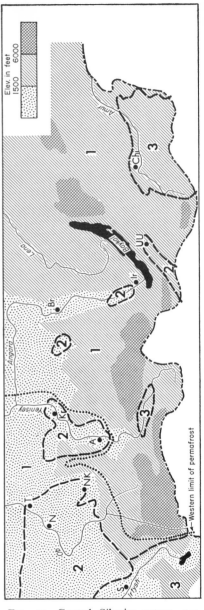

FIG. 40—Central Siberia: nature. 1=tayga, 2=wooded steppe, 3=steppe

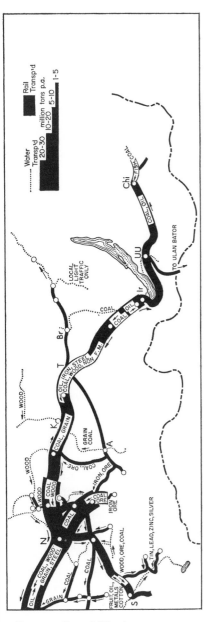

FIG. 41—Central Siberia: movements

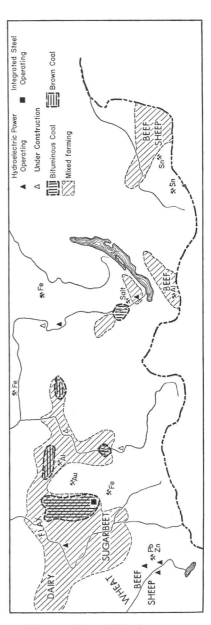

FIG. 42—Central Siberia: economy

ethnography, economy and rate of growth, largely because of juxtaposition. A case could perhaps be made for including this area, for hydrographic reasons, with the Soviet Far East, except that the northward bulge of Chinese territory effects a separation similar to that of the state of Maine between Quebec and the Maritime Provinces of Canada.

In spite of the exclusion of the vast northerly wastelands, this region is large and elongated. It covers much the same area as the inhabited part of Canada east of the Rockies and has the same population. Novosibirsk, the largest city of the region, is on the latitude of Edmonton, Alberta, and both cities are near the junction of steppe and boreal forest. With Novosibirsk superimposed on Edmonton, Irkutsk would be some four hundred miles north of Winnipeg and Chita at the southern tip of Hudson's Bay.

In its population numbers, ethnic make-up and recent city growth-rates it is very similar to the Ural–Ob region. Both regions have had a complicated record of Russian settlement which goes back at least to the seventeenth century, and yet the dominant characteristics of the present economy are of very recent origin. The new character of the Central Siberian region has not yet assumed as definite a form as in the case of the Ural–Ob, but the metamorphosis has begun in earnest.

This region, thin end of the Russian inhabited triangle as it is, is the most fluid and active of the Soviet industrial frontiers today. Its liabilities of natural environment and, above all, of sheer distance from the population centre of the Soviet Union apparently do not weigh heavily enough to prevent the development of its superb endowments in industrial energy.

THE NATURAL HABITAT (Fig. 40)

The physical pattern of this region is very broken and complicated and this has meant a restricted habitat for human settlement. It is also a transitional zone between the tayga and the steppe and the great variations of relief have produced the whole range of the natural zones within the region, from tundra to desert. However, the geological and morphological complexity has resulted in great variety and richness of metals and minerals and excellent conditions for water-power generation.

An eastbound traveller along the Trans-Siberian railway, after several days of an almost featureless landscape, could not fail to notice the increasingly hilly and broken relief after crossing the Ob. Next to the Mongolian border is a succession of deeply dissected mountains, trending generally more or less east–west, of which the chief are the Altay and Sayan, to the west of Lake Baykal, and the Yablonovy, to the east.

These mountains are really eroded plateaux, with general levels around

7,000 feet and dome-like summits, but there are occasional peaks which top 14,000 feet, which are glaciated and covered with permanent snow and ice. However, in general these ranges are less rugged, less high and contain far fewer glaciers than the mountains of Middle Asia to the south.

The immense geological dislocation which has affected the region is shown by the trench in which lies the 400-mile long Lake Baykal, measuring over 12,000 feet from the tops of the lake-shore mountains to the bottom of the lake—the deepest continental depression in the world. Earthquakes and hot sulphur springs are common and parts of the lake-shore are emerging or subsiding.

The giant rivers of Siberia—the Ob, Irtysh, Yenisey, Lena and Amur—all have their origin in this region or just over the Mongolian border and together with the Angara (Plate XIV), which receives the total overflow from Lake Baykal, they constitute a tremendous reservoir of power.

The greater distance from the Atlantic and the disjointed relief combine to give most of this region a more severe winter temperature and more intra-regional variations in precipitation than one finds in the plains of the Ural–Ob. The January average mean temperature decreases from around zero ° F. in the Kuznetsk basin to about −20° F. in parts of the Trans-Baykal region. The fact that patches of permanently frozen ground are common throughout the region, except in the Altay Steppe and Kuznetsk basin, testifies to the length and severity of the winter. The clear bright winter weather and the very thin snow cover contribute to the maintenance of permafrost. However, Lake Baykal exercises a notable moderating influence on the temperature. It does not freeze over until January and its temperature at that time is at least 15° warmer than at Ulan Ude, 50 miles to the east. The varied fish populations of the lake, and also the endemic seals, are able to move to deeper water during the winter. The Angara outlet never freezes and unequal freezing on the lake makes winter crossings hazardous.

The most widespread soil-vegetation zone is the tayga-podzol, both as a latitudinal zone in the north and an altitudinal zone in the south—predominantly pine and fir in the west and south, and larch in the north-east. However, there are small, populated enclaves of steppe and wooded steppe along the Trans-Siberian route west of Lake Baykal, and in particular the important Altay Steppe along the Ob. The latter has, for Siberia, an unusually fine and extensive spread of fertile deep black-earth coupled with relatively reliable and sufficient rainfall. It is also the only part of this region which has an accumulated heat budget equivalent to that of the wooded steppe further west, or even the districts just south of Moscow.

The westward-facing slopes of the Altay and Sayan, which receive over 60 inches of rain per annum and are well-clothed with forests (Plate XVI), contrast with the scrub or poor steppe of enclosed basins such as that of the upper Yenisey in Tuva, where the annual precipitation is only 7 inches.

Above the tree-line, i.e. about 5,000 or 6,000 feet, the bleak and often flat upland surfaces are variously classed as tundra or mountain meadow. They are largely covered with peat-bog, mosses and lichens which provide a habitat for wild reindeer, but can hardly be compared with the lush alps of Switzerland or the Caucasus.

THE PEOPLING OF THE REGION

When the Russian fur-traders first penetrated this region at the beginning of the seventeenth century they encountered a number of nomadic groups. The largest of these, the Buddhist Mongol Buryats, who had earlier displaced the Yakut and driven them into the northern forests, put up fairly stiff resistance. Moreover, the Russians, who had thus far travelled the great rivers of the Siberian forests without serious hindrance, came up against their first roadblock when they attempted to descend the Amur. This was the Chinese Empire, which held sway over what is now Mongolia, Tuva and the Altay mountain country, as well as Manchuria and what is now the Soviet Far East. Thus the Trans-Baykal area remained a frontier outpost of Russia against China for two centuries until the weakening of the latter allowed Russia to resume its advance to the south-east.

A string of trading posts was set up along the southern edge of the forests in the first half of the seventeenth century, to become the cities of today, among them Tomsk, Krasnoyarsk, Irkutsk, and Chita. But it was not until the eighteenth century that appreciable settlement occurred in the Altay Steppe and foothills—now much the richest and most populous agricultural part of the region. Settlement was soon stimulated further by the discovery of lead, silver and copper in the foothills area, which provided a growing local market, so important a consideration in an area as isolated from Russia proper. The Ob river, flowing northward through the fertile lands towards the main east–west Siberian post highway and the site for many towns, was also very useful.

These new settlements were still subject to raids from the south and a line of Cossack forts was built along the southern edge of the fertile land. Further, it should be emphasized that the scale of settlement remained small compared with that of the latter part of the nineteenth century.

The scene about 1900

The government restrictions on migration to Siberia following the end of serfdom strongly favoured the Altay lands over other areas of potential settlement between it and the Urals because they had become, for the most part, the personal property of the Tsar and were open for peasant lease when other areas were not. As a result of this and the unusual fertility of the area, the Altay attracted about two-thirds of all the migrants to Siberia in the last three or four decades of the nineteenth century.

The Trans-Siberian railway reached the Ob in 1896 and resulted in an unprecedented flood of migration accompanied by a rapid reduction of the proportion accruing to the Altay Steppe. During the latter half of the century the whole position of the Central Siberian region had been made less peripheral by the Russian acquisition of Middle Asia and the Far East. In the early years of the twentieth century, as the railway pushed on to the Pacific, and Russian interests were infiltrating Manchuria, there was tremendous population growth in the region.

In 1897 Tomsk and Irkutsk were the only cities of 50,000 but by 1911 Barnaul, Krasnoyarsk, Chita and Novosibirsk had been added, the two latter increasing seven-fold between these two dates.

The railway quickly opened up the area to export markets in agricultural products, but the trade was almost entirely confined to these products, in spite of the region's great wealth in energy and metals. The bottom had dropped out of silver-lead mining in the Altay foothills by the late nineteenth century and, although the coal of the Kuznetsk basin had been known and, to a very slight extent, mined since the eighteenth century, its use was still almost entirely confined to bunkering for the new railway.

On the eve of the Second World War

In 1930, the decision was taken, after prolonged arguments, throughout the 1920s and even earlier, to set up the Ural–Kuznetsk Combine. Thus, by transporting ore 1,500 miles from the Urals, the excellent Kuznetsk coking coal was brought into use on a substantial scale for the first time. A major steel industry was built up, and a remarkable growth of cities made possible in the western part of Central Siberia. Novosibirsk, in particular, grew faster than any other Soviet city of comparable size between 1926 and 1939—a period of rapid urban growth generally in the U.S.S.R.— and emerged much larger than the other cities of the region. Coal and steel cities mushroomed in the Kuznetsk basin, the most notable case being Novokuznetsk (then called Stalinsk)—a small village in 1926, which by 1939 had overtaken Tomsk—the largest town of the whole region at the beginning of the century. Except for Chita and Tomsk, all the other sizable cities of the region doubled their population in this period, but this was a commonplace among Soviet cities in that period. It was unequivocally the age of coal—in spite of the immense water-power resources of the region, not a single dam had been constructed by the eve of the war.

Individual peasant migration to the Altay Steppe had continued fitfully during the first Soviet decade but was prohibited in 1930. The subsequent urban growth provided, of course, a thriving local market especially in dairy produce, and the building of the Turk-Sib railway to Middle Asia from Novosibirsk in 1930 opened up another outlet for the grain surplus of Siberia. So the agricultural districts continued to prosper (rural population did not decline, as it did in most parts of Russia) and became more integrated with their region than they had been earlier.

THE PRESENT ECONOMY (Fig. 42)

The economy of this region is probably in a more active state of flux than any other in the country. It is at the farthest effective end of the Volga–Baykal zone along which the dominant wave of Soviet migration and economic development has been moving in recent decades. Further, the region can be divided into two parts as regards *stage* of industrial development: (a) the Kuznetsk–Ob–Altay part, which achieved its take-off point in the thirties on coal and steel and (b) the Yenisey–Angara–Baykal part, which is only just entering an era of cheap power and consequent power-intensive industries. These two parts have begun to grow together into a functioning unit capable of substantial industrial output and also an export of power to less favoured parts of the country.

Abundant energy

Within this region over half the Soviet *accessible* reserves of coal and over half the accessible potential water-power is stored up. This overriding fact is, more and more, guiding the character of the economic development of the region and its place in the national economy.

In terms of current output of energy, there is no doubt at all that coal takes pride of place. The Kuznetsk basin (Kuzbas) is by far the most important reserve of accessible good quality coal in the Soviet Union and has more than trebled its production since the end of the war. Although its production is still less than half that of the Donets basin (Donbas), it has contributed most to the weakening of the latter's formerly almost monopolistic position on the national scene; during the German occupation it necessarily became the chief energy reserve for the war effort. Although the two fields are about the same size, the Kuzbas, apart from its far greater reserves, can produce good coal at less than half the Donbas cost, owing to mechanization, exceptionally thick seams (sometimes about 100 feet), the good opportunities for open-cast mining, and the generally sulphur and ash-free nature of the coal. Half the Kuzbas coal is still shipped to other regions, notably the Urals. Although coking is the chief use to which Kuzbas coal is put, on the spot or outside, the recent emphasis on thermal power-stations is providing an increasingly important outlet.

This applies even more to the massive coal deposits which lie along the Trans-Siberian railway from the Yenisey to beyond Lake Baykal, in particular the black coal of Cheremkhovo on the Angara and Minusinsk, and the brown coal of the Kansk–Achinsk basin. The latter, which contains most of the accessible Soviet brown coal reserves, is being intensively developed for electricity production, in spite of the competitive presence of better quality coal on its margins, to say nothing of hydro-power.

The immense water-power potential of the upper reaches of the Yenisey and Ob systems has hardly begun to be developed. The extent to which this available power will be harnessed, and when, will depend much more on such matters as short-term policies in favour of thermal electricity from cheap coal, the suitability of the region for industrial growth and the technology of long-distance transmission, than on the physical excellence of the rivers *per se*, in terms of long-term costs, for power development.

Although giant hydro-electric dams played an important role in the Communist symbolism of the last years of Stalin, none had been completed on any Siberian river by the time of his death in 1953. Soon afterwards, however, stations of moderate capacity (about half a million kilowatts) were completed on the Angara (Irkutsk) the Ob (Novosibirsk) and two on the upper Irtysh. However, these have been dwarfed by the scale of the dams subsequently built, under construction or planned in the region, whose average ultimate capacity is to be 4 or 5 million kilowatts, which is larger than anything existing in the world at present. The first of these, at Bratsk on the Angara began producing power in 1961 and its twin at Krasnoyarsk on the Yenisey is almost finished (Plate XV). Three or four more on this scale are planned for the Angara and Yenisey, but they could be shelved at this early stage. Be that as it may, the large amounts of power which have become available in the early 1960s have already provided new opportunities for this region as an industrial base, as well as a large-scale exporter of energy.

Raw materials and the emerging industrial pattern

Many previously latent industrial raw materials have been turned into realistic resources by the advent of energy. Metals are much the most important of these and the region is being built up primarily as a 'third metallurgical base', essentially an easterly expansion from the Kuznetsk steel region. Most of the iron ore requirements for the latter now come from the southern margins of the coal basin itself, and not, as previously, from the Urals. But ultimately more important are the very large reserves of good iron ore in the region just east of the Angara at Bratsk, which may possibly be made the basis of an integrated steel works at Tayshet, as well as satisfying the growing needs of the Kuzbas. There is fuel and power in abundance for this new extension of the steel industry, with the Cherem-khovo and Kuzbas coking coals and the very cheap hydro and thermal electricity being produced in the vicinity.

Non-ferrous metal processing is a power-intensive activity which is quickly becoming attracted to the region. Of these aluminium is the most important and nepheline and other aluminium ores are already being reduced at several places in the Angara and Yenisey valleys, while Ural bauxites are processed in the Kuzbas. In addition there are two long-established polymetal areas in the region—the important lead-zinc-copper district of the upper Irtysh around Ust-Kamenogorsk, and the now rather less important silver-lead mines around Nerchinsk, east of Chita. Tin has now become the most significant metal of the Trans-Baykal area, south of Chita.

The chemical industry is another group which is rapidly being extended eastwards from the original coal-based nucleus of the Kuzbas to the Angara–Yenisey. Irkutsk in particular, with its nearby coal, hydro-power and salt, and its new oil refinery processing oil from the Volga–Ural fields, is scheduled for considerable development of a wide variety of chemicals. Another important raw material for the chemical industry, and more besides, is timber. The northern part of this region is becoming the most important timber-processing area of Siberia, and large-scale plants for pulp, cellulose and also furniture are operating at such power-rich sites as Krasnoyarsk and Bratsk.

Transport (Fig. 41)

Such a rapid regional transformation as the present one, with the Kuzbas looking increasingly east for its raw materials and a conscious effort being made to promote a new regional interdependence, is inevitably limited by a lag in the provision of adequate transport links.

There is still a contrast between the railway network west and east of the Yenisey. The Kuzbas was provided with an additional line to the Urals (the South Siberian railway) in 1952 and this has since been extended to the Yenisey. However, east of this river the old Trans-Siberian was still the only through line in 1964, although recently a very important link has been completed between the trunk line at Tayshet and the River Lena, passing through Bratsk and a rich iron ore region. Moreover an extension to the South Siberian was completed in 1965 from the Kuzbas to Tayshet, designed specifically to link up with Angara iron ore directly. Although insignificant when compared with the railways, the rivers are locally important as feeders for bulky goods, in particular timber, and such cities as Tomsk, Novosibirsk and Krasnoyarsk are notable transfer points. The Yenisey is navigable below Abakan, and the Ob and Irtysh are also in their inhabited reaches. The Angara is navigable from Lake Baykal to the Bratsk rapids but, by an oversight, the dam built at Irkutsk included no provision for locks, although this will no doubt be remedied. At present the middle third of the Angara is beset by rapids but, if and when the whole series of dams is completed, there will be a through waterway from Lake Baykal to the Arctic.

Coal, wheat and timber are the chief commodities going west on the Trans-Siberian and south on the Turk-Sib to Middle Asia, while oil, by pipe and rail, predominates in the opposite direction.

East of Lake Baykal eastbound freight, chiefly coal and oil, begins to exceed westbound, and the traditional connections with China and Mongolia are reflected in the branching off of main railways to Ulan Bator and Peking (built 1955) and from Chita into the heart of industrializing Manchuria (though the latter link is hardly living up to the expectations of a decade ago, or even those of 1900).

Farming

From the agricultural point of view the Yenisey marks off two worlds. To the west there is the Altay Steppe along the Ob—first-rate black-earth country, relatively mild and moist, long a Mecca for peasants and, in spite of the rapidly increasing local urban markets, still a notable exporter of food. To the east there are a few patches of farmland strung out like beads along the Trans-Siberian railway, with problems of drought, or permafrost or cool summers—marginal in one way or another.

Wheat and dairy products (especially cheese) are the chief farm exports from the Altay Steppe—Middle Asia being an important outlet—and in the neighbourhood of the industrial cities market-gardening and pig-breeding are combined with dairying. The area has played a major part in the recent Virgin Lands development. The snow-fed rivers are suitable for irrigation, and sugar-beet has been introduced on a considerable scale in the south, while the region has shared in the national maize promotion programme, at least as far as 'green mass' is concerned.

In the eastern patches wheat is also grown, but oats, barley, rye and buckwheat become increasingly widespread. The scarcity of tolerable farmland to provide the basic needs in fresh food for the rapidly growing urban population has been shown by the public clamour over the projected hydro-electric flooding of the Ilim valleylands. Beyond Lake Baykal beef cattle and sheep-rearing become dominant, and this is the traditional land of the Buryat Mongol horsemen. Some reindeer and yaks are reared in the mountains bordering on Mongolia.

THE PRESENT POPULATION

The population of the region probably doubled during the first quarter of the present century and has doubled yet again since then. By comparison this is what happened to the British population in the first and second halves respectively of the exceptional nineteenth century. Moreover, the region seems to be continuing to grow and in terms of trends, plans and resource opportunities, the development of the region may still be in an early stage.

The present numbers (some 16 million) are much the same as those of the Ural–Ob region and the city growth of the last two decades has also been closely comparable—they are certainly the two fastest-growing parts of the country. Both have two-thirds of their population concentrated in their western quarter—i.e., in the case of Central Siberia, west of the Yenisey.

Ethnically the population is overwhelmingly Slavic in speech and origin. However, the 5% or so who compose the native population form coherent entities in certain areas. The most important group is the Buryat Mongols, numbering a quarter of a million or as many as all the other native groups of the region combined. They are Buddhists and much of their homeland, east of Lake Baykal, was controlled by the monasteries, as in Tibet. They were nomads and have conducted for three centuries a stubborn but inevitably a losing battle against the onset of Russian settlement, and are now fully collectivized or employed in the cities.

The Tuvinians, some 100,000 people related to the Kirgiz and enclosed in their mountain basin, have been left on their own to a remarkable extent until recently. They had come under a vague Russian tutelage in 1911

NOVOSTI PRESS AGENCY

XII. A view of Novosibirsk on the Ob, the largest city of Siberia.

XIII. A blast furnace at an iron and steel works on Novokuxnetsk in the Kuznetsk basin.

NOVOSTI PRESS AGENCY

SOVIET EMBASSY, WASHINGTON

XIV. The Angara river near Bratsk before the building of the hydro-electric dam

XV. The hydro-dam at Krasnoyarsk on the Yenisey, under construction in 1963. Its ultimate capacity is planned to be 5 million kilowatts.

NOVOSTI PRESS AGENCY

and this situation was not changed appreciably during the period 1921–44 when Tuva (or Tannu Tuva) was nominally an independent State, like the Mongolian People's Republic. It was incorporated officially into the Soviet Union in 1944 and a road was built over the Sayan mountains linking the isolated community with the Yenisey at Abakan. Since then its integration into the Soviet economy has, of course, been strengthened, but its offside, cul-de-sac position is ensuring that it can maintain an identity more easily than other peoples whose homelands lie on the through-ways of Russian migration.

Other native groups, scattered and smaller, are the Khakass, Kazakhs and Altaytsy of the mountains and foothills of the Altay and Sayan. Although they were all nomadic herdsmen and hunters when the Russians arrived, there is evidence that the Altaytsy had decayed into this state from a one-time metal-working and agricultural civilization.

The rural distribution (Fig. 39)

About 4 in 10 of the people of the region are classified as rural, which is rather less than the national average. However, this overall figure masks the difference outlined above between the Altay–Ob country— the most densely peopled farmland of all Siberia, and the rest of the region, where rural settlement is meagre and patchy and decidedly overshadowed by the urban populations.

The main concentration in terms of density (at least 10 people to the square kilometre) is a north–south belt from the Irtysh near Semipalatinsk to Tomsk, and centred around Barnaul. This is essentially the Altay Steppe together with the Kuzbas, which is marked off on the west by the much poorer, emptier Kulunda-Baraba steppe region, on the east by the Salair range, and on the north and south by the tayga and the semi-desert respectively.

Leading off from this, like the handle to a pan, and following the Trans-Siberian lifeline closely, is a succession of small clusters of rural population of which the most important are the Yenisey valley from Abakan to Krasnoyarsk, the upper Angara around Irkutsk, and around Chita and Ulan-Ude, beyond Lake Baykal.

To the south, in the Sayan mountain area, is a large blank on the map of rural settlement, except for a few pockets such as the Kyzyl basin of Tuva. Similarly rural settlement quickly fades away beyond the coniferous forest fringes, and becomes, as everywhere in the northlands, an exceptional phenomenon subsidized to serve exceptionally valuable enterprises.

The cities

In dynamics and quantity, the pattern of cities in this region is similar to that of the Ural–Ob. Each of them has over a third of its population in cities over of 50,000, has more than doubled its city population since 1939 and also has added some three millions to its city population since that date. Each has about thirty towns of over 50,000 today, or double the pre-war number.

Novosibirsk has, however, outdistanced the other cities of both regions, may well become the metropolis of all Siberia and, with about a million inhabitants, is among the eight largest cities of the Soviet Union (Plate XII). Since 1939 it has grown faster than any other Soviet city of comparable size and is still doing so. It is a true child of the railway age, and symbolizes the opening up of modern Siberia in the same way as Chicago does for the Mid-West of the United States—in fact it is sometimes spoken of as the Chicago of Siberia.

Novo-Nikolayevsk, as it was then called, was founded in 1893, on a virgin forest site on the right bank of the Ob, at the point where the Trans-Siberian was to bridge the river. By 1926 it had 120,000 inhabitants, but it was still well behind Omsk, and its unequivocal arrival as a regional capital dates from 1930 when the Ural–Kuznetsk Combine was established and the Turk-Sib railway to Middle Asia was completed. The subsequent building of a double-track rail link between the growing cities of the Kuzbas and Novosibirsk set the final seal on its supremacy and gave it a similar position to Kharkov in relation to the Donbas, or Düsseldorf and Cologne in relation to the Ruhr.

Its position on the navigable Ob at about the junction of forest and steppe, at right angles to the railways and tapping some of the finest timber and farmland of Siberia, enhances its nodal position still further, and the recent arrival of oil pipelines from the west and the local building of a hydro-electric dam have strengthened its already favourable energy base. Thus the very advantageous convergence of routes on the city, effected largely in this century, has singled it out as the regional capital of Siberia, and also given it the largest, fastest-growing and most varied industrial base within a thousand miles radius or more. Steel and engineering products, especially tractors, cars and ships, make up the major industrial category, but meat packing (the original echo of Chicago), flour-milling, cotton, woodworking and chemicals are also notable. Consumer-goods for this very large city and its burgeoning hinterland—far removed from European Russia—are obviously becoming increasingly significant. Considering the city's necessary connections with the newly developing territories to the east, it is difficult to foresee a stop to its present astonishing momentum of growth.

The Trans-Siberian railway which gave birth to Novosibirsk almost dealt a death-blow to *Tomsk*. Like Novosibirsk today, Tomsk was the largest city of all Siberia in the late nineteenth century, possessing, for example, the only Siberian university. It is the oldest settlement of the region, having been founded in 1604 (just before Jamestown, Virginia, the first English settlement in North America, was being planted), on the high right bank of a tributary of the Ob, at the southern edge of the forest, a suitable point of departure to the east for the fur-seekers. Throughout the eighteenth and nineteenth centuries it was a key point on the Siberian post-road system. It was spared the fate of Tobolsk, which has stagnated for more than a century, by the building of a branch line to the Trans-Siberian and because of the Kuznetsk development immediately to the south, with which it has since been partly integrated. With a quarter-million people, it makes electrical and other equipment for the Kuzbas and is also a major wood-processing centre. It is still quite sharply differentiated from the young coal and steel cities to the south—though now, for practical purposes, in the Kuzbas industrial region, it is still not *of* it.

These Kuzbas cities, strung out over some 200 miles south of the Trans-Siberian, still maintain a recognizable separateness, and are not to be considered as a tightly packed Ruhr-type conurbation. Most of them have grown from villages, or less, during the Soviet period. The largest city is *Novokuznetsk* (410,000, formerly called Stalinsk), the centre of steel and aluminium making and also heavy engineering such as locomotives (Plate XIII). The two main coal-mining and chemical centres are *Kemerovo* and *Prokopyevsk* (each about 300,000), while there are five other coal-mining towns of rather more than 100,000 population.

A very different group of cities is that lying south of Novosibirsk, between the Ob and the Irtysh in the rich farmland of the Altay Steppe. They were generally founded in the early eighteenth century as outposts against the Kazakhs and centres for the beginning of farming or even mining activity. They are now mainly devoted to processing farm products such as grain, meat, wool and sugar, or manufacturing farm machinery, while they took up cotton manufacturing after the rail connection was made with Middle Asia in 1930.

The most important of these, situated at the point where the Turk-Sib railway crosses the Ob, is *Barnaul* (350,000), which is about double the size of the others—*Semipalatinsk*, where the Turk-Sib crosses the Irtysh, *Biysk* and *Rubtsovsk*, where a large tractor works was set up during the war. Mention should also be made here of the very different city of *Ust-Kamenogorsk* (180,000) upstream from Semipalatinsk, which specializes in metal processing, with two hydro-electric dams behind it, and copper, silver, lead and zinc nearby; it has grown eight-fold since 1939.

A very important regional focus, half-way between Novosibirsk and Irkutsk, is *Krasnoyarsk*, which is approaching half-a-million and has grown at much the same speed as Novosibirsk since 1939. It was founded as one of the easterly string of fur-posts in the early seventeenth century, in the very narrow strip of wooded steppe which lies between the northern tayga and the Sayan mountains, where the navigable Yenisey has high banks. It was the Hobson's choice for a settlement in the early days and again when the Trans-Siberian arrived. Further, on a railway map of the U.S.S.R., Krasnoyarsk stands out still as the only link-point between the western half of the country, which has a relatively dense network, and the eastern half with, until recently, its solitary Trans-Siberian trunk line.

The city's industrial potential is great and its development still at an early stage. It could hardly be better situated as to energy, since it stands in the middle of the largest and cheapest brown coal deposit of the country (Kansk-Achinsk), where open-cast mining and large thermal stations are producing much cheaper electricity than in the Kuzbas or places further west. In addition there is a giant (5 million kw) hydro-station approaching completion above the city, and the oil-pipeline from the Volga. Power-oriented industries like aluminium smelting (using nepheline from Achinsk) have begun to be attracted to the city on a large scale, with their by-products—for instance the cement development using silicon waste from the nepheline. Krasnoyarsk has an important chemical industry, notably synthetic rubber derived largely from wood, and also heavy engineering items like mining machinery. Its own resource base, together with its location in between the established Novosibirsk–Kuzbas area and the developing Angara–Baykal area, gives it a particularly bright future.

Irkutsk is another great developing regional focus, also with about half a million population (if we include the nearby new town of *Angarsk*), which has very similar industries, resources and expectations to those just described for Krasnoyarsk.

It was founded on the right bank of the Angara in 1652 at the point, some forty miles from Lake Baykal, where a valley-way crosses the Angara at right angles, giving easy access to the headwaters of the Lena and to Mongolia, as well as east–west. Thus it became the natural administrative and supply centre for the far-flung mining and other activities in Eastern Siberia. By the late nineteenth century it was second only to Tomsk among the Siberian cities, and the railway followed the left bank of the Angara to a point opposite Irkutsk before striking off south, with the result that Irkutsk now, like Krasnoyarsk, lies on both sides of its river.

The local hydro-electric station, the nearby Cheremkhovo bituminous coalfield and salt deposits, and the oil pipeline from the Volga have encouraged the growth of the chemical industry and aluminium smelting to supplement the traditional mining machinery and timber industries. The current development in the hinterland, especially the big dams built or planned further down the Angara and the possible steel plant at Tayshet, are bound to boost the future growth of Irkutsk and its neighbourhood.

In the extensive Trans-Baykal region, east of the Lake, there are only two cities with more than 30,000 population. *Chita* and *Ulan Ude* are almost the same size (just under 200,000) and each has grown by less than 50% since 1939, which is much slower than the average for the Siberian cities west of the Lake. Ulan-Ude (formerly called Verkhne Udinsk), where the Trans-Siberian crosses the Selenga, the main river feeding Lake Baykal, is the administrative centre for the Buryat Mongols. Locomotive building, glass-making and meat packing are the chief industries, and nearby is an old but reconditioned iron foundry at Petrovsk.

Chita is more central for the whole Trans-Baykal region, but slightly smaller than Ulan Ude. It has had a good deal of mining in its hinterland, and controls the fork of the two eastern railways which lead to the Pacific. However, the direct connection with Mongolia and Peking is now by way of the railway which leads south from Ulan Ude. The future development of both of these towns is dependent on an expansion of the rather meagre local resources, on the degree of economic activity in the Soviet Far East and on the long-term relations between the Soviet Union and China.

THE PROSPECT

The Pacific North-West of North America is sometimes called America's Last Frontier, indicating the furthest effective reach of the westerly wave of settlement and economic development which has made such an impression on that continent's history. Similarly the present evidence and that of the long-term plans seems to justify the identification of Central Siberia as Russia's Last Frontier. It is without doubt the most fluid of the country's developing regions, and its regional character has only just begun to crystallize recognizably. The maps of population growth, of accessible resources and of major construction projects, together give a clear impression of a frontier of feverish activity and plenty of realistic promise. But it is equally clear that this activity ends at Lake Baykal, and that the easterly industrial wave which has dominated Soviet history does not extend to the lands of the Amur.

Although most of the region is marginal agriculturally (always excepting the Altay Steppe) there is no question about whether it possesses a solid resource base for industrial development. With the lion's share of the country's accessible resources of coal and water-power, alongside large reserves of the metals, timber and other raw materials which can make use of cheap power profitably, the immediate material conditions for the creation of a major industrial base are there. What is more, the costs of producing such things as pig iron and electricity are stated to be so much lower than they are at places further west that even the fundamental draw-backs of distance from the population centre of the Soviet Union as well as the severe living conditions, can be neutralized. This remains to be seen— it depends very much on the continuance of the long-term government policy of the drive to the east, on technological developments such as the long-distance transmission of electricity and on success in using all the by-products of such substances as nepheline.

Be that as it may, the fact remains that the scale of capital investment and industrial growth in recent years has been so great as to indicate that the major decision to build up the region as the third national base for heavy industry, has become irrevocable. One can distinguish the fast developing core of Central Siberia between Novosibirsk and Lake Baykal, within which three distinct nuclei can be discerned: (1) the Novosibirsk–Kuzbas area, which is much the largest and most maturely developed of the three, with (2) the Yenisey region centred on Krasnoyarsk, and (3) the Angara region which is growing north-westwards from Irkutsk, as young regions on the threshold of massive expansion. Further, all indications suggest that these three nuclei are planned to grow together and become increasingly inter-dependent as parts of the functional complex of Central Siberia.

On an altogether different plane of intensity are the two peripheral agricultural sub-regions of Central Siberia, the fertile Altay Steppe be-tween Novosibirsk and the Irtysh, which will nevertheless continue to be vitally important as the main food producer for the industrial cities, and the Trans-Baykal lands, less important and less well endowed but containing some vital metals, such as tin, and a limited but still sorely needed agricul-tural base.

In the early Russian incursions into this region it was the forest edge of Yenisey–Angara–Baykal which first claimed attention, while the farm-lands and coalfields of the Ob came considerably later. In the modern,

Soviet stage of development, this order has been reversed—the Ob–Kuzbas area coming into its own in the 1930s, while the fifties and sixties are seeing the fulfilment of the lands between Yenisey and Baykal.

Here then, we have a young region, well over a thousand miles in length, which has the population of a Canada, its latitudinal sister, and which, like Canada also, has doubled its population in the first three decades of this century and again in the second three. Like Canada, too, it combines a harshly inhospitable natural environment with fabulous industrial resources and is tied, for markets and capital investment, to very much larger controlling centres of population elsewhere. Given national policies favourable to this region, its development could be very spectacular. However, as in other parts of Siberia and the Far East, problems of labour recruitment are likely to be chronic, and much hinges upon the answers to general questions of the regional allocation of scarce capital, and the degree of success attending the industrial developments of European Russia.

CHAPTER TWELVE

The Baltic Region

THE people of a substantial part of Eastern Europe have seemed to be fated to inhabit a shatter-belt, perennially caught between a number of rival expansionist empires. They have become used to finding themselves fought over, bargained for, and pillaged; but on the other hand they have, in the quiet intervals, realized the considerable opportunities for fruitful cultural and economic interchange inherent in this same location.

Such a marchland lies between the Moscow region and the Baltic Sea. Its area is considerably larger than that of present-day Poland, but its population of 22 million is considerably smaller. It displays a complexity in politico-military history and ethnic pattern which contrasts sharply with that of the Moscow region. It has been a meeting place for Germans and Russians, Poles and Swedes, for at least a thousand years, as well as being the home of several coherent national groups—quite distinct from these intruders. Virtually the whole region was over-run and, to a greater or less degree, devastated more than once between 1940 and 1945 and much of it has been effectively part of the Soviet Union for only twenty years.

It is a water-world—a convenient river network which in the early days provided a key to the rise of Novgorod and its empire, while later on the

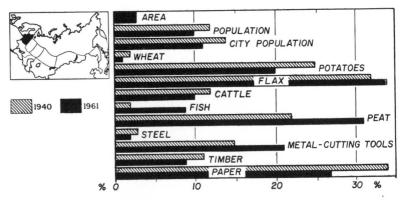

FIG. 43—Location and importance of the Baltic Region in relation to the Soviet Union as a whole, for certain selected items

prolonged striving by Russia for an easy outlet to the European seas eventually produced the phenomenon of St Petersburg—by far the greatest city of the region today. On the other hand, water stands about on the surface of much of the land to an embarrassing degree, which is unusual among the inhabited regions of the Soviet Union.

The Baltic, like the Moscow region, has farmland of indifferent quality and a dearth of industrial resources. But, unlike the Moscow region, it does not have, in today's Soviet Union, the compensating advantages of centrality in relation to the main streams of national development. Leningrad, it is true, inherited an immense man-made nodality but it is a lonely city today, without its extremely favoured Imperial position, and after a terrible wartime experience.

West of the edge of the Moscow region, from Bryansk, Kalinin or Rybinsk, there is a quite sudden falling off in the density of population and nationally significant economic activity. The same rather dismal outlook is evident looking north-west from the Ukraine above Kiev, and the region can therefore be marked off, from an essentially negative standpoint, as lying west of the heavily industrialized Moscow region and north of the wooded-steppe farmland of the Ukraine. Its western limits are necessarily the Baltic Sea and the Polish border. The North begins a very short way beyond the gates of Leningrad. However, on grounds of economic interdependence there is a case for extending the region to include Petrozavodsk, on Lake Onega, and Cherepovets, though on other grounds these towns could also be placed within the North and Moscow regions respectively. It is of interest that this region, as delimited above, coincides almost exactly with the area of the north-west electricity grid, which has so far been of a lower level of intensity than the main European Russian grid.

The contribution of this region is mainly in such products as flax, vegetables, butter and timber, traditional products of a moist and cool land. But, in addition, the inherited skills of Leningrad and one or two other towns have kept them as important manufacturers of specialized machinery, though of a much smaller scale and range than those of the Moscow region. This region's overall relative significance on the national scene has declined steadily since the Revolution and has been shifted off to one side, away from the major geographical currents of Soviet growth. If Leningrad, very much an exceptional case, were excluded, the population of the region would still be heavily rural, and relatively depressed rural at that. Its ethnic fragmentation, indifferent resource base, and minor contribution to the national economy, combine to relegate this region now to one of relatively marginal importance in the national context (Fig. 43).

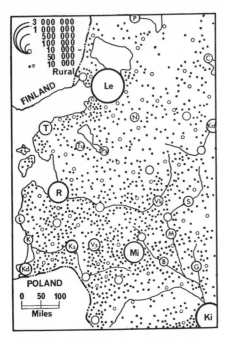

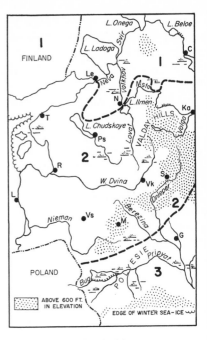

FIG. 44—The Baltic: population. Key to cities: B=Bobruisk, C=Cherepovets, G= Gomel, K=Klaipeda, Ka=Kalinin, Kd= Kaliningrad, Ki=Kiev, Ks=Kaunas, L= Liepaja, Le=Leningrad, M=Mogilev, Mi=Minsk, N=Novgorod, P=Petroza-vodsk, Ps=Pskov, R=Riga, S=Smolensk, T=Tallinn, Tu=Tartu, Vk=Vitebsk, Vs=Vilnius

FIG. 45—The Baltic: nature

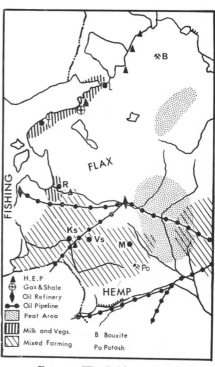

FIG. 47—The Baltic: economy

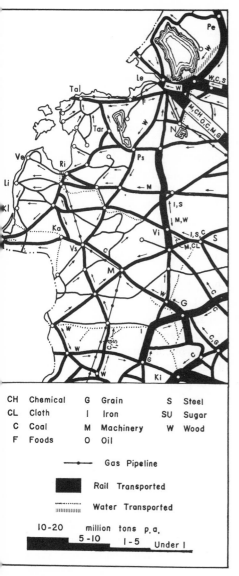

CH	Chemical	G	Grain	S	Steel
CL	Cloth	I	Iron	SU	Sugar
C	Coal	M	Machinery	W	Wood
F	Foods	O	Oil		

—•— Gas Pipeline

▬▬ Rail Transported

┅┅ Water Transported

10-20 million tons p.a.
5-10   1-5
Under 1

FIG. 46—The Baltic: movements

THE NATURAL HABITAT (Fig. 45)

Here, alone among the regions recognized in this book, precipitation exceeds evaporation everywhere. This condition, combined with the fact that most of the land is low-lying and has been drastically disturbed by glaciation, has produced, in general, a watery and rather dismal landscape. Actually the annual precipitation is no more than that of south-east England (19 to 25 inches), with a marked maximum in summer, but the summers are relatively cool (July, 63° F. at Leningrad). Moreover, although by Russian standards the winters are regarded as relatively mild, they are well below freezing everywhere. Leningrad is in fact slightly warmer than Moscow in midwinter, but a raw fog often prevails and the port is frozen from December to April (cf. the St Lawrence). On latitude 60° north, the city is famous for its midsummer 'white nights', but the general climatic amelioration towards the south-west is shown by the significant facts that the Baltic at Kaliningrad is completely ice-free and that the accumulated temperatures in the Pripyat (Pripet) marshes are 50% greater than at Leningrad.

The cool, damp conditions are reflected in the universal prevalence of leached podzolic soils, with a great deal of peat bog, and forests. The majority of the region is in the mixed forest zone, with spruce and pine predominating in the north and oak, birch and hornbeam in the south. North of Novgorod is the tayga proper, but a tongue of mixed forest extends to the Gulf of Finland, with Leningrad as its ultimate northern outpost, coaxed to the utmost by careful planting.

Most of the region is low-lying though not necessarily flat, as the glaciers have strewn about a great deal of material to form a hummocky, morainic landscape. The most prominent of these features is the terminal moraine running through Minsk to Smolensk and Moscow, along which the main lines of communication between Moscow and Western Europe run, and along which the soldiers of Napoleon and Hitler wearily tramped.

On the flanks of this ridge, in northern Belorussia and southern Lithuania, is to be found the only extensive zone of relatively dry land in the Baltic region. On the eastern edge of the region, the Valday Hills, an escarpment smothered by glacial waste and peat bog, form the birthplace of many great rivers—the Volga, Dnieper, Western Dvina and the Msta, upon which the early history of this part of Europe was made.

There are a number of shallow lakes, of which the largest are Chudskoye (Peipus), drained by the river Narva to the Gulf of Finland, and Ilmen, drained by the Volkhov to Lake Ladoga. Lakes Ladoga and Onega, in the hard rock shield country of Karelia, are larger and much deeper (several hundred feet in the north)—their connecting river, the Svir, is a swift hydro-electric stream, and their ultimate outlet, the Neva, only forty miles long, is a miniature St Lawrence, a mile wide at Leningrad.

The north coast of Estonia, with its high Glint limestone cliffs and rocky indentations, contrasts sharply with the low dune coasts and long off-shore sand-bars of Latvia and Lithuania.

THE PEOPLING OF THE REGION

Slavic-speaking peoples had begun to infiltrate this land of rivers and lakes by the fifth century A.D., combining shifting agriculture and stock-rearing with fishing and hunting, increasingly for furs. Fortified trading posts grew up at strategic places along the remarkable water-road which led from the Baltic to the Dnieper system, linking Scandinavia and the Baltic lands with Byzantium and the Eastern Mediterranean. Smolensk, Pskov and Polotsk were among these, but Novgorod, on the outlet from Lake Ilmen, at the edge of the great northern forest, emerged supreme. Founded in the ninth century, it became a powerful and civilized city state which had its emissaries in many lands and a special relationship with Kiev, at the southern end of the forested waterway. When Kiev declined, Novgorod continued to thrive and, in the twelfth and thirteenth centuries, before the rise of Moscow, was the most powerful and most populous city in Russia. Furs were much the most important exports, and Novgorod controlled a forest-empire which stretched to the Urals and even beyond. Honey, wax, flax and hemp were also significant items and farming remained the main occupation of most of the people of the region, whether Slavs or the Balt-speaking peoples further west. Germanic infiltration of the Baltic coastlands, which was to have such an impact for centuries, began with that of the merchants of the Hanseatic League in ports like Riga and Königsberg, and the Teutonic Knights frequently clashed with the men of Novgorod.

Although Moscow had fallen heir to Novgorod's dominions in the fifteenth century, it was kept away from the Baltic coastlands for a further two centuries. A loose but extensive Lithuanian State had emerged, with its capital at Vilnius, under strong Polish and Catholic influence, which eventually led to a Polish–Lithuanian merger in the sixteenth century. Since this state included a majority of Russians or Belorussians at one time, it was considered a serious rival to Moscow. In any case, it effectively blocked Muscovy's entry to the southern Baltic coast and Belorussia, while

Sweden, in control of Estonia and much of present-day Latvia, barred the way to the Gulf of Finland.

From the Russian point of view, these barriers were finally broken during the eighteenth century. In the early years Peter the Great triumphantly planted his new capital, St Petersburg, at the head of the Gulf of Finland and flanked it with newly conquered Estonia and Riga to the south and Karelian Vyborg on the north. This realized an age-long Russian desire for an outlet on the Baltic, facilitated closer contacts with western Europe and also brought into the Empire people (Estonians and Latvians as well as Baltic Germans) who were generally more advanced than the Russians themselves. Finally, towards the end of the century Lithuania and Belorussia fell under Russian control, completing the annexation of the whole of the region under consideration, except, of course, for East Prussia and the old German port of Königsberg.

On the eve of the First World War

Thus all these Baltic lands were bound up, willy-nilly, with the Russian Empire in its period of greatest expansion after 1780 and, through St Petersburg, were thrust into the forefront of this expansion. The canals, which were built to succeed the portages, had connected the Upper Volga with St Petersburg by three routes and also the Dnieper with the Western Dvina, Bug and Nieman systems. With the beginning of railway building, the end of serfdom and the developments in Siberia and the Ukraine from the mid-nineteenth century, trade, industry and cities grew rapidly. St Petersburg, already the largest city in Russia, grew from half a million in 1870 to over 2 million by 1914 and Riga from 80,000 to 350,000. Wheat and butter out from Siberia, cotton in from America—these were some of the major indices of a wider horizon for Russia and its impact on the Baltic. Industries ranged from shipbuilding to textiles and those based on the processing of imports, from esparto grass to sugar. One-third of all the metal-cutting tools and over half the paper made in Russia in 1913 came from the Baltic region. Several of the smaller old Baltic ports were also given a new lease of life, such as Liepaja, connected by rail with the black-earth region and developed as a naval port, which had a greater population in 1914 than it has today.

However, as in the Moscow region, the opening up of new rich lands elsewhere and contact with the international economy had a disrupting effect on the inefficient farming of the poorer lands of the region. The Black Sea ports had also begun to reduce the hegemony of those on the Baltic. Much surplus labour, apart from that which drifted to the towns, was employed in massive projects such as the drainage of swamps in the Polyesie.

Apart from the Russians and the Baltic peoples themselves, others were involved on quite a large scale. Many of the Lithuanian and White Russian cities had a large percentage of Jews, while the German influence was still strong in the cities (Tartu University still used German as the medium of instruction, for instance), and also in the country where 'Baltic barons' continued to own many large estates. But the whole region had become closely integrated economically with Russia during the nineteenth century and deliberate policies of Russification were pursued.

On the eve of the Second World War

About half this region was outside the borders of the U.S.S.R. during the twenty year inter-war period, and the Soviet boundary had reverted to the situation of about 1700, with only the single Baltic loophole of Leningrad. Estonia, Latvia and Lithuania had been granted their independence in 1918, following the principles of self-determination. The first two had never had an independent political existence before, while in all three countries the German influence was still strong and economic integration with Russia had been carried a long way. Moreover, the populations were overwhelmingly rural and the only important exportable commodities were primary products—flax, timber, butter, etc. Trade with the established Russian hinterland fell off, of course, and the populations of the major port cities declined. With populations of one or two million each, economies of scale were impossible, and financial borrowing difficult. Quite different from each other in religion and language, they found it impossible to federate—fear of German or Jewish dominance was also put forward as a factor against this. But they endeavoured to modernize their economies—particularly Estonia, the smallest of them—and found markets with countries in Western Europe, such as Britain, which preferred to trade with them rather than with Soviet Russia. But conditions were becoming increasingly competitive, especially in the depressed thirties.

The fragmented and unstable political structure of the whole of the Baltic region was exacerbated by the fact that Poland had unilaterally occupied large stretches of Belorussia and also the ancient capital of Lithuania, Vilnius. In 1939–40 Soviet troops reoccupied the areas of Belorussia taken over by Poland and later invaded the three Baltic states. There is little doubt that the latter were, like Finland, developing reasonably well as democracies, and that the bulk of the population did not want to return to Russian control. However, the long-term position of these little states was inevitably precarious on a hard realistic view, given the re-emergence of Russia in 1944 as a strong power in Europe, and the centuries-long Russian involvement, amounting at times to obsession, with the Baltic coastlands.

The tragic predicament of the Baltic states, inherent in their location, was made even more poignant when they were 'liberated' by their other age-long oppressors, the Germans. In this chaotic situation, many thousands of Baltic peoples were deported eastwards or fled westwards. The greatest physical devastation, however, fell upon the cities of Belorussia and particularly Leningrad, which had to withstand a long and bitter siege. Added to the former capital's demotion and relative stagnation in the Soviet period, Leningrad retained only a shadow of its former Imperial glory. Moreover, even today, the Baltic region as a whole remains de-populated in comparison with the position on the eve of the Second World War.

THE PRESENT ECONOMY (Fig. 47)

Owing to the continuing effects of the post-1918 political dismember-ment of the region, the diversion of the mainstream of Soviet economic development away from it, the continuing poverty in natural resources and, finally, the war, it is not surprising that the economy of the Baltic region has become marginal and relatively stagnant. The chief assets remain the historico-cultural legacies of skill, educational traditions, Western con-nections and a good transport network, but these are by no means as rare as they were in the inter-war period. The case of Leningrad is still in a class by itself, retaining many real if intangible advantages, and the considerable market in or near the region will probably ensure a continuing, if modest, growth in consumer-oriented industries and farming.

Farming and Fishing

Away from the vicinity of the larger cities along the Baltic, the region is still overwhelmingly rural, dependent on the fruits of a less than bounti-ful nature. About half the region is either still in forest or waterlogged, or both. Most of the usable farmland needs considerable investment in drain-age operations and application of fertilizer, especially lime, to maintain tolerable yields. Further drainage of the Pripyat (Pripet) marshes (Polyesie) is continuing, but it is slow and expensive and much of it is simply the repair of war-damaged systems. Because of the relatively favourable heat budget in this area, drainage, if successful, pays higher dividends than in the north. The zone of better agricultural land (relatively dry) lies in southern

XVI. The Sayan mountains of Southern Siberia in summer, clothed with pine and spruce, interrupted by snow-capped domes.

XVII. A street in Kaunas, Lithuania, on the river Niemen. The architecture here, as in the other Baltic republics, contrasts with that of Russia proper.

XVIII. The square in front of the Winter Palace in Leningrad, where the Bolshevik Revolution began in 1917.

XIX. The Summer Palace on the Gulf of Finland, originally built by Peter the Great, demolished in the Second World War, and rebuilt since.

Lithuania and central Belorussia, between the cool, wet, forested north and north-west and the Pripyat marshes. Rye is the traditional cereal, while potatoes (one-fifth of the national output) is the other staple. Sugar-beet is of minor importance in this more fertile zone. In addition, the fertile coastal strip of post-glacial marine deposits has given rise to intensive market-gardening developments.

One-third of the Soviet flax is grown in the region, mainly in the cool, wet north-west, but the market is not an expanding one and the labour demands are exorbitant. The wet south is also a traditional source of hemp, for which there is also a declining need.

Actually the majority of the sown acreage today is devoted to fodder crops—clovers, root crops and green maize, as well as oats and barley. Dairy cattle—for butter, except near the cities—and pigs are the main animals, and provide the chief farm 'exports' of the region and the ones on which the future health and expansion of Baltic farming seem most to depend.

Although the Baltic has never been one of Russia's greatest sources of fish, it has shared fully in the rapid post-war expansion of Soviet fishing operations, in lakes and rivers as well as on the sea. About a tenth of the Soviet catch, mainly herring, cod and sprats, has been brought in to the Baltic in recent years, part of it from the North Atlantic.

Transport (Fig. 46)

This region is probably better supplied with communication lines in relation to current demand than any other in the country. The first railways and major canals were built to converge on St Petersburg and a network developed through this patronage out of all proportion to the national trends of development of resources and economic needs. In addition the Baltic states built a number of additional railway lines in their period of independence.

Much the largest freight flows of the region today are into Leningrad—the most concentrated and well developed market. From the south come energy—coal and oil by rail, gas by pipe—and food, machinery, etc. From the north and east comes timber—the most important product by bulk—steel from Cherepovets and coal from Vorkuta. Outside the Leningrad orbit, rail freights are relatively small, reflecting the small degree of economic activity other than for local needs. Building materials, peat and wood, are characteristic items carried.

There is a considerable network of rivers linked by canals, but they are now mainly of minor or local significance. Of the three routes originally

cut from the Volga to the Baltic only one is now of more than local significance—the Mariinsk route via Rybinsk and Lakes Onega and Ladoga—
and it was so hamstrung by archaic, cramped facilities, that it has just been
revamped completely as part of a general deep-waterway system for
European Russia. The Baltic–White Sea canal, built in 1932, while
possessing considerable strategic significance, has been something of a
white elephant from the economic point of view. The Dnieper–Bug canal
is also to be revamped as part of a similar deep waterway from the Black
Sea to the Baltic—it already takes considerable loads of iron ore to Poland
and wood to the Ukraine. A link between the Nieman and the Black Sea
is also planned but there is still considerable doubt about the future of the
waterways in the pipeline age. Leningrad receives gas from the North
Caucasus, Cherepovets from the Volga and Riga, Vilnius and Minsk from
the western Ukraine. The 'Druzhba' oil pipelines from the Volga to Eastern
Europe pass through Belorussia. The north-west electrical grid is soon due
to be hooked up with the main European Russian grid.

There are many good ports in the region, above all Leningrad, but also
Riga, Tallinn, and the ice-free ones of Kaliningrad, Liepaja and Klaipeda.
The region has the greatest traditions and most experienced labour-force in
marine transport in the country, and the steady expansion of Soviet trade,
together with improvement in loading and processing facilities and pipelines, should rejuvenate many of these old ports.

Industry

Because of the paucity of local resources of energy and raw materials, industrial development depends heavily on a thoroughgoing
rehabilitation of the region's transit position and traditional functions
and skills.

The region does produce nine-tenths of the Soviet oil-shale (near the
Gulf of Finland), one-third of the country's peat (cut almost everywhere)
and a good deal of the firewood. However this is probably equivalent *in toto*
to no more than ten million tons of coal, and expensive coal at that. The
first hydro-electric stations in Russia were built on the Volkhov and Svir
rivers, but they are very small by today's needs and standards. Others
have been built on the Dvina, Nieman and Narva rivers. The oil and gas
revolution has rapidly spread to the Baltic with the pipelines mentioned
above and should fundamentally alter the industrial potentialities and also
the use of local poor quality fuel supplies. The chemical industries especially,
now largely confined to the Leningrad region, could be expected to
develop. The only mineral deposits of any importance are potash in

southern Belorussia and bauxite—the first to be exploited in Russia but secondary now—east of Leningrad (Boksitogorsk).

The most important indigenous raw material is timber, although its share of the national cut has fallen steadily since the war. The most important commercial timber zone is north-west of Leningrad, and timber products form an important export from that city. A quarter of the nation's paper is still made in the region, in several plants north and south of Leningrad and along the Baltic coast, but this compares with over half in 1913. Flax is the other traditional raw material of the region but it has long since taken second place behind cotton in the main textile centres, especially Leningrad.

Metal-using industries suffer from the high cost of Cherepovets steel, but the inertia of traditions of skill is illustrated by the continued role of Leningrad as maker of some of the giant turbines for the Central Siberian hydro-dams, as the chief shipbuilding centre of the country and as a processing centre for miscellaneous imported raw materials. This type of industry, plus chemicals, is clearly the chief hope of expansion for the region.

The tourist industry, whether based on the historical and cultural attractions of Leningrad, Novgorod or Tallinn, or the more hedonistic attractions of the sandy beaches of Latvia, has a great deal of scope for development as living-standards rise.

THE PRESENT POPULATION

There are now nearly 22 million people living in the region, still appreciably fewer than there were before the outbreak of war. This amounts to one in ten of Soviet citizens, compared with more than one in six before the Revolution. The population is increasing slowly again now, but almost entirely in the cities. There are now $7\frac{1}{2}$ million people in cities of over 50,000, compared with $1\frac{1}{2}$ million at the turn of the century. However, the relative decline is even more clearly indicated by the fact that the region's city-dwellers amounted to one in five of those of all Russia in 1900, compared with only one in ten today.

Probably no more than one out of three people in the region as a whole are Great Russians, of whom nearly half live in the Greater Leningrad region. Another one in three (7 million) are Belorussians, with their own language—significantly distinct from Russian—and more contact with Polish and Catholic traditions. The remaining third is mainly composed of: $2\frac{1}{4}$ million Lithuanians, $1\frac{1}{4}$ million Latvians, and 1 million Estonians, almost all of whom are found in their respective Republics, and who do not appear to have increased in numbers since 1930. There are also some quarter of a million Jews listed as living in the Baltic republics and Belorussia (mainly the latter)—a mere fraction of those living in these regions during the period of the Jewish Pale in Tsarist times and before the Nazi invasion. There are still more than ¾ million Poles—mostly in those parts of north-west Belorussia and south-east Lithuania which Poland held before the war. Several hundred thousand Karelians left the area southwest of Lake Ladoga which was annexed by the Russians in 1940, and were re-settled in Finland. No Germans are listed for the region now, but there were at least half a million of them before the war in the part of East Prussia which was incorporated into the U.S.S.R., and probably another quarter-million in the Baltic States.

It is a complicated ethnic picture, with a wide range of religious, linguistic and cultural differences, and a good deal of deep-rooted animosity—usually, though by no means always, directed against the Russians. The latter are to be found in the towns, often in key positions, outside their own Republic—thus they form a rather large proportion of the population of the urbanized Republics, i.e. Latvia and Estonia (27% and 20% respectively), as against 8% in each of the more heavily rural Republics of Lithuania and Belorussia.

The rural distribution (Fig. 44)

Half the people of the region are still classified as rural, and they belong, in general, to one of the hard-core depressed areas in the country, living in primitive conditions and probably with an abnormally high percentage in the older age groups. Three-quarters of them are in Belorussia and Lithuania, over half in the former alone.

The northern part of Estonia has a relatively intensive type of farming, similar to that of southern Finland across the Gulf—producing vegetables, meat and milk, and this kind of suburban farming surrounds Greater Leningrad, in spite of poor natural conditions. The eastern half of the region, in the Russian Republic, has a very sparse rural population, regardless of the fact that it lies between the two great metropolises of the country.

The cities

Of the 7½ million people who live in cities of over 50,000, nearly half are in Greater Leningrad and a further quarter are in four or five other widely scattered cities. The lonely eminence of Leningrad and the absence of any clusters of cities such as are found in the Moscow region or the Ukraine, are salient characteristics of the urban geography of the Baltic region.

Leningrad (formerly known as St Petersburg or Petrograd, 3½ millions) is for the Russians a unique symbol of their links with the West. Moscow represents something quite else—the immemorial Russian Russia. The two cities may be compared to Shanghai and Peking as symbols for China in some ways, except that Leningrad has not carried with it an image of humiliation by the West. The somewhat ironic culmination of the role of St Petersburg as a 'window on the West', and the link with the Soviet present, came when Marxist ideas from the West came in through that same window. The heroic role of the city in the Second World War added another dimension to its symbolic significance for the Russian people.

The foundation of St Petersburg in 1703 not only as a port but as the capital of a country which already possessed a traditional, almost hallowed, capital was, in the first instance, a tribute to the determined will of Peter the Great. The fact that, in little more than a century, it had become Russia's largest city—the commercial, financial and cultural, not just political capital—and one of the most lavishly laid out cities in Europe, was evidence of the immense authoritarian power of the Tsars, and their new orientation (Plates XVIII and XIX).

The freshly conquered site for this magnificent, planted city was anything but attractive—a swampy delta liable to floods from the wind-driven gulf; on the edge of the great northern forest, beyond the normal agricultural limits, with long, raw, foggy, dark winters (at 60° north) and the river frozen for five months of the year. It had indeed been, in far off Novgorod days, the end of the water-road from the Black Sea to the Baltic, but there is no evidence of there having been any settlement there.

Still, it symbolized the successful outcome of a long struggle for an outlet to the sea (other than by the even more distant and frozen Arctic) and its acquisition and the defeat of Sweden as a Baltic power, announced the entry of Russia into the ranks of the great powers of Europe. Archangel was deprived of its former privileges and was quickly reduced to insignificance. During the eighteenth and early nineteenth centuries, before the Black Sea trade began, the Baltic almost monopolized a much expanded Russian trade, and St Petersburg handled the great bulk of it. Russian timber, flax and pig iron were in great demand, especially for naval and military purposes, in Western Europe.

With the cutting of the water-links with the Volga, St Petersburg was put in direct contact with the Caspian and the Urals (where the great iron works were being initiated) as well as the heart of inhabited Russia. Power was supplied by imported British or German coal and a whole range of industries based on imported raw materials, such as cotton, jute, esparto grass and tropical oils grew up in St Petersburg, often with the backing of foreign capital and technicians. It became a repository of traditional industrial skills and cultural eminence, which have remained as its chief assets to this day. Having become fully established as the effective capital, it was able to compound its supremacy by making itself the focus of a rail net and, presiding over the remarkable agricultural and industrial renaissance in the Ukraine, Siberia and Middle Asia, grew from half a million to over two millions in its last half-century as capital.

Since 1918, by and large, it has been living on its capital (in the other meaning of the word). Following the Revolution and Civil War its population dropped sharply and probably did not regain its former level until 1930. The city, apart from losing its capital status, was shorn of its Baltic hinterland and was only a few miles from foreign territory. The country's overseas trade was drastically curtailed. However, its industrial skills, especially in engineering, were particularly vital in the period of the early Five Year Plans, when they were still so rare. The population had risen above 3 millions by 1939, but it was decimated dreadfully during the war and only by 1962 had the pre-war population level been regained. The city still has very much to contribute, tangibly and intangibly, to the country and, with the normal operation of historical momentum and natural increase, should, with its satellite settlements, maintain a gradual growth, in spite of the official discouragement of metropolitan growth and the marginal nature of its situation.

In the Baltic region there are a dozen other cities with more than 100,000, but with the solitary exception of Minsk, their overall growth since the early 1920s has been no more rapid than that of Leningrad, i.e. they have at most doubled in size. Half of these cities were in fact outside the U.S.S.R. for half this period and all of them suffered greatly from war destruction, migration, deportation and other hazards of the region's recent history. In general, the larger cities are along or near the Baltic coast, while the smaller and usually more stagnant ones are further inland towards the east and south.

Minsk (600,000) is the anomaly in this general situation, having more than quadrupled its population since 1926. In spite of being razed by the war, it doubled its population between 1939 and 1959—the only city of over half a million in European Russia (west of the Volga) to do so. If recent rates of growth continue, it is likely to replace Riga soon as the second city of the whole Baltic region. Lacking any particular local advantages of site or resources, its unusual growth is primarily explicable in terms of its political-regional function in the Soviet centralized system as the capital of the Belorussian republic, which is larger than the three Baltic republics combined. Between the wars, when it was very near the Polish border, it grew quite slowly by Soviet standards, but since 1939 it has been centrally situated in Belorussia, and has concentrated almost all of the urban-industrial growth of that republic, which had never had any real industrial tradition. It is also on the morainic route from Moscow to Poland. It now specializes in engineering products (tractors, trucks and machine tools), based on imported steel and gas fuel, but also, as a major regional centre, has a varied industrial structure composed of textiles, printing, and food processing.

The other secondary regional towns in the Belorussian area which have recovered very slowly from their wartime battering are *Gomel* (190,000), *Smolensk* (160,000), *Mogilev* (140,000) and *Bobruisk* (110,000), river towns on the Dnieper system, and *Vitebsk* (170,000), on the Dvina. Ancient foundations in general, they were very important in the days when the rivers were the highways. Now they are centres of rather depressed agricultural districts, with timber, flax and leather working industries. Smolensk, which celebrated its 1,100th anniversary in 1963, situated at the head of navigation on the Dnieper and also on the main land route to Moscow from the west, has a special place in the chronicles of Russian military history. Over several centuries, against the Poles, Napoleon and Hitler, it assumed the role of Moscow's shield and it seems likely that its most distinctive function, like that of *Novgorod* (70,000) and *Pskov* (100,000) will become that of a partly fossilized shrine of Russia's heroic past.

Along the Baltic coast, much the largest city south of Leningrad is *Riga* (620,000). Midway between Leningrad and the Polish coast, Riga is the nearest thing to a regional centre for all the Baltic republics and would have been the obvious choice for a capital if the three independent states had agreed to federate. On the other hand it is the Baltic city which has had the most contact with, and dependence on, Moscow and probably owes its greater size to this. Founded in 1201, near the mouth of the Western Dvina, leading directly to the lands of Novgorod and Moscow, it was first a Hanseatic port and later became a focal point, along with Tallinn and Vyborg, in the process of denial of the Baltic to Russia. It was finally taken by Peter the Great in 1721, but it lay on the very edge of Russian territory until the Polish partition at the end of the century. It was therefore during the nineteenth century that the full integration of the port with Moscow, by river and rail, was effected. Had St Petersburg not been there, with a prior claim and Imperial sanction to take most of the available trade, Riga might have proved a more suitable St Petersburg for a Moscow state, ice-bound only for a month or so, set amid reasonable agricultural land, and on a shorter route between Moscow and the ports of the West. As it was, Riga did prosper even on the crumbs from St Petersburg's table, exporting butter, eggs and Siberian wheat, and growing from 80,000 in 1870 to 330,000 in 1910. Its completely ice-free outport, *Liepaja*, was also developed rapidly as a naval, fishing and metal-working city, and had a population of 94,000 in 1914, more than it has today (80,000). Riga became the capital of independent Latvia (2 millions) between the wars but its population numbers remained static, as its traditional market was largely cut off. Since the war it has grown again quite quickly, with a varied structure of skilled metal industries, notably of the radio and electronic type, as well as more traditional textiles, timber and fish processing. The advent of natural gas from the Ukraine will help to solve a serious fuel shortage.

Like Riga, *Tallinn* (formerly called Revel, 300,000) concentrates about one-third of the population of its republic, Estonia, and has the same range of diversified industry and political functions. On a good harbour on the indented coast, it may be compared with Helsinki on the other side of the gulf. It has had a considerable German influence, as has *Tartu* (formerly called Dorpat, 80,000), an old university town.

Unlike Latvia and Estonia, which have only one dominating city each, Lithuania, for historical reasons, has two cities of about the same size, both inland. *Vilnius* (formerly called Wilno or Vilna, 260,000) was the capital of the great medieval Lithuanian–Polish Empire. The Lithuanians naturally regard it as their capital, but the Poles have looked on it as Polish and they annexed it by force in the inter-war period. Its population has long been an amalgam of Lithuanian, Polish and Jewish peoples. *Kaunas* (formerly Kovno, 250,000) is situated where the river Neris, on which Vilnius is situated, joins the Nieman (Plate XVII). It served as the capital of independent Lithuania after the Poles seized Vilnius. Lithuania's only port is *Klaipeda* (formerly called Memel, 100,000), at the narrow outlet from the sand-barred lagoon into which the Nieman debouches. It was basically an old and minor German port and was in fact annexed by Nazi Germany in 1939. The Germans have since been expelled as they have from the much larger port, *Kaliningrad* (formerly Königsberg, 230,000). This old Hanse port, formerly capital of East Prussia, had always been thoroughly German until 1945, when it was annexed by the U.S.S.R. on the defeat of Germany. The expelled Germans were replaced by Russian migrants (not Lithuanians) but the population is still only two-thirds as large as it was before the war. As one of the largest ice-free ports in the Soviet Union, nearest to the chief foreign markets, with good inland communications and facilities for naval and commercial shipping, shipbuilding and fishing, it is bound to take on increasing significance as the country expands its maritime operations. Since much of the long Russian history on the Baltic can be interpreted simply in terms of a struggle for warm-water outlets, and since the Germans have often been their chief enemies and rivals in this shatter-zone, the Russian occupation of Königsberg is a significant postscript to what seems to be the final achievement of ancient Russian ambitions.

PROSPECT

The weaknesses of this region are much more evident than its strengths, and do not suggest the likelihood that it will be anything but relatively marginal in the Soviet scheme in the foreseeable future. The damp, cool, podzolic conditions can hardly support a first-rate, economical agriculture and the large rural component in many areas only reinforces the impression of agrarian depression, inviting comparison with the under-developed world. The general poverty in competitive local resources of energy and industrial raw materials means dependence on outside sources, and puts an extra onus on the justification of industrial development, necessitating either extra efficiency or other overriding incentives. The plurality of culture and language groups, often with a record of internecine-hostility and recent political separatism, as well as the emigration, by one means or another, of many of the potential leaders of society, could inspire the same kind of lack of confidence one may find in the American South, or Quebec, or northern Britain. The war dealt most of the region a crippling blow, and it is a generally observable fact that wars tend to accelerate the decline of regions which were previously on the way down, while strengthening the resilience of those which were on the way up. The comparison of post-war trends in the Baltic region with, say, the Volga–Ural, except in some specialized and valuable industries, is not particularly encouraging to the former.

And yet one cannot condemn a region to death even on such apparently impressive evidence. Some of the foregoing negative attributes could apply equally to the Moscow region or to Finland or Japan. The Baltic region is certainly in the marginal category among the Soviet regions at present, in terms of relative contribution to the country as a whole. Even so, it is probably the most important of the marginal regions. Whether this relatively depressed position will change in the foreseeable future depends as much on national or even international developments as on those which originate in the region itself. Perhaps the most important of such questions is whether the Soviet Union will develop as a thoroughgoing world trading nation. The strong movement towards the realization of this, in the eighteenth and nineteenth centuries, was largely responsible for creating the major assets which the region is admitted to have—a fair tradition of skilled industrial labour, sea-going activities and good internal communications. If the international horizon were extended, the Baltic coastal area would stand to gain a great deal, but not necessarily the same places as before. The disproportionate supremacy and wealth-accumulation of St Petersburg are to some degree to be regarded as an artificial bonanza. Riga and perhaps still more, Kaliningrad could be expected, in a rational situation today, to gain a greater share. Much depends, too, on the character of developments in the economic relationships between the Soviet Union and the other East European Communist countries.

Much hope is pinned on the expansion of skilled engineering industries, but how long the labour pool can operate as a decisive locational factor in the absence of other things remains in doubt. For instance if, as seems likely, the major demand for large hydro-turbines continues to be in Central Siberia, will Leningrad continue to be the main producer of them rather than, say, Novosibirsk, with its much cheaper steel and fuel and a wide range of high-powered technical institutes? Might this not amount to subsidization, just as an increase of farming investment on the poor lands of the Baltic region might involve subsidization? Much depends on the actual extent and urgency of total demand, on the strength of geographical inertia, national policy with regard to continued disproportionate investment in the Eastern Regions, and so on. But the extent to which the Soviet Union feels strong enough to take the plunge into the international economy is perhaps the most crucial question in the long run for the Baltic region.

Empires have risen and fallen in this region in the past. Before Moscow or St Petersburg were heard of, the empire of Novgorod grew rich and powerful, but the city with its watery territory is now one of the more moribund parts of the Soviet Union, for which the future prospects are dim. It is only a very short time since the vastly greater city-power of St Petersburg was symbolically toppled. It has, in one way or another, slipped a long way in national importance, although its intangible assets should still not be under-estimated.

It would seem that little progress can be forecast for towns like Vitebsk, Novgorod, Smolensk or even Kaunas, but much more likely that Minsk, Riga and, secondarily, Tallinn or Kaliningrad, will develop rapidly. What happens to such places, and above all, to Leningrad itself, may well provide a useful index to various trends in national policy on regional and international questions.

CHAPTER THIRTEEN

Caucasus-Caspia

FOR all the stirring exploits, the seats of imperial and industrial power, the vast resources and the limitless horizons, there is an atmosphere of the sombre and the monotonous in the lands of Slavic settlement from the Baltic to the Pacific. Everything that sets off the American Mid-West from the Caribbean or the North European plain from the Mediterranean—and more—makes the Russo-Siberian plains a place apart from the Caucasian realm, between the Black Sea and the Caspian.

Nowhere else in the Soviet Union are the patterns of nature and man so complex. Eurasia in microcosm, it includes sedentary Georgian Christians, nomadic Buddhist Mongol Kalmucks, Turkish-speaking Moslems of Azerbaijan, Persian-speaking Ossetians and the highly individual Armenians, among scores of other linguistic and culture groups. Numbering no more than 2 million out of the total of 15 millions, the Russians are the newest arrivals and wield disproportionate influence, but the fires of nationalism have by no means died down. The national groups are ancient, certainly older than Russia itself, and their historical predicament has been very similar to that of the Baltic nations—unable to join with each other,

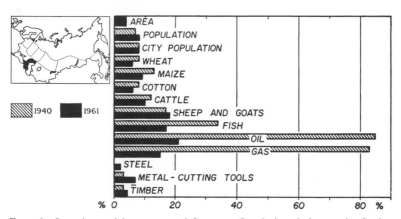

FIG. 48—Location and importance of Caucasus-Caspia in relation to the Soviet Union as a whole, for certain selected items

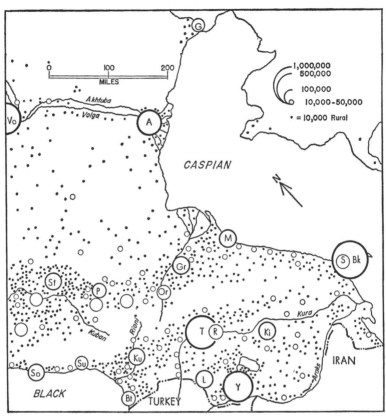

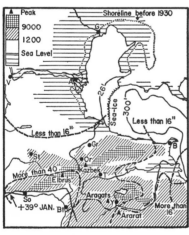

Fig. 49—Caucasus-Caspia: population. Key to cities: A=Astrakhan, Bk=Baku, Bt=Batumi, G=Guryev, Gr=Grozny, Ki=Kirovabad, Ku=Kutaisi, L=Leninakan, M=Makhachkala, P=Pyatigorsk, R=Rustavi, S=Sumgait, So=Sochi, St=Stavropol, Su=Sukhumi, T=Tbilisi, Vo=Volgograd, Y=Yerevan

Fig. 50—Caucasus-Caspia: nature

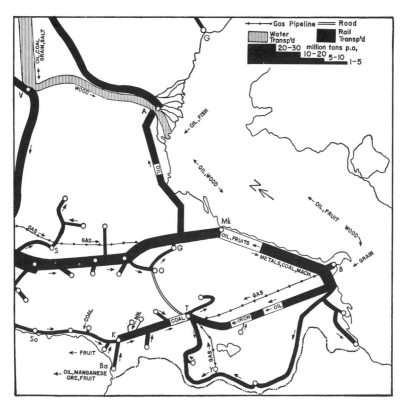

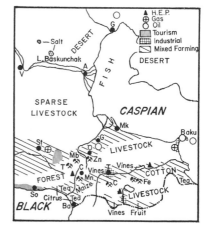

FIG. 51—Caucasus-Caspia: movements

FIG. 52—Caucasus-Caspia: economy.
Metals: C=copper, Mb=molybde-
num, Mn=manganese, T=tungsten,
Zn=zinc

and at the mercy of their bigger brothers—Turkey, Persia or, most lately, Russia.

Nature's labyrinth is fully as intricate as man's. Ice-capped mountains coexist in the region with salt flats below sea-level; sub-tropical swamp-lands with semi-desert and windswept plateaux; and the agriculture has responded with a variety unknown in Russia proper. The contrasts are great in the socio-economic sphere too, ranging from insulated peoples cast up long ago in high mountain cul-de-sacs to urban workers in the modern chemical complexes of Yerevan or Baku.

This exceptional heterogeneity of land and people, and its non-Russian character, provides, paradoxically, the chief criterion for delimitation of the area as a region. To the south the international frontier inevitably serves, although it marks no real boundary on either ethnic or natural grounds. To the east and west the Black and Caspian Seas also arbitrarily bound the region, and the eastern shore of the latter is strikingly negative by comparison with the western. However, in a departure from the conventional northern boundaries of this region, in both Soviet and Western geographical writing, one area has here been excluded and another included. The excluded area is the Kuban lowland, which is basically Russo-Ukrainian in its history, ethnic composition, natural conditions and agriculture and has been, with the lower Don, included in Ukrainia. A convenient natural boundary—orographic and climatic, is formed by the Stavropol upland, which fans out north from the Caucasus. Included in the region is the north shore of the Caspian, and in particular the braided Volga below Volgograd. The desert conditions, the diversion effect of the Volga–Don canal, the traditional Asian and Caspian outlook, the fisheries, and the general air of comparative decay—all these combine to differentiate the lower Volga and the lower Ural from the Middle Volga and the Ural regions proper.

It has been said that there is a general air of decline in the region, though as in the case of the Baltic, there are local exceptions to this generalization. Not long ago the fate of all Russia depended on the oil of Baku and the Caspian was the most vital of the Soviet shipping routes. In Tsarist times the region provided two-thirds of the Russian fish, nine-tenths of its oil, and some of its cotton. The proportion of all of these things has declined rapidly, especially since the Second World War—probably to a degree *because* of the war, which revealed the vulnerability and off-side location of the whole region and hastened the development of alternative sources, particularly of oil (Fig. 48)

The country does not now depend on this region to any critical extent for essential industrial or agricultural commodities. However, the rising national standard of living is making it increasingly possible for Caucasia to capitalize on those natural assets of which it has a permanent near-monopoly in the Soviet Union. Its relatively frost-free, sunny winters (on the Black Sea coast), combined with mountain and sea and a wealth of historical interest, could make it, in some respects, the Mediterranean of the Soviet Union.

THE NATURAL HABITAT (Fig. 50)

In contrast to Russia proper, it is the relief which is the fundamental element in the natural environment, not climate and vegetation, which are, in general, controlled by this overpowering skeleton of hills and valleys.

The main range of the Caucasus, an even grander Pyrenees, stretches from north-west to south-east between two seas, and forms a great barrier to human or atmospheric movement. It is a young folded range, with a rugged crest of over 10,000 feet, ice-capped in the middle between Kazbek and Elbrus, which rises above 18,000 feet. The easiest pass, following the Terek river and the Georgian Military Highway, climbs to 7,500 feet. Like the Carpathians, the Caucasus range is asymmetrical, falling steeply on its southern side, while descending more gently to the north. The eastern half (Dagestan) is more like a high plateau, contrasting with the rocky, icy and—lower down—thickly forested western half. Limestone topography (with caves and underground drainage), earthquakes and hot mineral springs are common throughout.

Separated from the main range by the hour-glass of the Kura-Rioni lowlands, and the bridge of the Surami uplands, are the disjointed ranges known as the Lesser Caucasus—lower and not so rugged, but still rising to 10,000 feet in places. Several snow-capped volcanic cones rise above the general level—the most famous being Ararat just across the border in Turkey. In the midst of them lies the Armenian Plateau, mainly between about 4,000 and 7,000 feet, cut into by rivers, in particular the Razdan, which drains the extensive, shallow and shrinking Lake Sevan, and empties into the Araks.

The latter river forms the frontier with Turkey and Iran before debouching into the Kura system, which drains four-fifths of the area of Transcaucasia, and into the Caspian Sea. The only other notable system is that of the Rioni, which receives the heavy rains and glacier-melt of the Black Sea-facing western Caucasus, leading to very difficult drainage problems in the flat Colchis (Kolkhida) lowlands. The great lowland surrounding the north Caspian, bounded on the west by the Stavropol and Yergeni uplands, is almost entirely below sea level. Most of it is without permanent drainage, but the Terek, Volga and Ural rivers do reach the sea.

These Caspian lowlands, including that of the lower Kura valley, are generally dry—less than 8 inches annually in Astrakhan or Baku—and the evaporation exceeds precipitation by at least three times. This situation is in striking contrast to the Rioni basin which, together with the tiny, freakish Lenkoran lowland on the Caspian, is the only part of the whole Soviet Union where precipitation exceeds evaporation and where the accumulated heat balance is also ample. Even Batumi, at sea level, receives 93 inches a year and malaria has been an endemic problem in the lowlands. However, the zone of excess moisture does not penetrate far to the east—in the upper Kura valley, only 100 miles from the Black Sea, irrigation is necessary, as it is in the valleys of Armenia and Azerbaijan. Apart from the Colchis lowland, which has a slight winter maximum, the whole region has a pronounced summer precipitation maximum.

Although the whole area, at low altitudes, has adequate accumulated heat for growth of maize, cotton, etc., the only area which is reasonably free of frost in winter (January average over 40° F.) is the Black Sea coast. The Caspian-facing lowlands are appreciably more continental and while the average January temperature may be above freezing (as at Baku) periodic cold blasts from the interior prohibit the growth of frost-sensitive plants. Thus the nearest Soviet climatic analogue to California or, rather more accurately, Florida (with summer rainfall) is the Black Sea coast and Colchis (Kolkhida) lowland. It is, however, stricken by killing frosts more frequently than Florida.

Obviously such varied climatic and relief conditions are reflected in a complex pattern of soil and vegetation, ranging from the red and yellow sub-tropical soils of the better drained part of the Colchis lowland where many monsoonal Asian plants are at home, to the *solonchaki* (salt crusts) of the Caspian shore, carrying almost no vegetation at all. Much of Armenia and Dagestan is dry steppe, but the western Caucasus is clothed with a dense growth of broad-leaved forest. The snowline on the south face of the Caucasus lies at from 10,000 to 12,000 feet.

The Caspian Sea problem

A major physical phenomenon, which raises many economic difficulties and questions, is that of the Caspian, the largest inland water-body in the world, the level of which has been falling steadily since 1929. This has happened before at various historical periods and seems to be related primarily to quantitative fluctuations in the effective moisture balance of the

XX. A tea plantation in the Kolkhida basin of Western Georgia, between the Caucasus and the Black Sea.

XXI. Tbilisi on the river Kura, showing the old town, the typical Georgian church, the cable-car and the semi-arid aspect.

XXII. A small settlement, with strips of grain cultivation and a church, on a terrace above the Aragvi river at about 3,000 feet on the south side of the Caucasus.

XXIII. The city and harbour of Baku, on the Caspian.

Volga catchment area, which provides the Caspian with three-quarters of its intake. This in turn has recently been affected by the construction of large dams, with their extensive reservoirs, on the Volga. Whatever the causes, the level is now about 8 feet below what it was in 1929—the lowest level, apparently, for several centuries. The great delta of the Volga, the culmination of the long braided channels below Volgograd (Stalingrad), has been extended about 20 miles out into the Caspian in the last three decades, causing serious navigational problems. In fact a wide strip of former sea bed has been left high and dry and, since the northernmost part of the lake ranges in depth from 10 to 25 feet, a continuance of the drop would extend the land area to a great extent. Apart from the navigation problems, this shallow part is the critical area for the fishing industry, which has in fact been declining alongside the drop in level, though not necessarily only for this reason.

Plans have been discussed at various times to divert water into the Caspian from the Amu Darya (Turkmen Canal), from the Ob system (Davydov Plan) and, most lately and feasibly, by joining the headwaters of the Kama and Pechora rivers to be able to divert into the Volga system water which at present flows to the Arctic. This would have the additional advantage that the extra water destined for the Caspian, or for irrigation in the arid lower Volga, would generate extra power as it passed through the various Volga hydro-stations. Another ambitious, probably too ambitious, plan involves the building of a system of low dams across the northern Caspian, cordoning off the shallow, critical, part and at least maintaining its level, while allowing the southern part to fall. The northern shallow part freezes regularly, and a minor argument for this dam project is that the annual damage caused to oil and port installations in the south by drifting ice floes would be avoided.

However, the crucial question is not whether the Caspian could be restored to its former level, but whether this would be desirable or at least justify the immense costs, at a time when the Soviet authorities are becoming increasingly conscious of short-term comparative costs and priorities. It has been suggested that the natural evaporating basin of Kara-bogaz Gulf, on the east side of the Caspian, might be allowed, or even helped, to seal itself off from the Caspian, thus considerably reducing total loss by evaporation without jeopardizing its sulphate-mining industry. Further, the striking opinion has been voiced that the agricultural potential of the gratuitous new delta lands being uncovered would more than offset any decline in the fisheries, in terms of food value. The fundamental question underlying all these alternatives is: how much is the health of the

Caspian worth *today*, not a quarter-century ago, in terms of overriding national needs and cheaper prospects elsewhere?

THE PEOPLING OF THE REGION

Most of the valley and plateau lands south of the Caucasus were settled, and often quite elaborately organized, before the Slavs had begun to make a mark at all in the European forests. The Urartu state, with its irrigation works, cuneiform writing and advanced numerical techniques, was centred on the Armenian plateau about the ninth century B.C. and extended some kind of control as far as the Mediterranean and Mesopotamia. The Armenians built up an early reputation as participants in the caravan trade of the ancient world, and well-organized urban societies grew up. There were two powerful alliances of Georgian tribes in Colchis and the upper Kura and a similar organization (the Albanians) in Azerbaijan.

But by the very nature of their position, at a crossroads of the ancient world, the local inhabitants of the Caucasus were constantly at the mercy of greater empires, and were trampled upon by armies in transit—Alexander, the Medes and the Romans, amongst others. There were Hellenic trading centres on the Black Sea coast and by the first century A.D. the entire Transcaucasus became a Roman dependency. Soon afterwards the Georgians and Armenians adopted their separate Christian Churches and found themselves in the middle of a power struggle between the Byzantine and Persian Empires. The city of Tbilisi, in the centre of Transcaucasia, was founded in the fourth century, but later, as Kiev was being founded to the north, the Transcaucasus was subjected to Arab rule. In the comparative lull between the ninth and the twelfth centuries—the Golden Age of Kiev Rus—there were considerable trading connections between the Slavs and Transcaucasia, and there was much agricultural development, especially viticulture, animal husbandry and sericulture, and also crafts, particularly iron-working. Baku dates from this period. For the Georgian state particularly, this was a Golden Age.

The Mongol conquest, which snuffed out Kiev, also laid waste the Transcaucasus, and for three centuries, until Russia gained control of the Volga and captured Astrakhan in 1556, there was no contact between Russia and the Caucasus. Thenceforth the Volga has been the main avenue between Russia and the Caucasian peoples—an additional justification, perhaps, for including the Lower Volga within the present regional boundaries. The Volga–Caspian was the main road for the coveted silk trade, and expansionist Muscovy's concern with it led to Cossack settlements being established along the Terek river, north of the Caucasus, in the seventeenth century. Peter the Great did hold Baku for ten years, but later retreated behind the Caucasus again.

The Caucasian peoples were in fact caught between the anvil of Turkey and the hammer of Persia and this eventually worked to the advantage of Russia, which became the lesser of three evils to such an extent that the Eastern Georgians of Tbilisi actually invited Russian protection in the late eighteenth century. During the first quarter of the nineteenth century Russia had established control over all of present-day Transcaucasia, except for Batumi and some of the mountain fastnesses. Several more decades were needed finally to subdue the mountain tribesmen (especially the Circassians) who were supplied with arms by the Turks and the British, and who seriously impeded the Russians in their building of the Georgian Military Highway across the Caucasus. By 1878 however, all was quiet, outwardly at any rate, and the Russians had taken not only Batumi but the Kars region of Turkey, which the Soviet Union does not hold today. At this time, Russia was also subduing Central Asia, across the Caspian, and Baku oil was beginning to flow. Russia's position as a Caucasian and Caspian power seemed assured.

The eve of the First World War

Transcaucasia had been in a backward state under the Turks and Persians and had also been riven by internecine feuds. Thus to be associated with Russia in its period of rapid industrialization after 1880 was in many ways an improvement. However, Russia did not attempt to improve relations between the various ethnic groups—rather the opposite—and repressive actions had kindled fresh anti-Russian sentiment by 1914.

The rate of economic development and population growth was rapid in many parts of the region. The greatest phenomenon was that of Baku, which by about 1900 was producing half the world's oil. Largely financed from abroad, it supplied (together with Grozny, north of the Caucasus) over nine-tenths of the Russian oil. Two-thirds of the Russian fish-catch came from the Caspian and with the new importance of its shipping as well —and as yet no problem of falling level—Astrakhan prospered. Georgia was also beginning to be developed with tea-gardens, citrus groves, cotton and metals, particularly manganese, while the traditional preoccupation with vineyards, sheep and goats was extended. In addition to the Military Highway, railways linked Baku with Batumi, via Tbilisi, in 1883, with Rostov and Moscow in 1900 and, through the Trans-Caspian railway, with Middle Asia. An oil-pipeline was laid from Baku to Batumi by 1900. There were three cities of over 100,000 in 1897—Tbilisi, the ancient centre of the region, which was still the largest; Baku, with the most hectic growth; and Astrakhan. Baku more than doubled its population in the first two decades of the present century, to overtake Tbilisi and become the fifth largest city in all Russia.

The eve of the Second World War

The years 1917 to 1921 had been at least as chaotic in Caucasia as in Russia proper. The Georgians in particular took the opportunity, like the Ukrainians, to press for independence, first under the aegis of Germany and later of Britain. The Turks took over Batumi, and the British, Turks and Germans each for a time attempted to control the Baku oilfields. Like the Baltic States, the three main Caucasian peoples found it impossible to federate, and the victorious Bolsheviks re-established Russian control over them all, in the face of considerable opposition, in 1920.

Thus the resource developments begun under the Tsars were continued and accelerated—above all that of oil. By 1937 Baku and Grozny still accounted for over four-fifths of the Soviet oil and gas, which was undoubtedly well known to the Germans, who all but reached Grozny several years later. Moreover, the total oil production was three times what it had been in 1913. Baku was a city of three-quarters of a million, half as large again as Tbilisi. The fishing industry had declined in importance, and Astrakhan, which had been the same size as Baku in 1900, was only one-third as large in 1939. Yerevan, with its new role as Armenian capital and with a major synthetic rubber industry, was almost as large as Astrakhan, having been very small in Tsarist days. The mining of Georgian manganese was greatly increased as well as other metals, such as the rare molybdenum and tungsten in the high Caucasus, which the Germans actually reached. The acreage of both tea and citrus fruits in Colchis apparently increased some fifty-fold between 1913 and 1937. However, in terms of the region's contribution to the national economy in 1940 it was oil which stood far above everything else, to the point of possessing, as it turned out, a life-and-death significance for the Soviet Union.

THE PRESENT ECONOMY (Fig. 52)

The most striking change since the war in the region's economy, looked at in the national context, is the decline in its contribution of oil and gas from four-fifths to one-fifth of a greatly expanded national output. Together with the reduction of the Caspian fish contribution to less than a fifth of the national catch, this means that the only distinctive and critical contribution of the region, apart from one or two metals, is in tea and citrus fruits. But these crops, marginal and exotic as they are, are beset with natural problems and are expensive in relation to imports. Thus it seems that there has been a relative reversion to regional self-sufficiency, on a much higher level than before 1880, of course, with chemical and engineering industries as well as the traditional maize, vines and livestock enterprises, but self-sufficiency nevertheless from a national standpoint.

Farming

Although the region is characteristically distinguished by farming rather than industry, only one-tenth of its total area is cultivated (Plate XXII). It is traditionally a grazing land, with time-honoured ways of combining, through transhumance, the winter pastures of the valleys with the summer alpine meadows. Sheep and goats are rather more suitable to the dry or rugged conditions and are found everywhere except in the Colchis lowland. Together they are twice as numerous as cattle, which are, however, spread over all but the very driest parts of the Caspian lowland. Pigs are common except in the Moslem east, while water buffalo are widespread as beasts of burden through Transcaucasia, and camels along the north Caspian lowlands.

Maize is a traditional crop and Transcaucasia produced half the Soviet output before the war, but is now relatively overshadowed by more northerly regions with a less than adequate heat budget for sure ripening. The vine is also a long-standing crop but in the last decade Transcaucasia's contribution has dropped from a third to a quarter of the total Soviet wine output, in the face of greater extensions in the Ukraine. The valley-lands of the Transcaucasus also grow other crops, like melons, rice, tobacco, sunflowers and winter wheat and this combination is carried over to the northern foothills of the Caucasus, but not beyond the Terek river. Irrigated cotton is grown, chiefly in the lower Kura valley, but again the regional proportion in relation to Central Asia has been declining since the war. Rearing silk-worms is still an important cottage activity in the Transcaucasus.

The sub-tropical agriculture of the Colchis basin and Black Sea coast is a unique phenomenon in the Soviet Union. It produces virtually all of the Soviet tea, citrus fruits, tung-oil and other sub-tropical crops (Plate XX). The Lenkoran district on the Caspian produces about 3% of the tea, but little of the other crops. Since tea is the traditional Russian drink and it is normally taken with lemon, the national demand certainly exists but, in spite of great efforts, the supply continues to fall short of it. Although the acreage has been greatly increased since before the war, periodic killing frosts (and also hot dry *föhn* winds) have taken serious toll. Moreover, although much of the swampy area has been reclaimed, this is expensive and only partly successful, because the rivers are often raised above their flood-plains, and because flat land is more liable to frost than the slopes. Since both tea and citrus fruits need well-drained, reasonably frost-free situations, there is considerable competition for the limited available good land. Other suitable crops, especially maize, are crowded out and the local food supply is disrupted. This region does apparently provide three-quarters of the estimated Soviet tea consumption, but no more than a fifth of that of citrus fruits. Moreover, it seems clear that the latent demand is by no means correctly indicated by the actual consumption, that much of the fruit is of poor quality, and that further imports from more suitable areas abroad might be less expensive.

Though the Caspian fisheries have undoubtedly been declining, absolutely as well as in relation to the national catch, they are still two or three times as important as that of the whole of the Black Sea and Sea of Azov, and one of the types of fish, the sturgeon, has a value out of all proportion to its weight, because of the demand for its black roe (*caviar*).

Industry

Although Baku oil is no longer of great national significance, its production, due partly to increased drilling off-shore in the Caspian, is not yet declining absolutely, but is remaining at a level which is twice the volume of 1913, though still less than that of 1940. Its sulphur-free character keeps it still in demand in other parts of the country. It is still regionally important as far as the character of industry is concerned, and provides refining capacity for oil from the north as well as export oil piped to the Black Sea. The Grozny field, the oldest in the country, has also a relatively stable production at a low level, but its oil is still in demand for its high quality. The small Guryev fields on the north Caspian are connected to the Urals. Natural gas from Karadag, south of Baku, and also from Stavropol has become a new factor in the Transcaucasus energy picture, being used in power-stations, and piped to Tbilisi and Yerevan. Output is expanding rapidly, and gas is becoming the chief source of power even in traditionally hydro-electric areas like Armenia.

Natural conditions are very good for hydro-electric power in Transcaucasus, especially the western half, and much development has proceeded in recent years. The Rioni, with a steep gradient and heavy rainfall, has three stations; the Razdan, a short river which drops 3,000 feet from Lake Sevan to the Araks, also has three as part of an eventual larger 'cascade';

while on the Kura there are several widely separated dams, the most important being at Mingechaur, in connection with irrigation for cotton, flood control and anti-malaria projects.

Thus the Caucasus area cannot be said to be power-deficient. Although the importance of oil is declining, gas is filling the breach very adequately at present and there is clearly much scope for further hydro-development, should other sources become immediately competitive. So far the Caucasus electrical grid system has been set apart from the main European grid, but eventually it is due to be hooked up with it and would be likely to be a net contributor, unlike the Baltic region, in spite of undoubted seasonal fluctuations in hydro-electric generation.

Most of the industries are concerned either with processing local raw materials or providing for regional self-sufficiency, or both. Oil has had a powerful influence on industrial character—the greater Baku and Grozny regions have a variety of petrochemical industries and are sharing in the national expansion of these. As already noted, the influence of gas is increasing rapidly, changing not only the industrial fuel emphasis but the raw material base for synthetic rubber industry, for instance at Yerevan.

The region has a variety of economic metal resources—the largest being the manganese of Chiatura in western Georgia (one of the largest in the world)—giving rise to ferro-alloy reduction operations nearby. Aluminium is smelted from Urals alumina at Sumgait, a suburb of Baku, where there is also a modern steel-tube works. However, the Transcaucasian equivalent of Cherepovets, i.e. an integrated iron and steel mill, is at Rustavi near Tbilisi. Based on coal from Tkvarcheli near the Black Sea and iron ore from Dashkesan, near Lake Sevan, its steel is even more expensive than that of Cherepovets. Donbas steel can be delivered there more cheaply, but Rustavi stands as a gesture towards basic self-sufficiency and relieving the overloaded railways.

North of the Caucasus the valuable zinc is reduced at Ordzhonikidze, as well as the molybdenum and tungsten ores from the mountains at Tyrny Auz. There are large and long-exploited deposits of common salt east of the lower Volga, especially at Lakes Baskunchak and Elton.

Throughout the region there are important industries processing food and fibre, such as tea, wine, cotton, silk, fish, and even the reeds of the Volga delta, which are made into cardboard at Astrakhan. Finally, there is the tourist industry. There are two groups of health resorts which have been carried over from Tsarist times and greatly expanded: (a) the resorts of the Black Sea coast, clustered around Sochi, Gagra and Sukhumi, where the attractions, as on the Crimean Riviera, are the combination of mountain, sea and winter sunshine; (b) the cluster of spas around Pyatigorsk, on the northern foothills of the Caucasus, where the warm sulphur springs are the main asset. A third type, hitherto less developed but also offering considerable potential, is the skiing and climbing-resort of the high central Caucasus. Since health resorts are now firmly part of Soviet governmental policy and since the Caucasus has quite unusually rich assets in the Soviet context, located quite close to the main population centres, great expansion of this industry here is almost certain to take place.

Transport (Fig. 51)

This region may be said to be well equipped, by Soviet standards and in relation to current needs, with the kinds of transport links, notably pipelines, which are most in vogue today. Today's two main transport axes—along the northern foothills of the Caucasus and through the Transcaucasian 'hourglass', from the Caspian to the Black Sea, were in operation in Tsarist times (both railways and oil pipelines). The Volga–Caspian waterway was also well developed, and these three main routes converged on Baku, which indeed was supplying most of the freight carried on them. Oil is probably still the single most important commodity carried by rail and pipe combined, but much less of it now goes north and some even comes south ('coals to Newcastle') via the Volga, to be refined at Baku. A second pipe is being built to Batumi for Baku oil exports. The gas pipelines from Karadag to Tbilisi and Yerevan and from Stavropol to Grozny, are the most significant new elements in the transport network. Railway building in Soviet times has been mostly confined to minor branch lines, e.g. to enable coal and iron to be assembled at Rustavi, but Grozny was linked to Astrakhan and a line built along the mountainous Black Sea coast. The most famous road in the region, over the Caucasus from Tbilisi to Ordzhonikidze, is only open during the summer, but takes a considerable freight and tourist traffic during that season.

Of the Caucasian rivers, only the Kura, as far as the Mingechaur reservoir, is used for navigation to any extent. Moreover, although the Volga river as a whole still handles about half of the river-freight of the Soviet Union, the trade of the reaches below Volgograd has shrunk, owing to the Volga–Don canal, the drying up of the stream of oil, the decline of the fisheries and the navigational problems caused by the falling level of the Caspian. Astrakhan is now 40 miles from the sea, navigation has been restricted to one channel (the 'Hooghly' of the Volga) and although a special fleet of shallow-draft boats has been built, costly trans-shipments are still necessary.

THE PRESENT POPULATION

Most of the region's 15 million people are still rural and the great majority are non-Russian, in spite of its crucial role on the Russian scene over the past three-quarters of a century. The region has roughly the same proportion of the total Soviet population as it had in 1926, but possesses a notably smaller share of the city-dwellers than it did then, and a greater share of the country folk. This relative disparity is likely to widen, although the rather high natural increase is likely to ensure that numbers will grow at least as fast as the national average, and the drift to the cities is a continuing force here as elsewhere.

The Russians number about a million in the Transcaucasus, mainly city-dwellers, above all in Baku. This is three times as many Russians as there were in this area in 1926, and they now number one in ten of the population of the three Republics, compared with one in eighteen then.

There are some thirty accredited ethnic groups, numbering at least 20,000 each, in the Caucasian region and many more distinct groups with smaller numbers—too scattered or isolated for separate recognition. Moreover, they constitute a veritable Tower of Babel—in the cities of the Transcaucasus one may see signs up in three or four different languages, each having a different alphabet.

The three largest distinct groups in the Caucasus—the Azerbaijanis ($2\frac{3}{4}$ millions), Georgians and Armenians ($2\frac{1}{2}$ millions each) have been allowed to form Republics, but each Republic contains a number of smaller minority groups. Only two-thirds of the populations of Georgia and Azerbaijan are Georgians and Azerbaijanis respectively, while nearly nine-tenths of those in Armenia are Armenians. On the other hand, very few Georgians, Stalin notwithstanding, are found outside Georgia, while Armenians are strongly represented in the other Republics, including the Russian, and indeed have, like the Jews, spread across the world. Thus only about half the Armenians of the U.S.S.R. are actually resident in Armenia. The smaller groups, such as the Abkhazians and Adzharis of the Black Sea coast, the Iranian-speaking Ossetians of the central Caucasus and the Dagestani peoples (a lumping together of many groups) have been formed into A.S.S.Rs within an S.S.R. Some of these A.S.S.Rs, such as that of Mongol Kalmucks, in the Volga semi-desert, and the Chechen-Ingush, in the North Caucasian foothills, have recently been reconstituted after having been abolished during the war. Stalin had accused these peoples of treasonable collaboration with the Germans and many were deported.

Thus the region is a veritable ethnological museum—a meeting-place, but not necessarily a melting-pot, for many of the languages, religions and races of Eurasia. The untidiness of the ethnic map hardly has its equal even in Europe, but intensity of national feeling is very variable—the Georgians would probably qualify as the most fiercely nationalistic of any major group. The Russians are increasingly represented as important members of the city population but, except for the Armenians, the Caucasian peoples have not taken part in the economic and migratory developments of the main Russian triangle.

The rural distribution (Fig. 49)

Most parts of this region, especially where the native population predominates, are still predominantly rural in character. The highest densities occur in western Georgia, in the irrigated parts of Azerbaijan and Armenia and on the northern foothills and valleys of the Caucasus. In sharp contrast are the dry steppe and desert areas between the Terek and the Volga and between the Volga and the Ural, as well as the high Caucasus, visited only seasonally by small numbers of nomadic men and animals.

The cities

About 4½ million of the region's people live in cities of over 50,000, compared with one-third of a million in 1900. Thus, in spite of its persisting rural character, the Russian period has been one of intensive urbanization. Three out of four of the city people live in the five cities of over a quarter-million—one in four in Greater Baku alone.

Baku (1,070,000, including its suburbs) has been the dynamo which has generated most of the urban and industrial activity of the region for seventy-five years, and the busiest routes still converge upon the city (Plate XXIII). Its fortunes between the last quarter of the nineteenth century and the Second World War were, of course, tied up with oil, and its growth may be compared with that of Dallas or Los Angeles. Before the great oil boom it had a long but rather dim existence. Founded in the eighth century on a south-facing embayment of a windswept desert peninsula jutting into the Caspian, it became a minor port of call on trade-routes between Europe and the East. Its position at the narrowest part of the South Caspian on the route between inhabited Transcaucasia and Middle Asia, and also on the way from the Volga to Persia, and the fact that it was ice-free, gave it considerable potential as a trading centre and fort, and it was stormed by Peter the Great, amongst others. But its desert environs and exposed position limited its growth, and it numbered only 13,000 in 1860. It was much smaller than Tbilisi even about 1900, when it produced half the world's oil, but experienced its real boom period in the first quarter of the twentieth century when, in spite of war, revolution and constant changes of control, it quadrupled its population.

During the early Five Year Plans, before the war, when it still dominated the country's oil industry, it developed a wide range of engineering and chemical industries and doubled its population again. In the last decade or so, its growth has inevitably slackened, alongside its fast-declining role in the Soviet oil world. Its industrial superstructure—of a type so much in demand today—the new gas fields nearby, the water supply piped in from the mountains for irrigation, and its man-made nodality, will probably provide enough momentum to maintain the city as a going concern, even when the oil finally dries up.

On the other hand, as the move towards regional self-sufficiency for the Transcaucasus proceeds, *Tbilisi* (formerly Tiflis, 740,000), stretched along the narrow valley of Kura (Plate XXI), is likely to strengthen the role of chief regional centre which it has traditionally held, and which, even in Baku's heyday, it only partially surrendered. Its title to this role comes from its unique focal position, with maximum accessibility to the three main concentrations of population south of the Caucasus—the lower Kura valley with Baku, the core of Armenia and the sub-tropical triangle of western Georgia. In addition it controls the only practicable road over the mountains. This situation has ensured that, since its foundation fifteen hundred years ago, it has always risen, phoenix-like, from the ashes to which many invaders reduced it. In 1865 it had 70,000 people and was much the largest city south of the Caucasus, with traditional craft industries based on silk, wool, leather, food and wine. The building of rail and pipeline enhanced the significance of its position, and it had grown to $\frac{1}{4}$ million by the Revolution, $\frac{1}{2}$ million by the Second World War and $\frac{3}{4}$ million today. It is the city of Transcaucasia with the most diversified industrial structure—engineering as well as textiles and food industries—the distinguishing mark of a true regional capital.

The most phenomenal rate of growth of any sizable city in the region has been experienced by *Yerevan* (580,000), the capital of Armenia. Although records of its existence as a fort and trading centre go back intermittently to the eighth century B.C., its arrested development reflected the harrowing history of the Armenian people. When Russia took it over in 1827 it had only 11,000 people—only half of them Armenians—and even by 1910 it numbered only 30,000. Its remarkable growth since then has been a measure of its role as the capital of a reconstituted Armenia in which it has developed an overwhelming concentration of political, cultural, industrial and even agricultural activities. Its position and rise may be compared with that of Minsk in the Belorussian Republic, which stands out as much in the Baltic region as Yerevan does in the Caucasus.

Its rapid growth has much to do with the river Razdan (Zanga), on which it is sited, which flows out of Lake Sevan. This river has provided irrigation water to turn the dry alluvial basin surrounding the city into a green and fertile land. It has also been harnessed by a string of hydro-electric plants, begun before the war and still not fully completed. These, combined with the nearby limestone, have made possible the production of synthetic rubber, Yerevan's first modern industry, which was added to the old cognac, woollens and tobacco enterprises. The supply of power is still crucial, but the gas pipeline from Karadag has greatly extended its scope. In spite of its *cul-de-sac* location near the international boundary, its exceptional resilience of growth since the war is likely to be continued.

The other cities of the Transcaucasus are much smaller—*Kutaisi* (140,000) an agricultural centre at the apex of the Colchis lowlands, which also assembles the commercial vehicles for the whole Transcaucasus; *Kirovabad* (130,000) the processing centre for the lower Kura cotton region; *Leninakan* (120,000) a textile town in western Armenia; *Batumi* (90,000) at the terminus of the pipelines and railway from the Caspian, processing and exporting oil, tea and citrus fruits; *Sukhumi* (80,000) a centre for sub-tropical botanical research, and capital of the Abkhazian people, and *Rustavi* (70,000) the steel town near Tbilisi. But larger than any of these in 1962 was *Sochi* (170,000), the centre of a string of coastal resorts which have seen a great increase in activity in the last decade or so. Granted that the city boundaries are extensive and that the midwinter census may have counted some temporary residents, the indications are that an incipient Floridan or Californian phenomenon is showing itself here.

North of the Caucasus, *Grozny* (280,000) is a miniature Baku, which has experienced about the same cycle of development, but on a smaller scale and with few activities not connected with the oil industry. It is on the oil pipeline from the Caspian port of *Makhachkala* (130,000) to the Ukraine and has also recently been connected with the Stavropol gas-fields. *Ordzhonikidze* (formerly called Vladikavkaz and also Dzaudzhikau, 180,000), where the Terek river leaves the mountains, and the terminus of the Military Highway from Tbilisi, is a zinc-refining centre (with plentiful hydro-electric power), set in a maize and vine-growing valley.

Further west there is the cluster of sulphur-spring, warm-bath resorts centred on *Pyatigorsk* (70,000) and *Kislovodsk* (80,000), which have not grown much since the war, in contrast to the Black Sea resorts.

Astrakhan (320,000), founded in the eighth century at the mouth of the mighty Volga, at the same time as Baku and Kiev, has played an eventful and significant role as a link between Europe and the East. When Caucasia was incorporated within Russia and Baku oil began to flow, its importance was greatly enhanced and in addition it was the hub of the Russian fishery industry.

However, since the Second World War, it has been dealt a number of simultaneous blows from which there can be no rapid recovery. Its immediate physical environment has been damaged by the falling level of the Caspian which has put the port further and further away from the sea, hurt the local mainstay industry—fisheries—and compounded navigational difficulties. But much more serious has been the diversion of the main stream of the Volga, in effect, to the Black Sea in 1954 and the sudden disappearance of the demand for its former main through-product —Baku oil. Melons and other vegetables are grown with irrigation on the delta and these are increasing in acreage all the time. Already the reeds of the delta are being made into cardboard products, and it seems as if Astrakhan will have to fall back, more and more, on the somewhat meagre resources of its vicinity, and will depend less and less on the through traffic which has served it so well in the past. *Guryev* (90,000), at the mouth of the Ural river, has much the same problems as Astrakhan in relation to navigation and its fishery industries, but its more important links are in relation to its oil-bearing hinterland and to the southern Urals, with which it has direct pipe and rail connections.

PROSPECT

Caucasia may be regarded as the most picturesque of the Soviet regions, with that infinite variety of nature and humanity, within a small compass, which is so untypical of Russia. With Riviera-type seascapes and snow-capped mountains, dripping forests and salt deserts, lemon groves and oil-fields, it is a match for California—most diverse of American states. But it also possesses what California altogether lacks—historical depth and an ethno-linguistic variety, fully as rich as that of the Mediterranean itself. These are the real attractions of the region, even though they may not be realizable in conventional economic terms, and they will probably come more and more to constitute its distinctive contribution within the Soviet realm.

On the other hand, there is an uncanny parallel, though only a slight functional connection, between the falling level of the Caspian Sea and the fall in the level of indispensability of the region to the national survival.

If another Hitler were to invade today, the Caucasus and the Lower Volga would hardly be the frenzied target which they were in 1941. If the various Republics were to secede now, the economic effect on the Soviet Union would be relatively slight, and no starvation of essential or much-needed commodities would be involved. The metals and fuel supplies of the Caucasus are also found elsewhere in the Soviet Union, although molybdenum might be short for a time. The one case of unique, specialized agricultural contributions—the tea and citrus fruits of the Black Sea coast—is more apparent than real, and indeed seems to involve questions of national pride, and autarchic conditioning, as much as strictly economic considerations. The serious natural liabilities of even this relatively favoured corner of the country, translated into long-term costs, might well lead the Soviet government to be content rationally with a token acreage of sub-tropical crops, while importing the bulk of the nation's real needs. Could not Italian lemons or Indian (if not Chinese) tea be procured more cheaply (and with more political fringe benefits) by a shipment of oil or manganese—or a steel plant—than by the worry and expense of investing in the risky climate of Colchis? National fisheries have, after all, been abandoned to a degree in favour of those of international waters. Such questions will undoubtedly be aired more openly as the Soviet Union feels stronger and more confident on the international scene, and they would have clear implications for the geography of this region.

Not that the Caucasus–Caspian lacks a future in the industrial or agricultural fields. The legacy of Baku has been munificent, and considering the trends to an oil-gas-chemical emphasis for Soviet industry, and the inertia of an elaborate superstructure of facilities for these things, it should be in a good position to hold its own. It is by no means deficient in fuel or industrial raw materials, as the Baltic region is, for instance, and it is not likely to be so for the foreseeable future. But its sights will be set more and more on self-sufficiency, and this will be gradually forced on it not only by lack of resources in quantities of 'All-Union' significance, but because of its peripheral location in relation to the main stream of Soviet economic development. This is particularly true of the Caspian side of the region, and one may expect the Black Sea segment, including Tbilisi and Yerevan, to develop relatively more rapidly, in contrast to the fifty years before the Second World War.

In fact it has been interesting to observe in recent years that national policy has been notably cautious in giving ear to expensive schemes for surgical operations to revive the ailing Caspian and lower Volga. Soviet leaders, even when speaking at Astrakhan, have discouraged talk of a further dam on the lower Volga, and the maintenance of a low economic level seems to be being tacitly authorized. The Caspian–lower Volga is thus quite likely to be allowed quietly to become an economic backwater, while available funds for investment go to more profitable lands in the Slavic homeland to the north.

However, there is one aspect of the modern economy of Caucasia which is almost bound to acquire an ever-increasing amount of 'All-Union' significance—the tourist industry—a massively organized and expanding one in the Soviet Union. The mountain and coastal resorts of the Caucasus and the Black Sea, together with the sedulously fostered historical attractions, may prove to be the most distinctive—and profitable—contribution of this region on the national, and even the international, scene.

CHAPTER FOURTEEN

Middle Asia

THE Russo-Siberian inhabited triangle fades away on the south-east into one of the emptiest of the deserts of Asia. Beyond, as across an ocean, lies the most isolated group of people of any size in the Soviet Union, and also the last to be brought within the Russian realm.

Superficially a number of parallels with the Western United States can be drawn. Soviet Middle Asia covers about the same area as the whole of the American West between the eastern foothills of the Rockies and the Sierra Nevada-Cascade Ranges, but carries more than twice as many people. Its northern edge lies in the latitudes of southern Montana, while its southern edge parallels northern Arizona and New Mexico. Both areas count drought as their all-pervading problem, and their predominantly yellow-brown landscapes are only occasionally streaked with the bright green of irrigated cotton or alfalfa.

The most fundamental geographical division of the United States occurs where the rainfall becomes inadequate and unreliable about the 100° W. meridian, and this still sets off the West as a world apart. However, although the American West was being 'won', and threaded with railways, at much the same time as the Russians were winning Middle Asia, the differences now become increasingly apparent. The whole of Soviet Middle Asia is hydrographically sealed off from the Oceans, whereas only a part of the American West is in this position, and such a natural insulation can be projected into the human situation. While beyond the dry American West

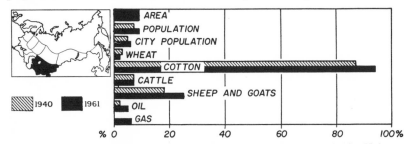

FIG. 53—Location and importance of Middle Asia in relation to the Soviet Union as a whole, for certain selected items

lies something more coveted—the Pacific Coast—Middle Asia is a dead end in the Soviet Union, and indeed was one of the world's backwaters in the period immediately before the Russian conquest.

Finally, whereas the American West was a young and empty land, now populated overwhelmingly by Europeans, Middle Asia is one of the earliest hearths of human settlement—and former centre of empires—where the controlling European Russians form only a small minority of the present population. It should not be forgotten that the region was annexed by Russia in the authentic manner of nineteenth-century colonialism, about the same time as most of the African colonies of France and Britain—almost all of which have now proclaimed their independence. The region stands as the largest group of colonial peoples in the Soviet Union and in the whole of the Moslem or even the Afro-Asian world, and is juxtaposed with the Middle East, India and China as well as Russia.

It still stands apart from the rest of the Soviet Union, in spite of the rail connections and a superficial sameness of political and social forms. It is the most rural and least industrialized of the Soviet regions and its main contributions to the national economy, as in Tsarist times, are products of the soil—above all, cotton (Fig. 53). Very recently the discovery and exploitation of natural gas on a large scale has altered this picture to some extent, but most of this gas is being sent out of the region, to the southern Urals. The gas deposits are said to be the largest and cheapest in the country, but the peripheral position is combined with a relatively retarded cultural pattern, and a population less mobile than that of Russia proper. It is still outside the main-stream of national development and does not at present have more than a secondary role on the national scene.

The boundaries of the region present less difficulty than those of any other. Its populated core is more concentrated than that of any other region, at the zone of contact of the two main landscape types—the desert and the mountains. On the south and east the international frontier inevitably serves, although it is not a clear ethnic divide and the Chinese section of the boundary does not seem as immutable as it once did. The eastern shore of the Caspian—much more starkly deserted than the other shores, marks the western edge of the region. On the north there is a broad latitudinal, empty no-man's land, which cuts the rather meaningless Kazakh Republic in half, running from the north-east corner of the Caspian through Lake Balkhash to the Chinese border, leaving the whole of the Aral Sea within Middle Asia. This neutral zone separates two distinct worlds; to the north the Russian world of the steppe, the Virgin Lands, coal, steel and non-ferrous metals—an integral part of the Soviet triangle; to the

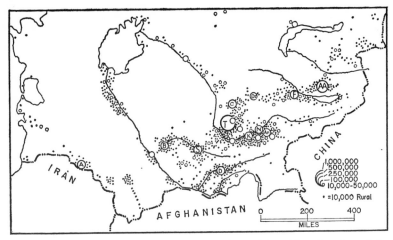

FIG. 54—Middle Asia: population. Key to cities: AA = Alma-Ata, A = Ash-khabad, An = Andizhan, B = Bukhara, C = Chimkent, D = Dushanbe, Dz = Dzhambul, F = Frunze, K = Kokand, N = Namangan, S = Samarkand, T = Tashkent

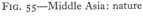

FIG. 55—Middle Asia: nature

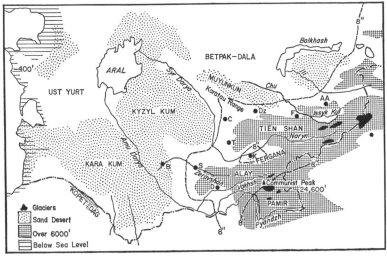

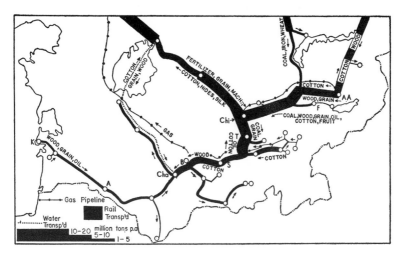

Fig. 56—Middle Asia: movements

Fig. 57—Middle Asia: economy. Minerals: C = coal, Cu = copper, M = molybdenum and tungsten, S = Glauber's salts, Su = sulphur

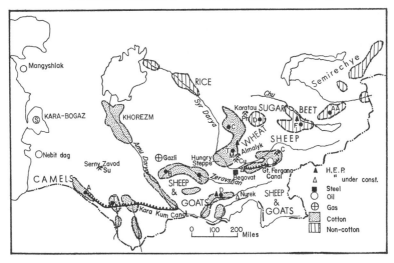

south the Asian, Moslem, ancient world of pastoralism and intensive irrigated farming, only partly integrated, economically and psychologically, with Russia.

THE NATURAL HABITAT (Fig. 55)

Middle Asia receives more heat and less moisture, in proportion to its size, than any other part of the Soviet Union. About three-quarters of the region may be classified as desert of one sort or another. But a population as large as that of Canada is supported on the remaining land. Availability of water is the key, but this in turn depends fundamentally on the pattern of the physical landscape.

Though the landscape does not display quite so many sharp changes within a small compass as does the Caucasus–Caspian region, there is no dearth of contrasts. Like the Western United States, it includes both the highest and the lowest points in the country—Peak Communism (formerly Stalin peak, 24,600 feet), in the Pamir, and a depression over 400 feet below sea level, in the Mangyshlak peninsula, a few miles from the Caspian. There are sand-dune deserts, lakes of salt and of fresh water (even both at the same time) deep beds of fine silty *löss*, bare slabs of hard rock, mud volcanoes and glaciers. Earthquakes are common throughout the southern mountain region—the city of Ashkhabad was destroyed by one in 1948— and all the cities take strict building precautions.

The mountain ranges of the south-east, part of the great system of southern Asia, radiating as well into China and India, rescue Soviet Middle Asia from an unmitigated desert condition. They intercept the depressions which come from the Mediterranean during the winter, storing moisture in the form of snow and ice, to be released into the lowlands in the summer. There are two main systems, both trending generally east–west and separated by the Fergana valley. On the north, the Tien Shan mountains, generally over 10,000 feet and rising to well over 20,000 at the Chinese border, give rise to various headstreams of the Syr Darya, which flow through the Fergana valley and eventually reach the Aral Sea. Many rivers also rise from its steep northern side, notably the Chu, which drains the large lake Issyk Kul and peters out in the sandy desert. The contribution of the river Ili, which empties into Lake Balkhash, is so decisive that the half of that long, shallow lake lying nearest to the river is fresh, while the farther part is saline. The Ili takes its rise in the Chinese part of the Tien Shan ('Heavenly Mountains'). South of the Fergana trough are the Alay ranges and the Pamir ('Roof of the World'), the latter a high plateau generally over 15,000 feet, flecked with many glaciers. However, the amount of precipitation which actually falls on these mountains, unlike that on the Black Sea slopes of the Caucasus, is limited. Most of the mountain area receives about 25 inches per annum, but the high Pamir, shielded as it is from the moist air of both the Atlantic and Indian Oceans, receives less than 5 inches and attempts have been made to increase the rate of glacier melt by dusting the ice with heat-absorbent materials. The forested areas are very limited in extent—most of the mountains are covered either with dry steppe vegetation or, higher up, alpine meadows, below the wastelands of rock and ice. However, these mountains and, to some extent, the glaciers do give birth to various tributaries of the Amu Darya, which carries much more water than any other Middle Asian river— twice that of the Syr Darya—and empties what is not captured for irrigation or by evaporation into the Aral Sea. It has been calculated that three-quarters of the water flowing out of the whole mountain area finds its way into the Amu Darya or Syr Darya systems.

Contrasted with the mountains are the lowland deserts which take up most of the region. Most of the desert is covered with sand and would be quite unsuitable for agriculture even if water were available. The Kara-Kum, south of the Amu Darya, is the most typical sand-dune desert, while the Kyzyl-Kum, between the two great rivers, is higher, with bare rock, devoid of sand, frequently exposed. A minor edition of the sandy Kara-Kum is the Muyun Kun, south of the Chu river. The Ust-Yurt, lying between the Aral and Caspian, and dropping in steep cliffs to each sea, is one of the most utterly waterless and empty deserts, being composed of thick horizontal beds of porous limestone. To the north of it, surrounding the Caspian, are the almost equally barren marshy salt flats, below sea level, the area of which has been substantially increased recently at the expense of the Caspian. Finally, north of the Syr Darya and the Chu rivers the desert (Betpak Dala) becomes more rocky and broken, eventually merging with the granites of the Kazakh uplands. Much of the surface of this area is covered with *solonchaki* (salt crusts) or *takyrs* (cracked-clay basins), as in other parts of the great desert lying north and west of the mountains of Middle Asia.

It would be wrong to think of this desert as absolutely useless, although a traverse conducted in the scorching parched summer months would certainly give this impression. Winter and spring, being cool and slightly rainy, bring out the peculiarly adapted desert plants, which have long been an essential part of the camel and sheep-herding nomad's economic environment, provided that they were able to make for higher latitudes or altitudes during the dead summer season. The *saksaul*, a desert tree of heavy hard wood, has been a mainstay for fuel in this generally fuel-deficient region with a cold winter. There is some fishing in the Aral Sea which, being recent, is only slightly saline—much less so than the Caspian. There are abundant deposits of salts, of many types, particularly in the Kara-Bogaz Gulf, which is tenuously connected, at the moment, to the Caspian, for which it acts as a giant evaporating pan. The great salt domes on the eastern shore of the Caspian are also proving, like their counterparts on the American Gulf Coast, to bear oil. Finally, there are the oases in the desert, notably in the lower Amu Darya valley (Khiva) and at the foot of the Kopet Dag mountains.

However, the really crucial natural zone, where most of the people live, is the piedmont strip, between 50 and 100 miles wide, which girdles the mountains. Here there are beds of *löss*, sometimes hundreds of feet thick, on which fertile soils have developed. The rainfall is typically about 12 inches a year, so that dry-farming can be practised but, with a multitude of short rivers fanning out from the mountains, the natural conditions are optimum for irrigation farming, given also the fertile soil and the long, hot growing season.

THE PEOPLING OF THE REGION

Irrigation farming, stock-rearing and city life—salient features of Middle Asia today—have been well-developed in the region, off and on, for several thousand years. The oldest recorded cultivators on the present territory of the U.S.S.R. have been traced to the southern edge of Turkmenia in the fourth millennium B.C. The first city, whose mysterious skeleton is still to be seen on the edge of present day Samarkand, in one of the earliest irrigated *löss*-lands—the Zeravshan valley—dates back to about 3000 B.C. By the beginning of the first millennium B.C. a powerful empire had grown up, based on the alluvial oasis of Khorezm in the lower Amu Darya, controlling much of Middle Asia, and proficient in irrigation agriculture, cattle breeding and iron working, with a slave-holding base.

Many of the beaten tracks of the Ancient World passed through the region, and along them the camel caravans plied their trade in silks, spices and other lucrative items. The two main routes from the East, one from Kashgar in the Tarim basin by a high pass to the Fergana valley, and the other through the Dzhungarian Gate from Urumchi and along the northern foothills of the Tien Shan, converged on the Zeravshan valley (Samarkand and Bukhara). From there they diverged again, one route going down the Amu Darya to Khiva (Khorezm) and on to the Volga; another following the foothills of the southern mountains, via the oasis of Merv (Mary) and the southern Caspian to the Black Sea and Mediterranean. The cities along these routes, and particularly Samarkand, stood to gain great wealth through their positions, but the other side of the coin was the constant danger (cf. Tbilisi, in Georgia) of being utterly destroyed by covetous or rampaging invaders. The utter destruction wrought by the Mongol invasion of the thirteenth century, which also laid waste Russia and the Caucasus, was the culmination of a succession of invasions and subjugations by Persians, the Greeks of Alexander the Great, Chinese and Arabs.

The zenith of Middle Asia came in the fourteenth century when, after the break-up of the Golden Horde, Samarkand became the capital of the far-flung Eurasian empire of Tamerlane and became a scientific, as well as a trading and military centre. But the discovery of the sea routes between Europe and the East had profound consequences for Middle Asia, sending it into a long decline. It was conquered by nomads—ancestors of today's Uzbeks, who took to agriculture and settled in the oases and cities of Zeravshan and Fergana. The region became more and more of a backwater, no longer on a main stream of world culture and technology, preoccupied with internecine disputes and breaking up into a number of Khanates of which Khiva, Bukhara and later Kokand were the chief centres.

Hard on the heels of the development of the Indian Ocean sea routes, came Russia's conquest of the Volga waterway and its first incursions into Asia. This fact increasingly oriented the foreign trade of Middle Asia towards this expanding power beyond the Caspian. Thus, although the economy of the region was generally decaying, and largely self-sufficient (grain, sheep, melons, etc.), what trade there was tended to be directed through Russia. Silk-worms had long been reared in the homes and cotton, which had been introduced from India in ancient times, was the chief Russian import from Middle Asia even in the early nineteenth century.

Thus, given decadence and lack of unity in Middle Asia and connections established over three centuries, it was not surprising that, in the age of imperialism rampant, the mid-nineteenth century, Russia should have considered the region ripe for colonial conquest. The Empire was already fully implanted in the Caucasus and had been gradually gaining control over the Kazakh nomads of the northern steppe. There was no natural frontier separating Middle Asia from Russia, as there was separating it from British India, for instance, or even from the Chinese Empire, which had exercised some loose control over the region in the previous century, to withdraw later, when it became weak. Looking at the physical map in the mid-nineteenth century, Russia's destiny in Middle Asia must have seemed as manifest as that of the United States in the same period. (Incidentally,

Americans were among the most fervent protagonists of Russia's civilizing mission in Asia at the time!)

The conquest of Middle Asia took most of the second half of the nineteenth century, as that of Caucasia had occupied the first half. The advance bases were prepared in the Aral–Balkhash deserts about 1853, while the final rounding out of the present boundary in the Pamir took place in 1895. But by 1875 almost all the heavily populated country had come under Russian rule, either direct or, as in the case of the vassal Khanates of Khiva and Bukhara, indirect rule, according to well-tried colonial practice. The first railway was built in the 1880s, from the Caspian to Samarkand, for explicitly military, rather than economic reasons, and the British certainly regarded it in that way. In any case by about 1890, just when the great resurgence of industrial activity in the Ukraine and Transcaucasus, as well as the agricultural migration to Siberia, were getting under way, Middle Asia was fully available for whatever Russia wanted of it.

The eve of the First World War

An improvement of communications between Russia and the populated parts of the region was an essential preliminary to either colonial economic development, or settlement on the Western Siberian model, both of which were projected for the region by the government in St Petersburg. In 1898 the railway from the Caspian reached Tashkent, which was much the largest city of the region (160,000) and had been chosen by the Russians as the capital. But the route was still very circuitous and in 1906 the completion of a direct railway between Tashkent, and Moscow provided a much more expeditious route, which henceforth carried the bulk of the exports and imports of the region. An extension into the very important Fergana valley was put through by 1916, but the Turk-Sib railway from Central Siberia, though planned, was left to the Soviets to complete.

The region was seen first and foremost as a source of the raw cotton needed for the factories of the Moscow region. Very dependent on American supplies, Russia had been hit by the Civil War. American methods were studied, American strains were introduced into Middle Asia, irrigation was extended and, as a result of various other incentives, cotton accounted for over half of the region's agricultural production by the early twentieth century. All the same, by the eve of the First World War, Russia's mills still acquired half their raw cotton from abroad. However, the cotton drive involved a radical disturbance of the self-sufficient character of the region, necessitating a dependence on food imports from the north—a situation which prompted the plan for the

Turk-Sib railway, to tap Siberian wheat. The new direct line also allowed for the sending of fresh fruit to Moscow, though the demand was small compared with that for cotton. Industrial employment in Middle Asia increased some twenty-fold between 1885 and 1914—mainly due to the establishment of cotton processing plants (the first American cotton grown in the region had to be sent back to the United States for ginning). This industrial growth, coupled with the advent of the railways and the importance of the Russian administrative machinery, led to rapid growth of cities. In particular, Tashkent became much larger than the old centres in the Fergana and Zeravshan valleys, numbering over a quarter of a million by 1914 (one-fifth of them Russian, housed in a completely new segregated quarter, contrasting sharply with the native old town).

There were some 400,000 Russians in Middle Asia in 1911, 6% of the total population, nearly half of them living in the cities. There was very limited scope for the agrarian settlement of Russians, because of the prior presence of the native peasants on the best land, although the government had grandiose plans for irrigation schemes, to make room for intensive settlement of Russian peasants. In fact, the only area where Russian rural settlement was feasible on any scale was in the northern foothills of the Tien Shan and Dzhungarian Alatau ranges (Semirechye region). Perhaps because of a severe climate (this is not cotton country even today) and more wooded character than the rest of Middle Asia, and security problems, there was only a sparse native settlement, other than the nomadic Kazakhs and Kirgiz of the drier steppe. Thus Russian Cossack families were settled on the land, and forts were established after 1850 (e.g. present-day Alma-Ata), with considerable government support, since this was seen as a strategic foothold and particularly as buttressing Russian claims against China. In fact a part of the upper Ili valley, now in Chinese Sinkiang, was held by Russia from 1871 to 1881. These settlements caused much trouble with the Kazakhs and seriously depleted the good timber reserves, but by 1914 there were probably about 150,000 Russians farming in this Semirechye region. They constituted the great bulk of the rural Russians in Middle Asia, but they were a small and isolated group, compared with the settlement to the north of the desert, in Siberia.

The native population had gained considerable benefits from the period of Russian rule, from a cultural and economic point of view and through the establishment of peace and order. But the depth of feeling against the Russian colonists and overlords was, nevertheless, demonstrated by the bitter revolts during and after the First World War, and the attempts to set up an independent state in Turkestan. As in Transcaucasia, traditional antipathies prevented such unity, but the Russians had certainly not been accepted as permanent rulers.

On the eve of the Second World War

The trends and processes which were set in train during the Tsarist time were generally intensified in the first two decades of the Soviet era. The Turk-Sib railway was finally completed in 1931, linking the Semirechye with the rest of Middle Asia and Siberia, while the capitals of the new Tadzhik and Kirgiz republics were brought into the rail net. Cotton output nearly doubled in the first Five Year Plan, making the country virtually self-sufficient, but this was achieved at the expense of food-crops in Middle Asia, which became even more acutely dependent on Russia for basic necessities. The Fergana valley was the scene of the most comprehensive irrigation scheme. Renewed immigration of Russians to the Semirechye (where sugar-beet was introduced), and above all to the cities, had substantially increased the proportion of Russians in the region by 1940, in spite of the high natural increase of the native population. Tashkent, with over half a million people in 1939, was still twice as large as any other city, but the relative growth of the other cities reflected the increasing Russification. Alma-Ata, which had been made capital of the Kazakh Republic, but was essentially a Russian city, grew with extraordinary rapidity to a quarter-million by 1939, while Frunze and Dushanbe (then Stalinabad), the similarly Russified capitals of the other Republics, were transformed from mere villages. By contrast the ancient native cities like Samarkand, Kokand, Namangan and Bukhara hardly grew at all during this period.

However, the paradox was that, in spite of all the efforts directed towards the transformation of Middle Asia into a gigantic cotton farm, its relative share of the Soviet cotton output was less than it had been in 1913, owing to the attempts to grow cotton elsewhere. In almost all other commodities its proportion of Soviet output had dropped, and acute deficiencies had developed. A little textile manufacture had been established and a small quantity of Caspian oil was being produced, but fundamentally the region was overwhelmingly agricultural and inextricably tied to the rest of the Soviet Union by the cotton-food exchange.

THE PRESENT ECONOMY (Fig. 57)

This basic economic structure and orientation has been preserved, with cotton making a greater contribution than ever, both relative (95%) and absolute on the national scene, while food crops have tended to decline, except for fruit. Manufacturing, even of textiles, is still relatively unimportant and, except for phosphates (for fertilizers), mining is not very significant. However, the energy picture has become much brighter recently with the discovery of enormous reserves of natural gas. This is already of marked benefit to the Urals, but what impact it will eventually have on the economic structure of Middle Asia remains to be seen.

Farming

Because of the limited amount of land which is both fertile and accessible to water, because the necessary heat and length of growing season hardly exist elsewhere in the U.S.S.R., and because of a deep-rooted desire for national self-sufficiency, cotton is King on the farms of Middle Asia. Output has risen five-fold since 1913 and cotton occupies about half of the irrigated farmland of the region. Nearly a third of the irrigated cotton acreage is in the Fergana valley, with the Tashkent oasis, the Zeravshan valley and the lower Amu Darya valley (Khiva) each about half as important as Fergana. Together these oases account for over three-quarters of the cotton, but several minor oases along the hot southern desert, in the Tadzhik and Turkmen Republics, have a rather higher yield. North of the Tien Shan the growing season is too hazardous and cotton is not grown, its place being taken by maize, alfalfa, sugar-beet and fruit, especially melons, peaches, grapes and apples. In the cotton belt, alfalfa is the chief rotation crop, restoring nitrogen, removing excess salts and helping to support a growing livestock (especially dairy) component, while rice is an important grain crop. Pigs, formerly taboo in this Moslem land, are now beginning to appear. Dry farming of wheat and other grains is practised in some parts of the *löss* foothill belt which have between 10 and 15 inches of rain but, as in the Virgin Lands to the north, with which it is associated, it involves a considerable gamble.

Outside the irrigated lands, the other traditional type of farming is stock-rearing, which is all that can be done with three out of four of the region's acres, and that quite precariously. Sheep and goats together outnumber cattle by at least five to one, and the wool and skins (particularly of the Karakul sheep and lambs) have long been the most lucrative livestock product from the region (Plate XXV). Cattle are on the increase though, while camels are declining and donkeys are the chief beast of burden, except in the desert proper.

Over many centuries of heart-breaking trial and error, particular nomadic groups had worked out a delicately balanced annual circuit, involving either latitudinal or altitudinal migrations by seasons—one which was fixed and by no means involved aimless wandering. Thus the incursions of Russian settlers over the last century or so, culminating in collectivization, dealt a very serious blow to the nomads, especially the Kazakhs, who at first resisted and later emigrated to China and other parts of Asia in large numbers. The native vegetation of mountain and desert is still the mainstay of many collective farms, but in the past a chance climatic disaster, such as the formation of a hard sheet of ice over the grazing grounds, frequently decimated the flocks. Recent developments have emphasized the crucial role of irrigated alfalfa from the cotton lands, as the chief reserve standby for the ranging animals.

Thus irrigation is clearly the key to the expansion of farming in the entire region, not excluding the traditional livestock sector, and great importance attaches to the prospects for its future extension. There are some 12 million acres of irrigated land in the region, compared with 7 million in 1913. Two-thirds of the total Soviet irrigated acreage are in Middle Asia, which of all regions provides the greatest incentive to this kind of agricultural investment, because of its unusually rich heat budget and because there is little temptation to try to get by agriculturally with unirrigated, low-yield agriculture.

It has been calculated that an area about four times the present irrigated acreage is irrigable land. However, most of this has poor-quality saline or clayey soils, which would hardly justify the heavy, continuing investment necessary, unless demand for cotton became suddenly much more acute. There are, though, several areas of relatively promising land where long-term irrigation projects are under way. Following on the pre-war Fergana project has come the extension of irrigation from the Syr Darya to the so-called Hungry Steppe south of Tashkent, and to the lowlands between Tashkent and the Karatau mountains (Arys valley) to the north, as well as extensions to the Fergana canal system. The Amu Darya has greater quantities of water available, however, and several fresh demands on it have been made since the Second World War. The Kara-Kum canal has been cut through the southern sandy desert, rather like the All-American canal in California, from the Amu Darya via the old oases of Mary (Merv) and Tedzhen to Ashkhabad. The latter oases get a good deal of snow-melt from the mountains of Afghanistan, but there are serious problems of uneven flow, involving storage reservoirs; in addition evaporation from the canal is intense and silting a major problem in the earlier stretches of the canal. Whether the canal will be continued to the Caspian is a moot point. This would probably be as economically unworkable as the Great Turkmen Canal project was eventually decided to be. The latter, one of

Stalin's grandiose plans, would have led off from the lower Amu Darya at Nukus, along the old Aral Sea spillway to the Caspian, but would have involved a demand for water which would have outrun the available supply, for very doubtful returns. In place of this a much more workable scheme now under way involves pumping Amu Darya water up to Bukhara, where the Zeravshan river peters out. Other major projects are under way in the valley of the Vakhsh, a tributary of the Amu Darya, in the Tadzhik Republic—in particular as a concomitant of the $2\frac{1}{2}$ million kilowatt high dam at Nurek.

All these schemes are primarily directed at the extension of the cotton acreage but will inevitably also broaden the base of the livestock industry. In addition fruit and vegetable growing is increasing, and should have considerable scope for expansion (cf. California) as national living standards continue to improve and a system of refrigerated transport is developed.

Transport (Fig. 56)

The policy of regional specialization on cotton has put considerable strain on the existing railway links with the rest of Russia, which traverse long stretches of commercially unresponsive country and have occasioned considerable problems of excessive coal use and of water deficiency. In spite of the expressed intention of bringing textile manufacturing down to the land of cotton, as in the U.S.A., almost all the raw cotton still has to be hauled over 2,000 miles to the Moscow region to be processed, most of it over the single-track direct line from Tashkent. The southward flow into Middle Asia of lumber, grain, pig iron, coal, fertilizers and other bulky goods greatly outweighs the northward. Since 1953 two additional rail lines have been built—one links Karaganda coal and steel and Virgin Lands wheat directly with the Turk-Sib, to the west of Lake Balkhash; the other links the important cotton oasis of the lower Amu Darya with the rest of the railway network—previously it was utterly dependent on the Amu Darya, which is a difficult and uncertain river for navigation, although the best in Middle Asia.

Tashkent is located strategically between the converging life-lines from Moscow, Urals and Siberia on the one hand, and the feeder lines from the oases of Fergana, Amu Darya–Zeravshan, Turkmenia and Tadzhikistan on the other. Middle Asia is probably more dependent on its railways than any other Soviet region, in a country where the railway is still dominant. The freight totals have grown rapidly in the Soviet era while the degree of self-sufficiency continues to decline, in spite of attempts to eliminate 'irrational shipments', and build up local industries.

The most important new factor in reducing the load on the railways through elimination of coal imports and stimulation of more home industry is the recent gas pipeline connection with Tashkent and other centres of population, though how far it will affect the region itself is still in doubt. The road network is being extended and a number of regular air-routes have put Tashkent within four hours of Moscow. Finally the effect of the immediate international situation *vis-à-vis* China remains in doubt. The completion of the Soviet section of the much advertised Sinkiang railway to Middle Asia, which was to have greatly increased international traffic on the Middle Asian rail system, has not yet been met by the Chinese. The latter's rail terminal is still Urumchi and the *Druzhba* (Friendship) station on the border looks rather forlorn. However, since Sino-Soviet trade has almost come to a standstill, and since the actual nature of the international commodities to ply this route was always rather shadowy, the concrete effects of a formal completion of this line, at this stage, would not be significant.

Industry

Middle Asia is much less industrialized, in proportion to population, than any of the other Soviet regions, in spite of considerable efforts, earnest intentions, and a steady actual increase in the numbers employed in manufacturing. It is very much an agricultural region and the industries are still, in the main, ancillary to agricultural needs.

Though, to a large extent, this has been due to locational, climatic and cultural reasons, comparative poverty in industrial resources has, until very recently, provided little stimulus for rapid development. The oil deposits of Nebit-dag near the Caspian continue to be very minor by national standards and are a long way from the main Middle Asian centres, while the oil and coal of the Fergana and neighbouring districts are even less impressive, though better located. Hydro-electric power has so far also been limited to several relatively small stations incidental to irrigation works, though the Nurek dam, now under construction on the Vakhsh, will be on an altogether larger scale. But the recent discovery of the immense natural gas deposits at Gazli, in the desert west of Bukhara has suddenly changed the picture of the region's industrial potential. It is said to be the largest single reserve of natural gas in the country, with perhaps a fifth of the nation's proven reserves, and in addition the cheapest to exploit. This gas is piped to the Zeravshan–Tashkent–Fergana core of the region but the greater part of it is now sent to the furnaces of the Urals. It seems that this is likely to continue to be the pattern and moreover the yearly increase in output is still much less than would seem to be warranted by its low cost and large reserves, and by comparison with that scheduled for the North Caucasus, Ukraine and the Volga.

Resources of industrial raw materials are also rather restricted. Various deposits of salts, sulphur and phosphates have long been worked and their output is likely to increase steadily because of their relevance to the new expansion of chemical industries and the great need for fertilizers for the cotton, much of which is still imported long distances by rail. The most important deposits are the phosphates of Karatau (formerly called Chulak-tau), the sulphur of Serny Zavod, in the Kara-Kum desert, and the Glauber's salts of the Kara-Bogaz gulf. The sulphur and phosphates are combined in several superphosphate plants in the cotton-growing belt, and a great effort is now being made to achieve self-sufficiency in this and other fertilizers.

The region is generally poor in metals, and pig iron has to be 'imported' to the region's only steel plant at Begovat. From a national point of view the molybdenum deposits at Almalyk, south of Tashkent, seem to be the most important. It may become the chief national source of this valuable metal, but quite clearly the whole production will be sent out of the region. Lead is smelted at Chimkent.

Processing of agricultural materials, especially cotton, silk, wool, skins and fruit, accounts for a major component of the industrial structure of the cities, but much of it is to be classified as primary processing rather than manufacturing proper. The most striking illustration of this is that, with over nine-tenths of the country's raw cotton, less than one-tenth of the Soviet cotton cloth is made in Middle Asia. The kind of shift in cotton textiles which has occurred in the U.S.A., from New England to the South, which the Soviet Union officially wishes to emulate, is still very far from being accomplished.

THE PRESENT POPULATION

The typical inhabitant of Middle Asia is still a non-Slavic, rural person, gaining a living on irrigated *löss*-land. Less than one in four of the population is found in cities of over 50,000, and a substantial proportion of these are Russians (probably a majority in some cities). Whereas in 1926 Middle Asia contained 5% of the Soviet city population and 7% of the rural, the percentages are now about 6 and 11 respectively. The population as a whole grew from 7 to 9% of the national total in the same period, indicating a relatively high growth-rate which may be ascribed, as in other under-developed parts of Asia, to a rapid reduction in the death-rate without corresponding reduction in birth-rates. The regional birth-rate is still

50% higher than the national average, while the death-rate is average. Other factors include immunity from war-ravages, and the war-time reception of many migrants, composed of many ethnic groups, both voluntary and involuntary. The destination of most of the ethnic groups deported by Stalin during the war, such as the Crimean Tatars, Chechens and Ingush, was probably Middle Asia.

The sharp difference between the nomadic and settled farmers, which has been fundamental throughout most of the region's history, has become blurred since the collectivization programme of the 1930s. This led to a considerable exodus, especially of Kazakhs, and the crucial dependence of the present herdsmen on a regular component of fodder grown on irrigated lands has effectively stabilized and controlled the nomadic groups.

There are some 2½ million Russians in the four Republics of Middle Asia (Uzbek, Tadzhik, Kirgiz and Turkmen) and probably rather more than a million in the southern part of Kazakhstan, so that they constitute between one-fifth and one-quarter of the people of the whole region. Only one of the other recognized ethnic groups, the Uzbeks, are more numerous (6 millions) but they are scattered and largely rural. Since the Russians are mainly in the cities and possess disproportionate influence in the industrial, political and cultural life of the region, they can fairly be regarded as the dominant ethnic group, as elsewhere in the U.S.S.R. However, they are, and will be for the foreseeable future, in a definite minority and this gives the region different characteristics and problems from those of, say, Siberia or northern Kazakhstan. The native languages are used in the schools, though they have been given Cyrillic script, but Russian is also compulsory and a *sine qua non* for anyone wanting to improve his position in society. The European and Asian peoples have limited contact socially and inter-marriage is still rare, while to some extent the living quarters are still distinct. This situation is culturally rather than legally induced, with traditional religious overtones still evident, and is a phenomenon well known in other parts of the world, even North America. But there has long been considerable intermixing between the various indigenous ethnic groups, greatly accelerated by urbanization, so that 'racial' criteria for distinguishing the various peoples of the region are becoming quite unrecognizable.

The rural distribution (Fig. 54)

The density of rural population shows sharper contrasts here than anywhere else in the Soviet Union. Most of the land is as empty as can be found anywhere in the country, possessing no settlement at all in the strict sense of the word. On the other hand the irrigated *löss*-lands have rural densities greater than those found anywhere else. Most of these high density areas (over 200 people to the square kilometre) are within a 200-mile radius of Tashkent. In all of them the population is overwhelmingly non-Slavic, the investment per acre is great, the main crop is cotton and the rural densities have been high for many centuries. Moreover, the rural population is less top-heavy in its age-structure than is the case in old rural parts of European Russia, and can be therefore expected to decline less suddenly than the latter in the foreseeable future. The chief outlier of dense rural population, where Russians are well-represented, is on the north-east foothills of the Tien Shan, around Alma-Ata and the Chu valley. Away from the *löss* foothills the alluvial basin of the lower Amu Darya (Khiva) is the most important outlier of relatively dense population (though less dense than the foothills)—the lower Syr-Darya is very thinly settled by comparison. In general the pattern is very similar to that found in the rest of Moslem Asia from Egypt to Pakistan and quite unlike that of Russia proper.

The cities

There are now 24 cities of over 50,000, compared with 6 in 1926. They house over 4 million people, less than one in four of the region's population, compared with less than three-quarters of a million, or one in eight of the population in 1926. Thus the drift to the cities has been a reality, as in the rest of the country. Nearly half the city population was in Tashkent in 1926 while, in spite of the consolidation of the latter's supremacy as a regional capital, it now claims only one-quarter. The new large cities are generally those with a predominantly Russian character, even though they are often also capitals of non-Russian republics. Those which have experienced a relative stagnation are those which were predominantly native, usually with ancient foundations, before the Soviet times.

Tashkent, with a million inhabitants, is one of the great cities of the Soviet Union, and the regional capital of Middle Asia. It is centrally situated with respect to the major population concentrations and route-ways of the region, in the oasis of the Chirchik river, close to its confluence with the Syr-Darya. It has certainly had thirteen centuries, and probably more, of life as a route centre—equally accessible to the northern and southern caravan routes between China and Europe. Before the Russian conquest it was frequently being fought for by the rival Khanates. It was already one of the largest of the Middle Asian cities (about 80,000) by the time of its conquest by Russia in 1865, but this set the seal on its supremacy within the region. The Russians made it the capital of all Turkestan and proceeded to build their own city next to, but aloof from the old one of low adobe (*löss*) houses. By 1910, after it had been connected directly to Moscow by rail, it had a population of a quarter of a million people, at least twice the size of any other city and it has remained much larger than the other cities since. Its accessibility and centrality is emphasized by the population map combined with the railway freight-flow map, which show it controlling the converging routes from the southern agricultural districts on the one hand and the northern lifeline from the Russian world—Moscow, Karaganda and Central Siberia—on the other. It is the most industrialized city in Middle Asia, and has been greatly encouraged by the recent gas pipeline from Bukhara, with cotton textiles and the machinery for them and for the cotton farms somewhat predominating. The diverse food and other consumption industries give the city in addition its character as the regional focus of the most isolated of the major Soviet regions. Implementation of long-term intentions of moving the bulk of textile manufacturing to Middle Asia would greatly accelerate its growth but, even without this, it is growing very quickly and has no foreseeable rival as a regional capital.

Alma-Ata (formerly called Verny, 530,000) is the largest of that group of cities which was virtually created by the Russians, and has been the second city of the region since the 1930s. It is situated, 2,600 feet high, in the foothills of steep, snow-capped mountains, thickly forested on their lower slopes, down which many small rivers, used for irrigation and power, cross the fertile alluvial plains to the Ili valley. Although there may have been an earlier settlement there, there was little left of it when Russian Cossacks founded the present city as a fort in 1854. It became the centre of the Russian settlement area of Semirechye and was also used as a penal settlement, but in 1913 the population was only 37,000, of whom three-quarters were Russians. Its period of rapid growth dates from the city's nomination as the capital of the Kazakh Republic in 1929 and the arrival of the Turk-Sib railway the following year. Its population reached a quarter of a million by the eve of the Second World War and has doubled since. It is in a good agricultural area and has developed a diverse group of industries—food and leather processing, textiles, ceramics and, most important, engineering—but its growth is to be attributed largely to its political function as capital of a large, rich and rapidly developing Republic. It is, however, right on the edge of this Republic and separated by a desert from the most important part of its dominions. If northern Kazakhstan were to be detached and joined to the Russian Republic, it is probable that

Alma-Ata's growth would slow down, but at present it continues to expand with great rapidity.

The capitals of the other Republics (other than Tashkent itself) may be compared with Alma-Ata. *Frunze* (formerly called Pishpek, 310,000) capital of Kirgizia, was founded in the nineteenth century as a fort, first by the Kokand Khanate and later by the Russians. Its situation, elevation, type of agriculture and history are almost identical to Alma-Ata's, but the many rivers fanning down from the Tien Shans converge on the Chu, which later loses itself in the desert. The city had only 14,000 people in 1911 and only 90,000 even in 1939. The Kirgiz republic dates only from 1936 and Frunze's main growth has been in the post-war period. Its industries are largely oriented towards agricultural needs. *Dushanbe* (formerly called Stalinabad, 260,000) has, like Frunze, tripled its population since the beginning of the war, and consisted of three villages totalling 5,000 people in 1926. Three years later it got its railway connection and became the capital of the Tadzhik Republic. It is situated in an irrigated cotton valley at the foot of the Gissar ranges and textiles are the main item of manufacture. *Ashkhabad* (formerly called Poltoratsk, 200,000), the capital of the Turkmen Republic, at the foot of the dry Kopet Dag range, was also a small village before being established in 1881 as a Russian fort and base for building the Trans-Caspian railway. Like most of the cities of Middle Asia, it is subject to earthquakes, and was destroyed by one in 1948. Like the other capitals, it is mainly a Russian city, with varied industries; it is also one of the chief film-making centres of the country. The city is somewhat isolated from the main concentrations of Middle Asian activity; it has grown more slowly than the other capitals and, were it not for its capital function, would be of little significance. Though not having a political role, two basically Soviet towns should be mentioned here, situated on either side of the Karatau range. *Chimkent* (180,000) near the junction of the Turk-Sib and Moscow–Tashkent railways, is the centre of a developing cotton-growing region and has textile manufacture as well as a large lead smelter. *Dzhambul* (140,000) is in a sugar-beet-growing region, where a branch rail line from the Karatau phosphate workings meets the Turk-Sib; its main industries, fertilizers and sugar-refining, reflect these endowments.

The old towns of the region were mostly sprawling, over-grown villages of low adobe dwellings in the irrigated *löss*-lands—some of them clustered around the crumbling ruins of the monuments of a more glorious past. They were, of course, the largest towns until the present century, but most of them have stagnated since. A very special case, both much older and more rejuvenated than the others, is *Samarkand* (220,000), where the

Zeravshan river, surrounded by dry mountain ranges (Plate XXIV), cuts through the thick beds of *löss*. This is certainly the most ancient, and world-famous, of the cities of Middle Asia where, cheek by jowl, there are earthworks of the precursor city, Afrosiab, perhaps five thousand years old; the wonderful mausoleums, theological colleges and a scientific observatory dating from the Golden Age of Tamerlane, dominating the city and sedulously taken care of by the Soviet authorities; and finally the apartments, factories and markets in the modern Soviet style (Plate XXVI). It was made the capital of the Uzbek Republic 1924–30 and has a definite regional importance—its present industries including silk and cotton textiles, chemicals, engineering and food industries. The recent arrival of gas from further down the Zeravshan valley should enhance its industrial potential. The tourist industry has very considerable significance and further scope.

The large towns of the Fergana valley—*Andizhan* (150,000), *Namangan* (140,000) and *Kokand* (120,000) have grown only sluggishly in the Soviet period, in spite of the considerable extension of irrigated land in the valley. Kokand in particular, which was the second largest city of Middle Asia in 1900, has hardly grown during this century. The same is true of *Bukhara* (80,000) which, with Kokand and Tashkent, was one of the three largest cities of the region before the Russians came. Its population in 1939 had shrunk to two-thirds of what it had been in 1900. Like Samarkand, it is a city of monuments, but has more significance for the Moslems and is much more completely a city of the past than Samarkand, with only a few small textile and handicraft activities. However, the great gas fields nearby, the increase in irrigation potential with the import of Amu Darya water, and the increasing tourist provision, should lead to a considerable rejuvenation of this ancient city in the immediate future.

PROSPECT

The sense of isolation, of a place apart, still pervades the region and its problems. In relation to the world of the twentieth century, it is more of a backwater or cul-de-sac than it was before the Age of Discovery. The fundamental insulator is the drought-blighted zone separating the inhabited core of Russia from that of Middle Asia, while the international boundaries to the south and east are also unresponsive, sometimes even hostile. Thus a certain cultural and psychological insulation persists, even though it is being modified continually by the new drift to the towns and the inevitable process of Russification in the key sectors of society.

Economically this outlying location expresses itself in a constant see-saw of public policy with regard to the conflicting claims of self-sufficiency and specialization for the region. The cost and congestion of rail transport in and out of the region provides every incentive for boosting internal self-sufficiency; yet the railways specifically opened the door to specialization and from the national point of view there is much to be gained by it. The degree of specialization does not seem to be decreasing and within this context the question becomes: what are the probable lines along which the character of this specialization will develop? It is almost certain to remain fundamentally agricultural for the foreseeable future, and irrigation will remain the key, but it is unlikely that investment in the extension of the irrigation area will go further than the relatively limited schemes now under way in comparatively favourable areas, such as the Hungry Steppe, Tadzhikistan, and Bukhara. Most of the land designated as irrigable is almost certainly destined to remain unirrigated. As elsewhere agricultural output will be increased mainly by improved methods in the good land already farmed, by intensification and by rearranging crop priorities. At present cotton is pre-eminent, but this may not be maintained. Apart from the incalculable effect on cotton of the new drive for synthetic fibres, might it not be advantageous, politically as well as economically, to import larger quantities of cotton from Egypt or other developing countries, to which the U.S.S.R. is sending considerable amounts of aid? Might it not be more rational, given an increase in national living standards and a chain of refrigerated rail cars, to use the irrigated lands more intensively for fruit, vegetables and live-stock perishables, which are greatly needed, which are of high value in relation to bulk and for which these areas are best suited? In other words is it not possible to conceive of Middle Asia as another California (melons and lettuce but not citrus), which is similarly separated from its main market by great stretches of desert? Combined with the implementation of the long-promised plan to make the region the main base of textile manufacturing, this could add up to a significant improvement in the efficient use of scarce railway capacity. The recent windfall of natural gas means that there is now no fuel bottleneck for industrial expansion, though the fact that most of this gas is scheduled for 'export' indicates that there may still be considerable disincentives, locational and cultural, to the creation of a full-scale industrial base in the region.

From the political point of view, Soviet Middle Asia presents an interesting case. The establishment of Russian control over the area was carried through in the classical colonialist manner and little reference was made to the wishes of the inhabitants either during the original conquest or the re-assertion of Russian control under the Soviets. The region now stands as one of the very few parts of the world where a minority of Europeans had brought a larger number of non-Europeans under its control in the nineteenth century, and which has not achieved its independence. Moreover, not only is there no prospect whatever of an independent Turkestan, but the Soviet government is posing, successfully, as the champion of anti-colonialism and even presenting Middle Asia as evidence that it is an Asian and Moslem power and therefore kin to the other peoples of Asia and the Moslem world. Undoubtedly great social and economic benefits have accrued, and the literacy and absence of poverty and beggary, in spite of a high natural increase, certainly contrasts with the countries to the south—a fact which is not lost on the frequent visitors from those countries. It is a remarkable fact that there is very little difference between the standard of living in this region and that of Russia proper, probably less than that between northern and southern Italy, or even the North and South of the U.S.A. or (reversed) England.

The Russians are clearly sensitive, all the same, to the charge of colonialism and since the war there has been a concerted effort by Soviet spokesmen to present the Tsarist conquest of Middle Asia not, as formerly, as an 'absolute evil' but as 'progressive' or even a 'reunion of brothers'. The greatest danger now, as the Russians see it, lies in the attitude of China, which has already attempted to bar the Soviet Union from an Afro-Asian Conference on the grounds that it is not an Asian State but only a 'conqueror of Asian peoples'. What is more, China also claims vague suzerainty over the area, has control of very similar country and peoples to the East, and has made it clear that, as in the case of India, the Sino-Soviet boundary is not to be regarded as sacrosanct.

However, the facts remain that Middle Asia is entirely dependent on and integrated with Russia, and has large numbers of Russian settlers, with no sea separating them from their kin, as in the case of, for instance, Algeria and France. Although the economic importance of Middle Asia to the Soviet Union is something less than vital, it can be expected to hold on to the region at all costs. Moreover, in view of the undoubted economic and social benefits which are continuing to accrue to them from the Russian contact, and the memories of former internecine conflicts, it is likely that the people of the region are, by and large, reconciled to permanent integration in the Soviet realm.

CHAPTER FIFTEEN

The Far East

THE Soviet Far East appears as the 'Ultima Thule' of inhabited Asia, and occupies a lonely position in the contemporary world. Its four million inhabitants live next door to the quarter of the world's people in China and Japan, while four or five thousand miles away from their own centre of government and the bulk of their kinsmen.

The first parallel with North America which comes to mind is British Columbia. In both cases, most of the people live a few miles from the border of a great neighbour-country to the south. They are both young in terms of settlement—virtually all within the last century—and had to await the arrival of a long-heralded trans-continental railway before any appreciable economic development could begin or political union with the 'motherland' be made anything like effective. Other similarities are the densely forested mountain ranges dropping steeply to the sea, a relatively high degree of urbanism, and the great significance of rivers whose development for energy has been held up by lack of international agreement.

But in the all-important factor of climate the analogy to be made is with the Maritime provinces of Canada, with their long raw winters and cool summers. The northern parts belong with Newfoundland and southern Labrador, and the entire sea-coast is frozen in winter, even though

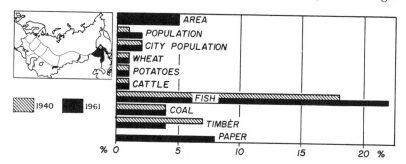

FIG. 58—Location and importance of the Far East in relation to the Soviet Union as a whole, for certain selected items

295

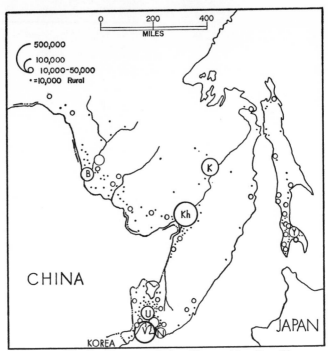

FIG. 59—The Far East: population. Key to cities: B = Blago-
veshchensk, K = Komsomolsk, Kh = Khabarovsk, N =
Nakhodka, U = Ussuriisk, V = Vladivostok, Y = Yuzhno-
Sakhalinsk

FIG. 60—The Far East: nature. 1 = deciduous forests, 2 =
mixed forests, 3 = tayga

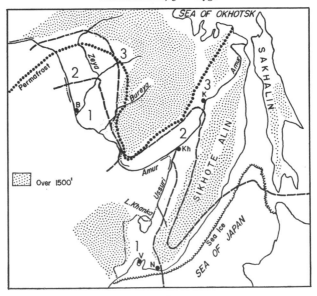

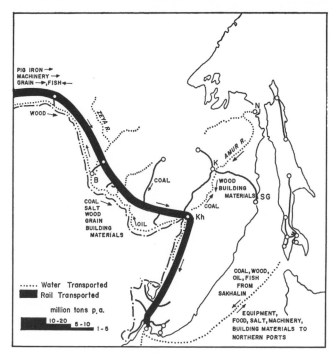

FIG. 61—The Far East: movements

FIG. 62—The Far East: economy. Minerals: C = black coal, Li = lignite, Pb = lead, Sn = tin

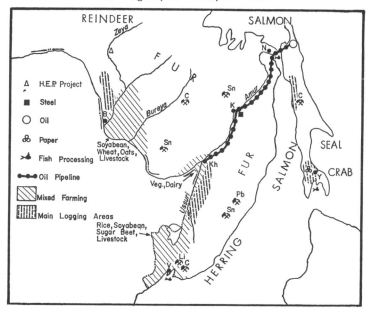

Vladivostok is a little further south than ice-free Halifax. This harsh picture helps to explain the long-time emptiness of the region and many of its present problems and limitations. In fact, when contemplating such handicaps, it seems remarkable that the population exceeds that of the Maritimes and British Columbia combined, having been almost empty a century ago.

Nevertheless, the region's development, always limited and difficult, has been severely stultified by the freezing of relations between the Soviet Union and China. The various schemes for another St Lawrence Seaway on the Amur have been shelved and it seems clear that the easterly movement of nationally significant industrial development does not extend beyond Lake Baykal. The long-drawn-out supply lifelines make self-sufficiency a desirable aim, but it is far from being achieved and the region depends heavily on 'imports' of food, steel and machinery. Its industries are largely primary, processing timber, fish and some metals. Since there is plenty of timber along the Trans-Siberian railway, the only major contribution of the region to the rest of the country lies in fish products (Fig. 58).

Although, therefore, the Far East looks insignificant in relation to the rest of the Soviet Union (with less than 2% of the population) or, still more, the Sino-Japanese world, it stands out in Siberia east of the Yenisey (half the Soviet area) as containing the only appreciable haven from permafrost and the most favourable pockets of farmland, poor though they are in an absolute sense. The region delimits itself quite naturally, standing out in isolation as it does. The North, in the form of the unrelieved, empty tayga, comes right down to the Trans-Siberian railway as it wends its way round the northerly bulge of Manchuria. The latter marks off the Trans-Baykal from the Far East even more surely than the similar northward bulge of Maine separates the Canadian Maritimes from Quebec. The northern boundary has been somewhat arbitrarily drawn from the crown of this bulge to the northern tip of Sakhalin, including the whole of the Amur drainage basin, even though much of this territory could objectively be characterized as the North. The Amur gives a unity to the region, and Sakhalin island is tied to it also while, for good measure, the Kuril islands may be included, although they could as well be bracketed with Kamchatka and therefore the North. The Soviet official economic region, 'The Far East', does in fact include the whole of the north-eastern corner of Siberia to the Chukchi Sea, but this is an unwieldy unit, which obscures the fundamental qualitative difference between the populated southern strip and the vast expanses of the empty north. It is this stark contrast which sets off, as clearly as anything, the identity of the region as defined here—a distinctive, if rather forlorn, corner of the Soviet Union.

THE NATURAL HABITAT (Fig. 60)

From their vantage point, the Chinese and Japanese must regard the Soviet Far East as almost beyond the pale from the climatic point of view. The whole of its coastline is frozen in winter, but the edge of the frozen zone coincides in an uncanny way with the Soviet frontier. Even Vladivostok is in the grip of the dry cold winds from the interior of Siberia, which keep temperatures below freezing for at least five months, with a January average of −6° F. The summers are in the 60s rather than the 70s or 80s and the summer monsoon rainfall (20–30 inches) is light and uncertain compared with those southern realms which intercept the bulk of it first. Raw fog, high humidity in summer and generally grey weather predominate—Sakhalin has a particularly miserable climate. For rice-growing peoples such a combination of climatic endowments looks rather dismal.

On the other hand these same endowments, at least those of the inhabited lowlands, look positively beckoning when viewed from the rest of the eastern half of the U.S.S.R. Freedom from permafrost (though only just), together with slightly higher accumulated temperatures (similar to the West Siberian steppe) and more effective moisture, make permanent settlement feasible. In response to the climate, the vegetation is mixed forest or meadow, and the soils, though still podzolic are somewhat richer in humus. However, the advantages are marginal and erratic; peat-bogs and soils with a very thin layer of humus, or subject to flooding, are widespread and created bitter disappointments for the early settlers. The areas with a tolerably good combination of soil, site and climate are very limited—in the main to the lowland where the Bureya and Zeya rivers join the Amur, and to the Khanka lake plain north of Vladivostok. Away from these two areas the lowlands tend to be marshy tayga, with clouds of biting insects. The mountains, which occupy most of the region (including Sakhalin) are thickly forested with a dense undergrowth, including a tenacious northern species of bamboo, and a varied fauna which includes tigers and bears. The most prominent of these ranges, the Sikhote Alin, has a general crest of 3,000 feet, rising occasionally to 6,000 feet, is deeply dissected and drops steeply to the Sea of Japan. The mountains of Sakhalin island, which is separated from the mainland by only four miles, are similar in character and elevation.

Virtually the whole region is in the drainage basin of the Amur—one of the longest rivers in the Soviet Union. Although this river is navigable, its usefulness is vitiated by several disadvantages: it is frozen for five or six months of the year; it turns the wrong way (north) below Khabarovsk and has a sand bar 12 feet below the surface at its mouth; its level in the late summer, swelled by the monsoonal rains, is 20 or 30 feet higher than in the spring, and floods can be disastrous. It is a river which cries out to be thoroughly tamed and its enormous potential put to work, but its present role as a cold-war barrier precludes such operations in the foreseeable future.

THE PEOPLING OF THE REGION

When the Russian fur-seekers made their marathon trek through Siberia to the Pacific in the seventeenth century they attempted to penetrate the lands of the Amur. But the armed power of the Manchu Empire, which claimed sovereignty over the region, blocked their way and for two centuries the Russo-Chinese boundary was fixed by treaty roughly along the boundary of the region as defined in this chapter. However, by the mid-nineteenth century the balance of power had greatly changed. Russia, by then a steppeland nation, securely established along the Black Sea and well into Europe and about to conquer Middle Asia, had become a Eurasian Imperial power to which a habitable foothold on the Pacific appeared desirable. Conversely the Chinese Empire was crumbling and being humiliated by the European powers, while Japan was only just emerging. Thus there was a vacuum, not only in the Amur but also in Manchuria, which was still an empty land. Americans were generally in support of Russia's 'destiny' on the Amur—particularly as a counterweight to Britain—and Russia was about to bow out from its American territories. However, even in this propitious atmosphere, Russia might not have taken the initiative in time, had it not been for a masterful proconsul, General Muravyov, who virtually took the law into his own hands and, without bloodshed, annexed the whole region. In 1860 the port of Vladivostok (Ruler of the East), with a good harbour, was founded.

The Amur lands were as empty as comparable parts of North America before the coming of the Europeans—there were probably no more than a few thousand native hunters, fishers and herders and, despite centuries of Chinese sovereignty, there had been no Chinese settlement. Settlement by Russians was clearly called for, if only to give credence to the territorial claim, but, in spite of the opening of the Amur for navigation, poor communications remained an obstacle. The sea-route around Cape Horn was still commonly used in preference to the land route from St Petersburg, and after 1880 peasant settlers from the northern Ukraine were sent out from Odessa to Vladivostok through the new Suez Canal. This mode of migration was something novel for Russia, having more in common with the settlement of Australia and New Zealand. The new peasants had extremely depressing experiences with the poor land (contrary to reports of its richness which, as elsewhere, were current in the migration literature), the isolation and the animal and insect pests. Most of the early peasant and Cossack immigrants, before the railway, settled in the Zeya-Bureya lowlands (Blagoveshchensk was the largest city in the Far East in 1897), but with the long-awaited arrival of the railways in the early twentieth century, the focus shifted to Vladivostok and the Khanka plain. Still, in spite of special inducements, the number of immigrants was very small, compared with Western Siberia, and the population of the whole region amounted only to some 400,000 by the end of the century. However this was ten to twenty times the numbers of forty years earlier, and the 1890s saw the beginning of a whole-hearted government drive to people the Russian Far East.

On the eve of the First World War

The migration and railway fever about the turn of the century has to be seen in the context of the Russian expansionism of the time and in relation to China and Japan. Much of China had come virtually under British or French control, which encouraged Russia to look upon Manchuria as its natural sphere of influence. At the same time as the first hundred thousand Russian settlers were laboriously struggling with the virgin lands of the Amur, millions of Chinese peasants were flooding into the much better lands of Manchuria which had been kept almost empty under the Manchu Empire. Following the recognized practice of the West European powers, Russia extorted permission from China to take a short cut with her Trans-Siberian railway, through the heart of Manchuria to Vladivostok, thus saving some three hundred miles as compared with the much poorer and more rugged route north of the Amur. In addition an extension was built to Port Arthur, an ice-free port which the Russians proceeded to fortify. Thus by 1904 Russia was largely in control of Manchuria, today the richest part of China, and the long-awaited rail connection with St Petersburg had materialized. This was the year in which the Russian Empire reached its all-time territorial high-water-mark and the British geographer Sir Halford Mackinder incidentally promulgated his theory of a 'pivot of history', then largely contained with this Empire.

However, the whole horizon for Russian power and settlement in the Far East was abruptly foreshortened the following year when a new power—

Japan—annihilated the Russian fleet in a lightning attack, and soon replaced Russia's influence in southern Manchuria, Korea and south Sakhalin. Russia still retained tenuous possession of the Chinese Eastern railway but, to all intents and purposes, retired behind the Amur and settled down to build the long All-Russian span of the Trans-Siberian, which was not finally completed until 1916. The years 1907–10, nevertheless, saw a rapid increase in the number of settlers arriving (64,000 as compared with 10,000 in the preceding four years) and the population probably doubled in the decade between the Japanese War and the First World War. The better land in Western Siberia had been taken up, and there were fewer incentives than formerly for migrants destined for the Far East to drop off *en route*. The government also introduced sterner measures to prevent this, and in 1907 one in five of the flood of migrants who crossed the Urals actually got to the Far East.

Within the region the centre of gravity of the population shifted rapidly towards the Ussuri valley. Blagoveshchensk, the centre of the Amur Cossacks and the largest town in the Far East in 1897, grew comparatively slowly (the Trans-Siberian passed it by) while Khabarovsk and Vladivostok trebled their populations between 1897 and 1911. By the war Vladivostok was much the largest city in the region—the administrative, military and naval headquarters of Russia on the Pacific, while after the revolution it became the entry point for Allied and Japanese intervention armies and the nerve-centre of a long-drawn-out Civil War.

On the eve of the Second World War

By 1926 Japan had evacuated the Soviet Far East, including north Sakhalin, and Soviet Russia had regained a major control of the Chinese Eastern railway. The Russia of Lenin and the China of Sun Yat-sen were probably on more friendly terms than these countries have been before or since with the exception of the early 1950s. The stage was re-set for the further development of this young—even raw—land. Immigration resumed and the population on the eve of the Second World War ($2\frac{1}{2}$ millions) was double what it had been in 1926. But at this stage the great bulk of the increase accrued to the cities. An attempt was made to promote both industry and regional self-sufficiency, the most spectacular example of which was the building of a steel base at Komsomolsk, which grew from a small fishing village to a city of 70,000 inhabitants by 1939. Fisheries were greatly expanded, and accounted for a fifth of the Soviet output by 1940. Some Chinese and Korean immigrants settled and developed rice and soy bean farming in the Ussuri and Khanka lowlands. A Jewish 'national home' (Birobidzhan) was set up in 1934, but less than 50,000 Jews had settled there by the eve of the war.

The relative maturity of the region and its increasing concern with its own internal development is shown by the fact that Khabarovsk, with the most focal location of any city, had become the largest by 1939, displacing Vladivostok, which had been twice its size in 1926. Khabarovsk had quadrupled its population in 12 years, but Blagoveshchensk stagnated. Half the people of the Far East were urban, compared with one-third in the nation as a whole.

But the rise of Japan continued to accentuate the real isolation of the region. Manchuria was overrun in 1931 and the Soviet Union was deprived of the Chinese Eastern railway. Japanese immigration into south Sakhalin was heavy and the population stood at 400,000 in 1940, while even the newly discovered oil in north (still Russian) Sakhalin was exploited under concession by the Japanese. By their possession, also, of the Kuril islands, the Soviet Far East was potentially as encircled as its Baltic or Black Sea lands. Had Japan decided, in 1941, to strike in support of its German ally, this region, with its single vulnerable life-line to the west, would have been easy prey.

THE PRESENT ECONOMY (Fig. 62)

During the first post-war decade the outlook seemed good for an economic renaissance of the Soviet Far East within the context of a new East Asian trading sphere. As a result of the brief war with Japan, the Soviet Union regained southern Sakhalin (after forty years of intensive development by the Japanese) and the Kuril islands (including the southern ones which had never been Russian and to which the Japanese are still pressing their claim). Since Manchuria had been Japanese territory, the Russians were able to occupy it and remove capital equipment as reparations; while also regaining their old rights on the Chinese Eastern railway and at Port Arthur. Then came the Communist victory in China and, in the warm glow of the new Sino-Soviet alliance, it seemed likely that the Soviet Far East and Manchuria would be economically integrated or that the Russians would at any rate have much influence again in Manchuria. When the Soviet Union in 1955 renounced its concessionary rights in Port Arthur it was assumed that they had become irrelevant. Plans were laid for another St Lawrence Seaway on the Amur as an example of socialist international co-operation.

However, in the early 1960s this vision turned out to be a mirage and Sino-Soviet co-operation in economic matters seems to have come to a standstill.

The Soviet Far East thus reverted once more to its rather cramped and isolated position, concentrating on exploiting its primary products, especially fish and timber. But because of distance on the one hand and international tensions on the other, it has become increasingly difficult to find satisfactory long-term markets. The problem of self-sufficiency is still acute and, on balance, the region seems to be an economic liability within the Soviet scheme.

Fishing and Forestry

There is no doubt that the region's major and most distinctive contribution to the national economy is that of fish. The horizon of this industry has been greatly extended since the war, notably because of the territorial acquisitions from Japan. These made the Okhotsk Sea virtually a Russian lake, and made available established bases and installations in Sakhalin and the Kurils. Also new treaties on fishing rights favoured the Russians against the Japanese in many of the best fishing grounds. Subsequently the recent phenomenon of well-equipped Russian fishing fleets appearing all over the north Pacific has effectively swelled the catch being landed at the Far East ports. Even leaving out Kamchatka, this region probably accounts for about a quarter of the Soviet catch. Salmon is the most important fish in coastal waters and particularly in the lower Amur, into which they come to spawn. Herring, cod, mackerel and crab are also widespread and expeditions for whales and seals also set out from the Far East ports. As elsewhere, complicated facilities needed for quick-freezing and canning and for the outfitting and repair of the modern fleets, are leading to growing concentration in the fishing industry. Vladivostok and its satellites around the 'Golden Horn' dominate the industry, with secondary foci at the mouth of the Amur and in southern Sakhalin.

The forest resources of the region could undoubtedly provide for a much greater timber-based industry than now exists, but the plentiful forests to the west in Siberia, the heavy transport costs on a bulky commodity, difficulty of obtaining long-term foreign outlets, and the small size of the local market, combine to inhibit its growth. The concentration of saw-milling is in the Ussuri valley, from Khabarovsk to the Lake Khanka plain. Good quality timber on the western slopes of the Sikhote Alin is floated down the many rivers. The pulp and paper-mills of the Far East are almost all clustered in southern Sakhalin, where they constitute a most valuable legacy from the pre-war Japanese development (Plate XXVII). Plans for extension of pulp and paper-making to the Amur valley have been slow to materialize.

XXIV. A settlement 6,000 feet up in the Zeravshan mountains, south of Samarkand. Maize growing in foreground and *makhorka* tobacco drying above.

XXV. Goats and fat-tailed sheep coming down from their summer pastures north of Dushanbe in the Tadzhik Republic.

XXVI. The collective farmers' market (formerly the bazaar) at Samarkand in early September.

XXVII. Logging operations in south-central Sakhalin. A variety of East Asian hardwoods are mixed with the conifers in this damp environment.

Other industries

Given favourable internal and external stimuli, the region's natural resources (other than forests and fisheries), though by no means outstanding, could probably support greater industrial development than now exists. The one steel works, at Komsomolsk (which has no blast furnace) supplies barely a third even of the limited local demand. There is a possibility that an integrated iron and steel plant will be constructed to allow for exports in addition to satisfying local demand, and the coking coal of the Bureya valley would probably be equal to underwriting such an operation. However, local iron ore reserves seem so far to be inadequate— the present steel works has to bring pig iron from Central Siberia. There are a number of deposits of other metals, and the one which has most national significance, because of its shortage elsewhere, is tin—mined in three locations, the chief of which is north-west of Komsomolsk. Lead is mined and smelted on the seaward side of the Sikhote Alin mountains. The other metals and minerals present in the region have hardly been touched so far.

The economic feasibility of intensifying the development of other metals present in the region hinges on the progress of long-laid plans for the generation of hydro-electricity. At present there is no hydro-station of any size operating in the region, although the Amur is supposed to have as great a potential as the Volga. In view of the fact that an improvement in Sino-Soviet relations would be required before the construction of any of the dams planned to span the Amur itself could be undertaken, the projected Soviet dam most likely to materialize is one on the Zeya river, which will counter-balance a Chinese one on the Sungari, a right-bank tributary of the Amur.

There is certainly a need for more energy in the region. Apart from the Bureya fields, lignite deposits are worked near Vladivostok and there is bituminous coal as well as oil on Sakhalin, but these are all limited. The Sakhalin oil output is very minor by national standards (one or two per cent) but has had considerable prominence because of being until very recently the only producer in Siberia. It is piped across the straits to the Amur valley where it is refined and supplies most of the local demand. There has been talk of increasing exports of Sakhalin oil, and at the same time talk of piping in oil *from* Central Siberia. This kind of contradiction epitomizes the uncertainty of industrial plans for the region, bedevilled as they are by shortage of labour, isolation, mediocre resources and international tensions.

Farming

There are only two agricultural districts of any importance, and they are economically marginal by ordinary standards, beset by natural liabilities and unable to meet the food requirements of the region. The first is the Khanka lake basin, north of Vladivostok, where the mixed farming combines Oriental elements—rice, soya-beans and sorghum especially—with the wheat, rye, oats, livestock and sugar-beet of the Russian and Ukrainian immigrants. The second is the Zeya-Bureya lowland, which is harsher, more subject to floods and frost, and has the rather poor grain-potato-livestock combination which is found on both sides of Lake Baykal. However, soya-beans are very important here too. This crop is the only one for which the Far East can claim to be the major producer in the country. In both districts the late arrival of the monsoon rains is a problem, often damaging crops at harvest time while necessitating irrigation in the early summer. There is limited scope for agricultural expansion and most of the Soviet Far East is quite beyond the limits of normal farming.

Transport (Fig. 61)

The Trans-Siberian railway, double-tracked just before the war, is the axis and lifeline of the region. The easterly flow greatly outweighs the westerly—being made up of a wide variety of food, raw materials, and manufactures—underlining the life-line aspect and the fundamental regional characteristics of liability and dependence. Fish and some wood products form the main westbound freight. The great majority of the people of the region live within 50 miles of the Trans-Siberian. The most important branch-line is to the steel city of Komsomolsk, which is also linked directly to the sea at Sovietskaya Gavan. This latter link was planned as part of a relief line for the Trans-Siberian. This was conceived under Stalin, particularly as a safeguard against the Japanese in Manchuria, but since its projected route follows rugged, permafrozen and uninhabited terrain, and since it is difficult to imagine what would be carried on it, it is most unlikely to materialize now. Largely owing to the Japanese, southern Sakhalin is fairly well served by railways.

The Amur was seen by some people (Americans as well as Russians) in the nineteenth century as a great continental artery—another St Lawrence, handling the trade of Siberia and north China, but even without the present Sino-Soviet quarrel, this flies in the face of economic and geographical realities. Although physically the Amur, Bureya, Zeya and Ussuri are navigable and used especially for local freight movements, they have serious problems, in their present untamed state, notably ice, sandbars and seasonal differences in level.

Sea-traffic is also overwhelmingly intra-regional, rather than inter-national. Vladivostok's almost ice-free outport of Nakhodka, now the terminus of the Trans-Siberian and the Northern Sea route, has, in fact, virtually replaced Vladivostok as a port, and would undoubtedly be the one to reflect most positively any new resurgence of international trading activity in the Soviet Far East (Plate XXVIII).

THE PRESENT POPULATION

The total population has grown more than threefold since 1926 to its present 4 millions, a rate of growth which has not been equalled by any of the other regions, as delimited in this book. This apparent paradox, for a region which has been characterized as relatively unimportant and poor, as well as suffering a labour shortage, is to be ascribed to the lateness of settlement and its predominantly urban character. Well over two-thirds of its population is classified as urban (as compared with half for the nation as a whole) and thus there is little rural decline to offset urban growth, as in other regions. However, it should be noted that the towns are generally smaller than average and that they have not grown as quickly as the other urban areas east of the Volga since the war. Moreover, *in toto*, the region's population is still diminutive on the national scale—less than 2%—a percentage which has been perceptibly decreasing in recent years. It is in fact the smallest of all the units considered in this book.

No more than 5% of the population is ethnically non-Russian or Ukrainian. There are only a few thousand of the aboriginal inhabitants, as there were before the Russian settlers came, and they seem to have become largely absorbed or engaged in their traditional hunting and fishing pursuits beyond the fringe of Slavic settlement. However, several attempts at colonization of non-Slavic groups were made in the 1930s. The setting up of the 'Jewish Autonomous Oblast' has not really achieved its end—there are only about 15,000 Jews there now, out of more than 2 million Soviet Jews and the majority of the population of their *oblast*, like the others, is Russian. There was a considerable settlement of Koreans in the Khanka plain in the thirties, where they made an important con-tribution to agricultural development, but, apparently due to fears of Japan (which had occupied Korea), Stalin deported most of these Koreans to Middle Asia and even in 1959 over two-thirds of the 300,000 Koreans in the U.S.S.R. were still there, far from their homeland. There was also some Chinese settlement, but the 1959 figures of 26,000 Chinese for the whole of the U.S.S.R. means that this is now quite negligible. Most of the

Chinese immigrants, as in western North America earlier, were single men, whereas the Koreans settled in families. In any case there is no ethnic pretext now to back up the Chinese claim to this region.

The rural distribution (Fig. 59)

There are a little over a million rural people in the region—a declining group, as elsewhere. Nearly half of them are around Lake Khanka and the upper Ussuri valley, while a further quarter are in the Zeya-Bureya lowlands. The densities are higher in the former district, with its partly Oriental agricultural character and Korean influence, than in the latter Cossack country, with traditionally meagre and extensive Russian farming. South Sakhalin, largely as a result of Japanese efforts, has an unusually high rural density for its natural conditions—composed of post-war Russian settlers who replaced the evacuated Japanese. Beyond a hundred miles or so from the Chinese border the rural population almost disappears—with less than one person to the square mile over most of the region.

The cities

The sizes of the larger cities are commensurate with the scale of the Far East as a whole and their shifting relative status in this century indicates the phases in the formation of the region. At the turn of the century the Cossack town of Blagoveshchensk was the largest; then, with the increase of government, military and shipping activity, the port of Vladivostok assumed that position. Finally the many-sided but inward-looking development of the region in the Soviet period has put Khabarovsk to the fore.

Khabarovsk (360,000) owes everything, in fact, to its focal location which gives access to all parts of the region, since its immediate surroundings are unprepossessing—swampy and harsh—much more so than the environs of Vladivostok. It is situated on the right bank of the Amur just below the point where it receives the Ussuri and makes its fatal right-angled turn to the north. It was the terminus of a railway from Vladivostok, built in the 1890s, and the completion of the Trans-Siberian from the west in 1916 created a situation of unrivalled regional centrality. Throughout the first quarter of the century it was only half the size of Vladivostok, but the impact of the pre-war Soviet Five Year Plans caused it to realize the latent assets of its position and enabled it to overtake Vladivostok. In particular the establishment of the steel base at Komsomolsk in 1932 added a new dimension to Khabarovsk—the former's major link with the outside world. Had the steel works been sited at Khabarovsk, which would have been more rational economically, the city might today have a population of half a million. In any case it has developed the characteristics of a regional capital, assembling and processing the local resources—engineering industries from Komsomolsk steel, chemicals with Sakhalin oil, and wood-working and fur processing—while also serving as a major supplier of consumer goods for the Far East.

Vladivostok (320,000), situated on a rocky peninsula jutting out into the 'Golden Horn', one of the Soviet Union's very few good harbours, grew up above all as a city of the sea—the country's most important outlet and base on the Pacific. Founded in 1860, it became, almost from the start, the government's main centre and port of entry for most of the early immigrants, sent out through the Suez Canal. It had only grown to 28,000 by 1897, but during the first decade or so of the twentieth century it experienced its most rapid growth, trebling its population and becoming much the largest city in the Russian Far East. The terminus of the Chinese Eastern railway and also of the Ussuri railway, at the time when Russian activity in Manchuria was at its height, it had also become a vital naval base.

During the Soviet phase it inevitably suffered from the national turn towards introversion and the fact that it was flanked on three sides by a rather unfriendly Japan. However, although Khabarovsk has assumed its role as regional focus, Vladivostok has also grown steadily, trebling its population since 1926. Its chief functions are connected with the sea, especially fish processing and packing, shipbuilding and catering to the needs of the fishing and naval fleets. The port is kept open by ice breakers in the winter, but has been superseded, to a considerable degree, by *Nakhodka* (70,000), which is almost ice-free. Its electricity needs are supplied mainly from the lignite fields at *Artem* (60,000) nearby. If these satellites are included, Greater Vladivostok would even today, turn out to be larger than Khabarovsk. With much better immediate environs than Khabarovsk, and being the centre of the region's most distinctive and lucrative industry, it should continue to grow, in spite of the currently unfavourable international trading climate.

The other cities are much less significant. *Komsomolsk* (190,000), supposedly built by the Young Communists in 1932 as a steel base in the wilderness of the lower Amur, is regarded as a symbol of Soviet development—a miniature Magnitogorsk. Although its original rationality could certainly be questioned, it is now a going concern, with expansion planned, not only in steel, but also in tin smelting, chemicals and timber processing. *Blagoveshchensk* (100,000), where the Zeya meets the Amur, was the centre of the Amur Cossack settlement in the late nineteenth century, but has stagnated since. It builds some river ships as well as having various food and forest industries. If the big dam planned nearby on the Zeya comes into being, the town would experience a new phase of expansion. *Ussuriisk* (formerly called Nikolsk-Ussuriisky and later Voroshilov, 110,000) is the centre of the Khanka agricultural district. It hardly existed in 1897 when Blagoveshchensk was the Far East's largest town and the fact that it has outgrown the latter reflects the southerly agricultural shift of emphasis. *Yuzhno-Sakhalinsk* (formerly called Toyohara, 90,000), is the centre of the cluster of fish and timber processing towns established by the Japanese, and the administrative capital of Sakhalin and the Kurils.

PROSPECT

Considering the circumstances and the short time-span involved, the presence of 4 million people in the Soviet Far East, where there were a few thousand a century ago, seems no mean achievement on the part of the Russians. And yet the upshot of the foregoing consideration of its present condition is that, on balance, the area is not particularly healthy. Its limitations are clear. The shortage of even tolerable farmland means a chronic food deficit. Its wheat needs are being met, as a long-term arrangement, by Canada rather than Siberia. The limited resources of energy (other than that of the hamstrung Amur) and industrial raw materials do not positively enforce industrial expansion, as other conditions are not favourable. The undoubted timber resources are of limited concern to a timber-rich national market thousands of miles away. The small size of the local market makes it expensive to promote that thoroughgoing self-sufficiency which the region's exceptional isolation and dependence on one lifeline would seem to require. Meanwhile a labour shortage seems to accentuate the vicious circle.

The only commodity on which the rest of the Soviet Union depends to any considerable extent, is fish. While the fishery industry is expanding and is traditionally important to the Russians, the new flexibility of the Russian fleets on the world's high seas—some more accessible to its main markets—makes even this item rather less than vital. Thus it seems clear that the assets of the Soviet Far East, from the national point of view, are modest, and probably outweighed by the economic liabilities.

Moreover, it is remarkable that the Soviet Union seems to have initiated hardly any capital investment undertakings of national significance in recent years, in sharp contrast to the lands west of Lake Baykal. The indications are that the Soviet Union is indifferent to its Far Eastern territory—which is in fact claimed by China—but it may be assumed that, at the very least, it is regarded as a strategic asset of no small order.

The long-term future of the region will probably hinge on the way in which the international scene unfolds in East Asia and the Pacific. The rosy future which was predicted a century ago for the lands of the Amur envisaged the combination under Russian control of the present region and also Manchuria, with a large trading hinterland. Indeed, had the Russians been in a position to consolidate their conquest and settle Manchuria in the 1860s before the Chinese migrations and before the rise of Japan, the Soviet Union's position on the Pacific would now have been radically different. As it is, although Russia has become one of the world's two great powers it has been balked of this 'destiny', first by Japan and most lately, by China. The Soviet Far East is thus peculiarly isolated and poor, without the necessary conditions for healthy growth.

At the beginning of this chapter, the region was compared with British Columbia. Apart from the important climatic difference, it would seem that one factor in particular sets them apart from each other. Despite some difficulties, British Columbia has made peace with its great neighbour to the south as a prime market and source of imports made attractive by economies of scale. Agreements on the international use of rivers for power and long-term markets for that power seem likely among other things to provide the capital necessary for the sustained exploitation of B.C.'s resources—timber, metals and fish, like the Soviet Far East—and for internal industrial growth. If the Soviet Far East could establish similar relations with its neighbour, China (or conceivably, Japan), its potentials would be more fully realizable and its internal viability and contribution to the Soviet Union enhanced. But then the question might be asked (as the same question sometimes is for B.C.)—might not economic or even political union with the southern neighbour appear as the next logical step?

CHAPTER SIXTEEN

The North

MOST of the large countries of the world—U.S.A., China, Canada, Brazil, Australia, U.S.S.R.—are made up of two quite fundamentally distinct geographical parts—the effectively settled lands and, beyond the fringe, the great open spaces. The latter, far from being forgotten, tend to haunt the national conscience. The 'outback', periodically advertised as possessing 'boundless potentialities', stands as a permanent reproach, and at the same time enters into the national folklore, symbolizing enterprise, virility and expansive opportunity. But the dead hand of climate, and the emptiness, remain.

In the Soviet Union, the North, beyond the effectively settled belt, occupies half the country, with an area larger than that of the U.S.A. or Canada. It has a population of nearly 5 million—2% of the national total. It is entirely in the zones of tayga and tundra and most of its ground is permanently frozen, so that agriculture can hardly exist without a subsidy. The harsh conditions and tremendous distances make the provision of transport a difficult and expensive problem. The North has long been associated in the Russian mind with forced labour camps and, now that they are apparently a thing of the past, shortage of labour is quite acute.

However, it would be a mistake to write off this huge area. It has played a crucial part in the growth of the Russian empire, enriching Russian coffers from the time of Novgorod to that of Peter the Great. Its geological variety enables it to play an important part in ensuring national self-

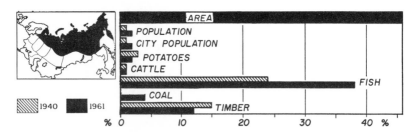

FIG. 63—Location and importance of the North in relation to the Soviet Union as a whole, for certain selected items

sufficiency in metals and minerals, while its great size has strategic advantages even in the modern world. Its population is now more than twice as large as it was in 1926 and it has continued to grow at an unusually rapid rate since 1959. Moreover, these people outnumber their counterparts in the North American equivalent territories by about fifteen to one. The scale of development, taken all round, is indeed considerably greater than in the Canadian North and Alaska, but it seems to be similarly condemned to a chronically pioneering economy and society, promising no permanent tenure, precariously specialized and dependent.

As in Canada, it is not very common to consider the North as a whole in the Soviet Union, in spite of its well-known common features, because of the fact that established political and other units cut across its boundary. The greater part of it is included as a kind of appendage in two official economic regions—Western Siberia and Eastern Siberia, the economic centre of gravity of each of which is well to the south. Apart from involving great problems of scale in mapping, this blurs the junction of fundamentally different types of human landscape. It will be necessary, of course, to differentiate and to some extent treat separately, the distinctive parts of the North. In particular the old continental boundary between Europe and Asia is still very meaningful here. The European North, covering 7% of the Soviet area, has $1\frac{1}{2}\%$ of its population, and the more permanent industries of lumbering and fishing loom larger than mining. The Siberian North, on the other hand, occupies about 40% of the Soviet area, with only $\frac{1}{2}\%$ of its population (Fig. 63). It is in a more raw state of pioneering than its European counterpart, and less well served by communications, with mining much the most important economic activity. In terms of its exaggerated problems of access, distance, severity of climate, and smaller population, coupled with a faster rate of growth, the Siberian North bears the same relationship to the European North as the settled part of Siberia does to settled European Russia.

THE NATURAL HABITAT (Fig. 65)

It is the climate which, in itself and through its effect on the soil-forming processes and the type of vegetation, has condemned this vast region to be largely devoid of permanent settlement. The basic lack is that of heat. The whole region has an accumulated temperature of less than 1,600° C. above the growing season threshold of 10° C. (50° F.), i.e. less than half the heat received in the southern Ukraine. This 1,600° line does in fact roughly coincide with the southern edge of tayga and the northern edge of economic agriculture, while nearly half of the North has less than 800°.

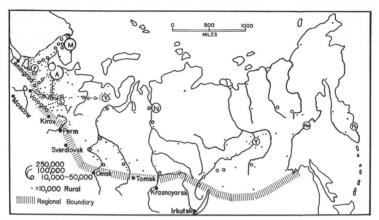

Fig. 64—The North: population. Key to cities: A = Archangel, M = Murmansk, Ma = Magadan, N = Norilsk, P = Petrozavodsk, Pk = Petropavlovsk-Kamchatsky, S = Syktyvkar, V = Vorkuta, Y = Yakutsk

Fig. 65—The North: nature

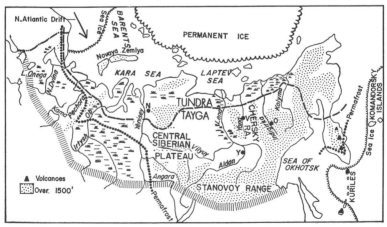

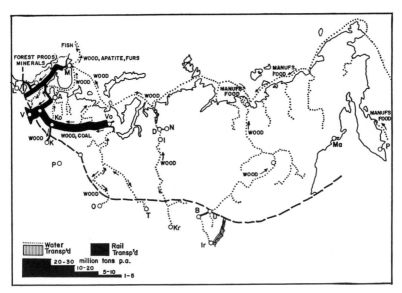

FIG. 66—The North: movements

FIG. 67—The North: economy. Minerals: Ap = apatite (phosphate) A = gold,
G = coal, Cu = copper, D = diamonds, Fe = iron, Ni = nickel

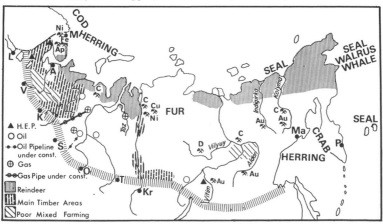

The winters are long and severe. Most of the Siberian part has average temperatures lower than 0° F. for more than half the year, and the temperatures drop rapidly towards the north-east, reaching —60° F. January averages in the enclosed valleys in the Verkhoyansk–Oymyakon districts. This intense cold, resulting from the high latitudes, vast area of land and distance from the Atlantic, produces a similarly intense high pressure system in winter. This effectively shuts out oceanic air, reduces snowfall to a minimum, and allows the cold to bite deep into the land, maintaining widespread permafrost. However, the European North is exposed to the snow-bearing Atlantic depressions as well as milder air—Murmansk is ice-free, like the ports of southern Alaska, while the whole of the rest of the northern and eastern seas are gripped in a deep freeze.

The winters are considerably more severe than they are in comparable parts of North America (as the much greater extent of permafrost suggests) but the summers are appreciably warmer, which is the critical factor in the northerly extension of the tree line. Away from the cool cloudy Arctic coast itself, the temperatures in the short summer may go very high— Verkhoyansk has recorded 100° F., which gives this place the distinction of having the greatest absolute annual range on earth (January minimum —90° F.). Together with the Midnight Sun, this means that some crops may be ripened in favoured sites even in a two-month frost-free season. But drought is another problem in the sheltered north-east. Although summer is the wet season throughout the North and, west of the Yenisey, most places receive at least 12 inches during the summer months, Eastern Siberia receives barely half as much. Combined with the summer heat and the meagre snow-melt, this means that places where agriculture is possible, such as around Yakutsk and Verkhoyansk, receive barely half the moisture needed to balance evaporation. In spite of the function of the permafrost in blocking percolation and so conserving moisture in the thin, thawing-out topsoil, irrigation is a major need in these places, as it is in similar situations in the Yukon and Alaska.

The short season in which any organic activity can take place in the soil, and the heavy leaching in most areas, results at best in an acidic podzol—at worst a quite unformed *gley* layer in the tundra—hardly worthy of the name of soil at all. The conifers which cover most of the North, while well-adapted to the climate, do not improve the soil much with their needles and cones. In Eastern Siberia, the larch, which is tolerant of the extreme cold and whose root system can adapt to permafrost, replaces the pine, fir and spruce which predominate further west. Beyond the tree-line, in the tundra, mosses and lichens prevail, with some dwarf birches and a mass of ephemeral flowers in the short summer. The tundra is alive with insects at this season and with migrant ducks, geese and plovers.

In no other region of the Soviet Union has the animal life been of such overwhelming importance to human living. The reindeer, seal, fish and fowl have been the traditional mainstays of the native peoples, while the small furry animals of the tayga first drew the Russians into the North and richly rewarded them.

The combined mantle of climate, soil and vegetation, ruling out close settlement, seems to render the character of the relief less significant than it would otherwise be. However, there is a great variety of physical landscapes in the 5,000 miles or so between Karelia and Kamchatka.

Bordering Finland, and essentially a continuation of the Finnish landscape, is Karelia, an ancient crystalline shield which seldom rises above 1,500 feet and has been heavily scoured by ice. It is pitted with lakes, which are often linked by 'hydro-electric' rivers. To the north, in the Kola peninsula, the mineral-rich Khibiny mountains do rise above the general level, to nearly 4,000 feet. The northern coast is carved into fiords, such as the one on which Murmansk is situated, in contrast to the generally low marshy shores of the rest of the Arctic coast.

Between the Karelian shield and the Urals is a low, often marshy, glacial plain of soft sedimentary rocks. The drainage systems of the Northern Dvina and the Pechora are separated by the low Timan range. The northern part of the Urals is the higher and more rugged half of this range, reaching 6,000 feet and continued in the equally mountainous, glacier-topped Arctic islands of Novaya Zemlya.

Between the Urals and the Central Siberian Plateau is one of the most featureless, swampy lowlands in the world, made up of recent fluvio-glacial and marine material. Most of it is drained, though very imperfectly, by the Ob–Irtysh system. The gradient of these rivers is imperceptible and the consequent sluggishness makes for extreme meandering, silting and, especially in spring, a virtual merging of the watercourses, old and new, into a vast swamp. The fact that the ice breaks up in late April in the south, while not until June in the north, exacerbates the chaos. Navigation can clearly be of only the most primitive kind except in the upper reaches and, for a short season, in the estuary of the river.

The Yenisey, on the other hand, flowing close under the scarp of the Central Siberian plateau, is much more valuable, making straight for the sea, with a good gradient and depth, and through generally un-waterlogged country. The timber is of much better quality and more easily accessible than that in the Ob basin. Like the Ob, the Yenisey empties into the Kara Sea which, in contrast to the sea on the eastern side of the Taymyr peninsula, is reasonably free of ice for two or three months in the summer.

The Yenisey marks the major physical divide of the Northlands. To the west the dominant landscape is that of non-permafrozen but glaciated lowland, with soft rock and excessive moisture, while to the east it is uplands or highlands of hard rock, deeply dissected, permafrozen but largely unglaciated and with a general deficiency of moisture. The eastern half must itself be divided into two parts, separated by the Lena valley.

The Central Siberian uplands consists of a plateau-like block, of hard rock, including thick lava-flows, with a general level of only about 2,000 feet, interrupted by the canyon-like valleys of rivers, mainly tributaries of the Yenisey. Just east of the metal-town of Norilsk, the Putorama mountains rise above the general level, to reach 6,000 feet. The plateau slopes down gradually to the flood-plain of the Lena. This river, though one of the longest and most powerful in the country, is paralysed by ice from October to June, and enters the severely frozen Laptev Sea through a delta in which ice may be a hazard even in summer. The fact that it flows entirely over permafrozen ground makes spring run-off exceptionally rapid, and flooding may be disastrous.

Between the Lena and the Pacific the landscape alters entirely—being composed of rugged Alpine ranges, sometimes rising above 10,000 feet, but without any regularity of elevation or trend. Several rivers, notably the Kolyma and Indigirka, flow between them to the swampy lowland of the eastern Arctic, where the pack-ice comes close to the shore, causing much peril to the passage of ships in the short season.

The peninsula of Kamchatka (with the Kuril islands) is a world of its own. It is the only part of the Soviet Union which has active volcanoes— one of them, Klyuchevskaya Sopka, being a cone 16,000 feet high. Hot springs and geysers abound, especially in the south and have begun to produce geothermal power. Earthquakes, often severe ones, are also common, particularly in the Kuril islands. Kamchatka and the islands are made up largely of volcanic material and form one of the most active sections of 'Rim of Fire' which encircles the Pacific.

THE PEOPLING OF THE REGION

The North is not a new land for the Russians. It has been part of their consciousness and an extension of their economic environment ever since their first attempts at political organization more than a thousand years ago. The tributaries of the Northern Dvina, leading to the White Sea and, via the headstreams of the Pechora, to the Urals, were accessible by easy portage to the boatmen of Novgorod and could feed in to the water-road 'From the Varangians to the Greeks'. The little fur-bearing animals were the chief quarry, but from the White Sea came also seal-skins, walrus ivory and whale-blubber. The forests yielded tar and pitch, while salt and potash were also obtained. These valuable products, gathered from an ever-growing territory, accrued to Novgorod, to be exported, through the Hanse merchants, to Western Europe and, where possible, to the Mediterranean. During the fourteenth century, men of Novgorod crossed the northern Urals—probably the first Russians to do so—and when Muscovy defeated Novgorod in the following century it inherited a vast, if loosely knit, forest empire stretching as far as the Ob.

The native population of the area had either been subjugated or absorbed, and Muscovy was able to intensify and extend commercial activity. In fact, during the next two centuries, the northern forests became the main source of wealth for the newly independent Muscovite nation, as well as its chief avenue of territorial aggrandisement and overseas trade. The sixteenth and seventeenth centuries—the Age of Discovery—saw the northern forests gain much the same significance in Russian national growth, offering epics of adventure and accumulation of treasure, as did the Americas and the Indies for Spain or Britain. It was partly a matter of necessity, since the Swedes and the Poles still barred the way to the Baltic and, even after the capture of the Volga, the southern nomads still made life difficult for the Russians. Richard Chancellor's English ships arrived at the mouth of the Northern Dvina in 1553 and inaugurated a new phase in Russian trading and national independence. For the next century and a half Archangel was the country's main window on the world.

The expeditions associated with the name of Yermak in 1580 marked the beginning of the thoroughgoing penetration of the Siberian forests. Little more than half a century later, Russians had reached the Pacific, founded many of the present towns of the region—Tobolsk, Turukhansk, Yakutsk, Verkhoyansk, Okhotsk—and claimed the huge territory for Russia. The rapidity of this extension of Russian control over the forests of Northern Asia can be explained by several factors, apart from the innate ingenuity and courage of the handful of adventurers involved. The rivers are well arranged for east–west as well as north–south travel, with easy portages between the Ob, Yenisey and Lena systems, almost to the Pacific. The natural environment and the needed skills were virtually identical with that to the west of the Urals, so no new adaptation was called for. The native peoples were few and far between, poorly organized and armed. They could even be put to work, and tribute of fur exacted from them. The political extension of the Empire was a very minor, and tardily conceived, factor—transcending everything was the obsession with the fur trade, comparable with the quest for gold and silver by the Spaniards in their New World. By the late seventeenth century, when European exploration of North America was in its early stages, the whole of the North, as delimited in this chapter, was controlled from Moscow, except for Kamchatka and the north-eastern tip of Siberia (which were, with Alaska, acquired soon afterwards). Russia's only sea-ports, albeit long-frozen ones, were in these northern forests—providing the gateways to further economic expansion in Europe and the Pacific. Seven-eighths of the whole Empire's area was in the North, which provided an indispensable source of internal revenue and export commodities.

But the place of the North in the Russian scheme of things declined steadily after 1700. The foundation of St Petersburg and the growth of Riga dealt Archangel a crippling blow. Mining, especially of iron, and new farming settlement were greatly stimulated and the centre of economic wealth moved steadily southwards to the Urals, the Ukraine and the Siberian steppe. There was a gold rush to the upper Lena (Bodaybo) in the mid-nineteenth century, while serf and later prisoner labour was used in the mines, but in Tsarist times 'Siberia' meant overwhelmingly South Siberia for miners and convicts, as well as farmers. In spite of the extent of the riches involved there was very little settlement in the North—the organization was vested in southern cities such as Irkutsk, Tomsk, Tobolsk and Perm in addition to St Petersburg and Moscow. As in North America the lure of the Northern forests became less powerful as the more lasting attractions of the south were uncovered.

The eve of the First World War

The North was therefore put in the shade by the great developments of the nineteenth century elsewhere in the growing Russian Empire. In 1897 there were no urban centres with as many as 25,000 people, although there were over a million people (1% of the national population) scattered across the vast area. The fur trade was still important and some timber was being floated down the Dvina, but the small size of even Archangel was indicative of the limited scale of operations. The potentially rich fishing-grounds of the Barents Sea were little exploited, although English salt herring was a staple import. Murmansk, on the ice-free fiord coast which had been Russian for centuries—during which time Russia had supposedly been searching for outlets to the sea—was a tiny fishing

XXVIII. The new port of Nakhodka on the Sea of Japan, the only virtually ice-free harbour in the Soviet Far East.

XXIX. The Aldan Highway linking Yakutsk with the Trans-Siberian railway, and the Siberian tayga as it looks for most of the year.

XXX. The main street in Norilsk, a mining city near the lower Yenisey, built on permanently frozen ground.

XXXI. Lena river barges in the bay of Tiksi, a port of call for the Northern Sea Route, in the brief summer.

village. There was no transport provision in the North except for rivers and the Kara Sea was still not ventured into, being known as the 'ice cellar'.

However, as in so many regions of Russia, there was a sudden upsurge of activity in the two decades before the Revolution. Archangel was connected by rail with Moscow, while Kotlas on the main junction of the Dvina's tributaries was connected by rail with the Volga, Urals and Siberia. Archangel was thus able to resume its former role—albeit now in a very minor capacity—as a national outlet, and Siberian wheat became one of its chief exports.

On the very eve of the Revolution, the St Petersburg–Murmansk railway was built, making possible not only year-round fishing and shipping activities but exploitation of the timber and minerals of Karelia and the Kola peninsula. Navigation by Russian and foreign vessels began in the Kara Sea and the delicate question of the limits of Russia's jurisdiction in the Arctic seas and islands came to the fore for the first time.

On the eve of the Second World War

The inter-war period saw a vigorous re-exploration of the North, which led to greatly increased economic exploitation—this time mainly of metals—and re-assertion of national control and sovereignty. Hitherto the Arctic had been explored by Scandinavians like Nansen and Nordenskjold, and the Arctic islands were hardly known. The so-called 'sector principle' of Arctic Ocean sovereignty was coming to be tacitly accepted, and the Soviet Union in 1926 evicted a group of Canadian claimants from Wrangel island in the Eastern Arctic, while formally annexing the other islands in its sector, such as Franz Josef Land, soon after. A Northern Sea Route Administration was set up, with jurisdiction not only over shipping but over virtually all the activities of the Siberian North, though this scope was reduced later. In the early thirties, for the first time, ships began to make the complete journey from Archangel to Vladivostok in one season. The effect was political and strategic, rather than economic, although it did stimulate the development of north-east Siberia. The bulk of the ships—many of them foreign—plied between the new Yenisey timber port of Igarka and the Atlantic margins.

Much primary land exploration was necessary (the rugged Chersky range in north-east Siberia was almost unknown before) and geological prospecting, with the aim of achieving rapid national self-sufficiency in strategic metals, was widely organized. Gold, from the Kolyma and Aldan fields, provided desperately needed foreign exchange, and all-weather roads were built, connecting them with Magadan and the Trans-Siberian respectively. Coal was proved to exist under much of the permafrozen north and was mined for the local purposes of the Northern Sea Route. The rich nickel deposits of Norilsk had only just begun to be worked by the Second World War. Iron, nickel and apatite were being developed in the Kola peninsula, and a little oil in the Pechora valley.

The Stalinist period of the thirties produced an unprecedented number of forced labourers, many of whom were transported to the Northern mining camps. Through their labour the Vorkuta coalmines in the European tundra and the railway connecting it with the south were operated from the beginning of the Second World War. Another transport link effected in the same way during this period was the Baltic–White Sea canal. The population of the North probably grew from 2 to 3 millions during this period, and expensive and highly publicized attempts to extend agriculture into many parts of the North, to subserve mining activities particularly, were made.

Fishing was greatly extended, particularly in the north-west but also in Kamchatka—nearly a quarter of the Soviet fish output derived from the North in 1940, compared with under a tenth before the Revolution. The expansion of the timber industry largely explains the growth of Archangel, which trebled its population in 12 years, to exceed a quarter of a million in 1939. Murmansk in the same period grew from 8,000 to 120,000, becoming by far the largest city in the world within the Arctic Circle.

THE PRESENT ECONOMY (Fig. 67)

In spite of spectacular projects, the North inevitably remains sparsely developed economically. With increasing attention being paid to costs, the expensive lack of adequate transport, agriculture and labour is an obstacle which can only be surmounted for exceptional reasons of resource availability and strategy. In the European North the proximity to the market stimulates the development of the timber and fish, but in Siberia as a rule only those metals which are either valuable or scarce, or both, are able to justify the allocation of investment capital. Vast natural riches such as coal, water-power or timber seem destined to remain insignificant as 'resources', in the proper sense of the term.

Mining and Power

For what they are worth, estimates have been made indicating that two-thirds of the coal reserves of the Soviet Union are to be found in permafrozen Northern Siberia, east of the Yenisey. However, only a fraction of 1% of the Soviet output comes from this area, although it is very useful for local purposes. The only coalfield of the North which has acquired national significance is around Vorkuta in the Pechora tundra. It is the main supplier of coking coal to Cherepovets, which provides steel for Leningrad. This field only came into production in 1942 when the railway reached it and, when the Donbas was over-run, it became vitally important for two or three years. However, its present position is far from secure—permafrost creates problems and the distance to the market is great, while the prisoner labour which has mined the coal from the beginning has been replaced by relatively highly paid miners. All this means high costs, and the arrival of natural gas at Cherepovets (itself under fire for high costs) should mean reduction of demand for Vorkuta coal. But it will probably escape being confined entirely to local needs, as are the other Northern fields, because of its railway, its position in European Russia and reportedly extensive reserves of good-quality coal.

The North also contains over a third of the country's potential water-power, and grandiose schemes are periodically discussed for building mammoth dams on the lower reaches of the great rivers. One long-discussed project is a dam on the lower Ob, which would incidentally transform vast areas of swamp into a lake and (the main intention of the original Davydov Plan) pump surplus water to Middle Asia. However, this project has encountered opposition and is no longer contemplated for the immediate future; the same fate has overtaken the projected dam just above the delta of the Lena. This is designed to be twice as powerful as the Bratsk and Krasnoyarsk dams combined, and the power is to be sent south along Direct Current 1,400 Kilovolt lines. Though the imagination boggles at such a project, its completion, suggested for the somewhat vague Twenty Year Plan (to 1980), cannot be entirely ruled out. Similarly, a great power-output would accompany the execution of the planned diversion of the headwaters of the Pechora system into the Volga. However, it is notable that, to date, there is only one hydro-station of any importance actually operating in the whole vast area of the North outside the Karelian shield. Moreover this one, at Mamakan, on a tributary of the Lena, is on the southern edge, has a very small capacity (one-seventieth that of Bratsk) and is used for local purposes, in the neighbouring gold fields. Natural conditions in terms of mild climate as well as good gradients, combined with accessible resources of metal and timber, have given rise to a cluster of hydro-stations in Karelia, especially around Kandalaksha, at the north-west tip of the White Sea.

Other sources of power which have begun to be experimented with in the

North are tidal power—in certain gulfs of the White Sea and Murman coast—and geothermal power in Kamchatka. But the most interesting question concerns the realistic potential of the North for oil and gas. Oil has been exploited for some decades in the Pechora region, but remains of small significance nationally. Geologically, regions such as the Ob and Lena basins offer good prospects for these products, which are increasingly coming to dominate the Soviet fuel structure, but until very recently prospecting had yielded no positive results, and pipelines were put through to Central Siberia from the Volga. In the early 1960s, however, oil has been discovered near the junction of the Ob and the Irtysh and also in the upper Lena, and there are plans to pipe this to refineries at Omsk and the Far East respectively. Gas deposits have recently been found in the lower Ob region (Berezovo) and this is scheduled to be piped 300 miles to the metallurgical industries of the northern Urals. Much the most prolific gas-fields are situated at the mouth of the Taz river, also about 300 miles from the metal centre of Norilsk, for which it is said to be destined. Swamp and frost conditions, as well as geological complications, are making these northern developments of oil and gas still uncertain, and much depends on alternative sources elsewhere.

This is increasingly true for the major contributing industry of the North—and consumer of most of its power—mining. Metals and minerals occur widely over the whole area, but actual mining of national significance is confined to three areas. (1) The Kola peninsula has the world's largest known deposits of apatite, a valuable fertilizer which is sent all over the country, while the Cherepovets steel-works depend on Kola iron ore. In addition, aluminium is made from local nephelite, while nickel, copper, titanium, zirconium and molybdenum are also mined. (2) Norilsk, on the edge of the Central Siberian Plateau, connected by a short railway with the Yenisey, is a very important producer of nickel, cobalt, copper and platinum and continues to develop steadily in spite of the harsh conditions. (3) In Eastern Siberia, within some 700 miles radius of Yakutsk, are several sites which produce most of the gold and diamonds which have recently made the Soviet Union the main rival of South Africa in this respect. The diamonds come from the Vilyuy valley, west of the Lena, while there are three main gold-mining districts—the upper Kolyma-Indigirka region to the east and the Aldan and Vitim areas to the south. Some tin and tungsten is also mined in the far north-east, while mica is plentiful in the south. In most of these areas, local coal is used in support of the mining operations.

Forest, Fish, Fur and Farm

Although most of the North is covered by forests, well over nine-tenths of the output of timber and timber products comes from the European part. This is a question of accessibility combined with superior quality. Since much of the logging is done along the southern margins of the region it is difficult to determine the North's contribution, but it probably amounts to about one-sixth of the national output. Logs are floated down the Dvina system, and Archangel is thus a great focus for timber assembly and processing. Much of the timber which is shipped from Igarka on the Yenisey—the only important centre in the Siberian North, finds its way to Archangel or abroad. Secondary timber foci are Syktyvkar and Kotlas, while Karelia, especially along the axis of the Baltic–White Sea canal, is, like neighbouring Finland, naturally good timber country. But it should be noted that there is little paper-making or similar refinement of timber processing in the North itself.

About a quarter of the Soviet fish catch is landed in the Northern ports and two-thirds of this comes into the ports of the Barents and White Seas. Half the catch of the Soviet North is landed in Murmansk and vicinity alone. It is mainly cod, herring and haddock, often from far afield and the processing of fish and the fitting out of the fleet accounts for most of the industry of Murmansk. The remainder of the Northern fish catch comprises mainly the rich salmon and crab harvest, as well as seals and whales, of Kamchatka (with the Komandorsky and Kuril islands) and the Sea of Okhotsk. By comparison the fisheries of the north coast and the rivers of Siberia are very under-developed, because of inaccessibility, but they remain a mainstay, as always, of the people living on their shores.

Northern agriculture has received much publicity—whether the out-size specimens of vegetables grown in the tundra, or the Arctic dairy herds. Breeding of frost-resistant varieties of crops and extensive use of hothouses has undoubtedly enabled notable feats to be achieved, and almost any investment in the provision of fresh foods for isolated communities seems justified. But, by definition, this region is beyond the agricultural belt, and the most that can be said is that the Russians have made great efforts on a minute scale and at a high price, by ordinary economic standards. Two areas are worthy of being singled out in a relative sense: (1) the Dvina valley area, with some dairying and flax, rye and buckwheat, a pale extension of Vologda and the upper Volga; and (2) the Middle Lena, where the Yakuts brought cattle and where frost-resistant wheat has been acclimatized, although summer drought is a major problem. The only branch of farming which may be said to be truly viable, enabling people for centuries to be self-sufficient, is reindeer-herding. There are still several million of these animals—almost all in the tundra and forest-tundra—the greatest densities being from the Kola peninsula to the Yenisey and north-east of the Kolyma.

Russia is still the world's greatest exporter of furs, as it has been for centuries, and for many of the Northern people this is the main source of cash income. But there has been serious depletion of the more valuable species, such as the silver fox and ermine, and fur-farms are now widespread in the North.

Transport (Fig. 66)

The fundamental difference in density of economic development between the European and Siberian North is reflected most dramatically in the map of freight flows. The European North is now fairly well served, by Soviet standards, certainly in relation to the population involved. The Murmansk–Leningrad and Archangel–Moscow lines, which were connected along the White Sea during the Second World War when Leningrad was besieged, are the two main permanent feeders to the south carrying lumber, fish and metals. The Dvina system, which is second only to the Volga in freight, is largely used for floating down timber. The Baltic–White Sea canal acts as a relief to the Murmansk railway, but its traffic, mainly wood, is rather thin north of Lake Onega. The Pechora, not yet connected with the rest of the Russian river system, is a minor feeder of timber to Archangel and foreign ports. Off to one side goes the remarkable Kotlas–Vorkuta railway, largely used for coal, but secondarily for lumber picked up from the rivers. Even more than in the case of the other railways of the region its southerly traffic greatly outweighs its northerly. The Vorkuta railway has been extended over the Urals to the Ob, but seems to carry very little traffic. Between the Ob and the Pacific, in an area as large as the United States, there is only one railway—the 70-mile line from Norilsk to the Yenisey at Dudinka. Permafrost is a hazard to railway-building, but the sparse population and the adequacy of the rivers for most purposes do not encourage their further extension. These rivers form the north-south part of a simple grid of which the east–west components are the Trans-Siberian (including its extension to the Lena) on the south, and the Northern Sea Route on the other side. The latter is open for two or three months in the summer but, while some ships do make the full journey from Murmansk to Vladivostok, the great bulk of the shipping stays west of the Yenisey. In spite of the new atomic ice-breaker, ice conditions are hazardous between the Taymyr peninsula and the Bering Strait and the amount of freight which needs to be carried along that stretch is very small. The service is essentially a supply operation for the northern peoples, the various bases for Arctic research and the meteorological stations (Plate XXXI).

Even here it is a moot point whether these places could not be supplied more economically and easily from the south. Since the inauguration of the Northern Sea Route, southern Siberia has become developed and quite well able to act as the base for Northern needs, via the rivers (downstream), which are crossed by the railways. Besides the rivers, all-weather roads play a vital part in the supply of the major development area of the Eastern Siberian North—the Aldan Highway from the Trans-Siberian to Yakutsk (Plate XXIX) and the Kolyma Highway from Magadan. Together these roads knit together this large region and tie it to the south. If, as is planned, a new east–west trunk railway is built some 200 miles north of the Trans-Siberian, the southerly pull would be made even stronger.

The general impression is still of great emptiness and, as in the Canadian Arctic or the Australian outback, the air is frequently the most convenient, if not the only way to supply outlying settlements. There is a considerable network of scheduled routes, mainly again from the south. Here the old supply bases—Irkutsk and Krasnoyarsk—appear in a new guise, but there are non-stop flights from Moscow and Leningrad to the northern posts, such as Tiksi at the mouth of the Lena. Finally, at the other end of the scale, the well-tried reindeer and sledge-dogs are still very important agents of transport in the North.

THE PRESENT POPULATION

Though the regional difference within the North can be no more than between sparse settlement and no settlement, there has been considerable increase in the population density in many places during the Soviet period. The present population of nearly 5 millions compares with some 2 millions in 1926 and this means that the North has increased at a rate considerably above the national average. During this period there was a large but unknown quantity of forced immigration into the region. However, as this process had not got under way on any scale by 1926 and seems to have been discontinued since 1953, the overall increase should not reflect it directly, although, of course, many of the forced labourers must have stayed on after their release, as their counterparts did after the abolition of serfdom a century earlier.

The increase has been almost entirely in the urban population and largely composed of Russians and Ukrainians. There has been a complete change in the general ethnic composition of the North. In 1926 the Russians numbered about the same as the total of the native peoples—about a million each. Today, the native peoples still number no more than a million, though this may be as much a result of assimilation or Russo-identification as of actual stagnation or decrease. Therefore the Russians now outnumber the native peoples by about four to one, and in the cities the disproportion is overwhelming. It is noteworthy that the whole of the North is part of the Russian Republic, though sub-divided into various national units.

There is a great variety of native groups, spread thinly across the North. The two largest and most coherent, separated by 3,000 miles from each other, are the Komi and the Yakuts, who together account for at least two-thirds of the non-Russian people of the North. The home of the Komi is in the forests of the Pechora and Vychegda valleys; they speak a Finnish language and have been in contact with the Russians for centuries. It may be added here that another, but more advanced, Finnish-speaking group, the Karelians, have been reduced in numbers considerably by the migration of many of them to Finland after the Second World War. Karelia's status as a Soviet Socialist Republic was abolished in 1956.

The Yakuts, speaking a Turkish language, inhabit the middle Lena and other valleys in the north-east, where they apparently settled after having been evicted from their former home, east of Lake Baykal, by the Buryats. They were cattle-herders, have remained quite distinct from the reindeer-based tribes who surround them, and have taken up some farming.

The other peoples are very widely scattered and probably amount, all told, to no more than 100,000. They are the oldest inhabitants of the North, being probably related to, and comparable with, the Indians and Eskimos of northern North America. They are mainly reindeer-herders, fishermen and hunters, ranging from the Nentsy and Khanty of the lower Ob to the seal and walrus-hunting and dog-breeding Chukchi of the far north-east, who number about 12,000, and the Soviet Eskimos, who are barely a thousand strong.

The rural distribution (Fig. 64)

The rural population numbers less than a third of the total and is concentrated, if that is not too positive a term, largely in the upper Dvina valley and secondarily in the valley of the middle Lena. Elsewhere it is based not on agriculture, except immediately next to the mining settlements, but on fishing, hunting and herding, and much of it may still be classified as nomadic. In the sense in which it is meant in the rest of the Soviet Union, a rural population can hardly be said to exist in the North.

The cities

The growth of the Northern population in the Soviet period means, in effect, the growth of the cities. There are now a dozen cities of over 50,000, containing over 1¼ million people, compared with one city (Archangel, 80,000) in 1926. They are the most northerly cities in the world, and the only appreciable group situated far away from tolerable agricultural land. Thus they share many basic problems, though they vary greatly in their functions.

The largest, containing nearly three-quarters of the Northern city population, are in the European part. *Archangel* (Arkhangelsk, 280,000) at the head of the deltaic estuary of the Northern Dvina, is the oldest and still the most important of them. It was founded in the mid-sixteenth century when, almost accidentally, English sailors stumbled on the Dvina and made their way to Moscow. Its position controlling the best water-route to Moscow and as a collection centre for forest products, quickly gave it almost a monopoly of the country's foreign trade, in furs, timber and flax. However, its Golden Age was short-lived and, shorn of its privileges by Peter the Great, it degenerated throughout the eighteenth and nineteenth centuries, becoming amongst other things, a penal colony. The completion of the railway from Moscow around 1900 marked the beginning of its resurrection, and it has increased more than ten-fold during the present century. Forest products dominate its activities—it is the largest saw-milling and timber exporting city in the country, but minor fish-processing and ship-building activities are also carried on. However, the White Sea fishing industry has declined relatively with the growth of long-distance operations, and Archangel has now fallen far behind Murmansk in the industry. It has, however, recently extended its shipping activities with a new naval base on the White Sea, *Severodvinsk* (formerly called Molotovsk, 100,000), which is connected with it by rail.

Murmansk (250,000) unlike Archangel, has an ice-free, deep harbour, 40 miles up a rocky fiord, but its tundra environment and the difficult journey overland to the south long balked hopes for its use as an outlet for Russia. Its existence as a town dates from the building of the railway from St Petersburg in 1916, the completion of which was rushed through in order to facilitate arms shipments from the west, an intention which was only to be thoroughly vindicated in the Second World War. It developed in the inter-war period as the centre of the expanded fishing fleets of the Barents Sea as well as the terminus of the Northern Sea Route and it also benefited from the mineral development in its hinterland. It had grown from almost nothing to 120,000 in 1939 and has doubled again since. The recent expansion of the Soviet North Atlantic fishing operations seem likely to ensure the city's further growth. It is already the largest fish-processing centre in the country and the various ramifications of this industry dominate the life of the city.

The other cities of the European North are minor regional centres, mainly occupied with the timber industry. *Petrozavodsk* (140,000), where the Murmansk railway touches Lake Onega, is the chief city of Karelia, and in many ways an outlier of the Leningrad region. It makes ceramics as well as equipment for the timber industry. *Syktyvkar* (80,000), on the Vychegda, is the Komi capital but nevertheless did not get a railway until 1960. It makes river ships and processes furs and skins as well as timber. *Vorkuta* (60,000) is the centre of the Pechora coalfield and was, after 1941, a notorious point of destination for German as well as Russian prisoners.

Norilsk (120,000) is the largest city of the Siberian North, and the only one within the Arctic Circle. It has arisen solely because of nickel, copper and other metal ores there; these must be very productive to justify such a rapid and continued development on permafrozen territory (Plate XXX). Its fuel base is local coal but there are plans for harnessing hydro-electric power in the Taymyr peninsula—and more feasible—piping in the natural gas of the Taz valley to the west. It is connected by railway with the deep-water Yenisey port of Dudinka, and therefore seems to possess the conditions for quite a permanent establishment, provided that the metals it produces continue to be in short supply elsewhere.

Yakutsk (80,000) is entirely different—a long-established trading fort on the Lena, which has become the regional centre for a very wide area of mining, hunting and even agricultural activity—and the political and cultural focus of the Yakut people. Apart from its central position within the Lena river system, it is a considerable centre of air-routes. *Petropavlovsk-Kamchatsky* (100,000) had an important role in the extension of Russian activities in the North Pacific, including Alaska, in the eighteenth and nineteenth centuries and was the scene of a naval engagement in the Crimean War. Its good harbour on the southern Pacific-facing coast of Kamchatka early made it a fishing, sealing and whaling base and the recent expansion of Soviet maritime activities in the Pacific has led to a rapid growth since the war. *Magadan* (70,000), on the Sea of Okhotsk, was founded in the thirties as the gateway to the Kolyma gold-fields. In addition to this function it is now a fishing port, with rich salmon-grounds nearby, but it suffers a long, exposed and severe winter.

PROSPECT

By comparison with its equivalents elsewhere, notably in North America, the Soviet North appears quite well developed. But it has to be remembered that most of this development was set in train in the Stalinist period, with methods of labour recruitment which would be inadmissible in North America and in a period of intense national stringency and acute shortages of industrial raw materials and foreign exchange, such as America has never known. Since the death of Stalin in 1953 the whole context within which the North is to be considered has been changing rapidly. Labour is now free labour and has to be bribed, as in North America, to settle in the North. The Soviet Union is now a developed and strong nation with ample supplies of most industrial raw materials in the south, and particularly southern Siberia. Although there is still a foreign exchange problem, particularly as a consequence of the recent wheat shortages, and gold is still very much needed, the whole problem is much less intense than it was in the thirties. National policies now tend to play down expensive symbols and long-term projects in favour of quick short-term solutions and more attention to the consumer.

In this new climate, what are the prospects for the North? Anywhere in the world, the reasons for establishing industries far away from an agri-cultural base, difficult and expensive of access, in an unpleasant natural environment and with high-cost labour, have to be compelling. The vicious circle of chronically pioneering, dependent communities, with a high labour turnover, can only be tolerated if the tangible returns are un-usually great or the government is prepared to subsidize the operation for strategic or ideological reasons. It is clear that the gold and diamonds of the Lena and Kolyma basins come into the first category, since they are the country's major producers of these precious commodities. Similarly one may assume that, although nickel is produced in other more accessible parts of the country, the continued expansion of Norilsk indicates that, for the present, the shortage is still acute. But the question of alternative sources will loom increasingly large in these matters, as suggested by the slowness and uncertainty with which the North's immense power reserves (not excluding oil and gas) are being developed.

The strategic, ideological and nationalist factors are also changing. When the Northern Sea Route was inaugurated southern Siberia was still un-developed industrially and Russia was deliberately asserting itself as a power in the Arctic. Now it is often easier to supply even the Far North from the south and, in the days of inter-continental missiles, the Arctic coast itself has no overriding claim to strategic importance. In any case the Arctic summer convoys, imprisoned in their ice-lanes, are nothing if not vulnerable, as well as expensive.

The more enduring forest and fishery industries may be expected to show a steady growth, with increasing international trade and internal living standards, and should complete the transformation of Archangel, Murmansk and perhaps settlements on the Yenisey or Kamchatka, into permanently established going concerns. The European North has a substantial and permanent advantage over the Siberian North for these reasons alone—that it is nearer the market and the farmland and has the best access to commercially favourable forests and fisheries. But the Vorkuta region shares some of the drawbacks and uncertainties of Northern Siberia. Even when the vast power resources of the North actually begin to be harnessed, they will almost certainly be fed directly into the southern Effective National Territory, rather than being used to support great industrial complexes at the point of origin. But the North will remain a considerable latent asset to the Soviet Union, as a reserve bank, a strategic insulator and an integral part of the national image.

PART III: CONCLUSIONS

CHAPTER SEVENTEEN

Soviet Strength in the Modern World

IT is more than likely that the present basic world power situation, in which two nations stand head and shoulders above all others, will remain with us for the foreseeable future. A super-state today has to possess many attributes—a great size and population, a wide range of industrial resources (including energy) and an adequate food base, coupled with a high level of internal unity, organization and technological development. The latter factors are without doubt the deciding ones, and it may be recalled that Britain managed to become the nineteenth-century super-state without benefit of some of the other factors. However, the circumstances of the world of the early nineteenth century were of course very different from those prevailing today. The world since then has become fully known, and the scientific knowledge to enable any nation to industrialize has been irrevocably diffused. Such things being equal, then, it seems very unlikely that a small nation will from now on be able to achieve super-power status, however impressive the Japanese or German 'miracles' may seem. The combined attributes listed above appear to be necessary, including sheer size—not least on grounds of strategic vulnerability. This alone, quite apart from doubts about internal coherence or resources, seems to make it unrealistic to speak of a European Common Market, present or prospective, in quite the same breath as the United States and the Soviet Union, just as it is difficult to envisage for quite a long time ahead a China, which has conquered its food/population problem and which has the independent technology and organization to carry it to the top rank.

The United States has been unmistakably a world power for several decades, and most intelligent Westerners probably feel that they have a fairly clear idea of its strengths and weaknesses. However, the case of the Soviet Union is much more novel and mysterious to many people. Before the war it would rarely have been rated a really top power—and rightly so. Only in the last decade or two, with the Cold War, the obvious obsession of Western foreign policy with the Soviet Union, and finally the symbolic bursting in on the public consciousness of the Soviet earth satellites and cosmonauts, has doubt finally evaporated from the Western mind about the location in Moscow of one of the two ultimate sources of world power.

But a measure of uncertainty persists, because of the sudden impact of the new situation, coupled with the traditional inscrutability of Russia, from the Western viewpoint. Insistent questions remain, and those which are directed at geographers have to do with things like inherent character and value of the land, meaningful quantities and qualities of resources, comparative regional rates of growth and mobility of population. Sooner or later two general topics tend to be brought up—the inevitable comparison with the United States, present and future, and the shadowy notion of a world-dominating 'Heartland', harking back to Mackinder. In this concluding chapter, each of these questions will be explored.

THE SOVIET UNION AND THE UNITED STATES

To attempt a comparative assessment of two countries with divergent traditions, values and economic systems, whatever similarity they may appear to have in size, population and resources, is always hazardous. All the same, while recognizing that such a comparison is bound to be impressionistic and subjective to a degree, it can hardly be avoided, when it is on so many lips or at least at the back of so many minds.

As suggested earlier, there are rather remarkable similarities in some tangible and measurable things. The parallel is usually closer with U.S.A. *plus* Canada, whose economies and cultures are in fact as closely intertwined as are those of some of the internal regions of the Soviet Union. In basic statistics, such as population, total area and sown area, the Soviet Union even slightly exceeds Anglo-America as a whole, but in capitalization, productivity or standard of living per head of the population it definitely lags behind at present.

There is no doubt that the natural environment is more severely restrictive in the Soviet Union than it is in Anglo-America as a whole. In comparison with the United States the U.S.S.R. is much less fortunate in the geographical coincidence of heat and moisture and, being cut off from tropical maritime air-masses, is less supplied with either. But the total significance of this can be exaggerated. The Soviet Union is now feeding its population adequately from its own land in normal climatic years, in spite of a hitherto low level of investment and of scientific methods in agriculture. It would be perfectly feasible, given an American level of investment and technology, particularly in the application of fertilizers, for the Soviet Union to provide its growing population with a varied diet for the foreseeable future, even from its generally second-rate land. Whether this would be wise national policy is another matter as the; country becomes a major exporter of industrial goods and raw materials

336

one would think it would be more economic to forego the doubtful blessings of complete national self-sufficiency and bring in from abroad a variety of cheaper foods.

Geographers have often tended to attribute to the natural environment a virtual veto power on the growth of national power. Thus the well known geographer George Cressey, 'from the standpoint of geography', which seems to mean largely the natural environment, concluded that it is very unlikely that the U.S.S.R. will ever overtake North America.[1] He may well have been correct, but the crucial question is not whether its agricultural capabilities are mediocre but whether its industrial prospects are, or are not, first-class, since the most powerful states in the modern world owe their power to industry rather than agriculture. Both North America and the U.S.S.R. are comfortably off in all forms of energy for industry, although the U.S. regularly imports oil while the Soviet Union exports it. In industrial raw materials the Soviet Union appears now to be almost self-sufficient, whereas North America has to bring in from outside vital items like manganese, chrome and tin.

An important question is the growth-rate and stage of development of the Soviet and American economies. The Soviet gross national product has grown three or four times as fast as the American in recent years and, if this continued in the same ratio, they could be expected to draw level during the decade of the 1970s.[2] On the other hand it is clear that the Soviet Union is in an altogether earlier stage of development (its experience of the last three decades has been compared to that of the U.S. from about 1870 to 1910) and can reasonably be expected to slacken off relatively from now on. Indeed a slowing down has recently become very evident. However, even if this trend continues while the U.S. picks up its speed somewhat, it is entirely possible that the next two or three decades will see the gap between the two economies more or less closed. Moreover, it is a well known fact that the technological time-lag between old and newly industrializing countries can suddenly disappear. Thus, although it is certainly true that important structural changes in the economy, such as from coal to oil and gas, rail transport to road and pipe, and steel to chemicals, inaugurated in the U.S.S.R. in recent years, are usually three decades behind the United States, many short-cuts can now be taken. In some fields, indeed, like long-distance electrical transmission, oil-drilling machinery, earth satellites and missiles, Russia is probably already ahead of America.

[1] Cressey, G. B., *Soviet Potentials*, Syracuse University Press, 1962.
[2] Bergson, A. *The Real National Income of Soviet Russia since 1928*. Harvard University Press, 1962, p. 296.

337

It should be stressed that national power and the individual wealth of a nation's citizens are two distinct matters, often but not invariably related. Consumption per head of goods and services in the Soviet Union may well be even today no more than half what it is in the United States, but such things are notoriously difficult to evaluate. In any case, it would hardly follow that America as a country was twice as powerful on the world scene. Is a resident of Los Angeles, for instance, who owns one or two cars and has to cope with traffic snarls and parking problems necessarily better off than a Muscovite (or New Yorker for that matter) who has access to fast public transport and taxis when needed? Can expenditure on, say, advertising be equated meaningfully with that on public services such as medicine, education or parks? On the other hand how does one put a value on such things as freedom to emigrate at will? One could go on endlessly—enough has been said to suggest the hazards of equating familiar indices of comfort with the realities of national power. The Soviet people are now reasonably well fed, healthy and educated, though still not well housed, and the standard of living has been rising steadily, at long last, since the death of Stalin. It is quite possible that in the next decade or two the gap between America and Russia—still a very real thing today—will wither away. However, such a result would have only minor repercussions on national power as such—in terms of military and economic might and influence abroad—in which there is probably already little to choose between the super-powers.

THE LEGACY OF MACKINDER

The most fundamental of all the elements of national power is sheer location on the globe. Although this is often regarded as absolute and immutable, it is in reality relative to the other parts of the world and its significance changes as they change, and therefore has to be constantly reassessed. However, probably the most famous of all statements of locational significance on a global scale, Mackinder's 'Heartland' theory, has appeared to possess, perhaps with some justification, an aura of permanence. Its influence on Hitler's wartime strategy was admitted and crucial, and Mackinder's ghost may even be encountered in the corridors of the Pentagon today! His idea has caught on with a wide public and may well have more significance than it is credited with in some quarters, although it can, conversely, very easily be exaggerated.

Mackinder's original 'pivot area',[1] which later became his Heartland,

[1] Sir H. J. Mackinder, 'The geographical pivot of history', *Geographical Journal*, 23 (1904), 421–37. Reprinted (with introduction by E. W. Gilbert), Royal Geographical Society, London, 1951.

was conceived in hydrographic terms, as befitted a writer from Britain, the water-borne power of the time. It comprised the apparently closed system of waterways which either failed to reach the oceans at all or emptied into the frozen Arctic (the Volga system was included in the area, but the Northern Dvina was not). This situation, it was argued, effectively denied access to ships from the outside world, while at the same time providing a natural sanctuary and springboard from which mobile horsemen from Central Asia were able for over a thousand years to launch attacks upon the settled margins of the Old World.

The date of this oracular utterance is significant. 1904 saw the high-water-mark of the Russian empire after several centuries of continuous extension of control over the 'pivot area'—they had spread near to the gates of Peking as well as of the northern approaches to India and the eastern approaches to maritime Europe. Russia had become the sinister bogey-man to the British, and indeed seemed to present a growing threat to their sea-empire.

However, the following year Russia's catastrophic defeat by Japan seemed to expose the clay feet of the colossus and thenceforth it stumbled from one crisis to another for several decades. Other changes in the world power balance were brought to a head by the First World War, notably the relative decline of British power and the rapid rise of the United States. Techniques of transport and warfare were transformed, with some implications for the validity of Mackinder's area. For instance more than half the Heartland was originally included because it drained to the frozen ocean. However, since the pioneering of the Northern Sea Route in 1932 and the subsequent development of atomic-powered ice-breakers, the Arctic coast has assumed a rather less negative face, and in fact a considerable summer traffic plies to and fro between the Yenisey and the Atlantic margins. Air-power had become crucial by the Second World War, but Mackinder claimed that this in no way invalidated his thesis, since air-power depends absolutely on the strength of its home base. This is certainly a point, but it might be said that air-power is able to achieve mass penetration into the Heartland, which sea-power, equally dependent on its own land base, is hardly able to do. This change has been underlined strongly with the arrival of nuclear bombs and inter-continental missiles. All the same, it would be wrong to imagine that the missile age has in some way neutralized the strategic advantages or disadvantages of particular areas or nations. Clearly countries with a large area, a dispersed population and also an interior fastness unusually far away from hostile bases, are even today relatively less vulnerable than those without these assets, though the

339

disparity has certainly ceased to be absolute, if indeed it ever was.

Some of the weaknesses in Mackinder's world view are illustrated by, if they did not stem from, his use of Mercator's projection, centred on Asia, with the Western Hemisphere on both edges, but cut in half. Mackinder did not seem to appreciate or anticipate the emergence of a moated continental stronghold in North America or the strategic significance of the Arctic as a major insulator and potential skyway between the two great seats of world power.

The interior lands of China, particularly Sinkiang and Tibet, plus Mongolia were included in Mackinder's Heartland and the last sentence of his original paper may be worth quoting now. 'Were the Chinese,' he says, 'for instance, organized by the Japanese, to overthrow the Russian Empire and conquer its territory, they might constitute the yellow peril to the world's freedom just because they would add an oceanic frontage to the resources of the great continent, an advantage as yet denied to the Russian tenant of the pivot region.' Two years after Mackinder's death the Communists came to power in China and proclaimed their solidarity with the Soviet Union, so that a closely knit political bloc of territory had materialized, comprising almost all the Heartland, *plus* the oceanic frontage, militantly organized and involving over a third of all mankind. This seemed to be the ultimate writing on the wall for the 'marginal powers' within the framework of the Heartland theory. However, scepticism about the permanence of this alliance was fed by the long history of antagonism between these two great powers, by their very different cultures, economic structure and stage of development, and by the great distances separating their core areas. A decade later the alliance did indeed begin to show signs of strain and seems now, to all intents and purposes, to have snapped. We now have the spectacle of both the Soviet Union and the United States (not to mention India) ostracizing China and actively delaying the attainment of her take-off as an industrial and nuclear power. The Heartland seems liable for some time to be a zone of, at best, tension—at worst, conflict.

When Mackinder first delimited his Heartland, it was very sparsely peopled and there was little inkling of the immense store of natural wealth which it contained. In fact the most remarkable thing about his area was that its geographical significance in the world power scheme was apparently almost independent of its population and resources, which imparted to it an almost mystical aura. However, in the depths of the Second World War, when Russia was almost prostrate, he did state that 'the Heartland is the greatest natural fortress on earth. For the first time in history it is manned by a garrison sufficient both in number and quality.'[1] This is surely a crucial point, presupposing as it must a solid base of resources for food and industry. Any witness of the terrible test of the German onslaught on Russia must have at least half believed in the existence of a charmed sanctuary in the Eurasian interior. However, it may be doubted whether an inaccessible but also *undeveloped* Heartland, devoid of natural resources, would have saved the day for the Russians, whatever value may be placed on sheer space for 'defence in depth'. The decisive contribution of the newly developed lands of the Urals and Siberia to the eventual victory was at bottom economic rather than strategic. The strength of the Soviet Union has undoubtedly been enhanced permanently by this extension of its national base to include the whole of its economically usable triangle, rather than just its long-established European end.

[1] H. W. Weigert and V. Stefansson (eds.), *Compass of the World:* A Symposium of Political Geography. Macmillan Co., New York, 1944, pp. 161–73.

CHAPTER EIGHTEEN

Patterns of Regional Change

THE geographical story of each region has been told in terms of its peopling and the economic realization of its latent assets—locational and natural. Thus the population map provides a cumulative summary to date of the relative valuation put on particular locations by man as an inhabitant. New notions about resources and needs, as well as new opportunities in other accessible regions, keep the population map in a constant state of flux. The time-lag between the introduction of the new conditions and their impact on the population distribution may be considerable. Accordingly an important element of the population pattern may reflect conditions of a former age which have since ceased to operate.

Therefore one can hardly exaggerate the importance of a historical approach to the study of regions. In the Soviet Union, as elsewhere, the concept of stage of development is most significant. There is a natural tendency for people to gravitate, given time, to areas with more favourable resources, in the broadest sense of the term, and Russians have been doing this steadily during the centuries since they began to get the upper hand over the nomads. The main set of the tide of migration has been first southerly and later easterly, and this represented essentially a colonization of land offering richer resources and greater opportunities. These movements are still evident in the growth of the North Caucasus and the Volga–Ural, though no longer much in the more outlying regions. But the process of drift away from the mixed forests of Central European Russia, while diminishing the latter's relative share of the national population, also greatly served to increase the wealth and power of its cities—Moscow and later St Petersburg. In the case of the Moscow region, this wealth, power and population has grown to such major proportions that it cannot be left out of any discussion of the distribution of Soviet strength, even though it is by no means a surplus or contributing region in terms of tangible natural resources—agricultural or industrial.

At this stage, then, it is necessary to recognize an economic spine, or Effective National Territory, of the country. These terms denote essentially that major part of the country which consistently produces a surplus in relation to its population and which, by implication, is therefore supporting the rest of the country in a real sense. In terms of output of food, energy and industrial raw materials this belt stretches from the Greater Ukraine, through the Middle Volga and Urals to Central Siberia, following the black-earth most of the way. But much of the wealth of this producing belt is diverted towards Moscow, and the map of freight flows indicates the true direction of the economic spine, from the southern Ukraine, *through the Moscow region* to the Middle Volga and Central Siberia. This includes five of the ten regions as treated in this book, while accounting for some three-quarters of the country's urban population and industrial and agricultural output and an even greater share of the accessible resources of energy and raw materials. Therefore, if the Soviet Union suddenly found itself divested of the remainder of its territories, the diminution of its national economic strength would be of only minor proportions. These remaining regions are, to a greater or less degree, marginal in the economic as well as the locational sense. They are either heavily rural and non-Slavic in composition, with a decidedly colonial character, or they are chronically pioneer regions of scattered and sometimes precarious communities, especially in the North. Although naturally the country values some specialized products of these regions, such as cotton, gold and diamonds, these peripheral regions are placed away from the agricultural and industrial mainstream and are in an altogether secondary category from the national standpoint.

THE ECONOMIC SPINE

The main contributing zone, outlined above, from Ukrainia to Central Siberia, is a generalization of expansive proportions, which includes many clusters of economic activity, distinct from each other not only in specialization, but also in stage of development, and frequently separated by large stretches of less intensively used land. A major division which has been discussed earlier in this book is that between the established cores of the Moscow region and the Greater Ukraine on the one hand and the more youthful Volga–Baykal zone on the other. Basically the productive character of the former was established before the Revolution, while that of the latter has been much more, though not entirely, a Soviet creation. In counterposing these two parts of the Effective National Territory, one must not lose sight of the fact that Moscow–Ukraine contains about 50% more people than Volga–Baykal. The latter has been singled out here because of its much faster city growth over the last quarter-century, coupled with plentiful and cheap industrial resources.

However, the fact remains that at least half the Soviet population is still found west of the Volga and, as in the case of the north-east quadrant of the United States, this area can be expected to remain dominant for the foreseeable future, if only through its inevitably greater annual natural increment. At present the Volga–Baykal zone has little more than a quarter of the Soviet population, and bearing in mind the increasing difficulty of skilled labour recruitment in Siberia, one cannot foresee a time now when it will house more than a third of the Soviet population, or the European area less than half. But the differential growth patterns, if persistent, become cumulative, so that it is vitally important to attempt to discern the long-term trends.

Volga–Baykal is to be seen above all *in conjunction with* the great established bases west of the Volga for which it has been the primary *funnel for expansion* as well as a storehouse of energy and raw materials and a reserve food bank. Thus the overwhelming majority of the functional links of Volga–Baykal are with the west—to its north, south and east it is flanked by economically unresponsive marginal regions.

HOW FAR EASTWARDS?

The easterly drift has been the dominant geographical process in Russia since 1880 and was at its most intense during the Second World War. Even though the European core has started to increase again after healing the wounds of war, the Volga–Baykal zone, in the early 1960s, was still growing at a slightly faster rate. But new factors are entering the situation, so that the question of the long-term pace of development of the Eastern Regions is becoming uncertain. It remains, however, of great significance as an indicator of national policies. Since the old-established European regions can be confidently expected to record solid growth from now on and since there is little evidence that the marginal regions will have more than marginal significance, the future of the zone between the Volga and Lake Baykal takes on more than local importance. It is too rich in resources and too much capital has already been sunk in it for it to be ignored for long, but its disproportionate growth seems to have come to an end for the time being.

VOLGA–BAYKAL AND ITS GAP

A fundamental two-fold division of the effective East can, however, be made on the basis of relative location—and above all distance—into the Middle Volga and the Greater Urals on the one hand and Central Siberia on the other. Between them there is a gap, not of negative country in the absolute sense, but of relatively less dense concentrations of activity.

This gap, and what can or should be done about it, is likely to play a crucial part in future Soviet locational policy. The Volga–Ural end obviously possesses more abundant locational assets in relation to the national economy and market than does Central Siberia, but the latter has very cheap and plentiful reserves of energy. Perhaps the most important current problem of regional development in the Soviet Union is that of ensuring a fruitful marriage between the population of the west and the energy resources of the east. The most promising key for opening up these resources seems to be long-distance, very high voltage transmissions of electricity, and the master plan for the current decade involves connecting the present European grid (which includes the Urals) with the Central Siberian grid. This would create a unified power system covering the whole vital triangle of the Soviet Union, with its apex at Lake Baykal, which encloses the great bulk of the population, industry, agriculture and accessible resources of the country. It would enable the low-cost coal and water-power resources in Central Siberia, already in the early stages of being converted into electricity, to be fully tapped, without straining overloaded conventional transport facilities. Moreover, the area of the gap itself is rich in a variety of metals and minerals, has moderately good farmland and a growing communications network, which would imply that it can look forward realistically to its own liquidation as a gap.

However, the question would remain, perhaps even more acutely, whether to intensify the concentration of industry in the European area and the Urals, virtually abandoning Central Siberia except as a reservoir of power, or to step-up the transfer of population and industry to the east to make use of the resources (not only energy) on the spot. A compromise seems to be the most probable outcome—it is extremely unlikely that the phenomenal scale and speed of transfer from west to east witnessed since 1939 will be approached, let alone repeated, but that a balanced industrial development, combined, perhaps, with a moderate, if necessary subsidized, easterly drift will become the long-term policy. There should in particular be an increase in the processing industries based on metals and timber but, except for ideological or strategic reasons—which should not be entirely ignored—no widespread establishment of labour-intensive industries in Siberia.

RETREAT TO THE WEST?

On the other hand, the forces favouring concentration in the west, probably in conjunction with the Middle Volga, have recently been gathering strength. The quick rise in the relative importance of oil and gas, coupled with the fact that the major centres of their production are situated between the Urals and the Black Sea, is very important. Given the required resources in sufficient quantity, these districts possess very considerable advantages. They are near the centre of gravity of the Soviet population, with Kuybyshev coming close to the ideal of a focal, well-connected centre in a national context. This has considerable market significance as the Soviet Union becomes more solicitous towards the consumer, although the ageing and impoverished rural population, in which much of European Russia is still top-heavy, counts for less in this respect than does the urban population. The problems of distance, and empty freight-cars, are minimized compared, say, with Central Siberia. Labour is generally more plentiful and more permanent than further east, where a more severe climate and fewer amenities have led to greater than average turnover of employees.

PROSPECT

Thus the east–west problem within the Effective National Territory shows some resemblance to a see-saw, with market and resource factors alternating in the amount of weight given them by the national planners. But we should beware of exclusive emphasis on economic factors. Even if the natural resource base east of the Volga had turned out to be only half as rich as it has, there is still every indication that the drive to the East would have been deliberately pursued. Although the early Leninists' forecasts that under communism the population would become evenly distributed have been given a decently quiet burial, there is little doubt that, other things being anything like equal, it is continuing policy to level up the developed and the under-developed regions, and that this fits in well with expressed government policies of decentralization and encouraging a measure of regional self-sufficiency. We cannot discount the idea that the industrial growth of the Volga–Baykal area is to some extent the statistical realization of an old Russian dream. The Virgin Lands project, for all its excesses, fits in here too; although there is little doubt that future agricultural investment will be put mainly, and justifiably, into the proven European black-earth, the centre of gravity of agricultural production is likely to remain permanently further to the east than it was before the war.

There are, however, many uncertainties. With the diffusion of industrial skills and education across the country, how long are Moscow and Leningrad likely to be able to depend on the inertia of a traditional labour pool, in the face of other high costs? How effectively will the present formal discouragements, through work-permits, to settlement in Greater Moscow be enforced? Alternatively, will the metropolitan area come to enjoy, whether officially or not, a kind of protection against outside price-competition? How far would the kind of climatic preference, very evident in the United States, favour, with more mobility and a rising standard of living, the southern Ukraine or the Caucasus? Are the ties between the Soviet Union and the other Communist counties of Eastern Europe weakening, and the plans for a Soviet-controlled economic unit from the Pacific to the Elbe beginning to evaporate? If so, would not this again be liable to shift the effective centre of gravity within the Soviet Union further eastwards? How would the re-emergence of a shatter-belt of small countries in Eastern Europe affect the strategic thinking of the Soviet Union? The Volga–Baykal zone has remained beyond the range of invaders ever since the ebb of the Mongols. What of the emergence of an expansionist, hostile China, accusing Russia of not being legitimately an Asian power, but only a 'conqueror of Asian peoples'? Is the Soviet response to Chinese provocation likely to be to intensify the drive to the East to fill up its open spaces (which the Chinese may well covet) and harness its resources, or to retire more and more behind the continental boundary of the Urals? Would the maximum dispersal of industry be an effective safeguard against potential threats, whether from America, Europe or China?

There are no simple answers to these questions, and the Soviet Union, in both its internal and external dealings is becoming less simple as time goes on. In general, it is by no means an overcrowded country—much more like America than like China or Europe—and this gives the government considerable flexibility in its regional policies, and makes it more susceptible to factors other than the strictly economic. The likelihood is that the economic spine of the country will even increase still further its already large share of the effective population and the effective wealth and strength of the country. Whether the balance will continue to shift eastwards within this national core is not clear. It may, as it still does to the west in North America, but probably more and more slowly. The great problem of distance, one of the severe handicaps that the colonizing Russians have had to suffer, is well on the way to being appreciably mitigated by the gas and oil pipe, the aircraft and the high-voltage transmission line. Much, perhaps most, of the Soviet Union, will remain of very little value; but the maintenance of the country's super-power status, in a competitive world, necessitates the comprehensive use of its effectively usable land—which covers an area almost as large as the whole of the United States.

Appendixes

Appendix I

GROWTH OF THE MAJOR SOVIET CITIES, 1897–1962

NOTE: Figures (in thousands) are all from official censuses, except for 1962, which is an official estimate. Where there is a blank entry, the population was less than 50,000 or, in particular cases, the city was not in Russia at the time.

	1897	1926	1939	1959	1962
Moscow Region					
Moscow	989	2,029	4,137	6,039	6,296
Gorky	95	222	644	942	1,025
Voronezh	84	122	344	448	516
Yaroslavl	71	114	309	407	443
Ivanovo	54	111	285	335	360
Tula	111	155	272	316	342
Kalinin	53	108	216	261	286
Ryazan	—	51	95	214	252
Bryansk	—	—	174	207	241
Kursk	53	82	120	205	228
Rybinsk	—	56	144	182	195
Lipetsk	—	—	67	157	194
Kostroma	—	74	121	172	189
Tambov	—	72	106	172	189
Dzerzhinsk	—	—	103	164	180
Orël	70	76	111	150	174
Vladimir	—	—	67	154	174
Kaluga	—	52	89	134	151
Vologda	—	58	95	139	149
Kolomna	—	—	75	100	125
Cherepovets	—	—	—	92	124
Novomoskovsk	—	—	76	107	114
Serpukhov	—	56	91	106	113

Ukrainia

Kiev	247	514	847	1,104	1,208
Kharkov . . .	175	417	833	934	990
Donetsk . . .	—	174	466	699	760
Dnepropetrovsk . .	121	237	527	660	722
Odessa . . .	405	421	602	667	704
Rostov . . .	120	308	510	600	661
Volgograd . . .	56	151	445	592	649
Zaporozhye . . .	—	56	282	435	490
Lvov	—	—	340	411	447
Krivoy Rog . . .	—	—	189	388	448
Makeyevka . . .	—	79	242	358	381
Krasnodar . . .	66	162	193	313	354
Zhdanov . . .	—	64	222	284	321
Gorlovka . . .	—	—	181	293	309
Lugansk . . .	—	72	215	275	306
Nikolayev . . .	92	105	169	226	258
Kishinev . . .	—	—	112	216	244
Taganrog . . .	52	86	189	202	220
Dneprodzerzhinsk. .	—	—	148	194	207
Shakhty . . .	—	—	135	196	201
Simferopol . . .	49	87	143	186	202
Kadiyevka . . .	—	—	135	180	192
Kherson . . .	69	59	97	158	183
Sevastopol . . .	51	75	114	148	169
Poltava . . .	53	92	128	143	154
Stavropol . . .	—	59	85	141	154

Volga–Ural

Kuybyshev . . .	92	176	390	806	881
Kazan . . .	132	179	398	647	711
Perm	45	120	306	629	701
Saratov . . .	137	220	372	581	631
Ufa	50	99	258	547	610
Izhevsk . . .	—	63	176	285	322
Orenburg . . .	73	123	172	267	288
Penza	62	92	160	255	286
Kirov	—	62	144	252	277
Ulyanovsk . . .	—	70	98	206	239
Syzran . . .	—	50	83	149	159

Sterlitamak	.	.	.	—	—	—	112	131
Berezniki	.	.	.	—	—	51	106	120
Uralsk.	.	.	.	—	—	67	104	109

Ural–Ob

Sverdlovsk	.	.	.	55	140	423	779	853
Chelyabinsk	.	.	—	59	273	689	751
Omsk	.	.	.	—	162	289	581	650
Karaganda	.	.	.	—	—	156	397	459
Nizhnii Tagil	.	.	—	—	160	339	359
Magnitogorsk	.	.	—	—	146	311	333
Orsk	.	.	.	.	—	—	66	176	199
Tyumen	.	.	.	—	50	79	150	174
Kurgan	.	.	.	—	—	53	146	173
Kopeysk	.	.	.	—	—	60	161	168
Zlatoust	.	.	.	—	—	99	161	167
Kamensk-Uralsky	.	—	—	51	141	152
Petropavlovsk	.	.	—	—	92	131	146
Tselinograd	.	.	.	—	—	—	102	127
Temirtau	.	.	.	—	—	—	77	123
Pavlodar	.	.	.	—	—	—	90	115
Aktyubinsk	.	.	.	—	—	—	97	111
Serov	.	.	.	.	—	—	65	98	102
Kustanay	.	.	.	—	—	—	86	102

Central Siberia

Novosibirsk	.	.	.	—	120	404	886	985
Krasnoyarsk	.	.	.	—	72	190	412	465
Novokuznetsk	.	.	—	—	166	377	410
Irkutsk	.	.	.	51	108	250	366	385
Barnaul	.	.	.	—	74	148	305	347
Kemerovo	.	.	.	—	—	133	278	305
Prokopyevsk	.	.	—	—	107	282	292
Tomsk	.	.	.	52	92	145	249	275
Ulan-Ude	.	.	.	—	—	126	175	196
Chita	.	.	.	.	—	62	121	172	185
Semipalatinsk	.	.	—	57	110	156	182
Ust-Kamenogorsk	.	.	—	—	—	150	181
Biysk	.	.	.	.	—	—	80	146	165
Angarsk	.	.	.	—	—	—	134	160
Rubtsovsk	.	.	.	—	—	—	111	127

The Baltic

Leningrad . . .	1,267	1,690	3,385	3,321	3,498
Riga	331	378	348	580	620
	(1910)	(1930)			
Minsk . . .	91	132	237	509	599
Tallinn . . .	—	130	160	282	305
		(1930)			
Vilnyus . . .	190	—	215	236	264
	(1910)				
Kaunas . . .	—	—	152	214	247
Kaliningrad . . .	—	—	316	204	232
			(1938)		
Gomel . . .	—	86	139	168	193
Vitebsk . . .	66	99	167	148	169
Smolensk . . .	—	79	157	147	164
Mogilev . . .	—	50	99	122	139
Bobruisk . . .	—	51	84	98	108
Klaipeda . . .	—	—	—	90	105
Pskov	—	—	60	81	98
Liepaja . . .	94	61	53	71	77
	(1914)	(1930)			
Tartu	—	70	57	74	77
		(1930)			
Novgorod . . .	—	—	—	61	72

Caucasus–Caspia

Baku	112	453	809	971	1,067
Tbilisi . . .	161	294	519	695	743
Yerevan . . .	—	65	204	509	583
Astrakhan . . .	113	184	254	296	320
Grozny . . .	—	97	172	242	280
Ordzhonikidze . .	—	78	131	164	183
Sochi	—	—	62	127	174
Kutaisi . . .	—	—	78	128	141
Makhachkala . .	—	—	87	119	135
Kirovabad . . .	—	57	99	116	126
Leninakan . . .	—	—	68	108	117
Batumi . . .	—	—	70	82	89
Guryev . . .	—	—	—	78	89

Kislovodsk . . .	—	—	51	79	83
Pyatigorsk . . .	—	—	62	70	74
Rustavi . . .	—	—	—	62	72
Sukhumi . . .	—	—	—	65	80

Middle Asia

Tashkent . . .	156	324	550	912	1,002
Alma-Ata . . .	—	—	222	456	534
Frunze . . .	—	—	93	220	312
Dushanbe . . .	—	—	83	224	260
Samarkand . . .	55	105	136	196	215
Ashkhabad . . .	—	52	127	170	197
Chimkent . . .	—	—	74	153	178
Andizhan . . .	—	73	85	130	145
Namangan . . .	62	74	89	123	138
Dzhambul . . .	—	—	64	113	136
Kokand . . .	82	69	85	105	117
Bukhara . . .	75	—	50	69	84

Far East

Khabarovsk . . .	—	52	207	323	363
Vladivostok . . .	—	108	206	291	325
Komsomolsk . .	—	—	71	177	192
Ussuriisk . .	—	—	72	104	113
Blagoveshchensk . .	—	53	59	95	101
Yuzhno-Sakhalinsk .	—	—	—	86	86

The North

Archangel . . .	—	77	251	256	276
Murmansk . . .	—	—	119	222	245
Petrozavodsk . .	—	—	70	136	142
Norilsk . . .	—	—	—	109	117
Petropavlovsk-Kamchatsky	—	—	—	86	100
Severodvinsk . .	—	—	—	79	97
Yakutsk . . .	—	—	53	74	79
Syktyvkar . . .	—	—	—	64	79
Magadan . . .	—	—	—	62	68
Vorkuta . . .	—	—	—	56	60

Appendix II

CONVERSION TABLES

° Fahrenheit	° Centigrade	Inches	Centimetres
−70	−56·7	1	2·54
−60	−51·1	5	12·7
−50	−45·6	8	20·32
−40	−40	10	25·4
−30	−34·4	15	38·1
−20	−28·9	20	50·8
−10	−23·3	30	76·2
0	−17·8	40	101·6
+10	−12·1	50	127·0
20	−6·7	100	254·0
30	−1·1		
40	+4·4		
50	10·0		
60	15·6		
70	21·1		
80	26·7		
90	32·2		
100	37·8		

Appendix III

SELECT BIBLIOGRAPHY

The bulk of the basic source material—primary and secondary—is, of course, in Russian, and the serious student of the Soviet Union has much to gain by acquiring some reading ability in the language. This will at the very least open up to him the rich world of the Soviet atlases and enable him to consult the now numerous statistical handbooks and regional monographs.

However, since 1960 a major chink in the Linguistic Curtain has been opened for geographers, in the form of the monthly journal *Soviet Geography: Review and Translation*, published by the American Geographical Society (edited and translated by Theodore Shabad). Particular articles which relate to the topics of this book are cited below; but there are many more on general topics which give invaluable insight into the ways of thought of Soviet geographers and the vigorous controversies in which they engage. In addition, the editor compiles News Notes, which form much the easiest way of keeping up with the rapidly changing geography of the country, and keeping this book up to date.

Abbreviations:

A.A.A.G.—*Annals* of the Association of American Geographers
Ec. Geog.—*Economic Geography*
G.R.—*Geographical Review*
S.G.—*Soviet Geography: Review and Translation*

GENERAL

BALZAK, S. S., VASYUTIN, V. F., and FEIGIN, Ya G. *Economic Geography of the U.S.S.R.* (trans. by R. M. Hankin and O. A. Titelbaum and ed. by C. D. Harris), New York, Macmillan, 1949 (for conditions just before the Second World War).

BARANSKY, N. N. *Economic Geography of the U.S.S.R.*, Moscow, Foreign Languages Publishing House, 1956.

COLE, J. P. and GERMAN, F. C. *A Geography of the U.S.S.R.*, London, Butterworth, 1961.

CRANKSHAW, E. *Khrushchev's Russia*, London, Penguin, 2nd ed., 1962.

D'ALMEIDA, C. A. *États de la Baltique, Russie*, Vol. 5 of *Geographie*

356

Universelle (ed. P. Vidal de la Blache and L. Gallois), Paris, 1932 (for conditions at the start of the First Five Year Plan).

EAST, W. G. *The Soviet Union*, Princeton, Van Nostrand, 1963.

KISH, G. *An Economic Atlas of the Soviet Union*, Michigan University Press, 1960.

LYDOLPH, P. E. *Geography of the U.S.S.R.*, New York, John Wiley, 1964.

Oxford Regional Economic Atlas of U.S.S.R. and Eastern Europe, London, Oxford University Press, 2nd ed. (with statistical addenda), 1960.

SHABAD, T. 'The Soviet Union' in HOFFMAN, G. (ed.), *A Geography of Europe*, London, Methuen, 2nd ed., 1961, 638–728.

CHAPTER ONE (Natural Habitat)

BERG, L. S. *Natural Regions of the U.S.S.R.* (trans. by O. A. Titelbaum and ed. by J. A. Morrison and C. C. Nikiforoff), New York, Macmillan, 1950.

GRIGOR'YEV, A. A. and BUDYKO, M. I. 'Classification of the Climates of the U.S.S.R.', *S.G.*, 1 (May 1960), 3–23.

KIRIKOV, S. V. and ISAKOV, YU. A. 'The Reserves of Wild Game; the Dynamics of Hunting and its Prospects', *S.G.*, 1 (Dec. 1960), 64–89.

L'VOVICH, M. I. *et al.* 'The Water Balance of the U.S.S.R. and its Prospects of Transformation', *S.G.*, 3 (Dec. 1962), 12–25.

SCHLOSS, M. 'Cloud Cover of the Soviet Union', *G.R.*, 52 (July 1962), 389–99.

SUSLOV, S. P. *The Physical Geography of Asiatic Russia* (trans. by J. E. Williams), London, W. H. Freeman, 1961.

TRUBE, L. 'The Arctic Ocean as a Factor in Eastern Siberia's Climate', *S.G.*, 2 (Sept. 1960), 64–6.

ZHAKOV, S. O. 'The Long-Term Transformation of Nature and Changes in the Atmospheric Moisture Supply of the European Part of the U.S.S.R.', *S.G.*, 5 (Mar. 1964), 52–60.

CHAPTER TWO (Historical Background)

FRENCH, R. A. 'The Making of the Russian Landscape', *Advancement of Science* (May 1963), 44–56.

FRENCH, R. A. 'The Reclamation of Swamp in Pre-Revolutionary Russia', *Transactions and Papers*, 34, Institute of British Geographers, 1964, 175–88.

JACKSON, W. A. D. *The Russo–Chinese Borderlands*, Princeton, Van Nostrand, 1962.

LYASHCHENKO, P. I. *History of the National Economy of Russia to 1917* (trans. by L. M. Herman), New York, Macmillan, 1949.

PARKER, W. H. 'Europe—How Far?', *Geographical Journal*, **126** (Sept. 1960), 278–97.

RIASANOVSKY, N. V. *A History of Russia*, London, Oxford University Press, 1963.

SUMNER, B. H. *Survey of Russian History*, London, Methuen: University Paperbacks, 1961.

TREADGOLD, D. W. *The Great Siberian Migration*, Princeton University Press, 1957.

MORRISON, J. A. 'Russia and Warm Water', *U.S. Naval Institute Proceedings*, **78** (November 1952), 1169–79

CHAPTER THREE (Farming)

DAVITAYA, F. F. 'A Natural Transmission Belt for the Year-Round Supply of Fresh Farm Products', *S.G.*, **4** (Feb. 1963), 25–31.

GERASIMOV, I. P. 'Reducing the Dependence of Soviet Agriculture on Natural Elements to a Minimum', *S.G.*, **4** (Feb. 1963), 3–11.

LAIRD, R. D. (ed.). *Soviet Agricultural and Peasant Affairs*, University of Kansas Press, 1963.

NEWTH, J. A. 'Soviet Agriculture: The Private Sector', *Soviet Studies*, **13** (1962), 414–32.

NOVE, A. 'Soviet Agriculture Marks Time', *Foreign Affairs*, **40**, 1962, 576–94.

SAPOZHNIKOVA, S. A. and SHASHKO, D. I. 'Agroclimatic Conditions of the Distribution and Specialization of Agriculture', *S.G.*, **1** (Nov. 1960), 20–34.

SOTNIKOV, V. P. 'Farming Problems in the Zones of the U.S.S.R. and the Tasks of Soviet Geographers', *S.G.*, **1** (Dec. 1960), 3–22.

CHAPTER FOUR (Transport)

KAZANSKIY, N. N. and LASIS, YU. V. 'Methods of Forecasting Freight Flows in Planning a Transport Net', *S.G.*, **4** (Sept. 1963), 3–18.

KISH, G. 'Railroad Passenger Transport in the Soviet Union', *G.R.*, **53** (July 1963), 363–76.

MAZANOVA, M. B. 'Marine Transport as a National Specialized Activity of a Major Economic Region', *S.G.*, **4** (May 1963), 3–9.

NIKOL'SKIY, I. V. 'Railroad Freight Traffic of the U.S.S.R.', *S.G.*, **2** (June 1961), 39–92.

VARLAMOV, V. S. and KAZANSKIY, N. N. 'Forecast of Average Length of Haul on Soviet Railroads', *S.G.*, **4** (Sept. 1963), 19–25.

CHAPTER FIVE (Industry)

BERNSHTEYN, L. B. 'On the Utilization of Tidal Power', *S.G.*, **4** (May 1963), 16–25.

GROSSMAN, G. (ed.). *Value and Plan*, University of California Press, 1960.

HODGKINS, J. A. *Soviet Power: Energy Resources, Production and Potentials*, New York, Prentice Hall, 1961.

HOLZMAN, F. D. 'Soviet Ural–Kuznetsk Combine: a Study in Investment Criteria and Industrialization Policies', *Quarterly Journal of Economics*, **71** (1957), 368–405.

LONSDALE, R. E. and THOMPSON, J. H. 'A Map of the U.S.S.R.'s Manufacturing', *Ec. Geog.*, **36** (Jan. 1960), 36–52.

LYDOLPH, P E. and SHABAD, T. 'The Oil and Gas Industries of the U.S.S.R.', *A.A.A.G.*, **50** (Dec. 1960), 461–86.

NUTTER, G. W. *The Growth of Industrial Production in the Soviet Union*, Princeton University Press, 1962.

OMAROVSKIY, A. G. 'Changes in the Geography of Machine Building in the U.S.S.R.', *S.G.*, **1** (Mar. 1960), 42–55.

RODGERS, A. 'Coking Coal Supply: Its Role in the Expansion of the Soviet Steel Industry', *Ec. Geog.*, **40** (Apr. 1964), 113–50.

SHIMKIN, D. B. *The Soviet Mineral-Fuels Industries 1928–1958*, Washington D.C., U.S. Bureau of Census, 1962.

CHAPTER SIX (Population)

DAVIDOVICH, V. G. 'Satellite Cities and Towns of the U.S.S.R.', *S.G.*, **3** (Mar. 1962), 3–34.

KONSTANTINOV, O. A. 'Some Conclusions About the Geography of Cities and the Urban Population of the U.S.S.R. based on the Results of the 1959 Census', *S.G.*, **1** (Sept. 1960), 59–74.

LORIMER, F. *The Population of the Soviet Union*, Geneva, League of Nations, 1946.

POKSHISHEVSKIY, V. V. 'Prospects of Population Migration in the U.S.S.R.', *S.G.*, **4** (Jan. 1963), 13–25.

INTRODUCTION TO PART II (A Scheme of Regions)

ALAMPIYEV, P. M. 'Problems of General Economic Regionalization at the Present Stage', *S.G.*, **1** (Oct. 1960), 3–15.

POKSHISHEVSKIY, V. V. 'The Role of Population Geography in Problems of Economic Regionalization of the U.S.S.R.', *S.G.*, **1** (Sept. 1960), 28–35.

SAUSHKIN, YU. G. and KALASHNIKOVA, T. M. 'Current Problems in the Economic Regionalization of the U.S.S.R.', *S.G.*, **1** (June 1960) 50–9.

TASKIN, G. 'Economic Zones', *Studies in the Soviet Union*, **1** (1962), 19–36.

CHAPTER SEVEN (The Moscow Region)

DOLGOPOLOV, K. V. 'Ways of Developing the Economy of the Central Chernozem Areas of the R.S.F.S.R.', *S.G.*, **1** (Mar. 1960), 33–41.

JACKSON, W. A. D. 'The Russian Non-Chernozem Wheat base', *A.A.A.G.*, **49** (1959), 79–109.

KAPITANOV, YE. I. 'The Kursk Magnetic Anomaly and Its Development', *S.G.*, **4** (May 1963), 10–15.

MISHCHENKO, G. YE. 'Satellite Cities and Towns of Moscow', *S.G.*, **3** (Mar. 1962), 35–42.

CHAPTER EIGHT (Ukrainia)

BONDARCHUK, B. G. *et al.* 'The Natural Resources of the Ukrainian S.S.R. and Ways of Using Them Rationally', *S.G.*, **2** (Jan. 1961), 12–34.

FOX, D. J. 'Odessa', *Scottish Geographical Magazine*, **79** (1963), 5–22.

GNATYUK, L. V. 'Some Aspects of the Economic-Geographic Situation of Odessa', *S.G.*, **4** (Nov. 1963), 43–51.

POPOV, V. P. *et al.* 'The Study of the Heat and Moisture Balance of the Ukraine as a Basis for Measures to Raise the Productivity of Agriculture', *S.G.*, **2** (Sept. 1960), 16–27.

CHAPTER NINE (Volga–Ural)

HOOSON, D. J. M. 'The Middle Volga—an Emerging Focal Region in the Soviet Union', *Geographical Journal*, **126** (1960), 180–90.

SAVENKO, YU. N. 'The Fuel Balance of Kuybyshev Oblast', *S.G.*, **2** (June 1961), 8–13.

STEPANOV, P. N. and SAVENKO, YU. N. 'Some Problems of Electric Power Development in the Kuybyshev Economic Administrative Region', *S.G.*, **2** (Mar. 1961), 73–9.

TAAFFE, R. N. 'Volga River Transportation: Problems and Prospects' in R. S. THOMAN and D. J. PATTON (eds.) *Focus on Geographic Activity*, New York, McGraw-Hill, 1964.

VARLAMOV, V. S. 'On the Economic Links of the Industry of Orenburg', *S.G.*, **2** (Mar. 1961), 54–60.

VARLAMOV, V. S. 'The Economic-Geographic Situation of Orenburg', *S.G.*, **2** (June 1961), 14–20.

CHAPTER TEN (Ural–Ob)

ADAMCHUK, V. A. 'The Problem of Creating a Kazakhstan Metallurgical Base', *S.G.*, **5** (June 1964), 20–35.

BUYANOVSKIY, M. S. 'On the Question of Iron and Steel Plant Location in Kazakhstan', *S.G.*, **2** (Nov. 1961), 44–59.

JACKSON, W. A. D. 'The Virgin and Idle Lands Program Reappraised', *A.A.A.G.*, **52** (Mar. 1962), 69–79.

KARSTEN, A. A. 'The Virgin Lands Kray and Its Prospects of Development', *S.G.*, **4** (May 1963), 37–46.

NIKOLSKIY, I. V. 'The Geography of Transportation of Kazakhstan', *S.G.*, **2** (Mar. 1961), 44–53.

ZHIRKOV, K. F. 'Dust Storms in the Steppes of Western Siberia and Kazakhstan', *S.G.*, **5** (May 1964), 33–41.

CHAPTER ELEVEN (Central Siberia)

LONSDALE, R. E. 'Siberian Industry before 1917: The Example of Tomsk Guberniya', *A.A.A.G.*, **53** (Dec. 1963), 479–93.

NAYMUSHIN, I. and GINDIN, A. 'Problems of the Angara Series of Hydro-electric Stations', *S.G.*, **1** (June 1960), 61–7.

VOROB'YEV, A. A. 'Problems in the Location of Transportation in the Southern Part of Eastern Siberia', *S.G.*, **5** (May 1964), 3–12.

YEGOROVA, V. V. 'The Economic Effectiveness of the Construction of Pioneering Railroads in Newly Developed Areas (as illustrated by the Lena railroad)', *S.G.*, **5** (Apr. 1964), 46–55.

CHAPTER TWELVE (The Baltic)

FRENCH, R. A. 'Drainage and Economic Development of Polyesye, U.S.S.R.', *Ec. Geog.*, **35** (1959), 172–80.

LOPATINA, YE. B. 'The Formation of Leningrad's Satellite Places', *S.G.*, **3** (Mar. 1962), 43–50.

ROM, V. YA. 'The Volga–Baltic Waterway', *S.G.*, **2** (Nov. 1961), 32–43.

TASKIN, G. A. 'The Soviet North-West: Economic Regionalization', *G.R.*, **51** (Apr. 1961), 213–35.

CHAPTER THIRTEEN (Caucasus–Caspia)

BOBROV, S. N. 'The Transformation of the Caspian Sea', *S.G.*, **2** (Sept. 1960), 47–58.

GELLER, S. YU. 'On the Question of Regulating the Level of the Caspian Sea', *S.G.*, **3** (Jan. 1962), 59–66.

GUMILEV, L. N. 'Khazaria and the Caspian (Landscape and Ethnos, Part i)', *S.G.*, **5** (June 1964), 54–68.

JENSEN, R. G. 'Soviet Subtropical Agriculture: A Microcosm', *G.R.*, **54** (Apr. 1964), 185–202.

CHAPTER FOURTEEN (Middle Asia)

AVSYUK, G. A. 'Artificial Intensification of the Melting of Mountain Glaciers to Increase the Stream Flow in Central Asia', *S.G.*, **4** (Feb. 1963), 46–51.

LEWIS, R. A. 'The Irrigation Potential of Soviet Central Asia', *A.A.A.G.*, **52** (Mar. 1962), 99–114.

PAVLENKO, V. F. 'The Transport-Geography Situation and Inter-regional Links of Central Asia', *S.G.*, **4** (Nov. 1963), 27–33.

PIERCE, R. A. *Russian Central Asia 1867–1917: A Study in Colonial Rule*, University of California Press, 1960.

TAAFFE, R. N. 'Transportation and Regional Specialization: The Example of Soviet Central Asia', *A.A.A.G.*, **52** (Mar. 1962), 80–98.

WHEELER, G. *Racial Problems in Soviet Muslim Asia*, London, Oxford University Press, 1962.

CHAPTER FIFTEEN (The Far East)

POKSHISHEVSKIY, V. V. 'On the Geography of Pre-Revolutionary Colonization and Migration Processes in the Southern Part of the Soviet Far East', *S.G.*, **4** (Apr. 1963), 17–30.

THIEL, E. *The Soviet Far East* (trans. by A. and R. M. Rookwood), London, Methuen, 1957.

CHAPTER SIXTEEN (The North)

ARMSTRONG, T. *The Russians in the Arctic*, London, Methuen, 1958.

ARMSTRONG, T. 'Population of the North of the U.S.S.R.', *Polar Record*, **11** (1962), 172–8.

BUYANOVSKIY, M. S. 'On the Question of the Prospects of Development of the Pechora Coal Basin', *S.G.*, **1** (Mar. 1960), 9–19.

D'YAKONOV, F. V. 'Productive Forces and Productive Territorial Complexes in the North-East of the U.S.S.R.', *S.G.*, **5** (Jan. 1964), 40–52.

GOROVOY, V. L. 'The Timber Industry of Northern European Russia', *S.G.*, **2** (Apr. 1961), 53–9.

HELIN, R. A. 'Soviet Fishing in the Barents Sea and the North Atlantic', *G.R.*, **54** (July 1964), 386–408.

KRYPTON, C. *The Northern Sea Route and the Economy of the Soviet North*, London, Methuen, 1956.

PARMUZIN, YU. P. 'The Zonal Character of the Cold Pole', *S.G.*, **1** (Jan.–Feb. 1960), 40–2.

SHISHKIN, N. I. 'On the Diversion of the Vychegda and Pechora Rivers to the Basin of the Volga', *S.G.*, **3** (May 1962), 46–56.

VENDROV, S. L. 'Geographical Aspects of the Problem of Diverting Part of the Flow of the Pechora and Vychegda Rivers to the Volga Basin', *S.G.*, **4** (June 1963), 29–41.

CHAPTER SEVENTEEN

(Soviet Strength in the Modern World)

CRESSEY, G. B. *Soviet Potentials: A Geographic Appraisal*, Syracuse University Press, 1962.

JOINT ECONOMIC COMMITTEE, CONGRESS OF THE UNITED STATES. *Dimensions of Soviet Power*, Washington D.C., U.S. Government Printing Office, 1962.

MACKINDER, Sir H. J. 'The Geographical Pivot of History', *Geographical Journal*, **23** (1904), 421–37. Reprinted (with an introduction by E. W. Gilbert), London, Royal Geographical Society, 1951.

CHAPTER EIGHTEEN (Patterns of Regional Change)

BUDTOLAYEV, N. M., NOVIKOV, V. P. and SAUSHKIN, YU. G. 'Problems of Economic Development of the West and East of the Soviet Union', *S.G.*, **5** (Jan. 1964), 3–14.

HOOSON, D. J. M. *A New Soviet Heartland?* Princeton, Van Nostrand, 1964.

Index

Figures in *italics* refer to the map on the specified page.
References in Roman numerals are to the photographic plates.